*if only*

# GERI HALLIWELL
## *if only*

**BANTAM BOOKS**

London • New York • Toronto • Sydney • Auckland

**IF ONLY**
**A BANTAM BOOK: 0 553 81293 9**

Originally published in Great Britain by Bantam Press,
a division of Transworld Publishers

PRINTING HISTORY
Bantam Press edition published 1999
Bantam Books edition published 2000

3 5 7 9 10 8 6 4

Set in 11/12pt Granjon by Falcon Oast Graphic Art

Bantam Books are published by Transworld Publishers,
61–63 Uxbridge Road, London W5 5SA,
a division of The Random House Group Ltd,
in Australia by Random House Australia (Pty) Ltd,
20 Alfred Street, Milsons Point, Sydney, NSW 2061, Australia,
in New Zealand by Random House New Zealand Ltd,
18 Poland Road, Glenfield, Auckland 10, New Zealand
and in South Africa by Random House (Pty) Ltd,
Endulini, 5a Jubilee Road, Parktown 2193, South Africa.

Reproduced, printed and bound in Great Britain by
Mackays of Chatham plc, Chatham, Kent

This is dedicated to my dad

## ACKNOWLEDGEMENTS

Thanks to my friend Michael, Mark
and all at Transworld

No two people see events the same way.
Everybody's truth is different. This is my truth.

If only there was a world with no pain . . .
 only love.
If only there was no fear.
If only . . .

# CONTENTS

Unless otherwise stated, the photographs are from the author's collection.

# Prologue

Maybe I should start my story here, lying beside a swimming pool in Beverly Hills on my twenty-sixth birthday, watching a spectacular sunset through the smog. Between my toes, past the tangled hedge, I can look across Coldwater Canyon at hundreds of sprinklers revolving on perfectly manicured lawns beneath the palm trees.

Winona lives down there somewhere, in a pastel-coloured stone-cladded mansion. Woody and Roseanne are there, too. You can get a movie-star map down the road for $3.50 from a guy who wears a pistachio-green baseball cap and has a mobile souvenir stand in the boot of his Cadillac. I should buy one so I can tell Mum about the neighbours.

The police blocked off Sunset Boulevard for twenty minutes last week because President Clinton was in town for a Democratic fundraiser. There were secret servicemen on every corner, and the traffic lights were set to green so the motorcade could sweep through without stopping.

I felt sorry for Bill Clinton. I know what it's like living in the 'bubble' – never having to dial a telephone, pack a bag or consult a road map. I remember hearing a story once about Ronald Reagan. For ten years the only time his motorcade ever stopped was when he had to get out. After retiring from the White House, whenever his car pulled up, even at a red light, he automatically moved for the door. There's something quite surreal about that.

There are people around here who have armed response teams hooked up to their alarm systems. Press a button and Rambo arrives. It's bad news if you forget your door keys. Others fill their swimming pools with mineral water and bring in bottled mountain air from the Rockies. My dad would have loved this place; no idea is too silly.

People say that LA is a plastic paradise and call it Las Vegas by the sea, but I love it here. Every person has a dream. Most of them want to live in a house like this, with a million-dollar view, a swimming pool and neighbours who get mentioned in *Variety*.

Look at that sunset. It owes as much to exhaust fumes as it does to Mother Nature, but that doesn't make it any less beautiful. You just have to know the difference between what's real and what's not. I think I can do that now.

I'm twenty-six and I've reached a crossroads. I keep thinking about how it all started in another place and at another time. I used to play music in my bedroom. That was me you heard singing into a hairbrush in front of the mirror, pretending to be Madonna. I knew the words to every hit song on the singles chart and watched *Top of the Pops* every Thursday night. And on Sunday afternoons I counted down the Top 40 on Capital Radio with Dr Fox.

I used to put a blank tape in the cassette player and record the songs because I couldn't afford to buy them. Then I learned the words by heart and sang them in the playground.

When I was twelve I went to a Wham! concert at the NEC in Birmingham on my sister Natalie's birthday. We were near the front and I remember George Michael singing:

> I don't want your freedom . . .
> I don't want to play around . . .
> I don't want nobody baby,
> Part time love just brings me down.
> I don't want your freedom,
> Girl, all I want right now is you.

He pointed somewhere in my direction as he sang the last line and my heart melted. I didn't scream like the other girls; I was in love, and I imagined that one day I was going to marry him.

I didn't think about what his life must be like. I thought pop stars did the occasional concert, or *Top of the Pops*, or a photo shoot for a teen magazine and were then put back in their box again. Now I know differently.

All my life I've felt as if I'm going to die tomorrow. That I'm running out of time. What if I don't finish what I set out to do? Even when I speak, I race to get things out. I'm very conscious of death, of an unseen clock ticking away in the background. Quickly, Geri, don't wait. You have to leave your mark.

It was also important to be loved. As a child I used to

go to my mother each day and ask her, 'Who has been the best girl today?'

I wanted her to say, 'You, Geri.'

I still find myself asking the same question of people, seeking their approval.

At a Blur concert in London with Melanie Chisholm, Sporty Spice, we stood on the balcony as the spotlights picked us out and the crowd of 2,000 turned and looked up. They began waving and we waved back, but I could see only one girl, who raised her arm and stuck up her finger.

Oh, my God, that girl doesn't like me, I thought. Why? What have I done to her? It ruined the night for me and sent me tumbling down.

I didn't always need *everyone* to love me. In the beginning I just wanted to show a few people that I *could* make it, like my mum and dad, brother and sisters, aunts and uncles, and friends from school. I wanted to shout, Hey, look at me!

Later it became a way of saying I told you so to the boyfriends who'd dumped me, the bosses who'd sacked me, the directors who hadn't cast me and the agencies who didn't sign me.

There's a battered brown Datsun parked just up the road with two photographers inside. I don't know what they look like because their faces are always obscured by cameras. Sometimes they change cars, or try to be clever by driving two or three cars behind when they follow me; they probably figure I won't notice them. Do they think I'm stupid? How many battered Datsuns are there in Beverly Hills?

I first noticed them in the rear-view mirror as I turned

onto Sunset Boulevard about five days ago. A friend and I were going to a gym in West Hollywood and I thought we'd managed to lose them. We found a parking space, but there were two dustbins in the way. I looked at Kenny and thought about the Datsun. 'I don't think I should move those.'

Kenny smiled and shook his head. 'I can see the headline, GERI'S NEW JOB.'

I stepped out of the Range Rover and looked up. The Datsun was parked about 100 yards further along the road, with a zoom lens poking from the rear window.

The boys were still there an hour later, with reinforcements in a second car.

'What do they *want* from me?' I sighed.

'The unguarded moment,' Kenny said. 'The new boyfriend or the bad-hair day . . .'

'I've just had an idea.' I grinned. 'Let's go to the Beverly Center.'

Kenny looked puzzled. 'The Church of Scientology?'

'I'm going to give them an unguarded moment.'

A short time later we pulled up outside a futuristic building, all concrete, chrome and glass. I pushed through the swing doors and strode past potted palms. A receptionist switched on an automatic smile. 'Hello, my name is Carly. I wish you peace and love.'

'Do you sell books?'

'Are you looking for the truth?'

'Pardon?'

'Are you looking for a new direction in your life?'

'No, just a book. Have you got some sort of bible?'

She produced a hardback the size of an atlas – *The Scientology Handbook* – and I handed her a credit card.

'That'll be one hundred and twenty-five dollars.'

'Wow! It must be a bloody great read.'

I tucked the book under one arm, making sure the title was clearly visible, and then walked outside. Someone had strung a banner across the street which asked, 'Is Anybody Out There?'

I paused just momentarily, and that was the picture that appeared in the *Daily Mail* the next morning. The headline read, GERI TURNS TO SCIENTOLOGY FOR A NEW CHAPTER IN HER LIFE.

The story announced that I had forsaken my skimpy Union Jack dresses and platform shoes to seek spiritual enlightenment in the Church of Scientology. This put me in good company because other 'cult disciples' included Tom Cruise, his wife Nicole Kidman and John Travolta, according to the article.

A source 'close' to me had apparently confirmed my search for 'happiness and peace of mind'.

Natalie arrived on Wednesday with my three-year-old nephew Alastair. He's running around the pool wearing inflatable armbands and playing with the waterfall. I really want to take him to Disneyland, although maybe he'll have to settle for the beach instead. I'll take Natalie shopping on Rodeo Drive.

Last night Kenny took us to a showbiz party in Santa Monica – one of those affairs where the waiters wear rented tuxedos with a screenplay tucked into an inside pocket, and everyone stands around trying to spot the celebrity and be discovered at the same time. Demi and Bruce were supposed to be going, according to the whispers. Someone thought they saw Sharon Stone in the bathroom.

But there were no celebrities. It wasn't much of a party, either, because nobody went there to have a good time. The place was packed with wannabes, so desperate I could smell it. I used to smell like that. I must have reeked of it.

Alastair has crawled up onto my knee with a bedtime storybook. He reaches up and touches my hair. 'No more red,' he says. I'm amazed that he's noticed; he's normally only interested in Batman and Robin.

My hair is almost back to its natural colour and the fancy-dress clothes have gone. I hardly wear any make-up these days. A lot has changed. Ginger Spice is no more. I wonder if she'll rest in peace.

# LOVE, KISS AND BROKEN PROMISES

Lee and Christopher were in the kitchen debating which of them was going to snog me. We were at my friend Shona's twelfth birthday party, sitting in the lounge listening to 'Move Closer' by Phyllis Nelson and 'Cherish' by Kool and the Gang – good snogging songs.

Lee said that because he'd been my boyfriend twice before it was only fair that he should kiss me. We were in the same class at junior school and used to play Truth, Dare, Double Dare, Love, Kiss or Promise in the stock cupboard. I would run my hand across his skinhead haircut and tell him it tickled.

Even at that age I was aware of sexual attraction, but in a very naive and childish way. I wore a green drop-waisted miniskirt, with my hair in braided pigtails, and when I looked in the mirror, I thought, Yeah you're looking kinda sexy today.

I had dropped Lee and started going out with Darren from Unit Six, who was one of those really bad kids that everyone said was a bit mental. Then my friend Tina started going out with Lee and I got jealous and wanted him back. It caused some tension.

From the kitchen I heard Christopher say, 'I'm gonna get off with Geri.' In our language 'get off' meant kissing with tongues.

'No, you're not. I'm gonna,' said Lee.

'I said I was gonna first.'

'She used to be *my* girlfriend.'

'But she's not your girlfriend now.'

'She is . . . er . . . sort of.'

'You broke up.'

'Well, she's more mine than yours.'

The whole conversation seemed totally absurd. I didn't expect kissing to be so premeditated; it took away all the excitement. I thought it just happened naturally and, besides, I didn't belong to anybody.

I made my choice. Lee was being a prat to assume a prior claim over me, so I chose Christopher. Shona had also said that he'd cry if I didn't pick him.

We snogged on the sofa and I remember seeing Lee out of the corner of my eye motioning to Christopher to put his hand up my top. I figured he was going to be rather disappointed because I had no bra to unhitch and nothing to grab.

He went to do it. 'I don't wear a bra,' I said, apologetically.

He mumbled something incomprehensible and kept kissing me.

Lee stuck his tongue out, signalling for Christopher to do the same. I was so shocked my mouth locked shut and his tongue went round my lips like a washing machine. I had to wipe the spit off afterwards. I found out later that Christopher told everyone I had a really small mouth. I was so embarrassed.

The next day I saw him hanging around on the corner after school, waiting for me. Shona and I were sitting on the brick wall, biting our nails. I just wanted him to go away.

I lived in the same house in Jubilee Road, Watford, for my whole childhood. It was around the corner from the Pakistani supermarket which had gum-ball machines and boxes of over-ripened fruit and veg out front. Eileen, who ran the greengrocer's opposite, used to target her discounts to make sure nobody bought veg from the Pakistanis.

There was no major landmark to help you get your geographical bearings in my neighbourhood. Every street looked almost identical, like the set of *Coronation Street*. Our two-storey semi had a flat front, set a few feet back from the road, and was plastered in a hideous pebble-dash, which my mother seemed to like. Every other house was the same, with a coal bunker, outside toilet and postage-stamp-sized back garden. The only unusual feature of our house was a single-car garage, and above the door my father had painted the words GARAGE ENTRANCE in large black letters. Heaven help anyone who parked across *his* driveway.

There were three bedrooms upstairs. Mum and Dad had the main one, overlooking the street, and I shared the next one with Natalie, who is three years older than me. We had a bunk bed – I slept on top – a wardrobe and a chest of drawers. Our brother, Max, who is two years older again, had a room the size of a broom cupboard at the very back of the house, overlooking the garden.

The three of us had some terrible fights in those years – real scraps, with no prisoners taken. Max gave Natalie a black eye with something he threw and another time I bloodied her nose. Although I was the youngest, I could hold my own, even if it meant biting and scratching.

When the air cleared, we nursed our bruises and began worrying about Mum finding out. Handwritten notes were slipped beneath bedroom doors, asking, 'Are you going to tell Mum?' There were boxes to tick for 'yes' or 'no'.

I don't remember my mother being home very often. She was always at work, cleaning offices and libraries. She left at 6 a.m., well before I woke up. I'd make my own breakfast and then kneel on a stool at the kitchen sink, looking in a mirror and trying to get the bunches straight in my hair.

'Do they look straight?' I'd ask Dad.

He'd grunt something unintelligible, without even looking up. Why did I bother? Normally he didn't get up that early, or would still be in the bathroom clearing his throat and spitting into the sink. Even when Mum was home I preferred to do my own hair. She used to pull the bunches back hard and say, 'You have to suffer to be beautiful, Geri,' whenever I complained.

Still balancing on the stool, I made my own school lunch, which was always crap compared to everyone else's. I used to be embarrassed when I opened my lunchbox, and jealous of those kids who got proper school dinners, or had mothers who slipped special treats into their schoolbags like salt and vinegar crisps and Marathon bars.

'Hello, welcome to *Home and Away*, the daily lifestyle programme for working mothers and home-makers,' I'd say, talking to the kitchen wall as if presenting *Blue Peter*. 'Today, I'm going to show you how to make the perfect peanut-butter sandwich. It's quick, easy and will have your children coming back for more . . .

'First, you need two slices of bread. You can use any type of bread – brown, white, wholemeal, although I prefer white – and I've found that your typical square slices fit much better into the lunch box.

'First spread a layer of butter on each slice – make sure you go right to the edges, otherwise you may find your child won't eat the crusts. Then you spread the peanut butter, again going right to the edges. Press the two slices of bread together and cut diagonally into large triangles. There, wasn't that easy?'

Also featured on my 'show' at various times were segments on 'How to make the perfect toffee apple' and 'Make your own perfume with flower petals'.

We all had chores to do before and after school, and Mum would check our efforts when she got home from work each evening. Normally, I had to do the washing up and clean the bathroom; Natalie tidied the sitting room and bedrooms, while Max did the vacuuming. To do the washing up, I had to once again kneel on a stool, trying to keep my balance. When I tried to empty the bowl, the water would splash back and drench me.

Meanwhile, the neighbourhood kids would be playing in the street outside. Although we weren't supposed to talk to them or join in, we often sneaked outside to play British Bulldog, racing back and forth between the footpaths, trying not to get caught by those in the middle. Another favourite game was Knock Down Ginger – ringing doorbells and then running away. We kept watch for

Mum's car at about 7.30 p.m., so we could dash inside before she spotted us.

She was always quite house-proud, which is often the case with people who haven't much money. She used to say to me, 'Geri, no matter how little we have, you're always clean and well fed.' And then she'd go on about how much she'd sacrificed. 'Look at me, I haven't been to the hairdresser in seven years. When was the last time I went out? I buy nothing for myself. No dresses, no shoes.'

I didn't hear the message, only the weary tone. Every chore she asked me to do, I regarded as a denial of my freedom. Hadn't child slavery been abolished?

My mother is one of seven children. She was born Ana Maria Hidalgo, in a small Spanish village near Huesca in the foothills of the Pyrenees in northern Spain. Her grandfather had been the mayor of Córdoba in the late 1930s, when the military overthrew the civilian government and General Franco seized power for the Fascists.

My great grandfather tried to convince the wealthy landowners to allow the starving peasants to grow food on the unused fields. The Fascists accused him of being a Communist and had him executed by a firing squad in the town square. His son – my grandfather – was sent to prison, where he met and married one of the prison guards – my grandmother.

I grew up hearing this story from my grandparents in Spain. Their lives had been so full of romance, tragedy and adventure that I wondered if anything in my life would be the same.

My mother was stunning in her youth, with long, thick black hair, high cheekbones, a lovely petite figure and striking looks. Her father had been only five feet tall and she was five feet one. At seventeen, she left home to work in a factory in Switzerland and later she became an au pair. She arrived in London just after her twenty-first birthday, excited about having seen the sea for the first time.

She met my father within days of stepping off the boat. He spied this beautiful creature walking in the street near Marble Arch. He straightened his tie, glanced at his reflection in a shop window and followed her into a pharmacy.

I can just imagine that first meeting – his salesman's patter, the wad of cash in his pocket and his supreme knowledge of how to impress a girl. The *señorita* didn't stand a chance.

Laurence Francis Halliwell was a car dealer, entrepreneur, womanizer and chancer. He was also a liar and a rogue. The fact that he was forty-four years old and divorced didn't come up in the conversation. Instead, he told my mother that his first wife had died in a car accident. He'd been left to raise two young children, Paul and Karen, alone. My mother's heart began melting.

She discovered the truth about his age seven weeks later at the registry office when they married. His ex-wife turned up another six months later – back from America rather than from beyond the grave. Yet, despite these surprises, Ana Maria had high expectations. She imagined her new husband to be a rich, successful businessman, but eventually she realized she had been wooed under false pretences.

Laurence could have been a very rich man, but for the fact that every way he found to earn money he found two ways to spend it. He was an Arthur Daley type – always looking for a new angle and dreaming about his next big deal.

He was born in Liverpool in 1922 after my grand-mother had a brief encounter with a Swedish merchant seaman who turned out to be married and disappeared home to his wife. My gran was left pregnant and abandoned in an era when single motherhood was a stain that didn't come out in the wash.

My surname might have been Sjovik if the sailor had hung around, but instead Gran married Mr Richard Laurence Halliwell. Dad always referred to himself as 'the bastard son', and I don't think his stepfather ever really accepted him.

The family moved to north London when Laurence was still a child. At the start of the war he became an engineer at RAF Northolt. He once told me that he'd managed to get out of the fighting by pretending he was gay and wetting his bed. I don't know if I believed him, although I can't see why he'd lie.

His entrepreneurial skills were already being sharpened. In a time of rationing, he took advantage of the thriving black market in ration coupons, nylons and chocolate. He also cashed in on the shortage of petrol by flogging bicycles to the American servicemen in exchange for sought-after luxuries.

Before long he'd made enough to buy his own car dealership and he had the potential to be a very wealthy man. But by the time he married my mother a lot of the big money had gone – soaked up by bad deals. His only asset was the house in Jubilee Road.

* * *

I was born at Watford General Hospital on 6 August 1972. Mum always said they gave her so much gas and air that she was delirious.

'"It's coming, it's coming," I tell them. And they say, "No, Mrs Halliwell, it can't be coming yet." And suddenly you shot out.'

I had visions of being propelled across the room like a cannon ball, with the midwife having to catch me before I ricocheted off the far wall.

My arrival at Jubilee Road wasn't cause for wild celebrations. I was considered just another mouth to feed. This gave me the sense of being a survivor and scrapping for attention.

My memories of those early years are a hotchpotch of fleeting images, like the photographs in a family album. Although I feel guilty about it now, as soon as I was old enough to have such thoughts I suffered from a cuckoo mentality. I imagined that I'd somehow been swapped at birth and placed with the wrong family. Max and Natalie did nothing to discourage this, and instead they'd dance around my bed like Indian braves, chanting, 'You're adopted. You're adopted.'

When I arrived Dad was fifty years old, with a dodgy hip, a growing waistline and receding hair. It took quite a bit of imagination to picture him as a ladykiller, although the photographs of him as a young man show he was quite handsome. I can only remember him as an old man, with a big belly and bad asthma, using his puffer all the time. He had striking grey eyes and a very turned-up nose, with a blob on the end, like mine. God realized my face wasn't screwed up enough, so he pinched the tip.

I'm a true mix of both my parents. Natalie got the

darkness of my mother, while Max is completely white-blond, like Dad. I'm in between, with mousy-brown hair, flecked with red. My complexion is edging towards olive, yet I have blue eyes and freckles on my nose – a mix of Swedish and Spanish.

I think I got both their personalities, too – the contained, cool Swedish side, and the fiery hot temper of the Mediterranean.

Another legacy was my diminutive size. I was so small as a child that my aunts in Spain nicknamed me 'la enana' – the dwarf. As the years passed I showed no desire to grow, and eventually, at the age of nine, my mother took me to a specialist.

The doctors took X-rays and ran a series of tests. They wanted to put me on human growth hormone, but thankfully common sense prevailed and I was left alone. As it turned out, I wasn't a midget – simply half Spanish.

Throughout these years I can't remember my father having a proper job. He damaged his hip in a car accident soon after I was born and moved with a ducklike waddle and a walking stick afterwards. Yet even before the crash he didn't do much, and afterwards he didn't even bother pretending. He claimed that all his bad luck stemmed from putting up an umbrella inside the house. I wondered if laziness could be caused by bad luck.

My mother took cleaning jobs to support us while Dad hung around the house and pottered in the garage. Occasionally he picked up a cheap second-hand car, fixed it up and then sold it off for a few quid profit. That's why he always drove an old banger, and I used to be embarrassed when he picked me up from school because my friends would see how poor I was and also that my father was so old. He looked more like my grandfather.

My dad would spend most of his days in the garage and emerge wiping grease from his fingers or picking dirt from beneath his nails. Mum would scream at him about oil on his boots when he came into the kitchen.

He was an intimidating figure who was famous for his outbursts about people blocking his garage driveway. The local kids would tease him, standing outside our house and chanting, 'Hitler has only got one ball,' and then scatter when he came out to challenge them.

Dad wasn't the type to play games with me or read bedtime stories. By then he was already regressing into his own second childhood. The two of us would wander down to the sweetshop, like two kids together, to choose our favourite ice cream. And when we had no money, Mum would occasionally find sweet wrappers under the sofa and realize that Dad had been holding out on us. Another time, he went off to pay a bill and came back with a little vase he'd bought instead because he thought it looked beautiful.

'Your father is a dreamer,' Mum would say. 'He lives in cuckoo land.'

I have some happy childhood memories of him. He brought home a game of Monopoly once – a really big deal in a house with no presents or games. And I remember one Christmas he crawled about on all fours, pretending to be a horse, and he let me ride on his back.

Occasionally, on a hot summer's day, he'd announce that we were off to the beach and we'd pile into the old banger – we had a series of Hillman Imps – and head for Bournemouth or Southend or Brighton. Dad would nominate a beach, and without fail we'd finish up somewhere different. Us kids would sit in the back on vinyl seats that stuck to our buttocks like Velcro and argue over whose turn it was to sit by the window and who was taking up too much space. But all would be forgiven when we splashed in the shallows and ate soft-whip ice-cream cones.

When I was about eight, Dad made me a doll's house, with doors that moved and stairs between the floors. My grandmother in Spain gave me £50 to buy the furniture, which I thought was a vast amount of money. It was. Natalie and I created a 'dolly land' and even Max would come and play, having made his own sock dolls. In miniature, we played happy families, although none of us knew exactly how a happy family was supposed to behave. Later, when I was by myself, I used to make my Sindy doll shag my teddy and wonder what their babies would look like.

I loved my father on his good days, but sometimes this was overshadowed by an unpredictable temper. He would pull his belt from his trousers and snap it through the air like a whip. As I lay hiding under the bed, I heard him shouting, 'Ready, ready red legs,' before he pulled me out and whipped me across the back of my thighs.

He was a very bright man, full of aspiration and goals, but ill-health and unfulfilled ambition had crept up on him, which left him sad and frustrated. When my parents fought, plates of spaghetti went flying across the kitchen and cups of tea stained the walls. Neither my mother's accent, nor her Spanish temper, diminished over the years, and she seemed to grow harder with age while he softened.

'Geri, you marry a rich man,' she'd say, as I helped her

clean up the broken dishes and wipe down the kitchen cabinets.

Both my parents seemed to be full of disappointment. I think Dad did truly love her, but she lost respect for him. The bitterness started and they began draining each other's energy.

Although she had been raised as a Catholic, my mother joined the Jehovah's Witnesses when I was very young. She never gave a reason, although I suspect she felt lonely and wanted to escape from my father. Clutching my favourite toys, yellow Ted and my black dolly Pippa, I sat through endless sermons at the King's Hall and learned Bible stories like Jonah and the Whale.

Afterwards, small groups stepped out to spread the word. 'From door to door to teach to preach . . .,' they sang. I stood on doorsteps, clutching my mother's hand. Nobody ever wanted to invite us inside, and some of them were quite rude.

The Jehovah's Witnesses didn't celebrate birthdays or Christmas, which is pretty difficult for a child to understand. Parties and presents matter at that age. I didn't go to friends' birthday parties because I didn't have a gift to give them.

Just as I grew old enough to be embarrassed by this, my mother abandoned her new faith in disillusionment. 'My expectations were too high,' she said later. 'They were a bunch of hypocrites who were just as materialistic and greedy as the rest of us.'

Ballet lessons and horse riding were beyond our family's means, although it didn't stop me asking for them. Ultimately, like most kids, I created my own happiness. I had daydreams that were like show-reels playing in my head, so vivid they seemed real. For example, after seeing Narnia in *The Lion, the Witch and the Wardrobe*, I used to climb into the back of cupboards and look for the secret doors. When I couldn't find one, I'd sit in the darkness and imagine I was there, surrounded by snow.

Another of my fantasies was perhaps less understandable. My dad was a true-blue Tory, a rare species in our neighbourhood. Margaret Thatcher was probably the first woman he ever truly respected. On the day she became prime minister he made me sit down and watch her speech on the steps of 10 Downing Street.

'Where there is discord, may we bring harmony. Where there is error, may we bring truth . . .'

Only six years old, I didn't understand most of what she said, but I knew she was famous. I thought to myself, that's what I'll be when I grow up: prime minister. I could see myself standing on a soapbox or addressing my adoring subjects from a balcony, Evita style.

I always wanted to be famous. Maybe I was born that way. At six, I imagined fame to be like a magic key that would unlock a door to a fantasy world where I wouldn't be lonely, poor or frightened. There would be no worries in this place – I wouldn't have to beg for money from Mum, or hear her go on about how much she'd sacrificed; I could buy whatever clothes I wanted, eat my favourite foods and have a fridge full of Marathon bars. I could even visualize having a chair like a throne and servants padding back and forth.

Another of my show-reels began with a red carpet with a gold-fringed satin canopy stretching above it. Thousands of people would wait behind barricades as a vintage car came to a stop and a chauffeur opened the door. The crowd would draw a breath when they glimpsed my elegant white evening gown and matching stole. Two men wearing tuxedos would be waiting to escort me. I'd wave a gloved hand and smile at the crowd before taking their arms and following the red carpet.

Where did it lead? I wasn't quite sure, but I knew it must have been somewhere far more glamorous than Jubilee Road, Watford.

I hadn't decided if I wanted to be a pop star or a screen siren. Compromising, I imagined living in a cream-coloured castle with a moat and a drawbridge. It wasn't a bad guess from what I've seen of Beverly Hills.

I still daydreamed about having been switched at birth. At any moment my real parents would arrive to collect me. One afternoon, as Mum dragged me through C&A in Watford, looking for bargain clothes from the cut-price carousels, I looked up and saw a picture of a beautiful woman wearing a polo-neck jumper and jodhpurs. She looked like Farrah Fawcett-Majors and was hugging two angelic-looking children in ski gear.

I turned to Mum and announced, 'That's my real mother.' I pointed at the picture. 'That's her! That's her!'

Mum tried to smile as the other shoppers began staring at us. She pinched my arm and whispered angrily, 'Wait till I get you home.'

Daily our family squabbles would come at mealtimes and food came to represent many things to me, including both praise and punishment.

Like all families we had our rituals. A plate of buttered bread took a central position on the table, and Dad would go ballistic if anyone dared put a buttery knife in the jam jar, or jam on the butter.

Mum tried her best to cook English food, like pork chops and veg, with mashed potatoes and gravy, but would always add a Spanish touch. Even her roast lamb, which I loved, came served with paella.

She shopped for food each Friday and had a 'goodies' cupboard where she put any extra treats she'd managed to buy. This remained locked to stop us raiding it while she was out. She would send me down to Eileen the green-grocer to pick up the vegetables – everything except for the bags of potatoes, which were too heavy for me to carry.

Occasionally she gave me an extra ten pence, which I could spend on a bag of penny sweets or go across to the Pakistani shop and buy a Mars bar. At other times, I would have to search the whole house for coppers until I scraped together twelve pence – enough for a chocolate ice cream.

My eating habits were terrible and another source of conflict at mealtimes. I hated almost all vegetables and dairy products. The term lactose-intolerant didn't figure in the Halliwell family dictionary, so I was expected to drink a glass of milk at dinner – which normally ended up in the pot plant. I was also made to stay at the table for what seemed like hours, making myself physically ill as I vomited up Brussels sprouts and cauliflower. I was then forced to re-eat them, with my mother holding my jaw shut.

Only Sunday lunches were free of arguments, perhaps because I normally liked the food or my parents treated it as a day of rest. When the dishes had been cleared and the gravy stains sponged from the tablecloth, Dad would say, 'Sing for us, Geri.'

Max and Natalie would roll their eyes.

I stood in the centre of the lounge and sang a Brotherhood of Man song, 'Figaro', with one of my legs twitching nervously. Mum would say, 'Come on, Geri, do Shirley Bassey arms,' and she'd try to show me, swinging her arms in time with the song.

Then we'd all squeeze into the front room around the TV, which was like a sixth member of the family. I loved the American soap operas, like *Dynasty* and *Dallas*, which were full of glamorous women with power suits and attitude. Compared to them, *Coronation Street* seemed boring and mundane; too close to home.

# 2

## 'I WANNA BE A NIGHTCLUB QUEEN'

Callowland Infant School was three blocks from Jubilee
Road, nestled beneath large trees in a nice part of
Watford. Often I walked to school by myself or rode in a
car with Roberto, a Spanish boy who lived up the road.
We sat in the back seat giggling at his father's copy of the
*Sun* and the topless girl on page three. Bare boobs are very
funny when you're six years old.

The school had no uniform and I arrived one day to
find everybody wearing their best clothes. The class
photographs were being taken and I'd forgotten to tell my
mother. I panicked. What if I wasn't wearing the right
clothes?

I looked like a scraggy kid at the best of times and the
social hierarchy of the school was determined by such
things. The scruffy kids were segregated onto what we
called 'the fleabag table', which normally had the
Pakistanis and really poor kids on it.

I found myself sitting there one day and wetting my
pants in the canteen. I was given a pair of knickers from
the lost-property box. They had fish printed on them and

proper elastic in the waistband. I was so pleased because they were far nicer than the hand-me-downs and jumble-sale knickers I normally wore.

Being small for my age and self-conscious about my height, I befriended several of the 'fleabags', including Tina, who *did* have fleas; Sonia, who used to pinch me under the desk, and John, who picked his nose.

In a bid to win friends and impress people, I became a compulsive liar. I used to tell people that we had sheep in our back garden to keep the grass short. I also claimed to wear contact lenses. When my teacher looked into my eyes and couldn't see any lenses, I explained to her that they covered my entire eyeball.

I was eventually cured of lying when I feigned a mystery back complaint which baffled doctors in Watford until a specialist at the hospital took my mother to one side and suggested to her that I was making the whole thing up.

Back I went to school. And from then on, like the boy who cried wolf, I had trouble convincing Mum when I was genuinely feeling sick.

My friends from the neighbourhood included Emma over the road, who suffered from polio and wore a brace on her leg. I was also allowed to join Max and his mates in a daredevil gang because I was small enough to get into places they couldn't. We used to climb on rooftops to show our bravery which, indirectly, led me to see our neighbour Percy wandering naked in his back garden. He smiled and waved. I nearly fell off.

During the long summer holiday, Max, Natalie and I would sometimes go to Spain to visit our grandmother, returning fat and bloated because she overfed us.

Dad normally stayed at home and Mum came with us.

On one such holiday my grandmother announced that we were off to find some snails. This is great, I thought. At home I used to collect snails and give each of them names before racing them from the centre of a circle. I didn't realize that my *abuela* – grandmother – intended to string them up and cook them. Horrified, I refused to eat them.

I considered bullfighting equally cruel. Our cousins would take us to the local bullring, and I'd cover my eyes when it was time to execute the poor tormented animal. The crowd would be cheering the matador's bravery, but Max, Natalie and I would shout down insults in our best Spanish. He wasn't courageous. He wouldn't even step into the ring until the bull had been exhausted and weakened by picadors and dwarves who danced out from behind the barricades.

My first experience of death was at one of the regular Sunday morning shows, when a baby bull was set loose in the ring. Dozens of teenagers would jump the fence and tease the animal, showing off to each other. One of them, a young boy, didn't move quickly enough and was trampled beneath the bull's hooves. His jaw was ripped out and he died in the arena. I was eight years old, and the violence of the scene branded itself on my consciousness. Yet I also had a strange sense of justice having been done. The contest would never be even, but at least the bulls had scored a minor victory.

At home during the holidays, Mum sometimes took me to work with her. As she vacuumed the Watford College library, I would stand on a table opposite a big mirror and pretend to be Marlene Dietrich or Rita Hayworth.

I had seen Natalie in a school play as a character who was a dowdy old housewife until someone sprinkled magic dust on her and turned her into a sultry nightclub singer. She sang a jazzy number, all low and husky, called 'I Wanna Be A Nightclub Queen'.

This is the song I belted out, imagining a huge audience watching me. In reality, if anybody had looked in they would have seen a goofy-looking kid with rabbit-like front teeth singing into a duster.

The life I wanted seemed to exist only in old musicals like *Singin' in the Rain*, *High Society* and *My Fair Lady*. I used to daydream about being Grace Kelly or Audrey Hepburn, and imagined that women like that really *did* look beautiful when they woke up in the morning.

My dad loved old musicals, and on rainy days we'd watch films about people putting on a show to save the old theatre or the old farm. Later, when I fell in love with the young Elvis, Shona and I would dance around the sitting room in our bikinis singing, 'Do the clam! Do the clam!'

By the time I moved to Walter de Merton Junior School, every girl in the neighbourhood seemed to be wearing rah-rah skirts and pink pedal-pushers. It was another mixed state school in a mainly working-class area, with a large council estate up the road.

Being cheeky and disruptive, I managed to find trouble occasionally. One really butch-looking girl, Gail, picked me up and threatened to throw me over the school fence onto the railway lines after I called her a boy. Dad had to come and straighten things out.

Junior school is where I first met Shona. I looked at her

fingernails one day and saw they were all broken and discoloured. My mum said it was because of malnutrition, an opinion I repeated at school the next day. Somehow it got back to Shona's mother, a gruff Scotswoman, who came storming up to the school, screaming, 'My daughter is not malnourished.' Again, Dad had to sort it out.

I played centre in the school netball team, and what I lacked in height I made up for with speed. In the team photograph I'm the one sitting in the front row, all teeth and rosy cheeks. Beside me is my friend Sarah. I used to sleep over at her house and we'd have midnight feasts of chocolate crunchies. Sarah's eldest sister used to practise snogging on her, which I thought a little weird. After all, most of us just practised on the back of our hand.

When I was nine years old I went to the headmaster and asked if we could put on a small concert each Friday afternoon. There were five of us, and we arranged the performances ourselves, writing the one-act plays, organizing costumes and practising in the sandpit during lunch break.

They were terrible plays, mostly improvised when lines were forgotten, and laced with melodrama that had people swooning and fainting when bad news arrived. Eventually, so many of the cast had been shot or had fainted there was no-one left to continue.

Afterwards I sang a pop song by Renee and Renato called 'Save Your Love', followed by a husky version of 'The Good Ship Lollipop'.

I once tried to reason why I went to such lengths to perform and decided it was probably because I never got picked for the major parts in the official school productions. Normally I'd be in the choir or playing a tree.

My only speaking role was in a play about creatures from outer space coming to Earth. I was cast as an alien child and had a single line. Sitting in the classroom with human kids, I had to ask, 'Has Earth got a dark side like us, then?'

I practised my line for weeks, panicking about the big night. It seemed so strange to want desperately to be in the play and then to be almost paralysed by fear and insecurity at having to perform. I forced myself, shaking in my alien shoes. How could I be famous if I suffered from stage fright?

I've always been pretty creative, and in those days I used to sit on the back steps, waiting to use the outside loo, writing poetry that rhymed and song lyrics. Dad loved listening to me sing and I think he had visions of me being a child star. He knew Mum would never approve.

One Sunday we sneaked out of the house and drove to see a theatrical agent in north London. Stella Greenfield had a rambling old house in Golders Green, with theatre posters and photographs all over the walls, as well as hundreds of books crammed onto her shelves.

Stella was ancient, with thick glasses that distorted her eyes and a creaky voice. She reminded me of Baron Greenback, the toad in *Dangermouse*.

I had a little dress with a cream jacket and I took off my coat and hung it over a small, child-sized chair. Stella asked me to read a poem from a book, which I didn't do very well, and then I put my hands on my hips and sang 'I Wanna Be A Nightclub Queen'.

My voice was quite deep and Stella seemed to like it.

'Well done, that was very good,' she croaked. 'Yes, we can do something with you.'

She wanted to put me on her books and send me to auditions for TV commercials and the West End revival of *Annie*. I went home in the car dreaming of fame and stardom.

We arrived at the house quite late and Mum realized something was going on. I told her breathlessly how I was going to be a movie star. She listened with her hands on her hips and her eyes fixed firmly on my father.

'I am not having my daughter becoming a Judy Garland,' she said. 'I know what happens to child stars: they commit suicide.'

'But Mum . . . but Mum . . .'

'No, Geri, you become a teacher. It's a good job.'

'But what about Shirley Bassey? You like her,' I pleaded.

'She grew up first.'

Eventually we compromised. Mum allowed me to take part in a charity concert at the Rudolf Steiner Hall in London which involved more than fifty children. It was billed as *The Stars of Today and Tomorrow*.

Most of the cast members were from various drama and stage schools around the country. At the start of rehearsals we each had to stand beside a piano and sing 'The Sun Will Come Out Tomorrow' from *Annie*. I didn't know the words and couldn't read music. The other kids had been brought up singing songs from popular musicals, while I was used to belting out Abba and Brotherhood of Man numbers to the mirror in Watford College library. They'd been to dance classes and singing lessons while I was pretending to be a nightclub queen. Not surprisingly, I ended up in the chorus.

They did, however, give me a bit part in one of the

drama sketches. I played the wind and had to wear a leotard with netted arms and long flowing strips of fabric. My big moment was when I had to dance across the stage, making appropriately windlike noises, and snatch a hankie from a girl's hand. I was so bloody ungraceful and clumsy that I risked bowling everyone over.

The other kids were absolutely fantastic, including the boy from the Curly Wurly commercial on TV who we all looked up to as a real pro.

Dad drove me to weekend rehearsals for three months. We put on two performances, mainly for an audience of family and friends. I was so excited, I borrowed my Mum's leopard-skin vanity case to carry all my bits and pieces of make-up.

As the curtain came up, I stood in the chorus wearing a horrible pink lurex leotard that stretched from neck to foot. The show opened with 'We Are Only Beginners' and then we sang 'You're Never Fully Dressed Without a Smile' and 'Tomorrow' both from *Annie*. We finished with 'There's No Business Like Show Business'.

My portrayal of the wind was an artistic triumph, which couldn't even be upstaged by the Curly Wurly boy wetting his pants in the wings, having suddenly suffered a bout of first-night nerves. It happens to the best of us.

Some time soon after that, my mum and dad decided to separate. It wasn't as simple as someone packing their bags and moving out. For months beforehand Dad stayed in his room most of the time, lying in bed watching TV, surrounded by smelly tissues. He had this disgusting habit of drawing back and clearing phlegm from his throat every morning, and spitting it into tissues, which he'd toss anywhere.

On Christmas Day Dad stayed in his half of the house, lying in his bed upstairs. He watched TV alone while we ate chips and chops for Christmas dinner in the front room downstairs.

I knew Mum didn't love him any more. I didn't blame her; he was a lousy husband.

Glancing up, there was a card on the mantelpiece that read, 'Peace and goodwill to all men'.

I remembered the Monopoly game and Dad crawling on all fours giving me 'horse rides'. Then I imagined him upstairs, alone on Christmas Day. I'd never felt so sad.

Soon afterwards, Max, Natalie and I were sent to stay with various relatives and friends. I went to my stepsister Karen's house. Karen and my stepbrother, Paul, had both left home by the time I was born, but I'd always been close to Karen.

She was married with two children and living in South Oxhey – the biggest council estate in Europe. I don't know how long I lived with them; it may have only been a few weeks, but it felt like much longer. I helped Karen change baby Mandy's nappies and do the housework. For the first time in my life I experienced what it was like to be part of a 'normal' family.

When Mum came to collect me from Karen's I cried because I didn't want to go back home. I wanted to stay with Karen and her proper family.

Dad had gone. He moved into a high-rise council flat in Garston, a rough area of Watford. The twin tower blocks looked like grey headstones against the skyline and I was frightened to go there alone. The lifts stank of urine and the rubbish chute reeked. Sometimes people just dropped their bags of rubbish over the balcony and they exploded on impact, littering the forecourt. Even their unwanted furniture went over the side, like sandbags dropped from a sinking balloon.

I saw the flat before Dad moved in and almost cried. Later, I would visit once a week and clean for him, washing the grease from all the kitchenware and utensils and making sure he had milk in the fridge. Sometimes I stayed to do my homework and he would make me a 'dusty salad' – so called because it seemed to be sprinkled with grit.

He wandered around in his underpants, not even bothering to get dressed.

The fact that our parents didn't have the best parenting skills in the world meant that Natalie, Max and I grew closer and relied more upon each other. I began to grow up very quickly.

I worshipped Natalie and wanted to be exactly like her. She was beautiful, whereas I was quite plain – cute at best. She had breasts, boyfriends and big brown eyes. She could dance to soul music and wear make-up. Completely in awe of her, I became her little shadow.

When Natalie worked at John Miller's bakery, I turned up to see if they'd give me a job, too. And I trailed after her when she went shopping with her friends, generally making a nuisance of myself. Nat had every right to complain, but she didn't get upset.

When she was sixteen, on a holiday in Majorca, she entered a hotel beauty contest and came second. In the photographs, I'm the flat-chested kid next to her with braces and a terrible perm. God, I envied her. I still do.

Boys were a complete mystery to me, yet they buzzed around Natalie like bees round a honey pot. She became the closest thing I had to an icon, until I discovered Madonna, the material girl.

Sex wasn't something my mother talked about openly or otherwise. Instead she adopted a rather Spanish way of dealing with the subject. 'You must be careful of boys because they make you pregnant.' That was it. No other details.

For this reason, my sex education was limited to discussions with Natalie after lights-out and the occasional lecture at school. I also discovered the steamier passages of a Jackie Collins novel and tore off the front cover to keep it a secret from Mum. Strangely, the bonking locations were so exotic that I couldn't imagine sex occurring anywhere as ordinary or mundane as Watford.

When I finally discovered the mechanics of sex it came as a shock. Thirty of us gathered to watch a video at junior school, sitting on a mat in front of the TV. I thought I was the only person in class who had absolutely no idea before then. All the boys seemed so cool and laid back. Although, saying that, I noticed most of them had their eyes sticking out on stalks during the video.

Afterwards, Mrs Flit, a teacher in her late twenties, who had curly brown hair and lipstick permanently smudged in the corners of her mouth, asked if we had any questions.

I wanted to ask her something but didn't want to put myself forward. Finally I plucked up the courage. 'So, with twins, does that mean you do it twice?'

Everybody laughed. I was so embarrassed.

My first crush on a boy was directed at one of Max's friends, who must have been about seventeen. Grant had been in our daredevil gang when I was much younger. On his birthday, I went round to his house with a packet of Liquorice Allsorts as a present for him. He opened the door and told me he didn't like liquorice. I felt crushed.

My other pre-teen love was Adrian Moore, who worked during the summer break in a Hoover shop on Leavesden Road. I dressed up in a leopard-print skirt, with a white handbag and too much lipstick, trying to look grown up.

'Where are you off to?' asked Mum as she caught me sneaking out.

'Just down to Woolworths.'

All afternoon I paraded up and down outside the Hoover shop, trying to catch a glimpse of Adrian. He didn't come out.

When it was time to leave junior school, I demanded to go to Watford Girls' Grammar School, even threatening to run away if Mum didn't send me there. Max and Natalie had gone to Leggatts, a rough school that took mostly poorer kids from the council estates.

Mum said I could apply to the grammar school and go to the interview, but I don't think she expected me to be accepted. I don't know why I was so keen to go. I suppose I wanted to be better. If I'd gone to Leggatts I might always have been the goofy kid with the beautiful older sister.

When the reply came saying I'd been accepted, I yelled and cheered. A friend of mine, Debbie, the vicar's daughter, had applied and been turned down. She was gutted.

Watford Girls' Grammar School was full of middle-class kids whose parents couldn't quite afford to send them to private school. I was the token poor kid from the rough end of town – a fact I was never allowed to forget, particularly by Mrs Case, the middle-aged English teacher. She enjoyed using me as an example of the school's noble policy towards the underprivileged. 'Do you know, Geri, you're very, very lucky to be here,' she'd say.

'I know, Mrs Case.'

'Do you?'

'Yes.'

Not surprisingly, I never stopped feeling like an outsider. For the first year I tried to be almost invisible and felt as though I'd moved to a new town. Wearing my second-hand blazer, tie and straw boater, I caught the bus every day from the end of Jubilee Road. Most of the kids were going to Leggatts.

It took a year before I gained the confidence to be my cheeky, chirpy self at the grammar school. The turning point came when some of the older girls decided to put on a talent contest at lunchtime. Mustering my courage, I put my name down and sang 'I Wanna Be A Nightclub Queen'.

I came second and it boosted my confidence enough for me to start being myself.

Encouraged by this success, I joined the school drama club and got the lead role in a play called, *A Day in the Mind of Titch Oldfield*. It was about a boy who had a wild imagination, and each time he imagined something it became real. I was chosen because I could mimic people and do a good impression of Margaret Thatcher.

Later, in grade three, I had a fabulous English teacher called Miss Medina, who looked like Diana Rigg and encouraged me to read. She often asked me to recite poetry to the class because she loved the sound of my voice.

One day I came to school wearing braces and she asked me to read.

'Pleathe, no, Mith. I've jutht had my bratheth fitted.'

'Come on now, you can still read.'

I recited the first few lines and spat and dribbled over the page. The rest of the girls were laughing at me.

'Oh dear, what have they done to you?' said Miss Medina.

The braces were to cause me no end of trouble. They consisted of a plate with a single metal band. At night I had to wear special head gear that looked like something out of *Star Trek*. One lunchtime I took my brace out to eat my sandwiches, hiding the plate in the waistband of my skirt. Being a goofy kid, I jumped up to catch a ball at the bottom of the playing fields and lost the brace.

I was distraught. Mum had already warned me, 'That brace costs twenty-five pounds. If you lose it, that's it, no more.' I had visions of me having to live with crooked teeth for the rest of my life.

After notifying the school office, the missing plate was found by a woman walking her dog. She'd found it in her dog's mouth when she'd arrived home. Surely, I couldn't wear it again. My mother had other ideas. She made me disinfect the brace and put it back in my mouth. How typical! I was always so clumsy. Why couldn't I be like Laura, the prettiest and brightest girl at school, and the star of the debating and drama clubs?

Having seen Laura perform, I didn't bother auditioning for any more school plays. My only performance had come prior to my braces being fitted, when Miss Medina had asked me to read a poem about Kathmandu. I forgot my lines halfway through and skipped to the end verse, which was the same as the first. The audience thought I'd gone back to the beginning to start again and nobody knew to applaud.

The next day, in English class, I hid under the desk because I felt so ashamed at having let my favourite teacher down.


I tried to see Dad once a week. I went round to his flat to do my homework so that he didn't get lonely. He didn't feel like a father; he was simply an old man in my life, who gave me money to clean his flat and was prone to random acts of kindness and explosive anger. Like a child, he imagined the world revolved around him.

Everything felt dirty in his flat, even the elephant statues and carvings he collected, which all faced the door because somebody had told him it was lucky. Dad would pick me up from school and ferry me between friends' houses. He took me to see my first movie, *Clash of the Titans*, which had a really scary Medusa. Years later I discovered that George Michael, a Watford boy, was probably working behind the confectionery counter at the same cinema, serving popcorn and soft drinks.

My relationship with Mum had become strained since the divorce, or maybe it was a teenage thing. Thirteen-year-old girls aren't supposed to get on with their mothers. I wrote in my diary:

## Saturday, 14 December 1984

*Last night I got in at 10.30 p.m. from Charlotte's place.*
*Mum went mental and has grounded me for two weeks.*
*The old cow. She makes me puke! She wouldn't even*
*listen. I can't wait to leave home.*

*This afternoon, when Karen phoned, I went outside*
*to get Max. Mum thought I was sneaking out. She gave*
*me a wallop. I HATE HER!!*

*I've ignored her since then. I'm sending her to*
*Coventry.*

Mum put a silver lock on our phone to stop us making
calls, but Max showed me how to hit the handset cradle
button the same number of times as each digit to dial a
number. She couldn't understand why our telephone bills
were so high until she came home and caught me in the
middle of 'tapping'.

We were all dragged into the sitting room and
punished with her flip-flop, which was less painful than
the wooden spoon.

Another time she caught me leaning over the kitchen
sink with a bottle of Natalie's peroxide in my hand. My
honey-coloured tresses had been bleached blond.

'What are you doing?' she cried, seizing the bottle.
'You silly, silly girl . . .' After a hard day at work Mum
couldn't summon the energy to say anything more.
Instead, she sighed tiredly and said, 'Whatever next?'

The new 'look' seemed to enhance my reputation at
school. The headmistress soon singled me out as *that* girl
with dyed hair, who wore hitched-up skirts, black eyeliner and kitten heels. The shoes were always too big for

me, so I wore inner soles and white fluffy socks to fit into them.

Although this makes me sound like a rebel, I was rarely in trouble with the headmistress. I could talk my way out of most things and worked just hard enough to pass my exams and assignments.

When dark roots began to spoil my blond hair it came as a total surprise. I hadn't read the small print on the bottle. To solve the problem I dyed my hair again, this time a Gothic-looking black with an almost bluish tinge. I tried to convince myself I looked like Snow White.

At fourteen I went for the Fifties look and put curlers in my hair. I'd go browsing round Camden market wearing my coolest clothes and this terrible home-made perm. Urgh!

Friends would come round after school and I'd back-comb their hair, putting on pink eyeshadow with blue mascara, or perhaps gold and blue.

Natalie had dyed her hair blond and had it cut to look like George Michael. We were both huge Wham! fans, but I didn't regard myself as a groupie. That was the term that described the girls at school who would gather outside Andrew Ridgeley's house in nearby Bushey as if worshipping at a religious site. Admittedly, there wasn't much else to do around Watford, apart from hang out at the park or go to the Odeon.

I still wanted to be famous, of course, although I didn't know exactly how I was going to achieve it. Probably by being a TV presenter, or a pop star or an actress, I thought. The precise details weren't particularly relevant to a teenager; it was simply going to happen.

And when it did I was going to buy a huge house, like

in *Gone With the Wind*, which would be big enough for Mum to live at one end and Dad at the other. That way I could be with them both, even if they couldn't live with each other.

In 1985 I discovered Madonna. She brought London to a standstill when she went jogging through Hyde Park. Fans queued for days, sleeping on pavements to get tickets to her concerts, or in the hope of catching a fleeting glimpse of her through a hotel window. This was public adoration on a huge scale. This was my dream.

I looked at the poster outside Watford Cinema and realized that I'd been staring at it for twenty minutes. There she was, the Material Girl, in jeans, a crop top and enough beads and bangles to kick-start Woodstock all over again. Madonna was starring in *Desperately Seeking Susan*. My school shoes shuffled on the pavement.

It just wasn't fair! I was her biggest fan. I knew every one of her lyrics and dance routines. I could identify every piece of clothing she'd ever been photographed wearing. But now I was being denied the chance to see her big-screen début.

The film certificate said fifteen and over. Normally anyone could get into a fifteen – you've almost got to be in nappies before they stop you. But not me! I didn't even look twelve. All my friends were inside, along with most of the older girls from the grammar school. Some of them were going for a second or third time.

Of course, I'd already tried to explain this to the lady at the ticket counter. I had shown her my encyclopedic knowledge of Madonna and explained that I was very grown up for my age.

'You're holding up the queue,' she'd said, with a heart that was as hard as her lacquered hair.

I vowed to everyone that I'd see the film – all my friends on the school bus and at the grammar school. It was a matter of saving face as much as seeing Madonna.

At home, I pulled on one of Natalie's sexy dresses and put on a bra. I shoved a pair of socks into each cup and stood side-on in front of the mirror. Not quite enough – maybe a second pair. No, that looks too lumpy. Suddenly, I had a brainwave: Max's football socks. Perfect.

I teased my hair and put on make-up. Tottering down the narrow stairs in my kitten heels, I called to Mum, 'I'm just off to see a film.'

'They're never going to let you in, Geri,' she said, laughing.

'Can I have some money for popcorn, please?'

I caught the bus to the cinema and waited in the queue. Even with high heels I could barely peer over the counter. The same lady looked down at me, peering through the lipstick and eyeliner. 'How old are you, dear?'

'Fifteen.'

'You don't look your age.'

'I am. Please let me in.' I thought I was going to wet my pants.

She knew I was lying, but she took my money anyway. The lights were still up as I walked down the aisle. I looked at the older girls from my school and smiled in triumph.

Two hours later I danced out, singing 'Into The Groove' with the biggest smile of satisfaction on my face. Mission accomplished.

# 3

## A MATERIAL GIRL

Madonna saved me from the worst fate that can befall a teenage girl: she kept me company when I was dateless and desperate. Being such a late developer, I took to lying about my periods and wearing a triangular-shaped bra that gave the impression I had a bust.

On sleepovers at Louisa Peg's house, we used to lift our T-shirts to compare progress. 'Oh, they're growing a tiny bit,' Louisa told me, trying to spare my feelings.

At church discos and birthday parties all my girlfriends got attention from the boys. They'd be getting groped in various corners while I had the lounge to myself. There never seemed to be enough boys to go round and, if there were, they often preferred to queue for someone else rather than consider me. Even Lee and Christopher had deserted me. Other girls had more to offer.

I turned on the stereo, put on Madonna's *True Blue* album and stood in the bay window of Natalie Smith's house with the curtains open. I danced and sang, imagining that I was Madonna. I'd even dyed my hair blond again and wore it in a topknot.

Fergie married Prince Andrew that summer, providing me with further proof that fairytales *do* happen. There was hope for me yet. That night, I lay in bed writing my diary. On the inside back cover I'd glued a picture of George Michael.

## *Wednesday, 23 July 1986*

*Woke up late. Watched the Royal Wedding in my nightie. Then Mum made me go down to the corner shop to buy onions. After the wedding Natalie and I went to hospital about my teeth, to tighten up my brace. We only just made it in time.*

*The dentist had this sander sort of thing that carved away some of the plastic bits. Bits were flying everywhere. On the way home two slags were giving me and Natalie dirty looks on the bus. I had a Crunchie.*

*Read Desperately Seeking Susan book – nearly finished.*

*Later, Natalie bought me a Marathon.*

*Good day. Mum keeps nagging me as usual.*

*Geri. xxx*

If there was nothing decent showing at the Odeon, I used to hang around Oxhey Park or the shops with my friends. Natalie had grown even more gorgeous. She had left school at seventeen and started a college course in tourism and finance. At night she worked at Paradise Lost, a discotheque that had been labelled the most beautiful in England. She looked fantastic in her sexy little dresses.

My two best friends were Lorraine, who lived in a house near the grammar school, and Louisa Peg, who spoke with a lisp. We fought constantly, of course, as best friends do, and talked mainly about music and boys.

I bunked off school only once, and Lorraine had the misfortune to be with me. We skipped a music lesson given by Mrs Rod – never a more apt name. Sod's law, of course, we were caught. Letters were sent home, lectures were delivered and Mum grounded me for a fortnight.

### Sunday, 27 July 1986

*Today woke up at 8.30 a.m. Got the bus to Louisa's house, although I had to wait three quarters of an hour. The bus driver was really rude. After lunch we went for a long walk up the river. We saw Julie, the fat cow.*

*Louisa wanted to go to the park and she got all dressed up – it was only because Donald was there. He doesn't even fancy Louisa anyway. He fancies Natalie Smith . . .*

*Julie and Louisa started calling each other names, so I encouraged Louisa to hit her. She punched her in the head. Julie burst out crying, and this boy called Ian, who was really ugly, pulled Louisa off and pushed her and she went flying. It was really funny.*

*Got back to Louisa's house. She said her back hurt and then the silly bitch told her mum that I'd encouraged her.*

*Madonna is still Number One with 'Papa Don't Preach'.*

*Not a bad day, I suppose. Went to bed at 11.30.*

*Mum made me fold my clothes away.*
*Geri.*

Money had become a problem. My lifestyle outstripped my resources and my weekly pocket money of £1.50 was never going to be enough for a 'material girl'. I needed a job.

My first part-time employment ended in disaster. The local newsagent gave me a paper round – seven mornings a week for £7.50. I spent hours calculating how long it would take me to save up for a sound system and a vanity case.

My first day was a Saturday, when the papers bulged with supplements. I struggled along Gammons Lane, weighed down by a massive orange shoulder bag that almost dragged on the ground when looped over my shoulder.

On Sunday morning, I discovered that the newspapers bulged even thicker. Halfway along Gammons Lane I collapsed into someone's front garden. That morning one householder had thirty newspapers shoved through his front door. I walked home in disgust.

My size didn't always count against me, although most restaurant owners thought I couldn't handle the heavy plates. During the summer I sold ice creams to tourists in Covent Garden and got great tips because people felt sorry for the little girl carrying a huge tray.

Later, I worked at a fish-and-chip shop at the bottom of Watford High Street. There was a dip in the floor on my side of the counter, which meant I had trouble seeing over the top when a customer came in to order. Sometimes they arrived and didn't realize anyone was serving until I spoke up. Then they'd peer over the bench-top and see the grease patch from the fish fryer on my forehead.

From the age of fourteen, every Saturday during the winter I worked on an open-air stall at Norford Market for Jimmy, a friend of my stepsister Karen's. I got up early to help set up the stall, and afterwards Jimmy bought us sausage sandwiches and big mugs of tea for breakfast.

He sold toys and dressing-up clothes and would get me to put on the different costumes. Some days I was a nurse, or a policewoman, or a cowgirl. I didn't realize until years later how kinky this might seem.

## 6 August. My Birthday

*For my birthday I got £31 and lots of clothes, a radio, a bra, three pairs of knickers, earrings, a necklace and two jackets. Wicked.*

*Spent the afternoon sunbathing in a bikini in the back garden, reading books from the library.*

*Natalie had a driving lesson. I can't imagine her on the road. Ha ha ha! I bet she'll cause other male drivers to crash while they're looking at her.*

*After dinner she styled my hair. At ten o'clock we watched Bonnie and Clyde. Really good movie. It's a true story about how they robbed banks and finished up getting shot by the police.*

*Love Geri.*

*PS. Mum's always picking on me.*

I lied about my age to get a job at Chelsea Girl, which I thought was a really cool clothes shop in Watford High

Street. From there I progressed to a better Saturday job, working in Next. The shop promoted in-store discount cards, and any member of staff who managed to sign up ten customers could go home early. With my gift of the gab I was home by three o'clock most Saturdays.

Of a Sunday I'd catch a train into London to visit Camden Market or Oxford Street. I'd buy discounted Levis 501s and T-shirts with American flag patches. I got my ideas from *Top of the Pops* and teen magazines.

Boys were still a mystery to me, primarily because I was a late bloomer. Breasts are like stop/go signs to adolescent boys, and I was so flat they didn't even bother to slow down. This didn't stop me falling in love at the slightest indication that a boy might fancy me. It only took a smile, or a shared bus seat, and I began filling my diary with the most frightful drivel.

### Saturday, 16 January 1988

*Dear John,*
*I just want to express my feelings to you.*
*    At first I liked you.*
*    Then I loved you.*
*    Then I was infatuated by you.*
*    Then I hated you.*
*    Then I loved you.*
*    Now a tiny part still does and always will. I thought you'd be the one – my first real romance . . .*

I can't remember anything at all about John. He was probably from Watford Boys' Grammar School, which provided most of our boyfriends, or, in my case, male fantasy figures. There was a gang of guys who used to hang out with us after school. On Friday and Saturday nights we'd find a party to go to, or gather at somebody's house when their parents were out for the evening.

## Friday, 29 January 1988

*Tonight I'm going round Splats. It's going to be bloody awful because I'll be the gooseberry again. Wag (Alison) is with Lloyd, Charlotte is with John; and Nicola will probably get off with Bod. I hope Nicki Jennings is coming, otherwise I'll be by myself. They're trying to pair me off with Barry who looks like Bruce Forsyth.*

*PS. Got in at 11.15. Mum knew I'd been drinking!! I can't believe I got off with Paul tonight. Puke! Puke! Not once, but three times. Barry saw me and I felt really bad.*

## Monday, 1 February 1988

*Today I thought I'd have to bunk class 'cos I hadn't done any homework – Maths, German and Textiles. But everything turned out all right.*

*Maths – I copied from Claire. Miss Baxter didn't even mark them.*

*German – she forgot.*

*Textiles – I showed the crap pom-poms I'd made. SHE SEEMED PLEASED!! Now to more important things. Who can I send Valentine's Day cards to???????*

*Think I'll send them to Lloyd and Jim. They're both so HOR—NY! Why is it that all the boys I like are going out with someone else?*

*I also want to dye my hair. What colour now??????*

The search for true love became all consuming. At school we talked about little else — even in the weeks leading up to our GCSEs. Romance was far more important than exams. There were constant feuds over which boys we liked, and love notes were passed between the various camps.

In the beginning, I couldn't decide what was worse, not having a boyfriend, or having one who didn't call. Then I discovered an even more embarrassing fate. Whenever a boy phoned me I suffered from either total amnesia or the inability to say anything remotely intelligent.

The entire course of a romance could be played out within a matter of days.

### Saturday, 7 May 1988

*Fell in love with Martin. We were all round at Charlotte's house. The boys came over and we had a water fight. I thought Martin fancied Amanda because he was getting her wet the most. I felt so jealous.*

### Tuesday, 11 May 1988

*Martin asked me to start going out with him. We were outside Boots and he said, 'How about it then?'*

'Yeah, OK then.'
'That's cool.'
'That's cool,' I replied.

## Saturday, 14 May 1988

*Martin wrote me slushy note. He got pissed tonight and acted a right prat. He grabbed my small/non-existent tits.*

## Sunday, 15 May 1988

*Martin put the phone down on me because I was horrible to him on Saturday night. I apologized.*

## Monday, 16 May 1988

*Went to stay at Charlotte's house. I had to hide in the cupboard from Martin. Decided I was going to chuck him. I went to the fair with Charlotte and Karen. It was really good. I saw Martin and chucked him. Later, on the Octopus, he was showing off and saying things about me that weren't true. I told him to get lost and we started fighting. I ran off, crying my eyes out. Later, I asked Max if he'd beat Martin up for me . . .*

## Wednesday, 18 May 1988

*Danny asked me out. I said no. I'm not over Martin yet.*

That summer I had to make a decision about whether to stay on at Watford Girls' Grammar or leave school. Although I never regretted going there, there was something very stifling about the place. Every morning we would sing a hymn and say the Lord's Prayer. Whenever there was a silence I had an almost overwhelming urge to stand up and scream an obscenity to fill the void and shake away the cobwebs. It terrified me that I might actually do it one day.

In my third year I was elected charity monitor, which meant I had to select a charity and organize the fundraising. I chose Aids Research – a rather controversial selection for an all-girls school. Announcing my choice, I told the assembled staff and teachers, 'I think it should be Aids because we're all going to have sex, you know.'

Jaws dropped collectively. Miss Medina giggled. I thought Mrs Case was going to have a heart attack.

I wasn't a naughty teenager, just cheeky and loud. And although I wasn't an A student, I managed to get Bs and Cs when I wasn't mucking about.

Much of it came down to personalities. If I liked the teacher, I liked the subject. Miss Baxter, who taught maths, could have stepped straight out of a St Trinian's movie. She had a huge bust, and when she turned around from the blackboard there were always white chalk marks on her breasts where they'd rubbed against the board.

Mr Hall, my chemistry teacher, looked like a pit bull terrier and fancied himself a bit. The girls liked to flirt with him. Miss Water, my grammar teacher, was an unfortunate-looking woman with flaking skin. Whenever her name was mentioned, we used to sing, 'Snowflakes are falling up your nose.' Sarah brought a condom to school one day and she made me leave it on Miss Water's desk.

All the teachers did their best, but I was destined to disappoint most of them.

On my report card in the spring term of 1988, Miss Baxter wrote, 'This examination grade is a reflection of Geraldine's casual attitude this half-year and not of her true ability. Whether or not she obtains a satisfactory result next term depends on how hard she is prepared to work.'

That pretty much sums up my schooling. The reports for each subject would begin with phrases such as 'lively and responsive', 'always enthusiastic' and 'full of good ideas'. But by the end these had been tempered by references to my being 'easily distracted', 'lacking concentration' and 'needs to pay more attention'.

We were the first year to do GCSEs and I spent most of the exams panicking and scrubbing out the right answers and replacing them with something wrong. I was so convinced I'd failed that months before the results were due I drew a gravestone in my diary complete with daisies:

*GERI RIP*
*In Memory of a Girl*
*Who Failed her GCSEs*

As it turned out, I finished with eight O level passes – not bad, just enough to get into a college if I decided to leave school. The results came in August, just after my sixteenth birthday.

In the Halliwell family, only Max had continued on to do A levels. Neither Mum nor Dad was particularly well educated – despite Mum's claims to the contrary. I looked to Natalie, who had left school and gone to college. She was earning money and saving to buy a car.

I didn't know what I wanted to do with my life, although I still had the show-reels about being rich and famous running in my head. Nobody had sat me down and shown me a way of achieving it. No-one had said, 'Go to drama school, Geri, or have singing lessons.'

What sort of fame did I want? I didn't know. Something along the lines of Marilyn Monroe, perhaps. She was 'discovered'. Whatever happened, I wanted to start living my life and begin experiencing things.

Natalie had done travel, tourism and finance at Casio College and seemed to enjoy it. I thought about doing hotel management, and then changed my mind and opted for the safety of following in her footsteps. So far she hadn't put a foot wrong.

I started college in September 1988, but immediately it felt more like killing time than forging a career. I didn't want to work in the travel industry, but being only sixteen I didn't have many choices. I wanted to go abroad and work in Spain, but Mum said I was too young. She wouldn't even let me go there on a holiday with two friends from school unless Dad went along as a chaperone. Eventually she backed down. I had to borrow £100 from Karen, £30 from Max, £50 from Dad – a year's pocket money – and get my birthday presents early –

cash only – to raise the money. It was worth every penny.

I met a Greek boy called Niko, who snogged me in a nightclub and said, 'I want to show you love, Geri.'

'Not likely, mate,' I told him as he pressed himself against me.

My next close encounter came after a dinner party for Natalie's twentieth birthday in February 1989. Her boyfriend had a mate called Andy, who must have been about twenty-one. I was sixteen. I had a bit to drink and he offered to drive me home to the YWCA where Natalie was staying. Stopping in the carpark opposite, he leaned across and kissed me. Pretty soon we were getting passionate.

I let him touch my breasts and wondered if he'd try to go further. He had the radio on and was listening to the Frank Bruno/Mike Tyson world heavyweight fight. It was round four, with Frank holding his own.

I thought about suggesting something more romantic – perhaps a music channel – but I feared that Andy might be more interested in the fight than in me. I spared myself any chance of embarrassment and kept snogging.

Andy didn't know I was a virgin. He unzipped his fly and pressed himself against me. I looked down at his angry-looking implement and sobered up instantly.

'Oh, my God,' I cried.

'What's wrong?'

I fumbled for the door, leaped out and ran across the carpark to the YWCA.

Andy shouted after me, 'What's up? What's up?'

Frank went down in the eighth round, but Andy had been floored in the sixth.

## Saturday, 25 February 1989

*I can't believe I almost lost my virginity. And in a carpark, for God's sake. How tacky can you get!*

*When I first ran off, Andy came after me, but his pride stopped him just like it stopped me. My head over-ruled my heart. I can't believe how close I came to making such a big mistake. Is God going to give me another chance? Yes or No?*

*Well, I pray you do, God. I don't want to die a virgin.*

## Sunday, 26 February 1989

*Spent the day with Natalie. Didn't tell her about this worry of mine. It would only ruin her holiday (she's going to the Seychelles). I can't face the fact that I may be pregnant or even have AIDS. I know Andy only put it near me, but you never know. I want to tie my legs together for ever.*

I couldn't sleep I was so terrified. Where could I turn for advice? None of the sex education classes could help me. I certainly couldn't talk to Mum. I woke at five in the morning on Monday and started praying. Please, God, what should I do?

That morning I went to see my family GP, Dr King. There were two old ladies in the waiting room who kept giving me dirty looks. I felt really anxious and wanted to get it over with. The doctor couldn't see me, so I went back to college. That afternoon, Dad took me back to the surgery. I lied and told him I was having my tonsils checked. Again, I had to wait for ages before Dr King finally ushered me into his room. I've always thought of him as quite handsome, in a middle-aged, fatherly sort of way, with big brown eyes and smooth hands.

'So what can I do for you, Geri?'

All my anxiety came spilling out in a tumble of words. I babbled about having sex and *not* having had sex, and about how I couldn't be pregnant, but I wanted to be sure.

Dr King seemed quite sad as he gave me a lecture about being careful and taking precautions if I was going to have sex. Tears were running down my cheeks. Here was a man who had known me since I was eleven years old. He had nursed me through childhood illnesses and watched me grow up. Now I felt as if I'd let him down.

I wrote in my diary:

*I'm going to think about God more. I know he's there. I think he made this happen to give me a warning; to make me aware of how bitter-sweet life can be.*

*I can't be a hypocrite and say I'm going to be a churchgoer from now on, because in a month's time I won't be scared. This has been a massive slap in the face. From now on I take responsibility for myself.*

*I can't say that I'll never have sex, but I do know that I must wait until I am ready. I am so glad my inner instincts told me to stop and think. But I hope and pray that when the right person does come along I will recognize him . . .*

In April I managed to get a weekend job at the Hilton Hotel in Olympia, London. I worked two shifts, the first from three to eleven on Friday evenings. Then they'd give me a room overnight – how cool! I'd start work again at seven the next morning. Mum was really impressed. She told all her cleaner friends that her daughter worked on reception at the Hilton Hotel.

It wasn't a bad job, although I hated missing Friday nights. The novelty of staying in a nice hotel room only lasted a few months. I quit in August, without telling Mum, and it took her a fortnight to find out.

She went absolutely mental. Raging in a mixture of Spanish and English, she screamed about me being ungrateful. Both of us were shouting and neither of us listened.

'I'm going to be somebody,' I cried defiantly. 'I'm going to be rich and famous. I am. Just you watch me!'

I ran out of the house, sobbing into the night. Mum couldn't chase me because she didn't have her contact lenses in. I kept running until I reached a council estate and got frightened. Then I called Dad from a phone box and he came to pick me up.

'I want to live with you,' I told him.

'What about your mum?'

'I don't want to talk about it any more. Let's just go home.'


### Friday, 25 May 1989 – Dad's flat

*It's now 04.37 in the morning. I can't sleep. This place smells of cat shit. I feel sick. I don't know if I can stay here. I feel I can't return to Jubilee Road. I would be betraying everything I argued for yesterday. Now it all seems meaningless.*

*All I need is somewhere to keep my clothes. But where?*

*Please, God, guide me and help me to do the right thing.*

I could understand Mum's frustration and anger. She feared for me. She had cleaned floors and toilets to feed her family, working horrendous hours for a pittance. And here I was, throwing away a perfectly good job for no reason.

I seemed to have been fighting with her since I was thirteen. My diaries were full of curses and complaints. Why couldn't she let me live my own life?

*Dear Mother,*
*Unfortunately, it has got to the point where my nerves can't stand up to the strain of non-stop arguing. I think it's best for both of our sakes that I move out because maybe then we might appreciate each other's company a bit more.*

*Hopefully, you'll understand that I need space. I expect you'll be happy now that you will have 'peace and quiet' without any 'rebellious teenagers' giving you unnecessary hassles with their 'immature behaviour'.*

On a college field trip down to Devon I met a boy called Mark and had a strange fluttering feeling in the pit of my stomach. I went bright red whenever I was near him and was completely incapable of intelligent conversation. Instead I giggled and talked utter bollocks.

This must be love. My feet barely touched the ground for those first few days. He was beautiful, polite, charming and unforgettable.

He didn't call me for two days after I got home. I made excuses for him. Love makes that easy. When he did call me, I felt happy and scared at the same time. 'I'll call you back,' I said. I didn't. This was about playing hard to get.

Two days later, back at college, I discovered that my one true love had made a pass at another girl on the same trip. The truth kicked me right in the teeth. Why do I get all the bastards?

He's gonna pay. Nobody takes Geraldine Halliwell for a ride.

'What are you going to do?' asked Natalie.

'I'm going to . . . to . . . to . . . learn how to drive.'

Precisely how this would 'show' him is a mystery to me, but it seemed to make sense at the time. I set about getting my licence.

After two driving lessons, I suddenly thought, This is easy. I was still living with Dad and I slipped out one night and took his car – a big Princess with a faulty starter. I could barely see over the top of the wheel.

I picked up a friend from college and we headed off to London. Madness! I could barely drive. It must have been nearly 5 a.m. before we finally got home.

Having got away with it once, I took the car again the next night and drove to a party in South Oxhey. When I picked it up again the next morning at ten o'clock I had to hot-wire the ignition to get it started. I got all the way home without incident and then scraped a panel as I parked beneath Dad's tower block.

Up until then I'd thought he'd never know, but I forgot about old men waking at absurd hours. He'd discovered the car was missing at 4 a.m. The keys were gone, I was gone and the car was gone – surely he realized I was responsible. No, not Dad. He called the police and reported the car stolen. A policeman sat waiting for me as I sneaked back into the flat. Busted!

Dad's punishment was far worse than the policeman's lecture: he tried to send me back home. I couldn't live at Jubilee Road, so I turned to Karen, my stepsister. She rented me a room in a house she owned in Queen's Road for £25 a week.

Although I passed my exams that first year, I still weighed up whether to go back to college. Several things happened that summer which altered my life dramatically. The first was physical. Suddenly – and it really did seem like overnight – my breasts began to grow. It was as though I came down to breakfast one morning and knocked over the cornflakes when I went to sit down.

There were raised eyebrows all round, not least among the lads at the Game Bird pub in Bushey. Before then I'd had trouble getting into a pub because I looked under age. Now, with a tight top and a splash of make-up, I could get in anywhere. My breasts, figuratively speaking, opened doors for me.

The second major discovery happened on a Saturday night in June, two months before my seventeenth birthday. At the Game Bird pub one Saturday night, ticket-sellers began moving through the crowd.

'What's it for?' I asked.

'A party.'

'Where is it?'

'We don't know yet.'

A group of boys convinced me to go and I spent £15 on a ticket. At exactly 11 p.m. a convoy of cars set off from the hotel and drove around the M25. I sat in the front seat of an old transit van, squeezed between four people as Adamski, the keyboard wizard, blared out of the van's stereo.

Glancing ahead and behind us I could see a small convoy of vehicles. We paused at a motorway service station on the M1 to receive new instructions via a recorded message on an answering machine. By then the convoy had swelled to more than a thousand cars and vans. There were two more checkpoints before we found out the location of the party.

We came to a halt in a farmer's field near Elstree, Hertfordshire. From a distance it was like seeing a sports ground lit up. And as I moved closer I saw thousands of people dancing with their hands in the air. There was an outdoor stage, with massive speakers and coloured lights that flashed to the beat of the music. Glancing in awe at the sea of moving bodies, it was as though someone had pegged down a massive silken parachute in patchwork colours and the breeze was rippling beneath it.

I danced all night to house music and acid-house beats. People smiled and embraced in a celebration of unity and love. There were stockbrokers and people from council estates – all colours and creeds. What's your name? Where are you from? – it was almost a catchphrase.

I thought peace had broken out in Hertfordshire and would spread to save the world.

I didn't leave until the last song had played on Sunday afternoon. A helicopter hovered overhead with a television crew covering the Woodstock-style phenomenon. Physically exhausted, I got home and collapsed into bed.

Natalie said, 'You look awful. Where have you been?'

I smiled and closed my eyes. 'I've found my people.'

# IS THAT IT?

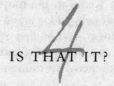

The whole rave culture exploded that summer, literally sweeping across the countryside. The tabloid press had a field day, portraying them as orgies of sex, drugs and hypnotic music that broke the law and corrupted the nation's youth. What better publicity could any movement have?

This was my summer of love.

I became a regular at the Game Bird and soon got to know all the ticket-sellers and 'runners'. My colourful raving friends were an explosion of tie-dyed floppy tops with overlong sleeves and smiley motifs. We had a new style of music, fresh fashions and a designer drug – Ecstasy.

Although I had no job and very little money in the bank, Barclay's Bank had been unwise enough to give me a Connect card with an overdraft facility. Life remained sweet as long as I had the necessary £10 or £15 to get into a rave. To make a little extra money, I would take my instamatic camera along and take photographs. The following week, I went back and sold them for a pound a print.

Mostly I made my own outfits – figure-hugging cat-suits, hotpants and cone bras that were designed to get me noticed. With my bleached-blond hair and my Madonna topknot, I was the wild child of Watford.

My new friends were older and far worldlier. Sean looked like Martin Kemp in the movie about the Kray twins. He wore a mobile phone slung on his belt, like a modern-day gunslinger, and he had a gruff Irish accent. Others, like Steve and Toby, were party organizers and determined to make their first million while still in their teens.

Although the raves gave the impression of spontaneity, the organization involved was enormous. Apart from the ticket-sellers and runners, there were marshals, location scouts, security guards and DJs. Tons of equipment had to be trucked in secretly to each new site. And every venue had to be kept secret until the last possible minute, to prevent the police from moving in to shut down the rave.

In the week beforehand printed handbills announced the all-nighters, which had names like *Sunrise* and *Biology*. Then hundreds of young people would gather at closing time at selected pubs near the M25. Ticket-sellers moved through the crowd, collecting money. Just before closing time the signal arrived and runners whispered the first instructions that set the convoys in motion. An intricate web of telephone numbers, names and addresses – some of them as far afield as the Virgin Islands – made it almost impossible to trace the organizers.

Each weekend another two or three would take place, with thousands of people cramming into disused warehouses, abandoned hangars and remote corners of the countryside. Permission was always sought from the farmers, but most of them had no idea of the sheer scale of the parties. Even if they did, they normally took the money and cried foul later when the police arrived.

My mother's warnings about boys had subconsciously done their job. For all my wildness and my racy outfits that screamed sex, I was still a virgin at seventeen. The most effective form of contraceptive a mother can give her daughter is guilt.

### Thursday, 29 June 1989

*I am only sixteen, yet it's a horrifying fact that I feel pressurized into finding a boyfriend, as well as feeling sexually deprived. I feel either left on the shelf or as though I'm missing out.*

*If I want a one-night stand it's almost impossible, because the next day it always leads to exchanging phone numbers and embarrassment.*

*Listen to me! I'm talking as though I'm twenty-one. Maybe I just worry what people think. Maybe I should just wait. But I'm fed up with waiting. What if the world ends tomorrow? I can't die a virgin.*

I waited until two months after my seventeenth birthday – 1 October to be exact. It was memorable for all the wrong reasons. Toby was a grey and sickly looking ex-public schoolboy with a toffy accent. After dancing till dawn in a muddy field, he took me back to a borrowed bedsit in Olympia. Trains rumbled past the back garden, rattling the sash windows and the unwashed cups in the sink.

There was a mattress on the floor. He tried to have sex with me, but couldn't penetrate because I was too rigid with fear. We fumbled about some more and finally it happened. Five minutes later it was over — and that's probably an exaggeration.

'Is that it?' I wondered. No romance, no passion, no joy. Not exactly *From Here to Eternity*.

Toby got up and dropped me at the station and I made my own way home.

Later he told me he was in love with a girl called Tamara and couldn't stop thinking about her. He kept on singing the Sinead O'Connor song, 'Nothing Compares 2 U', but it was all about her. It wasn't quite what I wanted to hear.

After a summer of such excitement and adventure, how could I go back to college? A different world had opened up to me, an undiscovered continent full of young, dynamic ideas and people. Forget the future; I might not live to see it. Enjoy the moment.

Not surprisingly, Mum didn't understand. There was no fighting this time, but I knew what she thought. I'd been given loads of opportunities and I'd wasted them. Where would I finish up? In her eyes, England was this marvellous country that offered free education. She hadn't had such advantages. She had sacrificed so much for me . . . worked her fingers to the bone . . . gone without things . . . wasted her youth . . . same old, same old. Guilt.

In early September I took a job at Video Collection, a company in Watford that checked the titles and classifications of each video before it was duplicated and put into the shops. It meant sitting in a darkened room and watching anything from the Smurfs to one of John Wayne's Westerns. I had to check each video for quality and put together the covers, making sure the copyright, credits and title were correct. The job paid seven grand a year and the boss seemed pretty cool.

On the Friday before I started work I invited a few people at the Game Bird pub back to my place for a party. By closing time word of mouth had guaranteed that 200 people descended on the small terrace house. They spilled out onto the street outside, blocking traffic and infuriating the neighbours. I couldn't even get inside my own front door. The party lasted until 3.30 p.m. on Saturday.

That night we went in search of a new rave called *Energy* up in Ipswich. We didn't find it until four in the morning, but stayed until 10 p.m. on Sunday night. The next day – my first at Video Collection – I arrived completely exhausted. I kept pacing back and forth to the coffee machine, trying to stay awake.

Karen was furious about the party. I had let her down and couldn't stay at Queen's Road. I went back to living with Dad for a while.

A lot of things were starting to slide. I bought a Mini for £70 and began driving it everywhere. A few weeks later it stalled at a roundabout and a Pakistani taxi-driver ran into the back of me. I brazenly got out of the car and declared, 'Look, mate, you're going to lose your no-claims bonus; give us a hundred quid and we'll forget about it.'

He gave me eighty and I drove away with a dent in the back of the boot.

Eventually, the Mini broke down at midday in the middle of a busy intersection, outside a pub in Bushey. I phoned a scrap-metal dealer and told him where he could pick it up, then I caught a bus home.

As the weather grew colder, the raves moved inside to old warehouses and railway workshops. The economic winds had grown chilly, with a lot of people laid off or unable to find work. We were Margaret Thatcher's children and we thought we were going to inherit the earth, or at least make a fortune.

The Government had brought in the Criminal Justice Bill to outlaw the massive raves, but it didn't stop the movement. If anything, it legitimized acid house, because instead of meeting up on motorway service stations or random patches of grass in the countryside, we queued outside new clubs like The Ministry of Sound in Elephant & Castle and the Wag in Soho.

We continued to be happy-hugging, gum-chewing, motor-mouthed ravers, dancing until dawn.

'Oh, no, the club's shutting!' someone shouted above the noise.

'Shite, where shall we go next?'

'We can't stop now.'

With so much energy to be used up, there was always an element of panic. It passed only when another party had been found or we ran out of places to go. Those hard-core few who remained went dancing through the streets, swinging off lamp-posts and climbing into fountains. I gyrated on the roof of a barge as it cruised down the Thames and climbed onto a shop awning.

Eventually, we crashed at some unfortunate sod's house, where the wind-down session began. We gently mulled and watched children's TV programmes that seemed especially bizarre. Meanwhile, I chatted endlessly about world peace and snogged people I would normally have avoided. They were funny times, but the unhappy endings were mandatory, because reality leaked in like the morning sun through the curtains and the dullness was blinding.

Many of the rave organizers were wide boys and budding entrepreneurs who were always on the make. Café de Paris in Leicester Square was a favourite hang-out, because it attracted such a glamorous crowd. You were always likely to see someone like David Bowie or John Taylor (who once asked me for a light).

I had started hanging out with a black guy, Billy, a forty-five-year-old who looked half his age and drove a flash new BMW. He carried rolls of money in his pockets and would peel off twenty-quid tips for waitresses. Billy had style, even though he lived in a little terrace house no different to the one I'd been raised in.

Our relationship was purely platonic. Billy already had a girlfriend and a mistress. I was his little sidekick, who rode shotgun in his van or BMW when he did his deals. Billy knew most of the wise guys in North London, all of whom seemed to drive flash cars but live in stone-clad houses. Nice wheels, shame about the taste!

Billy would trade in anything that turned a profit, wherever the opportunity arose. He saw himself as 'the boss' and loved playing the role. He wasn't a big man, but for all his sweetness he could handle himself. He always told me that people only messed with his friends once.

At the Café de Paris one night I met Niam. He was gorgeous. He had layered brown hair and fancied himself as a George Michael lookalike with his designer stubble. I was wearing a really tarty red dress and trying to get his attention.

We started chatting. Niam was so much more sophisticated and at ease with the world than me. Yet he came from a terribly rough family – one of the notorious criminal clans on the South Oxhey council estate in Watford. His mother had died when he was very young and he'd been raised by his father and brothers, who were known for their toughness on the estate.

Niam had a poet's heart and I saw him as a diamond in the rough. It didn't matter that he had a girlfriend and I was seeing someone else. These things could be sorted out later. And so what if he came from a broken family? That was an accident of birth.

I went home that night fantasizing about gangsters and their women. If Niam was Bugsy Malone, then I wanted to be his Tallulah.

Dad had a mild stroke that weekend and had to be taken into hospital. For a while I thought he was going to die. It happened near Southampton, and I have no idea what Dad was doing down there. I didn't visit him in hospital. I can make excuses: Southampton was a long way away; I had my job; Dad and I weren't very close; he hated my lifestyle. But in reality I was just too selfish and tied up with partying.

However, Dad's stroke did come as a shock. I suddenly thought to myself, 'What if he died?'

I'd spent most of my life fighting with him. Now was the time to make a fresh start. Maybe I could finally get to know him better.

Our relationship had changed over the years, partly

because of his age and creeping senility. He would tell me tales about his old girlfriends and how he had run away with his first wife when she was really young.

Dad was slightly deaf and it caused him to talk quite loudly. He spoke to me like an old mate he'd met down the pub, and I treated him like a silly boy who should have known better. I don't think he had any idea of how a father should behave because he had no role models. His own father had abandoned him and his stepfather had never been particularly close to him.

While he was in hospital I decided to paint his flat. I cleared out all his junk and had a car-boot sale to get rid of the rubbish he'd collected. I bought new rugs and cleaned the place from top to bottom. Niam managed to get me the paint and I repainted the walls white and every piece of furniture black. It was very Ikea.

When Dad got home I thought he'd have another stroke. He wandered from room to room as if he'd stepped into another person's flat. I think a part of him was grateful that I'd gone to so much effort, but I'd failed to understand how important his things were to him. I was only seventeen – what did I know of an old man's memories? I'd thrown away his life.

Strangely, I had the same feeling about my own future. What had happened to my dreams of fame and fortune?

I had been at Video Collection for nine months, catching a bus to the industrial estate every morning alongside dozens of office and factory workers. The novelty of working in an office and being normal had worn off. Apart from my regular Monday sickies, I'd taken to wearing a catsuit and trainers to the office.

A new guy had started work, Duncan, who had bright

ginger hair and an uptight attitude. It seemed to be his mission in life to snitch on me whenever I dozed off in the viewing room or overslept.

The boss eventually called me into his office and said, 'Geri, you really have to get your act together.'

He was right. Back at my desk, I glanced around the large open-plan office, with its computer terminals, phones, in-trays and out-trays. There was a *Gone with the Wind* poster on a pillar, showing Clark Gable carrying Vivien Leigh past a burning building.

'What am I doing?' I asked. 'This isn't my dream. I wanted to be a movie star. I wanted to be rich and famous.'

It felt like an important moment, as though I'd reached an intersection and had to make a decision about whether to continue along the same path or change direction. I stood up and walked over to Duncan's desk. He was at lunch and his grotty old cardigan hung on the back of his chair. I stapled up the sleeves and then walked out of the office. At home, I wrote a letter to the boss saying my father was very sick and I had to look after him. I didn't go back again. It was the May before I turned eighteen.

If I thought quitting my job would galvanize me into action, it failed miserably. Instead, I had more time to party with my raving friends. Billy would pick me up from Dad's flat of a morning, and I'd keep him company while he did his business deals. Of an evening, I'd go out with Niam and Billy to the Game Bird or to Café de Paris.

I was infatuated by Niam. He was a lovable rogue with a good heart and some questionable friends. Despite his tough exterior, he had a softness inside that showed when he wrote me poetry and bought me flowers. A bad person doesn't do that.

Every night became a party and every weekend we danced until we dropped. I forgot birthdays and failed to turn up for family gatherings.

Dad hated the direction my life had taken. I was unemployed and not even looking for work. I partied all night and slept all day. I'd gone wild and wouldn't listen.

Fed up with the arguments, Dad told me to leave. I couldn't go home to Mum, or stay with Karen. Natalie and Max confronted me about my reckless lifestyle and the company I was keeping. I told them to stop interfering.

Ever since Dad had left home, Max had tried to become the man of the house. He was only fourteen years old then, but had always been the sensible one who kept his head down and worked hard at school. I called Max straight, which is a nicer way of saying square.

Despite going to a rough school, Max went on to university and had nearly finished his science degree. He had turned into the perfect big brother, but I didn't realize it then. I told him to mind his own business. I could see the hurt in his eyes. He's such a big softie.

'I know somewhere you can stay,' said Niam's sister, Mary. 'It's just around the corner.'

'I haven't any money.'

'That's all right. This place is free of charge. It's a squat.'

Mary helped me break through a side window of a cute little granny cottage, which was part of the South Oxhey council estate. We put new locks on the door and Mary knew all about squatters' rights.

'They can't just kick you out,' she said. 'They need court orders and bailiffs.'

'But what about the owners?'

'The council owns the cottage. It shouldn't be empty, not with people homeless and living on the streets.'

South Oxhey was a terrible place, but I loved the cottage. It had central heating and loads of hot water. I fixed the curtains and cleaned the kitchen and bathroom until they were spotless. This is lovely, I thought, my own little home.

At the same time, I joined a promotion agency in Watford that provided staff for exhibitions and conferences. Companies were often looking for girls to hand out leaflets and brochures at motor shows and travel expos.

Straight away I was sent on a job. A huge fun day had been organized for hundreds of schoolchildren at a manor house in Oxfordshire. It was designed to be like *It's a Knockout*, with games, music and shows. I thought I'd be marshalling kids and arranging the party, but I ended up putting together hundreds of packed lunches on plastic trays.

The promotion agency needed pictures of me to send out with my CV, and they sent me to a photographer who had a studio off the Finchley Road in North London. I'd had experience of having my photo taken but was still quite nervous.

Karen had a friend Lilly, who was in a camera club, and in my early teens she'd asked me to pose for them. Dad drove me to West London and I sat on a stool with my hair in plaits, wearing a jumper, while a lot of middle-aged men and women snapped away. Normally they took photos of the countryside or still lifes, and a live model was a mystery to them. Afterwards they gave me £20.

Lilly photographed me again a few years later, when puberty had arrived in a rush and I had the curves to prove it. I'd just got home from a rave and she got me to pose in the back garden, lying on a blanket. I wore a figure-hugging white dress and had blond dishevelled hair. I look at the pictures now and wonder, Was I really only sixteen?

The photographer in North London took a few portrait shots for the agency and then suggested I put on a swimming costume.

'Sometimes the clients want swimsuit girls,' he explained.

I slipped on a strapless one-piece and he shot another roll of film.

'Do you want to take your top down, love?'

'No.'

I felt shocked. Bless me, I was only seventeen. In the changing room, I locked the door and quickly got dressed. Then I ran downstairs and all the way to Finchley tube station.

Why was I so shocked? Catholic guilt, perhaps, or my mother's lectures about nice girls and naughty girls. It wasn't as though I was shy about flaunting myself. The hippy clothes of my early rave days had been replaced by slinky catsuits, silver one-piece swimsuits and hot pants. They didn't leave much to the imagination.

But nudity was something very different. Only two boys had seen my naked breasts – Toby and Niam. Why would

I show a complete stranger, let alone a photographer?

Some rave organizers offered to pay me £30 to be a dancer on a Saturday night at the Crazy Club at the London Astoria. There were flyers posted all over Tottenham Court Road publicizing the club. I started work at 11 p.m., and had my hair dyed blond and wore a cone bra like Madonna's.

Standing on a speaker, dancing to the music, I imagined I truly was a superstar and that the crowd had come to see me. Sometimes I could pick out my friends' faces in the flashing strobe lights and mass of bodies, and for those few hours I could make-believe that all my little-girl fantasies and adolescent daydreams had come true.

And then the show would be over. On a rainy footpath, littered with drunks and hamburger wrappings, I trudged to the station and caught a train home to my illegal squat in South Oxhey. I had thirty quid in my pocket, a way-ward boyfriend and a family that felt far away. From the highs to the lows in the space of a few hours.

Often I wouldn't see Niam for days at a time, but Wednesday was always our night together. I'd go to the supermarket and get a bottle of wine and some nice food for a romantic dinner. I remember splurging on smoked salmon once, and lighting candles to create the right ambience. Niam arrived and announced, 'I don't like smoked salmon.' Then he fell asleep in front of the television.

Niam was a budding entrepreneur, always looking for the next deal. He wanted to get out of his crappy life. He had aspirations. I loved him for that. I also fantasized that we were like Bonnie and Clyde.

Even when I found out that Niam was still seeing his old girlfriend, I found a way of rationalizing my sadness. I was his bit on the side; the Mae West in his life; the showgirl mistress he lusted after while his boring 'wife' languished at home.

I loved Niam. More than that, I was obsessed by him. It wasn't just his charm and charisma. Even without my fantasies and show-reels, I knew we had connected. We were kindred spirits. We both wanted to make something more of our lives.

'He'll come round,' I told myself. 'He'll see that I'm the only girl for him.'

I spent my eighteenth birthday alone in the squat. Niam had dropped by with a bottle of champagne and then left because he had to attend to some business. I'd never felt so low and lonely. I lay in the bath, clutching a big bottle of rum, which scalded the back of my throat as I drank. Tears ran down my cheeks.

I wondered if I drank the whole bottle, would I drown in the bath? I really don't want to get old, I decided. Was I contemplating suicide? I don't know. Nobody would have cared, I thought. What an awful day.

Later I discovered a birthday card that Natalie, Max and Mum had posted. They had also given me £50. I wanted to buy a mountain bike that cost £120 and Billy gave me the rest. I took to riding around Watford wearing my silver swimsuit and little white hot pants. It certainly got me noticed.

Natalie had an ex-boyfriend called Rupert in Fairlawns, a nice area of town. He had a pet python that he used to take down to the pub, letting people pass it around and buy it beers. It was cruel and I told him so, but he just laughed.

I wanted to rescue the snake. I knew a young boy in South Oxhey who already had two snakes and he looked after them carefully. One night, when I knew Rupert was out, I put on my black catsuit, zipped up to the neck, black gloves and a beanie. Then I cycled the three miles from my squat to Fairlawns and left my bicycle down the street.

Imagining I was a cat burglar – like Cary Grant in *To Catch a Thief* – I circled the ground-floor flat and found a small window open. Crawling inside, I slid the glass lid from the tank. The python was about four feet long and as thick as my wrist. It squirmed suddenly in my hands, catching me by surprise. I knocked the glass lid, which tumbled to the floor. Surely it would break? It must have woken half of Watford as it settled on the floor in one piece.

I slid the python into my backpack. I could feel it squirming inside as I cycled home to the squat. That night I put it in a cupboard, and the next morning I gave it to the snake boy. Mission accomplished. Rupert never discovered what happened. He assumed that somehow the snake had managed to push open the glass lid and escape from its cramped tank.

The council pinned a notice to the front door, covered in plastic so the rain didn't make it soggy. It was written in a jumble of legalese, with references to 'illegal occupation', 'trespassing' and 'eviction'. I had been summonsed to appear in court.

I'd been in the cottage for two months and had done it

up nicely. It felt like home. I had two weeks before the court case. I don't know why I bothered turning up. Most squatters simply pack their gear and move out, letting the council resume control. Perhaps fired by Mary's zealous rhetoric about squatters' rights and bourgeoisie conspiracies against the poor, I decided to fight.

I knew I should wear a suit to court but I didn't have one, so Billy, who was quite short, gave me one of his. It was still way too big. When the case was called, I stood in court and introduced myself. To keep the suit pants from falling down, I had to keep my hands in my pockets, but that looked as though I was being cocky.

There were three black guys in the dock, waiting for another case, and they were giggling at me. I pressed on, explaining to the magistrate that I was homeless and that no-one had been living in the cottage when I moved in. 'I'm not damaging the place. I've actually done it up. Can I stay there, please?'

The magistrate shook his head. 'I'm sorry about your circumstances, but you can't stay. You have ten days to vacate the premises.'

As he issued the order I had tears streaming down my cheeks. It didn't seem fair. Feeling alone and homeless, I hitched up my trousers and cycled away from the court. Billy's shoes were so big they flapped against my heels.

Those next ten days were a blur of late nights. I partied as though it didn't matter whether I finished face down in the gutter. I thought about going back to live at home, but I couldn't face Mum. Natalie was living at Karen's place and there was no room for me there. I was the troubled teenager that nobody knew how to deal with.

Circumstances stacked up against me until one night I

found myself with nowhere to sleep. I knocked on Dad's flat. There was no answer. I ran down the stairwell, bouncing off the walls at each landing and trying not to stumble and fall.

At the base of the tower block, a wet, rotting sofa had been abandoned beside the big steel dustbins. I sat there, with my rucksack containing all my belongings on my back. I clutched Yellow Ted, my childhood toy, and let the tears fall on his worn fur and single glass eye.

'What the hell am I going to do? I have nowhere to go.'

I knocked on Angie's door, a girl I knew from various parties.

'Angie, I've nowhere to stay tonight, can I sleep with you?'

'I've had an argument with my mum.'

'Can't you sneak me in?'

'No. I'm sorry.'

Suddenly, it dawned on me that I had no real friends. They were all party companions who were just part of the scene.

That night I slept in my sister's boyfriend's car. In the morning, when his parents had gone to work, he let me into his house so I could have a bath and clean up. They say things always look better in the morning, but I drew no comfort from another cold, grey day. They also say that when you're at rock bottom there's only one way to go.

By that Christmas I'd moved into a bedsit above Autosounds, a car-stereo shop in Queen's Road. Niam had finally left his girlfriend and we were inseparable. Often we didn't see daylight for days on end. We partied, slept and then partied again.

I had no money. I tried to keep a little aside each week to pay the phone and gas bills when they arrived. This stash went missing one day after I'd saved more than £100. I tore the place apart looking for it. I felt sick. One of our friends must have stolen the money.

Three months later, British Telecom sent a final warning about disconnecting the phone within twenty-four hours for non-payment. I'd pleaded with them for more time, but my best excuses were wearing thin. Cleaning out my cupboards, I opened a shoebox and found a dozen crumpled notes crammed in the corner.

Here was my secret stash! I must have put the money in the box for safe keeping and then forgotten my hiding place. I felt as though I'd won the lottery. It was my lucky day.

On Christmas Eve I danced at the Crazy Club in fancy-dress costume, parodying the pantomimes of the season. I wore a tutu, silver tights and boots, a bustier, fairy wings and a blond wig with Vivienne Westwood ringlets.

I arrived home in the early hours and phoned Niam at 9 a.m. to wish him a merry Christmas. His dad picked up the phone.

'I don't want to wake him. He's with someone,' he said.

'I'm sorry?'

'You heard me the first time. I'm not waking him. He's got a girl with him.'

I felt sick, but the nausea was soon overtaken by anger. I ordered a cab and drove to Niam's house, telling the driver to hurry. He kept looking at me strangely in the rear-view mirror.

Knowing his father wouldn't let me in the front door, I slipped round the back and entered through the patio doors. Creeping up the stairs, I could hear the radio playing in the sitting room. My heart raced.

I burst into Niam's room, expecting to catch him in the act. He sat up, bleary-eyed, half asleep and *alone*. I looked like the Ghost of Christmas Present in my fairy costume and mascara-stained cheeks.

'I thought you were in bed with someone,' I exclaimed.

'Pardon?' He thought I'd gone mad.

'Never mind. I'm going home.' Sobbing, I ran out the door, down the stairs and through the house. The front door was deadlocked and I hammered on it in frustration. I turned and ran out through the patio doors.

Why would his father lie to me? What had I done to him? I knew the answer. Niam's former girlfriend had been well-to-do, with a cultured accent and manners. She came from a prominent local family, whereas I was a podium dancer from the wrong side of the tracks.

Back at the flat, I took a bath and tried to rationalize things. I wondered if perhaps there *had* been a girl in Niam's room. His dad might have tipped him off about my phone call and he could have bustled her out, or hidden her under his bed.

'Stop torturing yourself, Geri,' I told myself. 'Niam loves you.'

Mum had invited me to have Christmas lunch with the rest of the family – minus Dad, of course. After my disastrous morning with Niam, I turned up for lunch not exactly full of the Christmas spirit.

As Mum opened the door, I pushed past her, ran upstairs and threw up in the toilet. The girl in the mirror had black eyes and drawn cheeks. Her existence was futile. This wasn't fun any more. What had happened to that girl who was chatty and confident? It was as though I'd stayed too long at the party and the champagne had gone flat. Now I felt numb and lost.

The rest of the afternoon passed in a blur. I couldn't eat a thing. After dinner I fell fast asleep in the lounge. I didn't play Monopoly, eat mince pies, or watch *The Wizard of Oz* on TV. Another crap Christmas.

Just after New Year I had a party at my flat in Queen's Road. About forty people turned up, including someone with a police radio scanner, who monitored when the patrol cars were coming so we could turn down the music. Each time the officers arrived, they found us sitting and chatting as if we were holding a book-club wine-and-cheese night.

Niam came along and we seemed to be getting on fine. He stayed the night and I began to relax.

The following Saturday I danced at the Crazy Club as usual. Niam didn't come because he said he had mates to see. During a dance break, Laura, a friend of mine, said she had some news about Niam.

'I think you should know,' she declared. 'I'm telling you as a friend. I went round to Niam's house yesterday and his old girlfriend was there. They seemed pretty friendly.'

I knew it was true. That afternoon I confronted Niam when he arrived at the flat. I'd rehearsed it all beforehand – issuing the ultimatum and having him beg for my forgiveness. It didn't work that way.

Instead, I did the begging. It was humiliating and I hated myself. 'Please, don't leave me. I love you. Please, don't do this.' I was on my hands and knees, clutching his leg.

Niam prised my arms apart and walked out the door. He didn't belittle or ridicule me; I did that to myself. When he'd gone, I hugged my big furry gorilla and paced up and down the room, sobbing hysterically. My whole world had come to an end.

I didn't blame Niam for leaving me. We were going nowhere. The girl he'd chosen provided normality in his life. If we'd stayed together, who knows what might have happened? The only certainty is that the ending wouldn't have been as glamorous as my *Bonnie and Clyde* show-reel.

For two years afterwards I still thought about Niam. He was the first man ever to break my heart and, hopefully, the last. It taught me a painful lesson. From then on I believed that bastards bred bitches and bitches bred bastards. I would never let a man walk over me again.

I had visions of becoming rich and famous before seeing Niam again. Then I planned to invite him out to dinner and watch him squirm with jealousy and try so hard to impress me. Niam had always been a real wannabe and it would drive him crazy to think he'd missed his opportunity. Is it childish to want that sort of revenge?

It was time to *make* things happen rather than wait to be discovered. I enrolled in an A level drama course at Casio College for three days a week. I loved studying plays and dissecting roles, but struggled to overcome my shyness when performing. So much of an actor's craft is the ability to deliver true emotion, to reach deep inside oneself, to draw on the memories that can inspire sadness, anger, frustration or pity, whatever the scene demands.

Unfortunately I couldn't do this. I felt too vulnerable. I

wasn't confident enough of my own ability to open myself up in a classroom full of strangers who would later analyse and judge my performance. Just as had happened at grammar school, I felt like a scrappy little kid who didn't deserve to be there. I didn't belong. The other students were fresh from school productions or amateur theatrical groups. They were all very 'lovey', or were good at pretending to be. Most of the girls sounded like Helena Bonham Carter and the boys like Hugh Grant – or was it the other way round? By comparison, I felt like an impostor.

I tried hard. At a drama bookshop in Camden I bought books on acting and collections of monologues. I learned how to pace and project my voice. Eventually, I could deliver a reasonable monologue, but I could never let go and lose myself in a part.

On a night out at the Wag in Wardour Street, Soho, a cool-looking black guy thrust a card into my hand. It advertised a new music programme on BBC2 called *Dance Energy*, created by Janet Street-Porter and hosted by her boyfriend, Normski.

Trying to re-create the same ambience as a nightclub, the producers wanted a live audience to dance in the warehouse studio as the various bands played and video clips were shown.

Here was my chance to be on TV, I thought. Maybe I'll be discovered. I wore my sexiest outfit and trooped along to the large warehouse studio in Wembley. There was no payment involved, unless you counted the soggy trays of sandwiches laid on by the BBC and which disappeared within seconds.

Live acts like Mica Paris and Rebel MC were interspersed with video clips. Meanwhile, dozens of stylish club dancers and extroverts had turned up at the studio, dying to get on camera. We all danced our socks off, hoping to catch the attention of the cameraman who wandered around the floor.

*Dance Energy* aired every Thursday night, and I watched it religiously, hoping to catch a glimpse of myself. It rarely happened. Ironically, the only time I took Natalie along to the show she managed, without even trying, to feature half a dozen times. She was there doing her little shuffle dance, while next to her – out of shot – I was madly 'voguing'.

My place above Autosounds was basically just a room with a bed in the corner. One morning, as I put on my bra, I noticed a small, hard lump in my right breast. It was about the size of a Smartie.

I made an appointment to see Dr King, wanting him to check it out and reassure me. 'I'm booking you straight into hospital,' he said, without lifting his eyes from the notes he'd scrawled on a yellow form.

'Why?'

'We'll do a test to make sure everything is OK.'

'What sort of test?'

'A very minor operation, that's all.'

I trusted him implicitly. I didn't know much about breast cancer. Nobody I'd known had ever died from it, although I had a vague recollection of Mum mentioning an aunt in Spain who'd had a breast removed. I was so busy being young, it didn't even enter my head that I might lose a breast, or perhaps even die. This was a drama that didn't belong to me. It was a minor irritation; a fly in my soup. I would go into hospital, they would remove the lump and I would get on with my life – simple as that.

Mum drove me to Watford General Hospital at 6 a.m. Along the way, she kept telling me stories about giving birth to me at the same hospital. I had a little overnight bag containing a nightie and a book. All I kept thinking was, I've got to work on Saturday night. The rent is due on the flat. What am I going to do?

They took me straight into the operating theatre. The surgeon chatted to me. 'We're going to take a small sample of tissue from the lump in your breast. Then we're going to look under a microscope to see if it's cancerous.'

'How long before you know?'

'The results should come back in a few days.'

As I went under the anaesthetic, I can remember saying to myself, 'It's only a lump ... They're removing a lump. I'm not going to lose a breast ...'

At some point later that day I woke feeling groggy and disorientated. The chrome nightstand came into focus, and then the burnt-orange curtains around my bed. Suddenly, I remembered where I was. I looked down and saw a large pink stain on the front of my gown. Oh, my God, what have they done?

Nervously, I reached up and lifted the neckline of the hospital gown. Tilting my chin, I peered down. Both boobs were still there. Yes! The stain was an old iodine spill.

Getting out of bed, I wandered through the ward and down the corridor, hoping to find a nurse or a doctor who would tell me how the operation had gone. I didn't realize that I was wearing a backless gown and my bum was flashing.

When a nurse found me and steered me back to my bed, I thought she was being very sweet to put her hand on my back. Then I realized she was clasping the robe together so I didn't moon at any more patients.

Later in the day a young doctor came to see me. He told me how well the procedure had gone. The results would take another few days, but I was free to go home. Billy came to pick me up, and he tried to make me feel special by buying me a huge bunch of flowers.

I walked out of the hospital wearing my fake-fur leopard-skin coat that came down to my ankles, with my blond hair tied back and dark glasses shielding my eyes. I carried the bouquet of flowers and stepped into Billy's BMW.

The only thing missing was the paparazzi photographers, I thought, as I imagined myself to be Liz Taylor being whisked away from the Betty Ford Clinic.

Billy dropped me back at my bedsit. The hospital had given me strong painkillers and I floated about the place for the next day or two. Mum wanted me to stay in bed, but I was due to dance at the Crazy Club on Saturday night.

She gave me £30, saying, 'Please don't work; not this week. Here's the money. I'll pay it.'

I took her £30 and worked anyway: it helped to keep my mind off the test results.

They arrived a week later and were negative. The sense of relief was so enormous that it surprised me. For a while I'd tried to convince myself that I didn't care. It hadn't worked.

'That's it,' I told myself. 'It's time for Geri Halliwell to turn over a new leaf.'

Since leaving school my life had been a reckless series of experiments and aimless jobs. Mum blamed it on late puberty and all the resultant hormonal changes: I'd been as good as gold until I'd turned seventeen, she said.

But if I hadn't rebelled then, it would most likely have happened later. An unseen clock ticked inside me and time was running out. There might be no tomorrow. I had to experience things now just in case.

# 5

## DANCING QUEEN

A black girl with a gold tooth and Afro hair scooped up in a high ponytail tapped me on the shoulder. She was all painted nails and cleavage. The Crazy Club was heaving with Saturday night ravers and I had just stepped down from the podium. Swigging on a bottle of mineral water, I turned and smiled, wiping perspiration from my forehead.

'How would you like to dance in Spain?' she asked.

She had to repeat the question twice to be heard above the noise. Then she thrust a card into my hand for a night-club called BCM in Majorca. 'It's the biggest in Europe,' she said, shouting in my ear. 'We need three dancers for the summer season.'

By then I was the head dancer at the Crazy Club and handed out the wages each week.

'Are you interested?' she shouted.

'What's the deal?'

'Seven days a week, but you don't start work until late. The money's pretty good and we arrange your accommodation.'

I didn't commit straight away, although I knew immediately that this was just what I'd been looking for. What better way to clean up my act and make a fresh start? I could get away from places that reminded me of Niam and stop mixing with the wrong crowd. I could swim every day and eat healthy salads.

'Where do I sign up?'

I flew to Majorca in March 1991 with Shelly, an aspiring model, and Nicola, a trained dancer who could do stunning high kicks. Shelly looked like the lead singer in Roxette and was built like a beanpole – really long and thin, with bleached-blond hair. She had worked at the Astoria with me.

Initially, the three of us shared an apartment in town, but later Shelly and I moved to a lovely place in the hills, overlooking Magaluf, Majorca's best-known resort.

The apartment was about fifteen minutes' walk from the nightclub area of town, up a steep hill which provided stunning views of the surrounding beaches and the Mediterranean. From the balcony, I could look along the entire beachfront and walk down to it via winding stone steps.

I started work at midnight each day, when Des the DJ from Birmingham cranked up his mixing deck and his image appeared on a big screen. I stood on a podium, or sometimes in a cage, ten feet above the biggest, tackiest, loudest dance floor in Europe.

I danced for three records, and then rested before getting up again. For this I was paid 4,000 pesetas a night – around £20 – rising to 7,000 pesetas in the height of the summer.

The bars never closed in Majorca and the booze was

cheap. Regardless of how long the season lasted, each day felt like the first day of summer all over again. There were school-leavers and end-of-season sporting teams and backpackers from across Europe. By morning, some of them were too drunk to remember their own names, let alone where they were staying.

Shaz and Trace had found their spiritual home. Teenagers from across Europe were on a mission to go absolutely mental for two weeks. I watched them come and go in amazement as they got totally pissed and shagged each other.

I never tired of the absurdity of human behaviour, which saw normally quiet, subdued people turn into lager monsters. They were all on fast-forward, embracing the culture of wet-T-shirt competitions and impromptu sexual floor shows that were played out to the beat of novelty records. Eventually, they fell asleep on the beach and woke with sunburned legs and faces full of sand.

I finished work at five o'clock and was home by six. Then I'd make myself a cup of tea and put on Bob Marley's 'No Woman, No Cry'. I wound down, sitting on the balcony and watching the ocean. The sun had come up and I could see people having sex on the beach, or crashed out in their party clothes.

Normally, I slept until about midday and then padded about barefoot on the cool marble floors, doing the laundry or other chores during the hottest part of the day.

The fridge usually contained a few bottles of mineral water, a jar of olives, a selection of low-fat yoghurts and a big tub of pasta that Shelly had made. If I didn't eat the leftovers, I'd buy a baguette and munch on that.

Of an afternoon, Shelly and I would go down to the

beach. There was a whole community of ticket-sellers in Majorca, whose job it was to encourage punters into the clubs. We hung out with them, sitting in the beachfront cafés and bars while they dropped in and out. We could also go jet-skiing, or windsurfing, having befriended the guys who ran the boats and rented the equipment.

Most of the dancers in Majorca dreamed of being discovered and becoming famous. Nicola had trained as a dancer and wanted to be an actress. She had lovely long dark hair, a dancer's body and massive tits, but I could see the faintest tell-tale wrinkles around her eyes. She was probably in her early thirties, although she claimed to be much younger. God, I thought, I really don't want to be doing this when I'm her age.

Shelly wanted to be a model and had done some small jobs when she was still at school. She needed to be taken on by a good agency, but hadn't found one yet.

Ellena was another girl in our circle. She was Des the DJ's girlfriend. Whenever we talked about being discovered or getting our big break, Ellena would always have done things first. She loved name-dropping about soap stars she'd met and TV producers who'd promised her roles. Each of these stories was like a small victory over the rest of us and she clutched them like blankets that would keep her warm on cold nights.

I still imagined, or hoped, that one night some producer or director would suddenly come up and offer me a brilliant role. This might sound naive, but it still happens. A generation ago it was cigarette girls and waitresses who got discovered. Nowadays, somebody like Kate Moss is noticed by a model scout in an airline check-in queue. Things haven't changed that much. It's still a matter of being in the right place at the right time.

Spain gave me the chance to change my lifestyle. I ate healthy food and swam twenty lengths a day, as well as jogging and doing aerobics. I began to reflect on how I'd treated my family over the previous two years, particularly Mum. She had found herself a new boyfriend, Steve, and seemed really happy in her letters. I wanted her to come to Spain and visit me.

*3 May 1991*

*Dear Mama,*
Hola.

    *I miss you very much and I hope you miss me. You know what? I'm starting to realize the important things in life and that is to make you proud of me.*

    *I am really grateful for what you have done for me, Mum. I don't want to cause you any more trouble. I am so sorry for last year and what I put you through. I've grown up a lot since then and I'm learning how important it is to respect your parents. I want you to be proud of me. I want you to think, What a wonderful daughter I have.*

    *That's why I want you and Steve to come out and visit me. Hopefully, I can start paying you back for all that you've done for me. We can wipe the slate clean and start again.*

    *I don't know what I want to do with my life. I know that I won't work in a bank, that's for sure. I know that I'm different. I have this fear of being mediocre. I'm scared of getting old.*

*I understand why it's so important to you to keep the family together. And I know that you'll always be there for me. You have done so much for me, Mama. I love you with all my heart.*

*Asta la vista, Baby.*

*Love you.*

*Geri.*


Mum and Steve came out to see me in June. They had a riotous time, dancing at the club until the early hours like teenagers. I really liked Steve. The two of them seemed very much in love. Mum didn't say anything to me, but she sent me a letter afterwards.


### 21 June 1991

*Dear Geraldine,*
*How are you?*

*It was wonderful to see you. I came back with great peace of mind because I like the people you mix with. They all are very nice and they all look after each other. That is good.*

*I like the place you live, too. The girls keep it very nice and tidy.*

*Geraldine, this is very difficult for me to say, but when you were dancing, I was very proud of you. Please be very careful not to hurt yourself, especially to fall from the platform. I've been trying to find insurance for you here, but the cheapest is £13.90 a week ...*

*I liked the club. I've been showing everybody at work the leaflets.*

*It is very strange about life. Max went to a not very good school and ended up being a scientist. You went to a grammar school and you are a nightclub dancer!*

*I realize that you don't want an 8 to 5 job. Like any mother, I want you to settle down – it's only natural. I worry about you, especially after what happened last year. Whatever you decide to do, I will support you. But it must be respectable. I don't want you to get into any trouble.*

*Remember, we only have arguments if you are unruly. I respect your ambitions in life, but you must respect my life, too. When you come home, we're going to take it day by day and hopefully we'll sort things out.*

*I hope to see you soon,*

*Love,*

*Mama. xxxxx*

Max and his girlfriend Sue got married that summer. Sue wanted me to be a bridesmaid, but I told her to choose somebody else because my contract with BCM didn't allow me to take the time off. I couldn't guarantee that I'd be there, but eventually I managed to fly home for the day.

Mum was so excited about having the whole family together. She prepared my old room so I had somewhere to stay. Even Dad got dressed up and looked quite handsome. He'd been writing me letters in Spain that were typically eccentric. In one sentence he'd warn me about using a high-factor sunscreen, and in the next he'd tell me I shouldn't rush into marriage.

*The path to true love never did run straight, Geri. Your Mr Right will come along when you least expect him to. Don't panic. You have plenty of time to have a baby . . .*

*Between you and me, I think affection is just as important as sex. To go to sleep in each other's arms is a wonderful feeling.*

*Love and kisses.*

*I miss you.*

*Dad. xxxxxxxx.*

I think Dad assumed that, because Max and Natalie were both married, I suddenly felt left on the shelf. He really was going quite potty, I decided, but I quite liked him that way. He had mellowed into a charming old man, full of odd insights and strange stories about the war.

I loved my summer in the sun. The season stretched until September, and I got to know the other dancers and ticket-sellers. Of course, I had to put up with drunks propositioning me at the club, but most of them were good-natured.

Walking home one morning, two guys followed me up the hill. I was still dressed in my club gear. They asked me the time and then one of them grabbed at my breasts.

I'd always talked about what I'd do if I was attacked. I imagined lashing out and kicking him in the crotch. In reality, I was almost paralysed with fear. My attempt at fighting back was so feeble it was like slapping him on the wrist.

Thankfully, they ran off.

In that same week, I was shopping in town with Shelly when two guys began shouting insults from a car. They were kerb-crawling and calling out *puta!*, which means whore in Spanish.

I got really angry. 'How would you like it if someone called your sister a whore?' I told them. 'I'm somebody's sister and somebody's daughter. You shouldn't speak to me like that.'

By then they'd stopped the car. The driver got out and called me a whore again. I slapped his face. He tried to hit me and we finished up struggling in the street. Grabbing at my hair, he reacted in horror as my blond Madonna ponytail came away in his hands. It scared the living daylights out of him. I think he thought he'd scalped me. He dropped the hairpiece and ran.

Shelly and I often went shopping together, trying on different outfits and giving each other second opinions. She was so tall and skinny she could look good in polka dots and horizontal stripes.

'I think you're putting on a few pounds,' she said one day, but not in a harsh way. I laughed. Nobody had ever suggested I was overweight. I loved food and had never been weight-conscious. Yet suddenly I became aware of it. A few days later, I sat at a pub on the beachfront with Ellena and Shelly. As we chatted, I broke off chunks of bread and dipped them in a bowl of aioli – garlic mayonnaise. After a while I felt quite bloated and uncomfortable.

Excusing myself from the others, I went to the toilet and looked in the mirror. Am I fat? I must be. I've eaten too much. What can I do?

A Spanish girl came out of a cubicle and smiled at me as she adjusted her hair. She was plump and pretty. As she left, I went into the toilet and locked the cubicle door. The tiles were cool against my knees.

The idea of making myself throw-up wasn't something I'd heard about from anybody or read in a magazine. The word bulimia meant nothing to me. As far as I knew, I invented the idea that very moment, as I put my finger down my throat and vomited into the bowl.

I stood up and felt better. There wasn't much food left in my stomach; I wouldn't get fat. The tiles had left a crisscross pattern on my knees, which I rubbed with the palm of my hand as I rinsed out my mouth.

Afterwards, I rejoined the others, quite pleased with my ingenuity. I didn't plan to do it again. From then on I'd be more careful about what I ate. Naomi, another dancer who looked like a stick insect, began advising me. 'Geri, you should avoid eating cheese and salami,' she said. 'Maybe just have that sandwich before dancing, but don't eat anything afterwards.'

It wasn't that difficult. There was rarely anything in the fridge at the apartment because we were all too lazy to shop and carry groceries up the hill.

Shelly had just had some photographs taken for her modelling portfolio. A local photographer in Magaluf had done the shoot. She came back to the apartment with the contact sheets and a few dozen prints.

'Look! Look! Look! What do you think?'

She sat me down and we looked through the pictures. Many of them were nude shots, which surprised me because I hadn't expected it. None of the photographs was sexually explicit or sleazy – quite the opposite. Shelly didn't even seem naked in most of them, despite having no clothes on.

Instead of wondering what made a nice girl like Shelly strip off completely for a stranger with a camera, I found myself intrigued by her. The photographs made her look alluring and feminine.

'Wow! These are fantastic.'

Shelly beamed.

'Who did them?'

'Sebastian Amengual. Aren't they great?'

'Did you plan this?'

She grinned. 'Sort of. I wanted to see how they'd turn out.'

I flicked through the larger prints. 'Do you think he'd do some of me?' The question seemed to be halfway out before I had time to think.

'Sure. I'll ask him. He's really sweet.'

Sebastian was tanned, balding and had a head like a tortoise. He wore John Lennon-style glasses and seemed to wrinkle up his nose when he talked, as if he was constantly about to sneeze. Shelly introduced us and Sebastian seemed very professional and matter-of-fact.

To him it was another working day, while I had butter-flies fluttering in my stomach. We drove up into the hills in his car, stopping in the weed-strewn forecourt of an abandoned factory. The walls and roof had been stripped off, leaving the rusting iron skeleton and staircases.

It was a beautiful day, with the sun shining and a light sea breeze shifting the air.

'They used to make pottery here,' said Sebastian motioning to the ruins of the factory.

'What happened?'

He shrugged. 'It wasn't very good pottery.'

I helped him carry reflector umbrellas, lights and tripods from the car to the shade of the crumbling stone wall. The location didn't strike me as being particularly glamorous, but I assumed Sebastian had some artistic concept in mind. He casually handed me a chain-mail bikini and continued loading film into the camera.

Changing rooms were clearly not provided. Instead, I turned away and slipped off my skirt.

The bikini pinched me in all the wrong places, but it looked OK. I had a good tan and blond hair. Sebastian had me pose on the iron steps with my top on, getting me used to the camera and his instructions. In between shots, he chatted about local landmarks and gave me a brief history of Magaluf.

We changed locations and took some shots beside the river. There was an upturned boat on the bank and Sebastian got me to pose on the hull while wearing a bathrobe. As I lay on the boat, he asked me to pull the bathrobe back until my breasts were showing. I kept imagining that I was doing a skin-cream advert for Nivea.

'Look more towards me, Geri. Chin up. That's it. Now turn and look over your shoulder. Push your hair back . . . good, good, just a few more . . . Let your hair fall again and throw it back. Once more . . . Having fun?' The motor drive clicked and whirred.

Afterwards, Sebastian dropped me home and said he'd have the contact sheets ready the following day.

When I first saw the photographs, I thought, Wow! Is that really me? I looked tall, or at least in proportion, which meant you couldn't tell I was only five foot one and a half. I had never regarded myself as particularly attractive, but they were nice shots.

'Have you ever thought about modelling?' Ellena asked as I showed the girls the photographs.

I shook my head. 'I'm too short.'

'You don't have to be tall to be a glamour model.'

Suddenly, I twigged. 'You mean topless shots?'

She looked over my shoulder at the photographs. 'I could introduce you to an agency in London.'

'Have you done it?' I tried not to sound shocked.

Ellena nodded. 'Boobs and bums, that sort of thing.'

I kept thinking of the whole Samantha Fox phenomenon – the girl with the million-pound boobs. She'd had a virtual monopoly on page three of the tabloids for years. I also remembered giggling on the back seat of Roberto's car on our way to infant school, while looking at his Dad's copy of the *Sun*.

Here was a whole new world I knew nothing about. What would Mum say? She'd hate it. Dad would be cool. The dancing contract was nearly over. Come September, I'd need another way of making ends meet. Glamour modelling? Some of them were pretty famous. Look at Samantha Fox and Linda Lusardi. And a little nudity hadn't hurt Madonna's and Kim Basinger's careers. Both of them had posed for *Playboy*.

On a freezing October day, I stood in front of a big Edwardian house in Chiswick, staring at the bay windows and the paint peeling from the frames. This was the address of the modelling agency suggested by Ellena.

Pushing open the front door, I entered a reception area which had pictures of calendar girls and famous page-three faces on the walls.

'Just take a seat, love, I'll be with you in a moment.'

Ken was very tanned, with golden hair. He reminded me of a slim version of Chevy Chase.

I glanced around and noticed a box of files on a nearby desk that bore the label 'Dog Box'. I turned to the middle-aged secretary. 'What's that?'

'One of the little agency jokes,' she said, not looking up.

Ken answered for her. 'They're the models who'll do anything.'

'What do you mean, anything?' I asked anxiously.

'Don't you worry your pretty head about that,' he said, shaking my hand.

I wanted to be assertive, but felt too nervous. I sat with my knees together and my hands in my lap as he flicked through the photographs Sebastian had taken in Spain.

'These are very nice, as far as they go,' said Ken, 'but you'll need a far more extensive portfolio. Most of the first year of a model's life is spent putting a portfolio together and putting her name around the circuit. It's a very competitive business.'

I could tell he was trying to work out how committed I was.

'It means lots of "go-sees" – meeting various photographers and picture editors, building up contacts, that sort of thing.'

'Do you think I could do it?'

'Well, Geri, you've got a very nice little figure, but it's really up to you. How hard do you want to work? What sort of work do you want to do?'

He explained that the agency took a percentage of any fees. A page-three session was worth about £150 and a magazine shoot could be worth about £400 – more for glossy promotions or overseas calendar shoots.

'OK, let's get this girl going,' he said. 'I want you to go upstairs and one of our photographers will take some test shots. We'll see if we can't get you started, eh?'

Climbing a narrow staircase, I emerged on a landing and met Trevor, who was in his forties, with wiry grey and brown hair.

'Hello. Geri, isn't it?' He motioned me towards a chair.

Again, I sat with my knees together and my hands on my lap. He opened a desk drawer and pulled out a magazine. 'Now, this is what I do,' he said.

My eyes widened and almost popped out of my head.

He turned another page. 'Would you do this?'

I shook my head in shock.

'What about this?'

'No, really, that's not for me.'

Reality had been thrust in my face and it came in the form of no-holds-barred, full-penetration pornography. Trevor seemed to get the message and closed the magazine.

I was expecting him to take a few nice shots of me with my top off, just like in Spain. Instead, he gave me a crash course in the various schools of glamour modelling. I was smart enough to know what I did and didn't want to do.

'There's good money in porn,' he said.

I shook my head.

'OK, let's do some test shots. Get your gear off.'

He said it quite bluntly and I had a sudden panic. Then I realized he was testing me to see how committed I was. Did I have the bottle? There were no preliminaries. He directed me to a small changing room, where I stripped completely and put on a thin robe. My hair looked a mess, so I splashed water on it and put on a little more make-up.

As I came back into the studio, Trevor was burrowing in a wardrobe of props and outfits. He produced a mask made from peacock feathers and handed it to me.

'OK, let's get started,' he said, motioning to the black-and-white-tiled studio set. He stood behind the camera and waited.

'When you're ready.'

'Yes. OK.' I shrugged off the robe.

'Right. First get down on your knees, holding the mask just near your cheek . . . that's it . . . turn a little bit more towards me . . . with your head, not your shoulders. That's it.' As he fired off shots, he kept making suggestions.

'Squeeze your boobs together . . . shoulders back. That's lovely. Now lean back. Smile.'

It was all very stark and cold. I felt terribly aware of my nakedness and made sure, with every new position, that nothing could be seen of my chi chi – my grandmother's word for privates. Then he suggested a costume change, and held up a pink sequinned outfit that consisted of a G-string with a pair of braces coming up either side of my boobs.

'You'll look great in this.'

'You're kidding. I don't think it's really me.'

'Sure it is.'

'No, believe me. I'm not wearing that.'

'Relax, OK. Not to worry. I'll just shoot another roll. Let's do something different. What about this?' He held up a pair of crotchless knickers.

Before I could complain, he apologized with a grin.

'Why don't you spread your legs a bit?'

'I'm not going to . . .'

'Only joking, love. Give us one look, though?'

'No!'

'Just winding you up, Geri, that's all.'

The difference between nudity and nakedness is a subtle one. We see nudes every day in advertisements, on TV and in magazines. Nudity is a calculated form of artistic presentation. Nakedness is something very different – it's demeaning to women and makes them feel vulnerable and exposed. That's how the session in Chiswick made me feel – very, very naked.

When I stepped out onto the street, the crumpled leaves blew along the footpath and I pulled my collar up. 'What have I done?' I wondered out loud, walking to the train station in a daze. It was as though I'd crossed a boundary somehow, or done something I couldn't undo.

Ken was right and the work was hard to find. I went to half a dozen castings each week, chatting up photographers and hoping they'd take a few shots to add to my portfolio.

Most of the castings were a profound disappointment. The studios were grim, with wallpaper peeling off the walls and the smell of damp. And it was always a battle to maintain your dignity and say no to the cruder suggestions.

One job was advertised as a two-week shoot in the Bahamas to do a pin-up calendar. I arrived at the studio in Old Street in the City and found a derelict building. I had to weave through miles of corridors and climb rickety stairs to find the place. I arrived out of breath – not a good start. The two first rules of glamour modelling are not to wear a bra because the strap marks will show, and not to get flustered because your make-up starts to run.

A hundred girls had probably been through that morning and another dozen waited in the small changing room, applying lipstick and checking out the competition. Of course, a lot of photographers don't like a girl who has more than two brain cells, and pick ones with little between their ears.

Although I had very little experience, I already knew there was politics in glamour modelling. Sitting in one corner, with a foot propped on a stool and everything concentrated on painting her toenails, I noticed a regular *Sun* page-three girl. I guess you could call her a glamour supermodel. Opposite her, rarely making eye contact, was a girl from the other end of the spectrum – a porno actress from Leeds. She denied it, of course. Most of them do. The pictures and videos are sold in Europe and the girls are told they'll never turn up in the UK. I wouldn't believe a pornographer.

The photographer began calling us in one by one. I still looked flustered. The place was freezing because boobs are always firmer when they're cold. Upright and pert beats warm and saggy. That's why the studios are never heated.

'Geri Halliwell.'

I walked onto the white-painted set, showed my book to the photographer and handed him my zeb card – a photographic business card that includes a model's vital statistics. Then I dropped my robe while he took a Polaroid.

I walked off. That was it! Half a day it had taken. Perhaps I'd hear from them, but I doubted it. Call me cynical, but I got the feeling he was choosing girls who'd give him a blow job. I also knew that the two-week shoot in the Bahamas would probably end up being a week in Ibiza, staying in a fleapit hotel. The Trade Descriptions Act doesn't apply to the glamour industry. Which begs the question, Why is it called glamour modelling? What's glamorous about it?

To be fair, some of the photographers were very professional and the jobs could be quite classy. I was chosen for an *Esquire* magazine shoot to appear in a 1950s-style calendar advertising Katherine Hamnet jeans. I was Miss April, in cut-off denim shorts with a chain of flowers covering my nipples. It earned me £400.

I'll never forget the casting. I arrived at a house in Notting Hill Gate and waited with half a dozen other girls. Some of them were tall and skinny, without a smudge of make-up – they were fashion models and they looked down on glamour models as though we were beneath them.

You could always tell us apart, if only by the make-up. Glamour models had fake nails and eyelashes and loads of warpaint. Fashion models tended to dress down and look as though they existed on nothing but coffee and cigarettes. Of course, most of them did.

It was unusual to have a casting where both types were competing for the same job. We sat in silence in the waiting room until I couldn't stand it any longer. I started chatting away to a tall, skinny girl and asked to see her portfolio. The coldness seemed to disappear and she started smiling. I talked about her photographs and her wonderful high cheekbones. I tried to take away the competitiveness, because to me it didn't matter. I didn't feel like a proper glamour model, instead I seemed to be going through the motions, unsure of whether I wanted to be there.

* * *

A summons from Beverly Goodway's is always a big deal for a budding glamour model. He is arguably the Herb Ritz of glamour photographers, because he shoots most of the 'page-three stunners' for the *Sun*.

I sent him one of Sebastian's photographs and a month later the agency received a call asking me to come in for a page-three shoot. As I tottered through Leather Lane Market towards his studio, the barrow boys and market traders wolf-whistled and winked. 'All right darlin'?' ''Avin' a good day, then?' They were used to seeing models coming and going.

Inside the studio, an assistant did a short interview, asking me questions about what I'd been doing recently. This was so the *Sun* could caption the photographs in its typically pun-filled style. I mentioned that I'd been learning to drive. I could picture the blurb already: 'Geri Drives 'Em Mad! When today's stunner isn't getting her gear off, she's getting into gear. Geri, 19, of Watford, is learning to drive. Wouldn't you like to take her for a ride, fellas? . . . blah, blah, blah.'

Beverly Goodway wandered out of the darkroom and said hello. He was in his early forties, with round specs and a portly frame. I liked him immediately. He had a nice face and a gentle voice. He spoke to me in a fatherly way as he adjusted the lights and readied the camera.

My hair was now black, and supplemented with a horrible hairpiece because I thought it was too thin. I wore a G-string and Beverly had me put on gloves and a scarf. With traces of fake snow still dusting the floor, the *Sun* was obviously going for a winter look. The studio was certainly cold enough.

After shooting one roll of film, Beverly got me to put on a ski jacket, unzipped, so that my boobs poked out.

The session took about an hour and earned me £150. I had no idea when the shots would be used, if at all. Beverly photographed ten girls a week and barely half were ever used. The final decision rested with the editor, who would look through the photographs, going, 'Yes, no, yes, no.'

Each day I ran down to the newsagent, thinking, Is it going to be today? I bought my copy of the *Sun* and always waited until I walked outside before opening the first page. As the weeks passed, I stopped buying the paper and simply looked inside and put it back on the news-stand.

Beverly Goodway had sent me copies of the photographs for my portfolio. They were quite nice, although a bit of my hair was sticking up, which didn't look quite right. I showed the pictures to Ken, my agency boss, and asked his opinion.

'This is why you didn't get chosen,' he said, pointing just above my armpit with a ballpoint pen. 'Have you been swimming?'

'Pardon?'

'Swimming. You've developed another muscle here. See?' He made me look closely at the picture. 'This is muscle; this is boob. Muscle . . . boob. Muscle . . . boob.' He pointed to each in turn.

'You've got to be joking.'

'Nope. That's all it takes.'

I was amazed. I'd been swimming forty laps a day to keep trim. I thought my body looked great. Yet this is how particular they could be. On another job – an album cover for a band I'd never heard of – I had to appear naked, wearing nothing but a mask. Afterwards, Ken called saying I'd lost the job because I looked too fat. He didn't try to soften the blow or spare my feelings. Modelling is a competitive industry and clients can afford to be ruthless and seek out perfection.

It hurt to be rejected. I tried to convince myself that it didn't matter and that I'd eventually get a thick skin, but each time it preyed on my mind – the nagging insecurity and sense of being inadequate. I wasn't good enough.

Whereas once I never worried about my weight, now I couldn't stop thinking about it. Nothing makes you more body-conscious than taking your clothes off for complete strangers who may, or may not, choose you for their photo shoot. Rejection brings the obvious question of why? Is it because I'm fat?

Food became a focus – not just for the calories consumed, but for my own unhappiness whenever things weren't going well. Any rejection or slight could send me to the fridge. I'd binge on whatever I could find and then force myself to throw up.

In the beginning I had felt quite clever at having come up with such a good idea. This had been replaced by guilt. I remembered my mother's mealtime words: 'Think of all the starving people in the world.'

The very nature of the work depressed me – almost constantly having to battle with photographers who would try to push me a little bit further, or take explicit shots without my consent. One guy at a studio near Hammersmith tried to re-create the classic Seventies shot of Marianne Faithfull. I sat on the floor naked, with one knee lying flat and the other drawn up with my arms draped over it. Afterwards I discovered that he had angled the camera to see a lot more than I intended.

'You bastard!' I screamed, absolutely furious.

'I'm sorry, I didn't realize.' He threw up his hands and tried to make light of it.

'Bollocks you didn't!'

'If you're that worried I'll paint it out.'

'I'll make sure of it.'

I stayed until he'd used darkroom techniques to hide the exposed areas, but of course he still had the negatives. I told myself to be more careful next time.

However, it wasn't easy to be constantly vigilant. Some photographers made a habit of snatching extra shots as they asked me to change poses or props. It amazed me how provocative these sneaked photographs could be.

Similarly, because I needed to build up my portfolio, a lot of photographers knew they were doing me a favour. Occasionally, they tried to take advantage of the fact and had to be set straight. Others were blatantly sleazy, including a guy in north London who lived below a dilapidated studio by a train station and walked with a limp. He had a smelly dog and the whole place reeked of dog shit and mould. He gave me the creeps and I wanted to leave from the moment I arrived. Unfortunately, I couldn't afford to walk away from a contact who might provide future work.

After taking a few standard topless shots, he said excitedly, 'I've got the perfect thing for you. Just perfect. You'll love it.'

'What? What?'

Then he thrust a magazine in my face and started

laughing. The image was so disgusting that I felt sick. I collected my clothes and walked out.

'A lot of girls start out like you,' he shouted after me. 'They're all coy and Catholic. Wait till you need the money, love. You'll spread 'em.'

I was still shaking when I got home.

Looking back, I can't believe I put myself in such dangerous situations – going into dingy studios unchaperoned, never having met the photographer. If something had happened, it would have been his word against mine, and some might say that any girl who takes her clothes off for a living is asking for it.

What kept me going? Optimism. There were just enough good jobs, or possibilities of them, to hold my interest. For instance, I did a brilliant shoot with a freelance photographer who often worked for Athena, the poster shops. I also played a Victorian mistress having her bodice tightened on the front cover of the book *A Man with a Maid*.

Apart from the random good times, I had just the right mixture of naivety and burning desire to believe that someone would discover me. I had my goals, I just didn't know how to reach them. I couldn't see a ladder in front of me; it was more like a rock face, with a scattering of footholds.

When I first arrived home from Spain, I lived in a flat in Bushey with my best friend, Janine, who I'd known since our raving days and wild nights at the Game Bird pub. She is half-Italian and very down to earth. From a Saturday job at a hairdresser's in Watford, she worked her way up until she had her own salon.

Janine had come to visit me in Spain and had written to me regularly. Her letters had been full of local gossip about mutual friends, enemies and old boyfriends. One of them was a guy called Sean Green, who I'd been out with a few times before I'd left for Spain. Sean had been a rave organizer, but now he worked as a courier. I thought about Niam constantly and it could still bring me to tears, but Sean was thoughtful and gentle.

We didn't write or keep in touch while I was away, but when I got home, Sean phoned and said, 'Look, I really want to see you again.'

Being only nineteen, I was easily impressed by Sean. Like Niam, he had a great deal of charm and worldly experience. He had Irish blood, dark hair and piercing blue eyes, and he was always trying to come up with different schemes to make money – buying and selling mainly.

Sean didn't seem to mind my modelling. He would often drive me to go-sees and wait outside. He was a grafter, with big ambitions, and he really seemed to care about me.

Six months after getting back from Spain, Sean and I moved in together, renting a drafty old farmhouse with an Anthea Turner lookalike. The place smelled of dogs and had strange chills that seemed to sweep through the rooms. I'm sure it was haunted.

The modelling assignments were so random that I couldn't rely on them to support myself financially. I signed on for the dole and also got a part-time job working behind the bar at a golf club just up the road in Bushey.

An Irishman with a pot belly and terrible taste in nylon

shirts managed the club and he let me use the club gym when I wasn't working. Often I didn't finish until late and it was my job to turn off the lights and lock up.

Before leaving one night, I crept upstairs to the restaurant and manoeuvred around tables in the darkness until I reached the kitchen. I wanted to cook Sean a nice dinner, but I wasn't due to be paid until the following Thursday. I opened the freezer and took out a frozen steak. I didn't realize that the manager lived in a house opposite the club. He saw the lights from the fridge doors and became suspicious.

I put the steak inside my jacket, locked up the club and walked across the darkened parking lot to my mountain bike. As I rode towards the gates, this mad Irishman jumped out in front of me and wrapped his fists around my handlebars. I almost fainted.

'Was that you upstairs in the kitchen?'

'Yes.'

'Let me search you.'

'Why?'

'Money has been going missing from the till.'

'I haven't taken any money.'

'What were you doing upstairs?'

'Nothing. I thought I heard something.'

'Bollocks!'

He demanded that I come back inside with him while he called the police. Meanwhile, I kept trying to figure out how I could get rid of the frozen steak that was turning my stomach numb.

There's no way out of this, I realized. I had to come clean. Trying for sympathy, I turned on the waterworks. 'Look, I'm really sorry, I took this steak. I'm really hungry; I haven't eaten anything decent for days.'

The poor Irishman felt awful. 'I didn't realize. I'm sorry. I thought you were stealing money. I've gone and called the police.'

I gave him the steak back. My jacket lining was soaked.

We were standing inside the club secretary's office, unsure of what to do next. Finally he said, 'Go on, get out of here! Go home.'

What a relief. 'Does that mean I'm sacked?' I asked.

'Of course it does.'

It wasn't only the lack of money or the sleazy castings that depressed me. There were many days when I had too much time on my hands and the loneliness would leak in. I found it hard to go to Sean and say, I'm hurting, hold me.

When women need to feel better about themselves, they often go shopping or get dressed up for a night out. I dyed my hair. A new look for a new person – leave the old Geri in the salon. Normally, Janine did my hair, but she was away on holiday.

Instead, I took a train to London and visited the L'Oréal Colour Correction Centre in Kensington. The salon offered cut-price rates because most of the stylists were trainees who needed to practise tinting and high-lighting.

I had black hair with two-inch brown roots and wanted to go back to a honey-brown colour. The trainee stylists mucked about for hours with dyes and tints, turning it bright tangerine and then trying to get it back to brown. Come 6 p.m. they all wanted to go home to start their weekend.

'Oh yeah, it looks fine,' the stylist said.

'Really lovely,' echoed her workmate.

'I think it really suits you,' said the manager.

Ignoring my protests, they ushered me outside. I huddled in an overcoat and watched them lock the doors. Turning and walking towards the tube station, I glanced in a shopfront window and something from *The Rocky Horror Show* stared back at me. What had they done?

A few doors down, I stopped at a delicatessen and bought a pasta and potato salad in a plastic tub. Having scoffed that, I loaded up on sweets. On the station platform I bought crisps and chocolate bars from the kiosk and kept eating until I arrived home. Then I went straight to the toilet, fell to my knees and brought it all up again, vomiting away all my hurt and frustration.

That evening I went to Natalie's birthday party at an Italian restaurant. I'd barely eaten a thing until the cake came out, but I had a slice, went to the toilet and threw it up.

This became the pattern over the following weeks and months. Whenever I felt depressed or lonely, I went to the fridge. It started casually, with a cheese sandwich and then a biscuit, then another and another. The whole packet would disappear, along with the leftover Chinese, slices of toast, spaghetti and a box of after-dinner mints.

It always ended the same way: staring into the white porcelain bowl, retching until my nose ran and my stomach felt empty. Yet when that finger went down my throat, I felt like I was purging myself of more than calories. All my negative emotions were also flushed away.

Afterwards, I'd ask myself, Why am I so unhappy? What's wrong with me? But I couldn't answer, just as I couldn't stop. I was out of control and didn't want to deal with my emotions. Instead, I punished my weakness, using food as a form of abuse, just as others use alcohol or drugs.

Bulimia has nothing to do with being thin; it's about loneliness and low self-esteem. It's a very private disease that seems to create control out of chaos. I did this to myself, therefore I still have some say over my life. Of course, this isn't true. I was hurtling down a lift shaft, unable to stop or get off. What sort of masochist am I? I'd ask myself. Why do I put myself forward every day and risk rejection?

As summer approached, I found myself back in Spain on a modelling assignment in Marbella with two other girls. Cindy had massive boobs and told me that she'd taken a course of contraceptive pills to make them grow bigger. Although not particularly attractive, she had long legs and blond hair. Packaged together with her obvious other assets, she was a walking Barbie doll.

The other girl, Claire, was a waif in comparison, with a sweet little figure and the appetite of a bird. She seemed to be starving herself.

We were supposed to be body-painted for a calendar shoot, but the painter didn't turn up and the calendar finished up being a fairly standard topless and nude assignment. Some of the naked shots were more provocative than I was comfortable with, and eventually I refused to sign the release form allowing the pictures to be used.

The organizers of the shoot had other work for us and we finished up handing out fliers for a nightclub and wandering along the beachfront in club T-shirts.

Two other girls turned up at our apartment. Debbie and Julie were both northerners who had just come back from a dancing assignment in Italy. I thought they were nice, although they didn't talk a lot about the jobs they'd done.

That afternoon, I walked into town with them and we picked up some postcards and stamps. As we stood waiting in a queue at the newsagent, I absent-mindedly opened a men's magazine. It had become a habit because I'd sometimes see girls I'd met at castings. As I opened a page, I saw Debbie and Julie in a graphic lesbian clinch. I slammed the magazine shut and put it back.

'Anything wrong?' asked Debbie, who was writing a postcard.

'Oh! No, nothing,' I mumbled, completely shocked. My God, what am I getting myself into? I spilt all my change as I tried to pay for the postcards.

That evening I got dressed up and went to Puerto Banus with Cindy and Claire. It was a rich man's playground a few miles along the coast, with luxury boats and designer shops selling vastly overpriced goods.

Being three young pretty girls, we attracted quite a bit of attention from the local men and tourists. Eventually, a well-dressed man in a blazer and neatly pressed trousers offered to buy us a drink.

'How would you like to come to a party on a boat?' he said.

He pointed towards the bay, and I thought he meant a sleek-looking runabout tethered to the pier. 'It's not very big,' I joked.

'There's nothing bigger out there,' he said, surprised.

I looked again and saw the real boat. It was like a small

ocean liner, painted brilliant white and lit up from stem to stern with fairy lights.

'Is that yours?'

'It belongs to my boss.'

'Who is he?' squeaked Claire.

Cindy interrupted. 'More importantly, how much is he worth?'

'Who knows? You might meet him at the party,' said our well-spoken friend. 'Just tell them I invited you.'

There were dozens of rich Arabs at the party, pulling champagne glasses from a pyramid that didn't stop flowing all night. Images of white slavery flashed in front of me when I first stepped on board, but there were dozens of other women, many of them wives and girlfriends.

As we stepped back ashore, we were invited to another party that same evening. I still didn't know the host's name. We arrived at a mansion in Marbella overlooking the bay. Everything about the place reeked of extravagance, but not necessarily good taste. A butler showed us in and immediately I felt uncomfortable. Unlike the previous party, there seemed to be very few people and some of them were doing drugs.

The house had its own disco, with an underwater viewing window that looked into the pool, so you could watch people as they swam. Two men were teasing a girl and letting her try to swim away before catching her and pulling her back.

Elsewhere, I noticed some men kissing a girl on a settee. My radar started flashing a warning. This is not for you, Geri. Get out of here!

Cindy and Claire had picked up the same vibes. Men

had been eyeing us from the moment we arrived, as if the party could now start.

'I don't like the look of this,' I whispered to Cindy.

Our well-spoken friend in the blue blazer offered to take my coat.

'Sorry, I just have to go to the ladies' room. What about you, Claire?'

'Huh?'

'Didn't you just say you wanted to freshen up?' I nodded my head.

'Oh. Of course. Right behind you.'

All three of us paced up and down the arena-sized bathroom. 'I can't believe this place.'

'We're almost the only guests,' said Cindy, who couldn't walk past a mirror without adjusting herself.

'I don't know what happens at this sort of party,' I said, 'but I don't want to find out. I'm leaving.'

'Me, too,' said Claire. 'What are we going to tell them?'

'We'll say one of us isn't feeling well.'

'That'd be right. I felt sick just looking at some of those guys.'

We agreed a plan and made our bid for freedom. As we reached the foyer, our smooth-talking friend appeared and tried to talk us into staying. He grabbed me by the arm. 'Come on, just stay for a while. You've only just arrived. Have a swim—'

'No thank you. Please let me go. Cindy isn't feeling well.'

'We'll get a doctor to look at her.' I felt his fingers tighten.

I spun away from him and kept moving. 'No, really, that's OK, we'll take her home.'

We ran down the steps just as the bodyguards and chauffeurs began to take notice. They were leaning on luxury cars and chatting to each other.

Slipping through a side gate beside the driveway, the road outside was empty. How were we going to get home? Suddenly I spied a moped, ridden by a young Spanish guy in an open-necked shirt.

'Can you give us a lift?'

'All of you?'

'Yes please. Hurry.' I kept glancing over my shoulder, expecting the bodyguards to start chasing us. The moped started first time and we all climbed on, squeezing together and clinging tightly to each other.

Our saviour dropped us in the town centre and got a peck on the cheek from each of us. I'm sure none of his mates believed him when he told them the story. He's probably still fantasizing about having Cindy's boobs pressed against his back.

The next day I saw Debbie and Julie, the northern girls, tottering home after a long night out. They started telling me excitedly about a party they'd been to in Marbella with loads of rich Arabs.

'Look! See what they gave us?'

Both of them had diamond-studded bracelets with matching earrings.

'They said we could choose what we wanted,' said Debbie. 'You should have seen the jewellery. And this place . . .'

'Don't worry, I can imagine.'

There was no single, watershed moment that convinced me I wanted to get out of glamour modelling. A series of disasters seemed to hasten things. Despite the image of glamour models hanging out at nightclubs like Stringfellows, I only went to one party there. The agency had an open invitation to send girls along because Peter Stringfellow obviously wanted to see some fresh faces in the club.

David Sullivan, the owner of the *Sunday Sport*, was among the guests, and he had blonde, siliconed girls hanging off him – most of them drunk and spilling out of their dresses.

What am I doing here? This isn't me. For a long while I'd been wondering why I felt so different from the other girls. Finally it dawned on me. I wasn't really trying. It was as though I'd tested the water and been swept into the current. Ever since then I'd been swimming against it, trying to find a way out.

It's actually incredibly boring having your photograph taken. On one job, a photographer wanted to make a sign using different things, including a naked girl to form the letter 'N'. I had to crouch on my knees and pose for what seemed like hours. I realized then how tired I'd become of the whole thing – the castings, the sleazy photographers and the constant pressure to reveal more.

The final straw came on a nightmare job in Greece in October 1992. My agency had booked six models/dancers to help open a new nightclub in Patras, a port town about a hundred miles from Athens.

From the moment we arrived things began to unravel. Our luggage went missing during the flight and took two days to reach us. The club owner had sent a mini-van to pick us up from Athens Airport which arrived an hour late. It then took us another hour to find a hotel in Athens because one hadn't been pre-booked. We finally arrived in a fleapit that was so dirty I refused to even look in the bathroom.

Next morning, the mini-van drove us to Patras. We'd been promised modern apartments, and instead discovered a run-down hotel with no security, privacy, cooking facilities and one dirty toilet between six girls.

'Come on, come on,' said the driver. 'We go to club now.'

'But we've only just arrived,' I complained.

'No, let's go and complain,' said Caro, another of the dancers. 'I've just found something growing between the bathroom tiles.'

Back in the van, we drove into town. We expected Patras to be a popular tourist resort with lots of nice restaurants and bars. Instead, we discovered a fishing and commercial port that reeked of diesel and rotting vegetables. Instead of a glitzy nightclub, we were dropped in front of a half-built bar-cum-restaurant in a back alley between a warehouse and a fruit cannery. Rubble and bags of cement were stacked by the door, and electric wires stuck out of the walls.

The inside was dark and dingy and reeked of cigarette smoke. The floors were sticky with spilled Ouzo and covered in rose petals. I discovered that instead of breaking plates in traditional Greek style, the punters would throw rose petals every night.

I nicknamed the owner Medallion Man because of the chunky gold medallion resting in his forest of chest hair. 'Come on, girls, you dance for me,' he said.

'Not until we sort out a few things,' demanded Caro. Medallion Man shrugged off our complaints. He told us to take them up with Miles, the middleman in the booking, who was due to arrive that night.

Before leaving England we had put a few dance routines together, but it was obvious the owner had been expecting high-kicking showgirls. Instead, he finished up with six glamour models who could dance a bit – some better than others.

We showed him our routine to 'Missionary Man' by Annie Lennox and another to James Brown's 'I Got You (I Feel Good)'. He seemed satisfied. We also had to dance behind some Greek singers who were booked to perform at the club.

We rehearsed until the early hours and were then driven back to the hotel. The hard-to-pin-down Miles eventually arrived at 5 a.m. and moved us to a new hotel, which still didn't have private bathrooms.

I shared a room with Caro, who came from Chesham and was very well spoken and educated. Conditions were so awful that we had to laugh. We couldn't lock the door properly and somebody could easily have broken in. I put a chair behind the door and nearly killed Caro, who fell over it when she got up in the middle of the night to go to the bathroom.

Patras was clearly a rough town, with a lot of fishermen and merchant seamen. And while Greek men respect and honour their women, they have a long way to go before they discover equality of the sexes.

Medallion Man was very sly. After the first night of dancing he came to us and said, 'OK, sit down at the tables.'

He copped a chorus of objections:

'What? No way!'

'Like hell!'

'You've got to be joking.'

He insisted. 'You sit at the tables and say hello to people. It's agreed.'

'Not by us,' I said. I knew exactly what our job specifications were. Before leaving England, Miles had said that after the show we were to say a short hello to customers and sign autographs.

When I'd agreed to these terms, I'd imagined a glitzy nightclub full of fashionable people, not a bar full of sweaty, drunken sailors.

Medallion Man was having none of it. He had the bouncers virtually drag us to the tables – one dancer to each group of overfriendly men, who were constantly trying to move closer and grope us.

After that first night, we simply refused to visit the tables. If the bouncers tried to force us, we threatened to walk out.

There were other problems. Our stated hours were from nine to midnight, according to the contracts, but Medallion Man soon changed this from midnight to 3 a.m. He later extended this to 4 a.m., which meant that, by the time we'd had a drink at the tables, we didn't leave the club until dawn. Similarly, the 'set meal' promised every night finished up being a bowl of soup at 5 a.m.

The transport back to our hotel was also non-existent and we ended up having to pay for the fifteen-minute taxi ride each morning. On top of this, we'd been promised £200 a week for six nights' work, plus £15 for food. Instead we received 10,800 drachmas, including the food kitty, which added up to £180 in total.

I called the girls together for a war conference. We

discussed all our grievances and then I phoned up the agency in London, demanding they get us out of there. The agency tried to talk us into staying, and when that failed they jumped in with dozens of excuses for not being able to get flights or organize connections.

'Just stay for another week,' they pleaded, 'then I'll get you out.'

Most of the girls were lovely and we all had similar dreams. Skye had a lilting Scottish accent and looked like Faye Dunaway. She wanted to be a model, and for years afterwards I saw her in magazines.

One afternoon we climbed the crumbling marble steps to an old ruined temple on a mountaintop overlooking Patras. We could see fishing boats heading out for the night and container ships waiting to come into port.

Skye was quite spiritual and we talked about dreams and ambitions. I told her about the childhood fantasies I'd never outgrown. She smiled and squeezed my hand. 'Geri, you know, I see a star above your head.' It was so sweet.

The only girl I didn't like was a ballet dancer with a rakelike figure, who seemed to look down on me because I was top-heavy and it took me ages to learn a new dance routine. She finished by hooking up with a Greek bouncer who treated her appallingly. According to Caro, she became a stripper and never left Patras.

Despite our complaints, nothing improved. If anything, Medallion Man became more impatient and pushed us harder. The final humiliation came towards the end of the first week as I walked through town with a couple of the girls. I had my hair in curlers, in preparation for the show, with a scarf over the top, and I wore purple hot pants, sandals and a white shirt knotted above my navel.

We'd just been out for lunch, and had started heading back to the apartment when something made me turn. A man was right behind us. He had a pockmarked face, dark hair and penetrating black eyes. He exposed himself and began masturbating. We all screamed and started to run.

Back at the apartment, I told Caro, 'That's it. I'm going home.' I shoved the chair against the door.

'How?'

'I don't know yet, but I'm not staying here.' I began blindly throwing clothes into a bag.

Caro reached across the bed and grabbed a T-shirt from my hand.

'You're not going to stop me,' I warned her.

'Of course not, I'm coming with you. Just don't take any more of my clothes.'

Luckily we'd kept our passports when Medallion Man offered to 'keep them safe' for us. We caught an old bus back to Athens, with a suicidal driver who chain-smoked and constantly swerved round imaginary obstacles. Arriving at the airport, we tried to get on a flight. It was already evening and the last flights to London and Manchester were already fully booked with long waiting lists.

'There must be another way,' I pleaded with the clerk at the ticketing desk. 'We'll go via anywhere.' I kept glancing towards the doors, half expecting to see Medallion Man and his bouncers coming to drag us back.

'I can get you on a midnight flight to Budapest,' said the reservations clerk. 'From there you can catch a seven a.m. flight to Heathrow.'

'Budapest? Is that even in the right direction?' asked Caro.

'We'll take it,' I said, counting out the last of my money.

It proved to be a long night. Caro and I told each other our life stories and eventually fell asleep on a cold stone floor in Budapest Airport. Nothing was open at that hour and the coffee machine wouldn't take drachmas.

We arrived in London on 31 October 1992, and three days later I quit my agency and began looking for another. Yvonne Paul, a former Benny Hill 'angel', ran the most successful glamour modelling agency. I went to see her, hoping she might take me on.

My portfolio still looked rather thin and Yvonne Paul barely bothered to look at it. 'We don't need any dancers,' she said sarcastically. 'Oh, God, what's that on your head?'

'A hairpiece.'

She laughed and I felt humiliated. Thankfully, a girl in the office stood up for me. Later I discovered she was Sarah Jaffer, a well-known page-three girl and one of the few considered to have a brain as well as a body.

I signed with another agency, MOT – Models Out of Town – but ironically, a year later, when I'd done some good work, Yvonne Paul contacted me and said, 'Oh yes, we'll take you on, darling.'

By then I'd lost interest in glamour modelling and I couldn't forgive her rudeness. She was right about my hairpieces, though – they *were* dreadful.

# 6

## DANCING DAVE AND DIRTY HARI

Standing outside an old church in Marylebone Road, London, I looked at the newspaper advertisement again. This was the place. The Circle Line trains had been running late and I'd run all the way from Baker Street station.

As I walked up the worn stone steps, I saw a message pinned to the large wooden door: 'KIT KAT CLUB AUDITIONS – 11 a.m.'

The hall had high vaulted ceilings and every whisper seemed to echo as if delivered directly from the heavens. I could spot the wannabes from the gainfully employed. It takes one to know one. We all had eager-to-please smiles and wore our coolest children's TV presenter clothes. *The Kit Kat Club*, a cable programme, had advertised the position in *The Stage* newspaper.

*The Stage* had become my regular Thursday reading and potentially the high and low points of my week. Every Thursday morning, I walked out of W. H. Smith in Watford with a sense of anticipation. Clutching my copy of *The Stage*, I wouldn't look at it until I got to the car, and then I'd only glance quickly at the pages devoted to auditions and castings. I wouldn't read it properly until I got home, and then I'd study it far better than I studied anything for my school exams. Any likely-looking ads were circled with red pen and cut out. Then I began working on an application, redrafting my résumé and choosing a photograph.

I had my photographs copied at the same place every week – a colour copy shop in Market Street that had lots of boring still-life prints in the window in coloured metal frames. The lovely couple who ran the shop had got to know me.

'How's the search for stardom, Geri?'

'I've got an audition on Tuesday.'

'Good for you. What's it for?'

'A children's TV show.'

'You'd be perfect.'

Then I'd walk to the post office and stand in the queue to buy envelopes and first-class stamps. Posting the résumés and photographs was the second highlight of the week. For those next few days I could bask in the glow of my great expectations.

'All right, I hope you've all given your names to Martha.' A middle-aged, slightly balding producer type clapped his hands three times, as though he was about to conduct a school orchestra.

'Thank you all for coming. I'll say that now because most of you won't be here long enough for me to get to know you, or indeed to say goodbye.' He smiled at his sense of humour. 'This is an audition for *The Kit Kat Club*, which I'm sure that you'll all tell me you never miss, whereas in truth you've never laid eyes on it. I don't care.

We're looking for someone who has talent, flair, spark, charisma and wit. Can you follow a script? Can you work a live audience? Can you waffle for three minutes when a guest doesn't turn up?'

The questions echoed off the rafters and I shuffled nervously. I might have been smiling on the surface, but underneath I was paddling like crazy.

Martha took over, waving a clipboard and separating us into pairs. She walked like a ballet dancer and had her hair pulled back so severely I thought she'd had a face-lift. I recognized one of the other hopefuls. I'd seen him in *Grange Hill*, where he played a spotty teenager. There were planks of wood with more acting ability and I kept sending mental signals to Martha, Please don't put him with me. Please don't put him with me.

It didn't work. Acne Boy came loping over and introduced himself. To his credit, he didn't make out that I should have known his name, but I was still pretty pissed off.

Martha began giving us roles to play. 'OK, couple one, you're both cats – an alley cat and a Siamese – and you're both stalking the same bird. Couple two, I want you to be an old married couple, sitting on a park bench feeding the pigeons.'

She turned to me and Acne Boy. 'I want you two to be dogs – a poodle and a big mutt – and you're flirting with each other.'

My heart sank.

At least we didn't have to go first, although that only delayed the inevitable humiliation. Why couldn't I be the old couple? Why did I have to be a dog?

When it was our turn, I dared to hope that Acne Boy,

as a professional actor accustomed to this sort of challenge, would unleash his full range of dramatic skills. Perhaps *Grange Hill* hadn't been his best work.

'When you're ready,' said Martha.

I looked at him expectantly and knew immediately that he didn't have a single original thought in his head. Acne Boy's idea of improvising a horny dog was to drop on all fours and try to sniff my butt. What a nightmare! We were dreadful. Pathetic. Simply not funny.

I crawled about, yelping like a poodle and batting my eyelids. Acne Boy gave me nothing to vibe off, no signals or lines. Oh, for God's sake, you're an actor; you're meant to be good at this. Do something!

Martha put an end to our suffering and called time. A large cardboard box was pulled into the centre of the hall, full of props like cowboy hats, feather boas, plastic helmets, whoopee cushions, wigs and hand puppets.

'You are live on TV and you have one minute to improvise because a guest hasn't turned up. You have to explain why, but you have to be funny.'

My heart pounded. Despite my dancing and modelling work, I still felt nervous and insecure about performing, particularly alone. All that practising in the kitchen, hosting my imaginary lifestyle programme, now came back to me. I wasn't brilliant, but I managed to gab for a minute without repeating myself.

One of the other young hopefuls had a really animated face which he could blow up like a balloon or twist into various expressions to match his funny accents. He looked familiar. Where had I met him before? It wasn't until the end of the audition that I remembered. He'd put on weight and obviously grown older, but it was definitely the Curly Wurly boy who'd wet his pants in the wings a decade earlier.

Neither of us got *The Kit Kat Club* job, although I did see him on children's TV a few years later, still blowing his face up like a balloon.

Sean and I had moved out of the farmhouse because we couldn't afford the rent. We stayed with his mum and dad in Rickmansworth, along with his younger brothers and sisters. It was a typical Irish Catholic family. His mum cooked me porridge every morning and made me proper dinners. She treated me like a daughter and I loved being part of a close family.

Sean would lend me a tenner if I needed it and he still drove me to auditions. Our relationship was just physical at first, but now it had grown deeper. I think I needed Sean more than he needed me, particularly when I was modelling. I wanted his reassurance that I was beautiful when I faced so much rejection.

Very few relationships are perfectly balanced, where both people love each other equally. I think Sean grew to love me more just as I started to need him less. This was healthy. We both had our dreams and neither of us had to sacrifice our future or carry the other.

I tried not to get disappointed when I didn't get picked at auditions. I told myself that it was early days. I simply had to persevere and my turn would come.

Mum thought I was being foolish. 'Be a schoolteacher, Geri. It's a good job. Don't waste your life dreaming.' But Dad took totally the opposite view. He became a one-man fan club and would often drive me to auditions or photo shoots in his old banger. He never doubted me or tried to lower my sights. If anything, his faith was more un-wavering than mine.

I used to visit him once or twice a week to clean his flat and tell him about my latest try-outs. The tower block still depressed me. Abandoned cars littered the parking lot and the grass surrounds had been turned into compacted mud by kids kicking soccer balls to each other. It was scary going down the hallway, and even worse in the stair-wells when the lifts were broken.

Dad didn't complain. 'I've got a bird's-eye view,' he'd say, as he gazed over the playing fields of Garston Comprehensive School. He was right because there were pigeons everywhere, including one that nested on his balcony. Baby pigeons must be the ugliest animals ever created, but Dad didn't have the heart to get rid of them.

I had inherited Dad's interest in car-boot sales and flea markets. He would look in the local paper and make a note of the various sales on at the weekend and then ring me up. 'OK, we have to get cracking early to make sure we get the bargains.'

Dad's brown Mazda had worn carpets and stuffing spilling out of the seats. He drove everywhere at 20 mph, even on the dual carriageway. Lorries would zoom past us.

'Can't you go any faster?' I'd complain.

'What's the hurry?'

'I'm growing old in the slow lane.'

'Well, I'm saving petrol.'

As well as the cracked, torn seats, the door handles routinely fell off and the glove compartment wouldn't shut. Toying with the cigarette lighter one morning, I aimlessly pressed it into the seat, burning a neat circle into the vinyl.

'Jesus Christ, what are you doing?' bellowed Dad.

'Sorry.'

'This is my bloody car. What were you thinking?'

'I didn't think it worked. Nothing else on the car works.'

'Cheeky devil.'

Dad liked to arrive early, just as people were unpacking their gear but hadn't yet set up their displays. This was his territory. He used to say he grew up in jumble sales and I guess I'm the same. It's where he learned how to do business.

'Be shrewd,' Dad would say. 'Never show you're interested. Be prepared to walk away.' He would glance over people's shoulders as they unpacked their boxes, when none of their gear had price tags.

'How much for the toaster?'

'Three quid.'

Dad made a clicking noise with his tongue. 'It's a new one, is it?' he said, with just a hint of sarcasm, softened by a smile. 'I'll give you a quid. Take it or leave it. I'm not coming back.' He had the money ready. That was another of Dad's mottos: 'Don't give them too long to think about it.'

Dad would give me a wink. Then he'd waddle away with his walking stick in his hand and a toaster tucked under his arm. I'd always be hurrying him along and helping him carry stuff back to the car.

Dad also used to buy old coats.

'You'll never wear them,' I'd say.

'That's pure wool, that is,' he'd reply, running his fingers over the sleeves. 'Pure wool.'

It didn't matter that the coat was moth-eaten, vile and

ill-fitting, as long as it was pure bloody wool. He also bought loads of second-hand books, which he'd give away as presents, and anything electrical that he thought he could fix. His flat was cluttered with broken toasters, carved elephants and paintings of seascapes that were stacked six deep against the walls and never hung.

I would concentrate on finding jewellery at the car-boot sales and kept a lookout for original platform shoes or designer labels. I'd been wearing platforms since I was seventeen, when I started going to Camden Market and discovered a pair of Mary Quant replicas for £10.

On the drive home, Dad would reiterate how much money he'd saved and what mugs some people are. 'No bloody idea of the value of things, some people.' Usually he'd invite me back to his flat for a cup of tea, so I could help him carry his broken toaster and musty overcoat up the stairs. Then we'd sit at the table and dunk biscuits while going through the TV guide to see if there were any old black and white movies being rerun on Channel 4.

'Oh, look! Jimmy Stewart in *Harvey*. I must have seen that at least twenty-two times.'

'What's it about?'

'A six-foot white rabbit. There's this wonderful scene in a bar where Jimmy Stewart orders two martinis – one for him and the other for this rabbit. He's just sitting there, talking away to nobody . . .'

That was so typical of Dad. He'd start off telling me the plot and then get tied up on small details that made no difference at all. 'It's on at three o'clock. You'll love it. Please stay and watch.'

He was lonely. Since I'd got home from Spain, Dad and I had been much closer. Having never been a proper father to me, he had now become my friend. He had mellowed and become more childlike. I don't think it had anything to do with guilt. I'd always been Dad's favourite, and now he could live his dreams through me.

One Saturday morning he drove me to an audition at Pineapple Dance Studios, just off Oxford Street. Dad was a bit disappointed at missing the car-boot sales, but he was adamant that my career took precedence.

The advertisement in *The Stage* said, 'Funky street-style dancers wanted'. The producers of *Sesame Street* were planning a live stage show for the pantomime season. Upstairs in the studio it looked like a circus. People were roller skating, juggling and doing somersaults.

Most of them had full routines and wore proper dance shoes, whereas I had high heels and a vague notion of doing a freestyle routine in my own unique way. My God, this was serious stuff. What was I going to do?

I ran out into Oxford Street and found a shop that sold fake-looking patent-leather jazz shoes that had a mirror-like shine. I slipped them on and put my high heels in the plastic shopping bag.

Right, I'm going to treat this like an aerobics class. I'll keep bouncing and stepping to the music.

As I waited my turn, I noticed something odd about the girls who were getting picked to stay. None of them was particularly attractive, but they could all do back-flips and somersault like gymnasts. I couldn't work out the reasoning until I reread the advertisement. In small print at the bottom were the words, 'To appear in skins.'

Did that mean we had to show a bit of skin? I was used to that.

Hold on. Nudity? *Sesame Street*? It didn't make sense.

Then it dawned on me. They wanted people to wear costumes and play Big Bird, Elmo and Oscar the Grouch.

'Stuff that for a game of soldiers,' I told myself, as I picked up my shopping bag and headed for the stairs. 'I want to be famous. I'm not going to wear a costume where nobody even sees my face.'

Although trying to concentrate on show business, I hadn't entirely abandoned glamour modelling. Poverty wouldn't let me. I still called the agency once a week, or they called me.

I liked the sound of one job: a game-show hostess. An independent production company was behind shows like *The Price is Right*, *Every Second Counts* and *Bob's Full House*. It also had the rights to an American game show called *Let's Make a Deal*, and it had sold the franchise to a new TV channel in Turkey.

'They are looking for three girls to be hostesses,' explained the agency. 'You know the sort of thing – a bit of glamour, personality, lots of smiling.'

'Where is it filmed?'

'Istanbul. It's a three-week shoot. All expenses paid.'

After the horrors of Patras, I didn't believe many of the promises. But it did sound encouraging. I took down the address and found my way to the television company's Camden offices. Howard, the boss, was in his mid-forties and looked a little like Jimmy Tarbuck, but with thick-rimmed glasses. He was a northerner and the king among game-show producers. Girls had been in and out of his office all day and I could see the pile of zeb cards on his desk.

'You've got a great name, Geri. It suits TV.'

'Thank you.'

'I'm looking for girls with personality and sex appeal, but they need a bit of old-fashioned glamour about them. Game shows are about entertainment and escapism. Most of the women watching will never get to wear an evening dress, and the men are never going to have a girl as pretty as you. But we can all dream, can't we, Geri?'

'Absolutely.'

'OK, right, let me look at my diary. I've got some important TV types flying in from Istanbul tomorrow. I've promised to let them meet some of the possible girls. I think you should come along.'

I liked Howard. He took a genuine interest in the work I'd done and seemed to have a warm heart to match his relaxed northern sense of humour.

We arranged to meet the following day at the Hilton Hotel in Park Lane. I wore a blue and white striped top – my lucky one – with little black hot pants, knee-length socks and big high shoes.

I rang from reception and Howard directed me to a suite. As I walked down the corridor, I passed a girl in the hallway who was dressed to kill and had obviously come from the same suite. We made eye contact, but she didn't smile.

Howard answered my knock. 'Geri, perfect timing. I've told them all about you.'

There were room-service trays stacked up inside the door, and three rather swarthy men were sitting in comfortable chairs by the window, drinking coffee and smoking.

'Isn't she wonderful,' said Howard. He handed my portfolio to a man with a thick handlebar moustache.

'Hi, my name is Geri Halliwell, pleased to meet you.'

There was an awkward silence.

'Have you done any TV work before?' asked one of them.

'Bits and pieces,' I lied.

The man with the moustache leaned across to Howard and whispered something in his ear. Howard nodded.

'Geri, could you just pop into the bathroom and slip your clothes off. They want to see what you look like in your underwear.'

I didn't question him. I was so used to taking my gear off at modelling auditions that it seemed almost routine. Closing the bathroom door, I pulled off my striped top and slipped out of my hot pants.

As I came back into the bedroom, all eyes turned towards me. The man pouring the coffees stopped mid-cup. I started talking to hide my nerves.

'I'm quite good at ad libbing and I've had experience working in front of crowds,' I said.

Howard motioned with his hand for me to turn around. Then he cupped his hands on his chest and indicated that I should take off my bra.

Just before I reached to unhook it, I thought, Hang on a second! What have my naked breasts got to do with being a game-show hostess?

'Don't be ridiculous,' I said, glaring at Howard. Then I spun on my heels and strode haughtily back into the bathroom. As I dressed, I caught sight of my face in the mirror. I looked furious. These so-called hotshot TV executives were trying to get their thrills at my expense. How many girls had stripped for them?

I brushed past Howard as I left, too angry to speak. He

followed me down the corridor. 'I'm sorry about that, Geri. I'm just trying to keep them happy.'

'You're a dickhead.'

'I'm sorry. That actually went very well. You're in with a chance. Let me take you to lunch. Do you like sushi? There's a great Japanese restaurant downstairs.'

By the time I reached the lift he had said all the right things and I had calmed down. We went to lunch and had a nice time talking about the different shows he'd produced and the various TV presenters we admired.

'It's a very good career, particularly if you're young,' he said. 'Right now, you have everything going for you – the looks, the personality. There are new shows being made all the time, particularly for the youth market. That's where you have to aim.'

Like a sponge, I soaked all of this up, trying to learn what I could about the industry.

'I could probably help your career, Geri. In the right hands you have a lot of potential.'

'That's really nice of you to say.'

'I think you should come to LA with me.'

'What for?'

'I could introduce you to some people.'

I laughed and pretended that I didn't take him seriously. A small red warning light began flashing in the back of my mind. After lunch, I offered to drive Howard back to his office because he didn't have his car. Squeezed into my Fiat Uno, we drove up Park Lane towards Marble Arch.

'So have you thought about LA?' he asked.

'You still haven't explained why. I don't have any experience. You haven't seen me on camera. Why me?'

'We could have some fun.'

I slammed my foot on the brakes in the middle of Marble Arch roundabout. Buses, cars and black cabs swerved. Hands thumped horns.

'Thanks for the offer.' I laughed nervously. 'But I'm going to make it with or without your help.'

Howard didn't bluster or bleat. He simply muttered something about a misunderstanding as I dropped him at his office. He said he'd be in touch about the job.

I didn't blame Howard. He was simply trying it on, which men and women have done ever since Eve convinced Adam to eat the apple. Of course, I didn't expect to hear from him again.

Such rejection didn't bother me, because there were always other options. Every week, as I looked through *The Stage*, my hope was renewed. You can't beat that feeling of sending off a CV and thinking, Maybe this time they'll choose me.

It came as a total surprise when Howard phoned the agency on the following Friday and said that I'd been chosen. Filming began a few weeks before Christmas in Istanbul, with enough episodes pre-recorded to last through until the summer. If the show proved popular, they planned to extend the contract and make more.

Television was still quite a novelty in Turkey and the game show was a flagship programme for a new station. The studios were in a big warehouse on the outskirts of Istanbul.

There were two other girls, Cheryl and Sarah, who were both from up north. Sarah always felt her surname didn't quite fit with her glamorous profile and she eventually changed her name to Levi Trammel, which sounds like a character from *Santa Barbara*.

The hotel they put us up in was fabulous, with bellboys in immaculately starched white uniforms and room service that could deliver ice cream in twenty-eight different flavours. Istanbul was a smoggy schizophrenic city. Some areas were quite beautiful, particularly on the Bosporus, but other places looked as if they'd been bombed out or abandoned when only half built.

What a crazy place. Every driver seemed hell-bent on going to meet Allah, racing along half-built roads in rusting cars. It seemed to take hours for the mini-bus to reach the studio. We almost collected half a dozen pedestrians who stood at the side of the road frantically trying to wave down a lift. The studios were new and the dressing rooms fully staffed with make-up girls and hairdressers. This felt more like what I'd expected.

The young producer ran through the format of the show and we had a dry run without the studio audience. Straight away I realized we had a language problem. The entire show was recorded in Turkish, which meant that Cheryl, Sarah and I had very little idea of what was going on. The solution was simply to keep smiling. Each time the host said 'Geri' and the camera light came on, I flashed my pearly whites and struck a pose.

The game show consisted of three doors, with a girl at each door. The studio audience was mostly made up of farm labourers, peasant women in scarves and grizzled old men with crumbling teeth. They could have been bussed straight from the fields, or perhaps their carts were parked outside. About a dozen specially chosen contestants were put in fancy-dress outfits and made to sit at the front.

The portly middle-aged host, Ehran, had a sunbed tan and dyed black hair, parted at the side. He came bounding onto the set to wild applause, before telling a few jokes and flirting outrageously as he introduced each of his assistants.

The first contestant was an old woman dressed as Little Bo Peep. She had the option of choosing one of the three doors that had a mystery prize waiting behind it. She kept turning to the crowd as they yelled advice.

'OK, let's make a deal,' said Ehran, producing a wad of cash. 'You can take the money, or you can choose a door. What will it be?' He spread the cash into a makeshift fan and cooled his fevered brow.

The crowd kept shouting:

'Door two. Door two.'

'The money, the money.'

'Door three. Door three.'

The poor woman didn't know what to do. She would have been overjoyed to win a matching set of his and hers bath towels. Caught up in the excitement, she chose a door.

'Are you sure? You can still take the money. Final chance.'

She shook her head.

'OK, Geri. Let's see what's behind door number one!'

Drums rolled and the door opened to reveal a bald car tyre. The audience groaned, the music went, 'Wah, wah, wah, waaaaah,' and I gave the thumbs down. Little Bo Peep shrugged her shoulders, but she didn't stop smiling. At least she'd been on TV.

Not all of the doors concealed 'zonk' prizes. Sometimes I revealed a 'fantastic fridge', and I had to love that appliance like I'd never loved anything before. The contestant danced about, hugging the host, and the audience went wild.

We looked like three princesses in our evening gowns, and after the show scraggy-haired men and teenage boys would wait beside the set, hoping for an autograph. I always gave them a kiss on the cheek because I was so grateful that anybody wanted my autograph.

We pre-recorded three shows a day for three weeks – enough to last the station at least six months. The show proved to be a hit, and eventually I became a minor celebrity in Turkey. The publicity department for the show kept feeding the demand by releasing photographs and stories about my beauty secrets and exercise routines.

It didn't feel like fame to me. Being a minor TV star in a country where I didn't speak the language and nobody I knew would ever see me didn't seem to count. I wanted to be able to say, 'Hey, look at me,' to my family and friends. Instead, I told myself, This is just a stepping stone. I took the money, hoped they would make more shows and, in the mean time, kept looking for my big break.

Some of the auditions were worse than others. When the musical *Oliver* was returning to the West End, I went along to the cattle-call without a specific role in mind, although I knew the words to 'Oom-Pah-Pah' and thought I might make a good Nancy.

The theatre in Shaftesbury Avenue already had huge banners and billboards advertising the show. Jonathan Pryce had been tipped to play Fagin and the media were eager to see which newcomers would be cast as the orphan Oliver and the Artful Dodger.

Dozens of wannabes had crowded into the foyer and

two tables were set up to take down names, addresses and details. I had a reasonable voice, although it wasn't classically trained. Most of the characters had to talk and sing in cockney accents, which wasn't difficult for me. I'd always been quite a good mimic.

As I waited to be called, I went to the ladies' room and quickly straightened my skirt. A girl came in after me, who had classical English looks and long, shining hair which was beautifully groomed. She carried a tape recorder and carefully set it down beside the sink. Pressing the 'play' button, she looked in the mirror and began singing her scales to a warm-up tape.

What a voice! Like an angel.

Oh, my God, what am I doing here? I am so out of my league. I'm a prat to think I can do this. I walked out and took the train home to Watford, feeling very depressed. When I closed my eyes and rested my head against the window I could still hear her voice, holding the high notes with such purity and strength.

My next chance came from another advertisement in *The Stage*, this one advertising for an actress. It appeared in the classified section, so I assumed it wouldn't be a big-budget affair.

Writer/director seeks actress for new British film.
Must be aged between 18–25.
No theatrical or film experience necessary.

An actress? I should be demure, I thought. I can't get away with wearing hot pants to the audition. Instead, I opted for the arty, contemporary look – a second-hand floaty cotton dress, which was white with blue flowers. I looked at myself in the mirror and said, 'Yes, very Helena Bonham Carter.'

Unfortunately, I couldn't do a thing about my shoes; I seemed to have nothing but Mary Quant platforms. Tying my hairpiece back into a ponytail, I briefed myself on being an actress, trying to slip into the role. I had to talk like a lovey and project my voice.

The address was in Hackney and I imagined it was probably a warehouse studio or a dance hall. Instead, I found an old council house, with net curtains and milk bottles waiting for collection on the front step.

I knocked on the door and a man answered wearing a cardigan and too much hair oil.

'Oh, hello, are you Mr Markham? I've come for the interview.'

'Good, I've made you lunch,' he said.

'That's OK, I'm really not hungry,' I said, slightly taken aback.

'I've made it anyway.'

He led me through to his kitchen, which had worn lino on the floor and a cat-litter tray in the corner by the fridge.

'Call me Dave,' he said, as he put a fried veggie burger on a limp piece of lettuce. He must have been in his mid-thirties and had a thin, wiry frame and arms that he didn't quite know what to do with when he paused between mouthfuls.

My veggie burger did circuits round my plate before I finally pushed my knife and fork together.

Dave dumped the plates beside the sink and suggested we go into his office. This turned out to be the sitting room, which had a desk, a settee and an old-fashioned lampstand.

'All right, I want to see how you dance,' he said, putting on a record.

'Oh, I thought I'd be interviewed. Can you tell me a little about the film?'

'All in good time. Come on, dance with me.' He held out his hand and gave me a gap-toothed smile. He looked like Leonard Rossiter.

I didn't want to dance. I went stiff as a board as he tried to hold me close. We waltzed around the room to the sounds of Mozart's Piano Concerto in E Flat. Oh, my God, this guy is a nutter! If he tries anything, I'll knee him in the balls.

'Loosen up, Geri.'

'I've really got to go. My boyfriend is coming to pick me up. I'm going to my judo lesson.'

'Listen to the music. Let the music move you.'

'What's the time? He'll be here soon.'

Dave was humming along to the music and seemed to take no notice.

'About this film. Have you actually got any funding? Or a script? Or a camera?'

The music had carried Dave away and I doubt if he even heard me. Exit, stage left, I decided. 'One more dance,' Dave said, draping himself across the doorway, trying to block my escape. I slipped under his arm and was outside before his dancing feet could react.

Of course there was no film. Dancing Dave from Hackney wasn't a writer or a producer. He was a lonely heart, or a pervert, who put ads in *The Stage* so he could get girls to come to lunch and dance with him.

Sean and I had been together for a year and a half and

were still living with his parents. He seemed a lot happier when he had work. Otherwise, he tended to sit in front of the TV watching the soccer all day, letting the empty crisp packets and soft-drink cans pile up on the coffee table.

Although he remained supportive, he no longer took much interest in my auditions or my eternally optimistic search through *The Stage* each Thursday. A lot of the time he didn't seem to be listening when I pointed things out or asked him whether I should try out for a show. I even wandered about in front of the TV in my underwear trying to get him to pay me some attention.

'Do you mind? You've only made me miss a bloody penalty.'

'So what! They'll show a replay.'

'That's not the point. I'm watching this.'

'And I want to talk to you.'

'We'll talk later.'

'We never talk. You ignore me.'

'Don't be such a stupid cow.' He opened another can of drink.

I stormed out of the house and went to visit Karen. I figured that if I stayed away for a night Sean would miss me and plead with me to come back. It didn't work. He barely noticed I'd gone.

The following day I had a phone call from my agency. A European media boss wanted to meet me in London to discuss a job. He owned the rights to a game show and wanted me to be the next hostess. Caro, my friend from the nightmare dancing assignment in Greece, came with me to the interview. She had recently started working on the Turkish game show with me.

We met Hari at a posh old hotel in Holland Park, with

Chesterfield sofas in the lounge. He was approaching fifty, with silver-grey hair, green eyes and a strong jaw. Clearly, he'd been very good-looking in his youth and had aged into a Blake Carrington from *Dynasty* style figure. Hari was charming and sophisticated, with a taste for Italian designer suits, silk ties and hand-made leather shoes. 'Just call me Hari,' he said, as I sat down. 'Your photographs don't do you justice.'

Caro giggled and I had to hush her.

There were other TV bosses with him, and they talked about having seen me on *Let's Make a Deal* in Turkey. The feedback was very positive and the meeting informal. Hari walked Caro and I back to the car before saying goodbye.

He called me the next day from his home in Paris. 'Geri, I would like you to come to New York.'

'What for?'

'We need to talk business.'

'Why can't we talk in London?'

'Because I want to take you to New York.'

'I can't do that. I hardly know you.'

There was something rather familiar about this script and I could sense where it might be heading.

'We really need to talk,' said Hari. 'It's important for your career.'

'OK, I'll tell you what. I'll come to Paris with you and we'll have lunch.'

'Good idea. Come tomorrow. I'll organize the flights and have you picked up from the airport.'

I quite liked Hari. He had a puppylike enthusiasm and seemed to make decisions on the spur of the moment. I could picture him waking up in the morning and deciding over his grapefruit segments that he fancied going sailing in the Mediterranean. By lunchtime, he'd be dressed immaculately in a blazer and peaked cap, bobbing up and down on his private yacht off St Tropez.

I arrived in Paris feeling rather unwell. I had the raging flu and kept sneezing and sniffling. I still had doubts about Hari's intentions. He picked me up in a green Rolls-Royce with a walnut dashboard and we drove towards the centre of Paris.

Hari told me that he owned two banks and a TV station in Greece, but spent most of his time in Paris. I could see why as we pulled through the gates of an amazing house surrounded by a walled garden.

Suddenly, Hari announced, 'Geri, I must apologize. I have brought you here under false pretences. I am in love with you.'

I laughed.

'I am serious. I want you to stay with me. I will make you very happy.'

I felt totally overwhelmed. Hari held my hand and looked at me like Pepe le Pew, the amorous cartoon skunk. He was quite handsome for a man approaching fifty and he had a youthful sense of fun.

'I'm going to have to think about this,' I said, through a blocked-up nose. I had sniffled through lunch at a restaurant near Montmartre and sneezed when he bought me roses from a barrow on the banks of the Seine. I was more in need of a new box of tissues than an ageing Romeo.

Hari proved to be the perfect gentleman and, perhaps for the sake of his health, he said goodbye with a peck on the cheek.

As I flew back to London club class I felt like crying. I don't know why. My mother's words kept coming back to me. 'Geri, you gotta marry a rich man,' she had told me, as she struggled to keep us fed by cleaning floors. Now I had a rich man who wanted to marry me. Should I go for it? There are worse ways to spend a life than jetting between homes in London and Paris. I could be like Jacqueline Onassis. Imagine. There would be front-row seats at the Paris fashion shows; sailing in St Tropez; skiing in St Moritz . . .

I didn't love Hari; I didn't even know him. Did that matter? What were the alternatives? I had a boyfriend who had lost interest in me, a catalogue of unsuccessful auditions and a folder full of rejection letters.

Back at home I told no-one, although it soon became difficult to keep it secret. Hari besieged me with phone calls three times a day and sent me flowers and notes via Karen's house.

Finally I agreed to spend a weekend in Paris with him. I reasoned that if we spent time together, either he would discover that I wasn't the love of his life, or I might find out whether he could possibly be mine.

The green Rolls-Royce was again waiting at Charles de Gaulle Airport. Hari kissed my hand and sat holding it as we drove through the Friday evening traffic towards the house. His hands were beautifully manicured and he smelled as though he'd spent all day in a cologne shop.

'Where do you want to go? I will take you anywhere.'

'You decide.'

'No, I insist.'

The only place I associated with Paris nightlife was the Moulin Rouge, but I had no idea it had topless dancers.

Hari didn't bat an eyelid. We watched the show and afterwards dined at a little restaurant in the Latin Quarter. Hari said that he'd been married once before, but that his wife was dead. He had a son and a daughter, both of whom were at boarding school in Switzerland.

Changing the subject, he insisted on talking about me. 'I want to know everything, Geri. What is your favourite colour? What flowers do you like? Do you like music?'

Hari had rather unexpected musical tastes. He played Brazilian samba music in the Rolls-Royce as the chauffeur drove us back to the house. As we pulled through the large iron gates, Hari drew closer and tried to kiss me. I suffered a panic attack. This had been a huge mistake. What on earth was I doing? At that moment, I wanted to be back in Sean's house with my inattentive boyfriend.

'I'm sorry, Hari, but I can't do this. I can't stay.'

'It's OK, Geri. But it's too late for a flight. Stay tonight. No strings. You have your ticket to go back in the morning. My driver will take you to the airport.'

He was being such a gentleman that I didn't mind his company.

'I will get us a drink. Brandy?'

'Mineral water will be fine.'

As I waited in the lounge, I began flicking through magazines on the coffee table. One of them was *Hola!*, the Spanish version of *Hello!* magazine, which contained features on Europe's richest and most glamorous people. As I picked it up, the magazine fell open on a picture of a tall, striking woman in a strapless evening dress. Pictured next to her was Hari, in a dinner jacket, holding a champagne flute.

He looked every inch the media tycoon, and the

woman next to him, according to the caption, was Mrs Media Tycoon.

That bastard! What a fool I'd been!

As much as I wanted to go storming off into the night, I knew there were no flights until the morning and the gates outside were locked. Hari had been so clever and conniving, would he *let* me walk out?

'Here I am, Geri. I hope you haven't been lonely.' Hari had changed into a smoking jacket and looked like a portly version of Hugh Hefner. I jumped in fright and quickly closed the magazine.

'No, not at all,' I said. 'I'm actually very tired. I'd like to go to bed. Can you point me to my room?'

'I'll show you.'

'No, that's OK, just point me in the right direction.'

I found a bedroom upstairs that clearly belonged to his daughter. Rather than choose another, I stayed. I figured Hari was less likely to try to seduce somebody in his own daughter's room. Just to be doubly sure, I barricaded the door with a rocking horse and kept a Sindy doll plastic horse by my pillow. If he came near me, I'd give him a whack.

Somehow I managed to fall asleep and didn't wake until 9 a.m. I thought I heard Hari leaving the house, so I went downstairs to the kitchen. A maid was mopping the floor and I chatted to her as I munched a croissant.

Suddenly Hari came down the stairs chatting on his cell phone and wearing a very short bathrobe, tied at the waist. I was still wearing my striped Aquafresh men's pyjamas, with an old-fashioned pointy bra underneath. Although not the most revealing of outfits, I still felt vulnerable.

I could see Hari's love handles bulging above the towelling belt of his bathrobe. How could I have even contemplated sleeping with him?

Before he finished his phone call, I slipped upstairs to get changed. Wearing just my skirt and a bra, I turned as the door opened. Hari tried to sweep me into his arms.

'Come here, Geri.'

'Get off! Get off!'

He tried to kiss me.

A few weeks earlier I'd done a single self-defence class with a friend, and the instructor had taught us how to break a grip. Instead of automatically pulling away, the most effective method is to move closer and pull upwards.

I did this, successfully breaking Hari's hold, but at the same time I went flying across the room and smacked into a chest of drawers. I scrambled up and rushed into the bathroom, screaming, 'Go away! Go away! Leave me alone!'

My aggression shocked Hari. He threw up his hands and announced, 'You crazy, crazy girl.' Then he stormed downstairs.

I dressed, packed my things and made sure I had my ticket. I passed Hari at the bottom of the stairs and tossed back my head in disgust. 'Hmmmph! I have half a mind to tell your wife.'

Outside, with my heart pounding, I jumped into the Rolls-Royce and told the driver, 'Take me to the airport.'

I didn't see Hari again, although occasionally I'm sure he still pops up in *Hello!* He's one of those guests at celebrity functions and charity balls who is never at the centre of the photograph, but clings to the edges or squeezes his head over a shoulder.

He taught me a valuable lesson: I wanted to make my own money and establish my own name, rather than live off anybody else. And if I did marry, it would be for love.

# 7

## BUMS AND TUMS

Very little in my life seemed to have any sort of direction or control. It had been like that since I'd left school. I had run out those front gates and embraced whatever chances came my way, as if I was trying to catch falling leaves.

I had all these dreams and ambitions, but no clue how to achieve them. Even if I had stayed at college, there is no way I would have been happy working for a hotel or a travel company. And despite Mum's ambitions for me, I didn't have the patience to be a teacher. Instead, I'd drifted for four years, never quite in control of my life. Even getting to grips with bingeing had been a struggle. If alcoholics fall off the wagon, what does a bulimic do?

Food had always been a very emotional thing for me. As a child it had been used to comfort, bribe or punish me. The most turbulent times of day were at the dinner table, when tears were spilled into every sauce and tempers seasoned each mouthful.

Now it became one of the few things I could control in my chaotic life. I started a new regime of exercise and healthy eating. Calories were the enemy. Fat had to be burned.

Sean and I had moved into a flat in Hempstead Road. I joined a gym and became fanatical about doing a certain number of miles every morning. Mum's words would come back to me: 'You have to suffer to be beautiful.'

Eventually, I bluffed the gym manager and convinced him I was a trained aerobics instructor. In truth, I'd studied a few videos. Soon I had fliers printed and posted up about town.

Go for that tight bum, flat tum and firm body.
Burn the fat with
MISS MOTIVATOR.
Aerobics with Geri. Tuesday 7.30. Friday 6.00.
£3 including free sauna.

A little of my dad had rubbed off on me when it came to spotting the opportunity to make money. It was all about knowing a man who knew a man who could get things cheap.

I'd joined a new casting agency in London, and discovered that they had plans to put together a directory of their 200 clients. These were mostly extras who were looking for bit-parts, TV commercials or – the big score – a few days' work on a film or drama series.

'I can do that,' I told them. 'I know a photographer.'

I'd met Steve during my modelling days when I was trying to get my portfolio together. He mainly took wedding shots, but aspired to be the next Helmut Newton, shooting glamorous women in exotic locations. I approached him with an idea: I would do the make-up and he could take the pictures.

We shot the entire directory in a day. I felt bad about having only two sponges in my make-up kit and using them on 200 people. Not surprisingly, I threw them out afterwards.

We made a handsome profit on the deal, with Steve getting the lion's share to cover the cost of the film.

'We should go into business, you know,' I said.

'Doing what?'

'Make-overs. Girls love that sort of thing. I'll do the make-up and you can shoot them soft focus.'

We decided to put together a portfolio of 'before and after' pictures so we could advertise in the local papers. I convinced friends to come along and most of them seemed pretty happy with the end results.

Interestingly, one of the keenest girls was Sarah, the girlfriend of Sean's best mate, Greg. Of all our acquaintances, Greg had been the most critical of my topless modelling. He'd told Sean, 'I don't know how you put up with it, mate. There's no way I'd let Sarah show her tits to the world. It's disgusting having other blokes perving over her like that.'

Sarah arrived for her make-over and Steve took the 'before' shots. I did her make-up and she went back into the studio looking really pretty.

Afterwards Steve said to me, 'You'll never believe that.'

'What?'

'She took her clothes off.'

'You're kidding.'

'No way. She was right into it. I didn't say a word. She just pulled off her top and started posing.'

I couldn't stop laughing. It's true what they say about not judging a book by its cover. I felt like putting some of the prints in a plain brown envelope and posting them anonymously to Greg.

All of these jobs helped pay the rent, but strangely they also gave my life meaning. By keeping busy, I couldn't dwell on a failed audition or another rejection letter. I'm sure that having too much time to think was half the reason I started bingeing in the first place.

Now I didn't ponder on my set-backs, I simply kept working and picking up *The Stage* each Thursday. The more auditions I attended, the more people I met who were just like me – desperate to be discovered and have their name in lights. An army of wannabes marched in step with me, most of them surviving on fortnightly dole cheques and 'if only' stories.

I drew a lot of comfort from these wannabe musters in dance studios and theatre foyers because I knew I wasn't alone. If my dream was fruitless and foolish, then a lot of other people had the same problem. We couldn't all be wrong.

At each new cattle-call I networked for contacts and came up with new ideas. At one of them I heard about a Radio and TV presenter's course run by the Reuters news agency. The one-day course cost £200 – a huge amount for me.

I'd been living on a shoestring budget for months, pinching toilet rolls from the gym and scouring the bargain bins at the supermarket. Mum would have been proud of how far I could make a few pounds stretch.

Somehow I scraped together the necessary funds for the Reuter's course. Eight of us were taken through the various techniques of interviewing and being interviewed, as well as how to introduce a programme. We were also confronted with the challenge of doing a live news report from the scene of an accident.

All of these were taped and played back to the class, so that we could relive our mistakes publicly and cringe all over again. My most memorable moment came during a 'live cross' to Geri Halliwell at the scene of a bomb blast outside a department store in London.

'Can you tell us what is happening there now, Geri?'

'Well, yes, thanks, Jeremy. Police have confirmed that four people died in the blast which rocked Oxford Street a little after seven this evening. Eleven people were injured, three of them critically, including a seven-year-old boy whose mother died in the blast . . .'

I thought I'd done quite well until they played the tape back, then I noticed a serious flaw in my technique. Throughout my entire news report I had smiled like a game-show hostess who had just revealed a fabulous fridge.

'Perhaps you could be a little more sombre in your approach,' said the tutor, being very kind.

Upon finishing the course, I sent my tape to an agency called Talking Heads, run by Anthony Blackburn and TV voice-over man John Sachs, who worked on *Gladiators*. Surprisingly, they asked to see me, which triggered my usual few days of debating what to wear and how to act.

How will I play it?

Bubbly but switched on.

What will I wear?

Something that covers my breasts. I want to be taken seriously. My lucky striped top and a cream jacket.

Talking Heads had an office in Barnes, just by Hammersmith Bridge. As soon as I walked through the door, a Labrador bounded across and began humping my leg. I tried to push it away casually, but it had really taken to my tailored black trousers and was slobbering over my thigh.

They acted as though the dog didn't exist. I knew that John Sachs had enjoyed a long career in radio and TV, mainly doing voice-overs. He and Anthony were both really sweet.

'I know I haven't got any experience, but what I lack in experience I make up for in enthusiasm,' I told them. I'd said it so often it had begun to sound like a mantra.

Everything seemed to click. I didn't get tongue-tied or talk too quickly. I sounded bright and witty. My God, these people really seemed to like me.

Tony Blackburn had another appointment and apologized for having to leave. 'I don't think we need to discuss this,' he said, glancing at John Sachs, who shook his head. 'Right. We're agreed. You're going on our books, Geri.'

I was so shocked that I almost forgot to say thank you. Skipping down the stairs, I went running outside to where Sean was waiting in the car. I had a huge grin on my face. I wanted to scream at the top of my lungs, I'm going to make it! And I'm going to be famous! That's how I felt. For the first time I had a good agent. Now, surely, it was only a matter of time.

Four weeks later, in May 1993, I saw an advertisement in *The Stage* for a *Disney Club* audition. The Saturday morning children's TV show was looking for a new presenter who could fit easily into the existing team.

The audition was at a studio near Marble Arch. The rag-tag queue stretched down the stairs to the café and contained some familiar faces. They weren't just unknowns. I recognized an Australian girl from *Neighbours* and a guy who'd starred in an episode of *Inspector Morse*.

After much thought, I'd decided to wear hot pants, a Mickey Mouse T-shirt and my hair in bunches. I was looking for 'cheeky and accessible', like someone's cool older sister who tells them secrets. After waiting for nearly two hours, I finally got my turn.

'Just look into the camera and pretend you're talking to an audience,' said a rather bored-looking woman with an American accent.

'What do I have to say?'

'Just talk about yourself. You've got thirty seconds.'

A video camera had been set up in the adjoining room. As each aspirant gave their spiel, the pictures could be seen on a TV monitor outside.

'OK, next.'

I shuffled inside and waited for the red recording light.

'Hello, boys and girls, my name is Geri, and we have a fabulous show for you today. I hope you like cartoons. I do. Can you guess my favourite character?' I looked down at my T-shirt. 'That's right – Mickey Mouse!'

So far so good. What else can I say?

'I'm new to the show, so you don't know me. Let me tell you my favourite things. I love music, horse-riding, sunny days and watching cartoons . . .' If I didn't stop soon I'd be singing about raindrops on roses and whiskers on kittens.

The red light went off. Phew! I'd made it.

'That was very good,' said the American, 'but it's a bit *Play School*. You seem to be talking to a younger audience than our target group.'

'I can fix that,' I said eagerly.

'OK, I'm putting you on the shortlist. Here's an address in Soho. I want you to be there next Friday morning. In the mean time, come up with an idea for the show, a segment that you can present on Friday. Think like a seven-year-old.'

I spent the next few days racking my brain. Sean was typically hopeless. 'Why don't you just read 'em a story,' he said.

'Yeah, right. Very original.'

'Shame you can't do balloon animals.'

'Very funny.'

Suddenly, I had an idea. Animals? Kids love them. Particularly baby animals that are all cute and fluffy. Like . . . like . . . ducklings!

On Thursday afternoon I went to the pet shop and bought a baby duck, all fluffy and yellow. I found a cardboard box and put straw in the bottom. It slept in the kitchen of the flat that night, and the next morning I drove to the audition in a Soho studio.

I tied the box to a pull-along shopping-trolley bag and felt very pleased with myself as I wheeled it into the dressing room. I noticed only three other applicants.

'Where is everyone?'

'This is it,' said a roly-poly girl with bouncing curls.

My God, I'd made it down to the last four. I'm almost there, I thought, as I glanced through the air holes in my cardboard box. I bet nobody has an idea as good as mine.

Before we presented our individual segments, we met

the actual presenters of the *Disney Club* and ran through some comedy sketches and routines. I'd been given a script to learn about a couple called Norman and Norma Nerd, who were looking to buy a second-hand car.

I dressed up as Norma in an overcoat and thick glasses with a sticking plaster over one lens. *Disney Club* presenters played Norman and the car salesman. I felt quite excited about working with people who were actually on telly for a living.

Having managed to be suitably nerdy and not forget my lines, I watched the roly-poly girl have a turn. She improvised better than I did, but that didn't matter – I had my secret weapon waiting in the dressing room.

Eventually the time came. I retrieved the cardboard box and took a quick peek to make sure my bundle of fluff was ready for his début performance.

'Ladies and gentlemen, boys and girls, I want to introduce you to the latest member of our presenting team. This is Disney Duck!' I held aloft the fluffy yellow bundle.

The producer and director looked horrified. My poor little duck had been sweating in the cardboard box and looked set to expire.

'I think it needs some water.'

'Give it some air.'

'These TV lights are too hot.'

'How cruel.'

I could almost hear the music going, Wah, wah, wah, waaaaaah, in the background. Nobody cared about my segment; they were too worried about the duckling. My hopes were leaking away. Roly-poly girl got the job, but I didn't stay long enough to see her segment.

Loading my cardboard box and trolley into the car, I drove back to the pet shop in Watford and handed back the duckling.

'We don't give refunds,' the owner said.

'That's OK. Make sure he gets a good home.'

My search for a presenter's job carried on, despite the inauspicious start. My new agents at Talking Heads had been disappointingly quiet, but I told myself to be patient and to persevere.

I sat watching *The Big Breakfast* on Channel 4 one morning, eating my low-fat cereal and skimmed milk. I loved anything that Chris Evans hosted. He is such a brilliant improviser, tailor-made for live TV.

This particular day, Evans announced that Channel 4 was launching a new magazine-style show called *Trash Talk* which would be about all things trashy, cool and American. They were looking for presenters over the age of seventeen to host the show. Anybody interested should send in an audition tape.

It was perfect for me. I loved American fads and fashions – everything over the top. All I had to do was come up with the perfect video introduction and knock 'em dead.

I knew that *Trash Talk* would have some tie-in with American Football, which was one of Channel 4's most popular programmes. This gave me an idea. Just down the road from me, a gridiron team called London Thunder trained several nights a week. I borrowed a camcorder from a friend and turned up at the ground. It was pouring with rain and bitterly cold for June.

The coach wouldn't let me interrupt training, but said

I could talk to the players afterwards. Eventually, I convinced two enormous line-backers to help me, although both of them just wanted to hit the showers and dry off.

'OK, if you just stand each side of me. What are your names again?'

'Ritchie.'

'Joel.'

'OK, right. Ritchie and Joel, if you just stand either side of me – er, with your helmets on – I'll do a piece to camera.'

The rain teemed down, running into my eyes and plastering my hair. I had a plastic anorak over the camera and kept wiping the lens with a soggy tissue. Water had leaked into my boots, which squelched when I walked.

'Listen, love, how long is this going to take?'

'Not long. Not long. Won't be a minute.'

I pressed the 'record' button and squeezed in between them. 'Hi, my name's Geri and you're watching *Trash Talk*. Yeah. I'm here with Ritchie and, er, er . . . What's your name?'

'Joel,' muttered the line-backer.

'Yeah, Joel. OK, we've got news, reviews and interviews coming up. OK. We'll tell you what's cool, what's hot and what's not. OK, right. We've got some wonderful stuff for you. Don't go away. OK, stay tuned. I'll see you right after the break, OK, yeah.'

I'd tried to do it so quickly that words tumbled out in a rush and I couldn't remember any of my script. Ritchie and Joel wouldn't do another take, so it would have to do. I trudged back to my car with mud sucking at my boots.

Unbelievably, I had a letter from Channel 4 asking if they could have permission to play my tape on *The Big Breakfast*.

Oh, my God. This is it! They want to play it. For a week I seemed to walk a foot off the ground, telling everyone I met that I was going to be on *The Big Breakfast*. I told the couple in the colour copy shop and all my friends.

Unfortunately, on the day it was due to be shown I had to go to a casting. It was a waste of time, particularly when I knew I was missing *The Big Breakfast*.

Thankfully, Karen taped it for me and I rushed back to her place.

She tried to warn me that it might not be what I expected. What could she mean?

'For the last few weeks we've been telling you about an up-coming show on Channel Four called *Trash Talk*,' said Chris Evans, leaning forward on a sofa in his trademark floral shirt. 'We're giving you the chance to be a presenter on the show and we've had a huge response. This morning we thought we'd show you a few of the audition tapes that have been sent in. Have a look at these.'

The first showed a Jamaican guy in a bedsit who seemed to be almost head-butting the camera as he swayed back and forth, going in and out of focus. He spoke in such a heavy accent that I couldn't understand more than a few words he said.

The second hopeful was a sixty-five-year-old pub landlady from the West Country, who stood behind the bar and recited one of her poems.

Finally it came to me, looking soggy and pathetic, with make-up staining my cheeks. My mouth ran amok: 'OK, right. We've got some wonderful stuff for you. Don't go away. OK, stay tuned. I'll see you right after the break, OK, yeah.'

At the same time, Ritchie and Joel were making rude

gestures behind my back and pretending to grab my arse.

Back in the studio, Chris Evans and co-host Gabby Roslin were almost holding their sides with laughter. As the tape ended, Gabby carried on, 'OK, you. OK, you. See you OK. Coming up at you, wouldn't want to be you, no, no, no.'

The whole exercise had been a massive piss-take. I was horrified. I'd told everyone to watch. How could I show my face again? I sat on Karen's sofa staring at the blank TV screen.

'It wasn't so bad,' she said. 'It was a great idea.'

'Do you think so?'

'Yeah.'

'But they laughed at me.'

'No, you *made* them laugh. That's a good thing.'

Yeah, right! I thought.

Not all of my grand plans ended in complete disaster. Each time I seemed to make just enough forward momentum to feel that I was still heading in the right direction. It wasn't so much a case of one step forward and two steps back, more a question of treading water and hoping the current would take me where I wanted to go. It helped to be busy. I didn't want to count failures. And at least I had Natalie and Dad believing in me. They knew when to say nothing.

Rather than pondering failure, I set myself new goals every day. I called it my traffic-light syndrome because it started each morning as I drove to the gym. 'If I get through these next three lights without them changing to red, then everything will be all right,' I said. And further down the road: 'If this light turns green within ten seconds, then everything will be OK. If the next song on the radio is an up-tempo song, good things will happen.'

At the gym, I pushed myself to run another mile on the treadmill, or do another set of weights. 'If I do that, then I'll get what I want.'

Over time, the challenges grew more difficult. I would dare myself to go up to a complete stranger and strike up a conversation, or I'd knock on an unfamiliar door and pretend that I'd lost my cat. All the while, a voice inside my head kept saying, 'Come on, Geri, if you can do this, you can do anything.'

I couldn't dismiss or back out of a challenge. Once the voice had uttered the words, it was too late. Subconsciously, I had acknowledged the dare, and if I didn't fulfil it then my life would be altered totally; my dreams would not come true.

This superstition served a purpose: it helped overcome any shyness and insecurity I had. Equally, it seemed to empower me and reinforce the belief that I had control over my life.

So I persevered, rolling up to auditions and answering the same question: 'What acting experience have you got?'

'Well, I've done some fringe theatre,' I blagged. This was a total lie, of course, but I'd quickly realized that acting is about making things sound like the truth.

'And, of course, you know my surname is Halliwell, don't you? Well, the *Halliwell Film Guide* was written by my great uncle.'

'Really?'

'Yes. It took him twelve years. They say he watched over ten thousand films.'

This was all invention.

Talking Heads called about a magazine-style programme being planned by a new cable channel L!VE TV, due to be launched the following autumn. The idea was to create a live twenty-four-hour-a-day TV channel with the style and content of a tabloid newspaper.

The director of programmes at L!VE TV was Nick Ferrari, who was also deputy chief executive of the Mirror Group, publishers of the *Daily Mirror*. This is where we arranged to meet because L!VE TV still had no headquarters.

The decision about what to wear took on great importance. I couldn't think of the *Daily Mirror* without page-three girls coming to mind. OK, let's titillate them a little, I thought, choosing a tight black catsuit.

Nick Ferrari sat in his office overlooking Holborn Circus. Hanging on the walls were framed front pages of the *Daily Mirror*, reporting events like the Royal Wedding and the Brighton bombing.

'The show is called *London Live*,' he said. 'It's going to have loads of different segments on restaurants, theatre, music. Bright and breezy stuff. One of the spots is called "Fashion Police" and we're looking for somebody to front it.'

The format sounded like a low-budget cross between *Treasure Hunt* with Anneka Rice and *The Clothes Show* with Selena Scott. Basically, fashion victims were going to be arrested in the street and offered a make-over.

'We're gonna turn some pumpkin into a princess,' said Nick. 'It's good TV. Women love that sort of thing.'

*London Live* was still in development and the producers making various pilot episodes to see if the format worked, particularly live and uncut.

Although I knew I'd made a good impression on Nick Ferrari, it still came as something of a shock when he phoned a fortnight later to say that he wanted me to host the pilot of 'Fashion Police'. I couldn't control my excitement. Again I told everybody, even complete strangers in the newsagents. My own TV show! Part of one, anyway.

The downside, of course, was that L!VE TV was still more than a year away from broadcasting and would only be seen by subscribers.

What am I going to wear? It has to be sexy and hip. Black? Certainly. Figure-hugging? What else! I chose leather trousers, a black body and a zip-up jacket. I still wore a hairpiece, which I poked through the back of a baseball cap.

Nick gave me some last-minute advice before setting me loose with a camera crew.

'Whatever you do, Geri, just keep talking. Keep the show moving. Don't let it flag.'

'Do I get a practice run?'

'No, I don't want things to look too slick or staged.'

That was it. Twenty minutes later I stood in Oxford Street, outside Hennes with a cameraman, a sound recordist and a researcher.

Thankfully, the spontaneity of the show went straight out the window. Our fashion victim had been set up in advance, with the co-operation of Hennes and the editor of *More* magazine.

With the camera rolling, I burst from the door of a black van, blowing a whistle and pointing as I ran along the street.

'This is the fashion police and, baby, you're busted! What's your name?'

'Maria.'

'Maria, what are you wearing? You are in serious need of a make-over. I tell you what, if you're willing, we have a fashion editor, a stylist and a clothing store at your disposal. D'you want to do it? Let's go for it. Yeah!'

The puffing cameraman followed us into Hennes, getting some weird angles when he tripped over the soundman. My mouth ran riot for the next fifteen minutes. Meanwhile, Maria was transformed from a dowdy frump into a hip chick.

Considering I'd had no practice, I thought I'd done pretty well. Nick Ferrari said my clothes were too fussy and I had too much going on, but that could be fixed.

'We'll get back to you,' he said.

I almost believed him.

In the mean time, I had other possibilities. A writer/director casting a new play had asked me to read the script and try out for one of the lead roles. I'd met David Cadogan once before, six months earlier, through an advertisement in *The Stage*. Back then, he'd been casting a film. He was an interesting character, with a crippled leg and a frail body, but he had the most fabulous mind. He had written a political satire and thought I could play the naughty nurse. It was set in a lunatic asylum where Pol Pot was the consultant looking after three MPs – a Tory, Labour and Liberal Democrat.

The play was very funny, and I was invited to meet the director and cast for a reading at a rehearsal studio in Hammersmith. Although I felt nervous, it was exciting. I really wanted to do it. Yes, it was a silly part, but this was a proper play, something worthwhile, which might move to the West End.

I'd lost a lot of weight since David had last seen me.

'What happened to your curves?' he asked, looking horrified. 'You look malnourished. I want you to be buxom, not a bag of bones.'

David got me to read twice for the part. I was in competition with another girl.

'I'm afraid you've missed out, Geri,' he said. 'Joanne simply has more experience than you. Besides, what was the last thing you read? I bet it was *Cosmopolitan*.'

He laughed at his little joke. I felt angry and humiliated, but I knew he was right. Once upon a time a comment like that would have sent me straight to the fridge. Not any more. If I felt angry, I should do something about it. I had left school at sixteen and I wasn't well read.

The following day, I contacted Watford College and asked about its A level courses in English Literature. Geri Halliwell was going back to school.

Sean and I had been together for nearly two and a half years and our relationship had grown comfortable, if a little tired. We didn't seem to be on the same wavelength any more. I went out every day, doing various jobs and going to auditions, trying to make something of my life. Meanwhile, Sean seemed to have forgotten his ambitions. He lay in front of the TV, unemployed and uninspired.

For a while I pretended to be the perfect wife, cooking him dinners and doing his laundry. The novelty didn't last. This was partly due to boredom, but also a loss of respect. I cared about Sean. I could probably have spent my life with him if he'd shown a little more hunger and interest in me. Instead, I had a nagging doubt that wouldn't go away.

My twenty-first birthday was approaching, and I knew that Sean was planning some grand gesture. I didn't want him to invest too much emotionally in me. My life was going nowhere fast, but I was determined to change things.

On the day I picked up the entrance forms for Watford College, I also collected a reading list. I bought copies of *Sons and Lovers* and *Hamlet*, as well as the study guides. I began reading one of these in the college cafeteria. It talked of Hamlet's 'paralysis of analysis'; how he hesitated and procrastinated over avenging his father's death because the act was so unpleasant and painful.

When I arrived at the flat in Hempstead Road, Sean was still lying on the sofa. I doubt if he'd moved more than twelve feet all day. Although there is never a right time to leave somebody, I suddenly realized that Sean and I would be better off apart. Like Hamlet, I had delayed and made excuses, but the time had come to act.

'What do you mean, you're leaving?' he asked as I collected my things and loaded them into the car. All my worldly possessions could fit in the back of a Fiat Uno.

'We're heading in different directions,' I said.

'Since when?'

'For a long time.'

Sean asked me not to leave. I knew he loved me and I could so easily have stayed; he was so comfortable to be around.

I could see him standing at the window as I drove away. I almost wavered and turned back. But I was right to go. It proved to be the best thing for both of us. By leaving, I gave Sean the kick in the pants he needed to finally get his life together.

I moved into my own place – a studio flat in Fairlawns. Ironically, it was the same flat I had once broken into when I stole the snake from Natalie's former boyfriend Rupert. He still hadn't discovered the truth when he rented it to me.

I loved my new home. It was in a pretty cul-de-sac, with lovely gardens and well-established trees. I made the flat look really nice by sponge-painting the walls and re-carpeting the floors. The kitchen, dining room and lounge were open plan. It had one bedroom, with built-in wardrobes that were falling apart until I fixed the sliding doors. I had no furniture apart from a beanbag and an old stand-up piano that someone had left behind. For the first few weeks I slept on the floor, wrapped in a quilt. Later, I bought a double mattress and lots of cushions.

The electricity worked on a pre-paid key-card system. I had to put pound coins into a machine in town, which put credits on my key card. Then, at home, I put the card into the electricity meter and, hey presto, I had light and heating.

On my first night alone, I stood in front of a mirror adjusting a bustier dress I'd bought in a second-hand shop. I was always designing and making my own clothes, normally by cutting and pinning until I transformed an outfit into something new. It was 10 p.m., and I had a mouthful of pins and a half-completed hem when there was a click and suddenly everything went dark. I had an overwhelming sense of being alone and frightened. I didn't have Sean to help me. What if someone was trying to get in?

I opened the bedroom curtains and saw that the

neighbouring houses still had power. My credit had obviously expired and I needed to put more money on the electricity key card.

Fumbling in the dark, I found my car keys and purse. Then I drove into town, with pins jabbing my thighs each time I used the clutch. I didn't feel frightened any more; this was simply another challenge. If I could do this, then good things would happen.

Taking control of my life, I adopted a new regime. It started at six each morning, when I opened the gym and did a twenty-minute run before anyone else arrived. I still taught aerobics twice a week and would ride my pushbike home via the supermarket.

I had a food budget of £10 a week and lived on a diet of bean sprouts, onions, coffee, apples, yoghurt, jacket potatoes and baked beans. For months I'd avoided family dinners and other gatherings, because I knew my mother would try to make me eat. Each day I stripped naked and measured myself with a tape measure. I didn't trust bathroom scales. Afterwards, I couldn't wait until the next day because I'd be that much thinner.

So little had happened in terms of show-business success, there had to be a reason. I had a folder of rejection letters that was two inches thick. Perhaps it would make a difference when I was thinner, I told myself, as I thought of new ways to burn calories or cut them out completely.

I now washed hair every Saturday at a barber shop in St Albans, earning £20 for getting wrinkled fingers and all the latest gossip. I had to make coffee for the customers and it always seemed to have bits of hair floating on top.

On a busy afternoon, I was asked to dye a man's hair.

He was in his late thirties and quite fancied himself as a ladies' man. His hair had already started to thin, and he'd brushed it across his scalp like a single blanket trying to cover a double bed.

I put on the dark-brown dye, and he sat for a while, reading a magazine. As I started washing it out, I noticed a strange thing – the dye seemed to have stained his head. He had a neat brown rim across his forehead and down past his ears, as though someone had simply picked him up and dunked him head first into hot chocolate. No matter how hard I scrubbed, it simply wouldn't wash off.

He looked mortified and I felt terrible. The only thing that stopped him complaining was that the room was full of men and he didn't want to draw attention to himself. Instead, he tucked a newspaper under his arm and strolled outside as if nothing had happened.

Immediately after finishing at the barber shop, I would nip over the road, and fifteen minutes later I'd start work at an Italian restaurant, serving drinks and puddings. Then, during the week, I cleaned two houses – one in Rickmansworth and the other in Chorley Wood.

On top of this, a jeweller friend in Hatton Garden had a batch of fake TAG watches which he was trying to sell. I always carried a selection whenever I went to auditions or worked at the gym. I proved to be a pretty terrible saleswoman.

In September I started my English Literature course. It proved to be a revelation. I felt as though I'd rediscovered a gift that had been missing for years: my love of reading. I lost myself in Shakespeare, D. H. Lawrence and Oscar Wilde. I spent hours doing the essays and loved every minute of it – something that had never happened at school.

Most of the other students were seventeen or eighteen, having a second stab at their A levels because they failed to get accepted by the university they wanted. Although older, I didn't feel like an outsider and made some friends.

The classes were three days a week, and occasionally I went to the library afterwards. The large mirror still hung on the wall, and I couldn't walk past it without thinking back to when I used to stand on the table and sing 'I Wanna Be A Nightclub Queen' while Mum cleaned the library after hours.

From being an average student at sixteen, I became an excellent one at twenty-one. Instead of struggling at exams or growing bored with assignments, I revelled in the workload. It just goes to show what a few years of growing will do. People peak at different times.

At the same time, the game show in Turkey had been so successful that the station wanted to air it live every weekend. Because of my profile in the local media, I was offered the chance to go back. Cheryl and Sarah didn't return, but Caro had joined the team. We flew to Istanbul each Friday afternoon, filmed on Saturday and Sunday, and then flew back to London on Monday morning so I could go to college. It was perfect – I spent two days living it up in a swish hotel, with plenty of time to do my assignments.

The format of the show hadn't changed, although Ehran, the host, had grown a little rounder and smarmier with his elevation to top-rating TV star. Our interchanges grew more sophisticated. I had to write down a Turkish phrase on the inside of my arm, then he'd introduce the

Mama and her little girl at Whipsnade Zoo. I inherited her Spanish temper, but not her looks.

Playing 'happy families' with Natalie and the doll's house that Dad made. I ended up with the pudding-bowl haircut after catching fleas. Mum had to chase me round the garden with the scissors!

'I Wanna Be A Nightclub Queen'. Two early performances in the back garden at Jubilee Road.

Standing out in a crowd at
Watford Girls' Grammar, 1988.
Well, it wouldn't be hard
in those socks!

Ready to rave!
At seventeen I was the ultimate
wannabe, posing here in my
home-made outfit.

On holiday with Dad. He
was already an old man and was
mistaken for my grandfather.

Dancing up a storm in
Majorca and dreaming of being
'discovered'.

Making up with Mum for
all the worry I'd caused her. She
blamed it on my late blooming.

Max – the perfect big brother.

| HEIGHT | BUST | WAIST | HIPS | DRESS | SHOES | HAIR | EYES |
|--------|------|-------|------|-------|-------|------|------|
| 5'8 | 34C | 24 | 34 | 10 | 3-4 | Red Auburn | Blue |

**MOT**

Baring almost all on my first glamour shoot. I kept imagining I was modelling for a skin-cream advert. *Eduardo Pin*

My modelling zeb card. Notice the little fib about my height.

An early modelling shot –
a very anorexic moment.

A Beverly Goodway Page
Three special for the *Sun*. Can
you spot the flaw? Not just the
swimming muscle but the bad
hairpiece! *The Sun*

My Marianne Faithfull look.

Behind the scenes…

…and on the set of
Turkey's top-rating game show.

A cover girl at last –
although it's hardly *Vogue*.

Ms Motivator – Geri the
aerobics instructor.

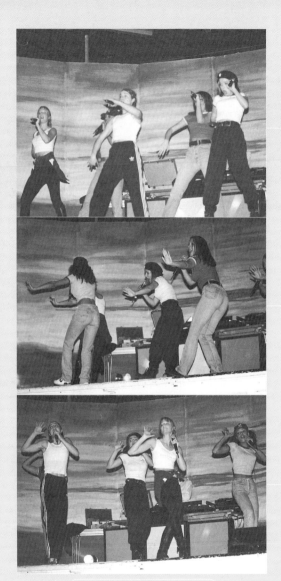

Spice – the début
performance at a church hall in
Finchley in 1994.

show and ask me a question. Like a good straight man, I'd answer and he'd drop the one-liner that had them rolling in the aisles. I still didn't have a bloody clue what he was saying. I just smiled and pretended I got the joke.

On 6 August I celebrated my twenty-first birthday in Istanbul. As the show ended, a large cake was wheeled in and the studio audience sang me 'Happy Birthday'. The photographs appeared in all the Turkish papers the next day. Oddly, I found this quite embarrassing. I didn't mind being in the spotlight when I sought attention, but when it came unexpectedly, or without me asking, I felt awkward and uncomfortable.

Back at the hotel that night, Caro and I were bouncing on the beds and trying to decide how to celebrate.

'This is my year,' I told her. 'If I haven't made it by my twenty-second birthday I'm going to streak at Wimbledon.'

She laughed. 'What makes you so sure?'

'I feel it in here.' I touched my heart. 'It's like an ache.'

Caro had a far more realistic view of her future. If it happened, great. If it didn't, then so be it. 'Not everyone succeeds, Geri. Somebody has to miss out.'

'I know. But that "somebody" isn't going to be me. I can remember being eleven years old and sitting in the back of a car with a friend of mine. We were singing "Careless Whisper". I told Lorraine that I was going to be rich and famous. She said exactly the same thing as you just did: "How can you be so sure?"'

'And what did you say?'

'I bet her fifty quid.'

Caro laughed. 'If you streak at Wimbledon it'll cost you a lot more.'

'I know.'

My fantasy of fame had changed over the years, but not the desire. Once it had been dominated by material things, because I hated being poor and having to scrape pennies together to pay the gas bill or buy someone a birthday card.

I wanted to be rich because I knew it would free me. I would never have to clean floors like my mother or wash people's hair at a salon. At the same time, I knew instinctively that money alone would never stop the ache inside me. If it could, I might as well find another tycoon like Hari, or buy lottery tickets with all my earnings.

When I visualized fame, I wanted people to recognize my face and know my name. I wanted them to like me. Even more importantly, it was the best form of revenge, the ultimate way of saying, 'I told you so,' to all the boyfriends who'd dumped me, the bosses who wouldn't employ me, the directors who hadn't cast me and the agencies who didn't sign me.

My joy came from imagining their faces. All of those people who had ever been rude to me or rejected me or laughed at me. I could go all the way back to Lee and Christopher who snogged me at junior school, through to Adrian Moore at the Hoover shop and Mrs Case at Watford Grammar. It didn't matter how small a role they played. Even the ticket-seller at Watford Cinema who belittled me when I tried to see *Desperately Seeking Susan*. All of them would get an 'I told you so'.

I wanted to prove to them that I could make it. Likewise, I wanted everybody to love me. Some people can go through life not particularly caring what others think of them, but I cared desperately. And the more rejected I felt, the more it fuelled my desire.

* * *

My life now ran to a complicated timetable. On Friday afternoons I flew to Istanbul and returned on Monday morning. Then I had college, the gym, auditions and all my various part-time jobs.

Being so busy, I didn't see much of my family. Sometimes I'd get home from work late and find a note from Dad on the front mat with the mail. He would have driven all the way from Garston to let me know about the highlights of that night's TV viewing.

He had handwriting like a doctor and would scrawl messages about a Jimmy Stewart season on Channel 4, or a BBC wildlife documentary about lions in the Serengeti.

I found him on my doorstep one chilly evening in mid-November.

'How long have you been here?'

'Only just arrived,' he said gruffly, pushing the half-written note into his coat pocket.

'You look half frozen. Come and have a cup of tea.'

While I got changed, Dad wandered around the flat, trying to spot any new purchases. The place had been furnished from jumble sales and the cupboards were full of old-fashioned champagne flutes and dinky teacups that didn't match.

In the open-plan kitchen, Dad paused to look at my collage of photographs and motivational thoughts for the day. I had photographs of Charlie Parsons, the TV producer, and Chris Evans, along with black-and-white shots of Marlene Dietrich and Marilyn Monroe.

Alongside these, I pasted quotations and little bits of inspirational verse. These helped to reassure me whenever I started getting nervous or disheartened.

I made two mugs of tea and listened to Dad reminisce. He was talking about Joyce again, the great love of his life. He had dated her in his youth, but let her get away. She married somebody else, but Dad had never forgotten her. He still saw her occasionally for afternoon tea. They were now both in their seventies, so it was hardly an illicit affair. They were just old friends.

Dad's mind used to wander and he didn't stay on any one subject for too long. He sat buddhalike in the corner with a mug of tea perched on his bloated belly.

'I've been reading this book,' he'd say, never remembering the name. 'It's a story about a bloke who finds a lost city of gold in the Amazon jungle.' Then he proceeded to tell me about the story, ignoring the plot entirely and focusing on some small detail about how wide a piranha can open its jaws and how quickly they strip flesh from bones.

I started mucking about on the out-of-tune piano. I knew only three tunes, including 'Chopsticks', but Dad roared with laughter and almost spilled his tea. He didn't want to go home. That night we watched *It's a Wonderful Life* with Jimmy Stewart.

# HAMLET'S MADNESS

Someone from the English staffroom interrupted the class. I had a telephone call downstairs.

It was Max. 'You have to come home, Geri.'

'Why, what's happened? You sound terrible.'

'I can't tell you on the phone. Just come home.'

I left my books and drove to Natalie's house in Ascot Wood. Max was standing in the doorway as I parked the car.

'Geri, Dad's dead.'

We looked at each other as I fought back the tears. I tried so hard to hold myself together. As soon as he put his arms around my shoulders I knew I was lost. Sitting on the front steps, I burst into tears. Max kept me company.

No, this couldn't be right. Dad can't be dead. When was the last time I saw him? What was the last thing we said to each other? Did I give him a hug? How did he seem?

Someone, somewhere, had made a dreadful mistake. This wasn't supposed to happen. I hadn't planned for this. Not Dad. Not now.

Later that day, I went back to college to collect my things. I told the teacher, 'I'm sorry, I can't join class this afternoon. My father has died.' The words sounded as though someone else had spoken them. Not me; it couldn't be me. How could he die? We'd only just got to know each other.

The previous day, Karen had celebrated her thirty-eighth birthday and the family had arranged a surprise party. I couldn't go because I was in Istanbul. Everyone else had turned up except Dad. They'd wondered why, but he was becoming a little senile and had most likely forgotten the date. He'd probably turn up next week asking, 'Where's the party?'

On Monday morning, Karen went to see how he was, but got no reply from his flat. She called the police and a young constable arrived. They managed to get the door open and found Dad lying naked on the floor with a nicely wrapped present beside him. He'd been getting ready for the party when he'd had a heart attack. He was seventy-one.

I went to see him at the hospital; I suppose I wanted to say goodbye. He lay there, with his face sunken and purple and his nails blackened. He looked like Danny de Vito playing the Penguin in the second Batman film.

Oh, Dad, I don't want to remember you like this. I tried to picture the last time I'd seen him, on that chilly November evening when he'd sat in the corner of my flat with a mug of tea perched on his belly. I'd been mucking about on the piano and Dad thought it was great.

That's just it; he thought everything I did was great. He was a dreamer, just like me. He had mellowed into sweet old age and I had grown up and matured. We understood each other. He enthused about my dreams and I empathized with his. He had always wanted to write a book; I still have the first three minutes on tape, which is as far as he got.

We had never had a standard father/daughter relationship. He was more like a grandfather and I was a little Shirley Temple. We were mates who loved car-boot sales, books and old movies. We debated and agreed to disagree over government spending on the health system and education. He taught me to love old cars, like MGs and Aston Martins.

Now he was dead. I felt gutted, angry, hurt, denied and deprived. I felt robbed of something that was mine. He belonged to me. He was my biggest fan. In my selfish grief, I could think of only me, me, me . . .

I went to the funeral parlour in St Albans Road on Tuesday afternoon. Dad lay in his coffin in the gloomy chapel. Electric candles flickered on a side table and organ music played on a continuous tape.

I edged closer and peered inside.

Dad?

The undertaker had pumped him up and put make-up on his face. He had clown-like red spots on powdered cheeks, thick eyeliner and salmon-pink lips.

I started laughing hysterically.

'Oh, Dad, what have they done to you? You look like a drag queen.'

My tears began falling, splashing onto the polished wood.

That night I went to the theatre. My English class had arranged to see a production of *Hamlet* in the West End. For a few hours, at least, I was transported into another tragedy. Alan Cumming played Hamlet brilliantly, spitting and crying with a tortured madness as he mourned his father's death.

The next morning, two black cars arrived at Karen's house in Chorley Wood to take family members to the funeral. On the drive to Garston Crematorium, I refused to cry. I wanted to get through it without breaking down.

Several times I wavered during the service. Particularly when they played 'Danny Boy' as the curtain came down and the coffin disappeared. It was awful.

Afterwards, the others went to look at the wreaths and condolence cards, but I went for a walk through the grounds. Only when alone, out of sight, did I start to cry.

I felt as though my tears were for Dad and no-one else. My number one supporter had gone. Now he'd never see me finally make it. I was wrong about fame being the ultimate form of revenge; it was also the best way of repaying those people who had never lost faith in me. Dad had been first among them.

In the weeks that followed, I wandered about in a daze. My weight had fallen to a little over six stone. I lived on a diet of apples, crushed ice and black coffee. Natalie and Karen were pressuring me to eat more. Secretly, I liked the attention.

When I picked up Natalie from work she said I looked disgusting.

'I'm fine.'

'What have you eaten today?'

'I've had two apples.'

'Geri, you have to eat! You're gonna get sick.'

Mum would arrive at my flat with home-cooked pasta

and meals designed to build up body fat in underweight people.

'I'm not eating that,' I said as she unpacked it.

'At least have the pasta. It's vegetarian. Hardly any calories.'

'Not after I've gone to all this trouble to get thin.'

I had added a new job to my collection – working at Shakers, a wine bar in Market Street, opposite the colour copy shop. I wore black tights and hot pants to work, trying to make myself appear thinner. I didn't see the horror on people's faces when they told me I was too skinny. Instead, I took the comments as compliments. Yet inside I felt almost paralysed by sadness and exhaustion. At home, I sat for hours staring at nothing and could barely bring myself to open my mail because I didn't want to read any more rejection letters. The worst times were late at night, when the depression seemed almost suffocating.

A month after Dad died, I wrote in my diary:

*I am enjoying being single. The selfish part, living just for me. But I am lonely – I just can't help it. I start thinking, What will I do?*

*Mmmm, eat?*

*No, I try not to binge through boredom. Eating for the sake of it is just an attempt to fill a gap.*

*I hate my lack of control. I am a fat bitch. I am so tired of life.*

*Come on, Geri. Time to dream. Dream of paradise – an island somewhere with the sun shining. Far away from any pain and sorrow. I'll have loads of energy and laughter. But my ambition just won't let go. I have to keep trying.*

During the days I tried to be positive. The plan was still the same – to fill my life with adventure, a career, fortune and fame. But at night I went tumbling down again.

Christmas made things worse. It had always been a depressing time for me, since the days of the divided house in Jubilee Road, eating chips and chops downstairs while Dad stayed in his bedroom.

Trying to lift my spirits, I made a conscious effort to get out and visit friends and family. For some inexplicable reason, I put on a bridesmaid's dress belonging to Amanda, my niece. She had worn it at Max's wedding when she was barely ten years old – that's how much weight I'd lost.

I didn't notice the shocked looks when I arrived at each new house wearing the blue dress with puffy sleeves. People spoke to me, but I wasn't listening. Nobody could reach me. Something had died inside.

## Saturday, 12 March 1994

*Hello diary, three months have passed since I last wrote and I am sinking. I am drowning in my sorrow, such self-absorbed tears. I feel such conflict, pain, sadness, misery, loneliness and helplessness.*

*Where is that Geri I used to know, full of ambition and motivation? These days the blues are surely over-taking. I know I have this thing sitting on my shoulder. I am ashamed, so ashamed of it. It haunts me, holds me, traps me. I am imprisoned within my own head. It feels like a weight pulling me down. These past few months I can honestly say have been the most miserable time of my life.*

*It's 11.26 p.m. I cancelled yet another date tonight for an early night, but I'm still awake.*

*Depression!!!!!!!*

*I feel so soft and tender-hearted; I can crumble at someone's touch. Why is Karen so strong – she hasn't had it easy – and I am a pathetic heap? I could slap my face. Wake up, Geri!*

*Am I just moaning? Is this part of the process of grieving? Am I normal?*

*My system feels like it is shutting down. It wants out. I've had it.*

*I think of killing myself, but then I think of my family and how selfish it would be. I'd probably mess it up and just look like an attention seeker.*

I decided not to do any more modelling or game-show hosting as they hadn't led anywhere. With so little energy, I had to concentrate on one particular thing – make one big push and see if I could achieve something worthwhile.

What about music? If I could have a hit single, on the strength of that I could get a presenting job or become an actress. I could change my life.

I found a recording studio near Watford Junction that would help me put together a demo. It would cost £300 for two songs – money I had to save, so I took on more jobs. I now had six, although I got sacked from one cleaning job for eating their cookies.

One song had been chosen. I wanted to do a cover of the old Seventies hit 'A Lover's Holiday', by a group called Change. A songwriter at the studio had offered to write me a second song, but it turned out to be slushy rubbish.

'I'll come back in a few hours,' I told him.

As I left the studio I saw a motorbike accident. A young guy, still with L-plates, went over the bonnet of a car that had pulled out of a driveway without looking. It must have happened just before I arrived, because the back wheel of the crushed motorbike was still spinning. The rider lay in the gutter, with one leg twisted impossibly beneath him. Blood covered his neck and he didn't seem to be conscious.

This terrible image stayed with me. Lost in thought, I drove past Fairlawns and into the countryside. Eventually, I parked on a muddy track covered in autumn leaves. It seemed to be an ancient wood, with old trees that groaned as the branches shifted in the wind.

Finding a pen and a piece of paper in the glove compartment, I wrote down the words to a song. I can only remember snatches of it now.

Love to love, live to love, that's what you've got to do.
Live to love, love to live, try to see it through . . .

Back at the studio it was put to music, ready to be recorded the following day. That night I came down with a terrible cold. My head felt so stuffed up that I could hardly hear myself talk. How typical! Having worked six jobs to get the £300 for the studio I was going to sound terrible.

I chopped up six cloves of garlic and mixed it with honey, swallowing the lot. It burned all the way down my throat, but seemed to clear me out.

The recording studio was a dreary old room with a creaking wooden stand. I had no idea how the process worked, but how different could it be from singing into a hairbrush? I'd had plenty of practice at that.

'We're going to take the song line by line,' the producer said.

'Don't I sing it right through?'

'No. Just do a line.'

Each song was broken down into parts and I sang them over and over. I lost count of how many takes I did. The entire process felt alien and discouraging. It was almost mechanical in its coldness, with no chance of getting emotion or passion into a song.

The demo wasn't great, but I didn't expect miracles. As long as a record company took a closer look at me that would be enough.

Anthony Blackburn had a contact at EMI and he sent him the demo, along with my old modelling zeb card. At the same time I found a music manager called Derek Price, who had an office in Kensal Town near the Grand Union Canal. He wore a wig that made him look like an Elvis wannabe.

'Yeah, Geri, faaaabulous. I'm gonna make you the new Betty Boo,' he exclaimed. 'You're gonna be big, Geri. B–I–G!'

Derek had all sorts of angles and ideas. He saw himself as the next Stock, Aitken and Waterman of Music Factory fame. He claimed to know all the top songwriting teams and A & R reps for the big labels.

Not entirely believing his patter, I sent the demo to another agent, Richard Foster, who I'd met a few months earlier. Although not a big name, Richard seemed especially interested in me and encouraged me to write more songs. He had a house in Chiswick and was very level-headed and sensible, particularly when compared to Derek.

With so many positive vibes, I began to cheer up a little. My depression seemed to come in waves, so I had good days and bad. On the bad days, I would go to the supermarket, buy the most fattening food and then puke it up before going straight back to bed. Then I'd simply lay there, staring at the ceiling for what seemed like hours.

The only time I broke free of my depression was during my English Literature classes. I felt no pressure; I was good at it. On my mid-year report card, the English tutor wrote:

'An enthusiastic and hard-working student, capable of perceptive insight of literary texts and penetrating analysis of the central themes. Geri is able to think for herself and express ideas of her own, expressing them often in a most engaging and interesting manner.

My old modelling agency MOT called me unexpectedly. They had a job for me on a video shoot for Pink Floyd. Although disillusioned with modelling, I thought I might make some useful music contacts.

The production team had set up in a warehouse in Acton, West London. They were trying to film backing visuals to be used during Pink Floyd's 1994 UK concert tour. I was cast because I had a Forties, sweater-girl look, although I'd lost so much weight that I looked more like Twiggy than Betty Grable.

They dressed me as a wartime factory girl loading bullets into tins on a production line. The shoot took half a day and I met a guy called Dave, who seemed quite nice. He was a male model and said he had a Levis contract, which I didn't believe.

The worst ones are always those who haven't quite made it, because they always talk up their experience. Occasionally I did that sort of thing at auditions, but never with other wannabes. Dave didn't seem to differentiate, as I discovered on my one and only date with him a week later.

He picked me up from the station at Greenwich in his black Mini, having just passed his driving test. Then we spent a few hours wandering around the antique shops and markets. Pretty soon it became evident that Dave was all beefcake and not much else.

It had been eight months since I'd split up with Sean, but I wasn't ready for another boyfriend. I had enough trouble dealing with my own insecurities, without trying to sort out Dave's problems. I pecked him on the cheek and said goodbye, expecting to never hear from him again.

The advertisement in *The Stage* read:

TANK GIRL AUDITION
The MGM Trocadero, Piccadilly.
WE ARE SEARCHING FOR THE STAR OF THIS
FUTURISTIC ACTION FEATURE FILM!
*TANK GIRL*

'... A stunning woman in her twenties – spirited, sexy, quick-witted, irreverent and tough, possessing a rugged rock & roll spirit! Able to take care of herself in most situations, both physically and mentally, and rides a water buffalo ...'

The queue outside the Trocadero stretched along the street and around the block. I arrived at 10 a.m. and it took two hours to reach the front doors of the cinema. I'll be really inventive, I thought, as I spent hours preparing my costume of ripped fishnet tights, with denim shorts over the top, a cut-off T-shirt and big air wear boots. I did my hair in tight nodules.

'Not bad,' I thought out loud. Then I saw the other girls. There must have been a hundred of them dressed up as Tank Girl, all of them wearing almost identical outfits to mine.

Inside the foyer, I gave my name and address at a registration desk and was given a number. Thankfully, I could now sit down. My feet were killing me and I hadn't eaten all day. I sat opposite the snack bar and rested my portfolio between my knees.

A tall, tanned girl with long brown hair and a smart suit pushed through the doors. She stopped suddenly, took one look at the competition and announced in a cockney voice, 'I didn't know we 'ad to come as Tank Girl, did I?'

She took a number and found a space beside me.

'Hi, I'm Geri,' I said.

'Victoria.'

She glanced around at the various Tank Girl lookalikes. Another girl sitting near by asked about my portfolio and I started showing her my photographs. Victoria took an interest, and soon I was telling them about glamour work, trying to put a positive spin on the whole thing.

I was so hungry I felt ready to faint. My blood sugar level had dropped. The snack bar was across the foyer, but I'd left my money in the car. I just needed something to tide me over.

Glancing from side to side, I checked the coast was clear. Then I sauntered over to the unattended snack bar and casually took a packet of Butterkist popcorn. My hands were shaking as I opened it. Then I shared it with Victoria and my other new friend.

At that moment, the attendant – a woman in her mid-twenties wearing a uniform and a permanent scowl – came back. She was obviously pissed off with all these people messing up her foyer. Her life would be a lot easier if nobody went to the movies.

'You stole that,' she said, loud enough for most of Piccadilly to hear her.

I turned red.

Next to me, Victoria whispered, 'What have you just done?' She looked horrified.

'You stole that!'

Everyone was staring at me.

'You stole that popcorn. You're a thief. I should call the police.'

I wanted to explain, but I couldn't find the words. Anyone could see I was anorexic. I would have paid, I just didn't have the money.

The woman stormed off, and I half-expected her to summon the manager or the police. For goodness' sake, it was only a bag of popcorn! I smiled apologetically at Victoria as we both ate the evidence.

Ten girls at a time were being called by number and escorted into the cinema. There must have been another exit, because no-one ever came back out into the foyer. I couldn't get an inkling of what was happening inside. Did they want a reading? What sort of voice would Tank Girl use? I'm pretty good with accents.

A young student type with a clipboard poked his head round the door. 'Numbers one seven one to one eighty.'

I walked down between the rows of cinema seats and stood in a line-up at the bottom. The seats were tiered, and about ten people were slouching, sitting or propped forward in the front row, already exhausted. I felt as if I was in a police identity parade, but tried to ooze sex appeal and screen presence from every pore.

'Hi. OK, girls, relax. I know you're probably very nervous.' An attractive woman in her thirties, with a ponytail and an oversized jumper, began explaining about the audition. 'First we'd like to know a bit about each of you, so starting from the right, can you tell us a bit about yourself?'

Christ, what am I going to say! I hate it when they do this. Why don't they give me something to read? Then I won't sound like an idiot. Think, Geri, think!

I tried to script something in my head, but I couldn't help listening to the girls before me. Oh, that was good. I wish I'd said that. Oh no, it's my turn next. I don't know what to say. Aaaarrrgh!

'Hello, I'm Geri Halliwell, I'm twenty-two and a Leo. I'm loud and I'm proud and I think I'd make a great Tank Girl.'

And that's it. That's what I said! My big chance to be Tank Girl and I said something so soppy and stupid as 'loud and proud'. Yuk! A Leo? For God's sake!

Not that it mattered. The girl after me made sure that I was eminently forgettable. She didn't have to say a word. Instead, she simply lifted her top up and showed her tits. Victoria, who was next to her, turned her head in shock, her mouth agape, and said, 'Well, I can't beat that, can I?'

My sentiments exactly.

Outside, a television crew was doing interviews about the auditions. Already I felt that the whole day had been a set-up to get advance publicity and funding for the film. It made me angry that so many girls had just been used.

'How did the audition go?' asked the reporter.

I turned to the camera. 'Good, if you're a bald-headed lesbian who looks like a weightlifter.' I strode off in a huff.

The dark cloud that had pervaded my life since Dad's death refused to lift. Each time a ray of light broke through, something happened to snuff it out.

The worst times were when I was alone at night; I'd sink so deeply into depression that I lay on my mattress, struggling to breathe.

I wrote in my diary:

### Thursday, 12 May 1994

*It is crippling me, I cannot move. It paralyses my rational thought. My body, my inspiration, my motivation. I enjoy nothing. I am existing in a lonely world of turmoil and confusion. I have no voice, only tears.*

*The world is spinning, but I'm drifting aimlessly, unable to get on board. I want to, but it's spinning too fast. I have neither the will nor the energy.*

*Is this just a lesson in life? Am I normal?*

*I want a recess. Call a time-out.*

The next morning, I scribbled the postscript: 'Hello, I'm still here.'

Later I watched the movie *Groundhog Day*, starring

Bill Murray, and had a good laugh. It made me realize that I should live each day as though it was my last. I should strive to be better and learn from my mistakes.

Glancing at my reflection in the bedroom mirror, I scolded myself for being so negative. Then a scrap of newspaper caught my eye. I had taped it to the mirror weeks earlier, after tearing it from *The Stage*.

R U 18–23 with the ability to sing/dance? R U streetwise, ambitious, outgoing and determined?

An all-girl band was being put together. I'd thought it was a good idea but hadn't gone to the audition. I remembered why: I'd been to Spain for a few days to see my uncle and his family, and they had taken me skiing in the Pyrenees and I'd managed to get horribly sunburned. My face had swelled until I looked like the Elephant Man.

I looked at the advertisement again. I don't know why I'd kept it. I'm always sticking reminder notes on mirrors, or writing phone numbers on scraps of paper.

The audition had been nearly two months earlier. Surely they wouldn't still be looking. Forcing myself to be more confident and optimistic, I dialled the number.

'Hi. Look, I'm sorry to call out of the blue like this. I kept your ad about the all-girl band. Are you still auditioning?'

The guy on the phone sounded quite young. 'Yeah, we're pretty much done.'

'So, I'm wasting my time?'

'We're down to the last twelve. They're auditioning next week.'

'I couldn't make the first try-out; I wasn't feeling well. I'd be really good. I've done some singing and modelling.'

'OK, you can come along. I'll put your name on the shortlist.'

Amazing! Hundreds of girls must have replied to the ad. Why did they suddenly let me jump the queue when I was two months late? Instead of being elated, I had doubts. These guys were obviously amateurs. No professional operation would be run like that.

The final audition was planned for Wednesday at a studio in Shepherd's Bush. I couldn't get excited. My weight had fallen to six stone and I barely had the energy to get out of bed. I cancelled my gym class on Tuesday and didn't want to leave the flat.

Dragging myself up, I went to the shops and bought a doughnut. Straight away it came up again. I couldn't keep any food down.

A friend Sue Joblin dropped round in the afternoon. She was Karen's ex-lodger and now had a big house in Fairlawns. Sue had once suffered from anorexia and bulimia and had recognized the symptoms in me. Although others, like Natalie and Mum, were worried, they didn't realize how bad it had become.

Sue tried to show me pictures of herself when she was anorexic. She also had a diary that she had written. She wanted me to read passages so that we could talk about them. I still hadn't admitted to having a problem, although I realized that people were worried about me. Instead of taking them seriously, I quite liked the attention.

'Geri, you have to accept that this is an illness. You're not well. Seek help.'

'I'm fine. I'm just depressed. Too many rejection letters.'

'What else have you eaten today?'

I couldn't remember. I tried to have breakfast and then I went back to bed. The doughnut came later.

'This is ridiculous, Geri. I want to call a doctor.'

'No, I'm OK. It's just a bad day.'

As far as I was concerned, it wasn't the lack of calories or my revolving-door stomach that had caused my lethargy and depression, I was simply sick of failing. I couldn't fight any more.

'I'm not going tomorrow,' I said, too tired to even contemplate it.

'You have to go. It's down to the last twelve girls. Five get chosen. They're great odds.'

'No. I'm not up to it. Look at me.'

For a moment I could see a hint of acceptance in Sue's eyes.

'Pick yourself up, Geri. You don't want to die wondering.'

'No. I've had enough.'

That night I lay in bed and wrote:

*I feel like a saturated flannel is covering my face, soaking into me. What the hell is going on? Why am I like this? I just want to wake up and feel my old self. I feel as though I'm getting on everyone's nerves – my sullen face, my sunken smile and my continual frown. I'm always on the brink of tears. It's crippling me, I can't move. I enjoy nothing. I'm just existing.*

*It would be easier if I had no will left. I could join Daddy. No, I can't be a bloody quitter.*

*I can count on one hand how many times I've laughed this year. Really laughed – truly, madly, deeply.*

*Now I just want to be happy for the moment – not in the expectation of things to come. I hate being so pathetic. It's like a disease. I've caught Hamlet's madness for self-analysis and introspection.*

I managed to sleep and woke when I heard the milkman's rattling float. I lay there, staring at the clock. To go or not to go, that is the question.

Maybe I'll just go as far as the kitchen and make a cup of tea. Then I'll decide.

# 9

## 'IF ONLY'

The narrow backstreets of Shepherd's Bush don't surrender parking spaces very easily. I squeezed in on a corner and quickly checked my make-up. 'OK, Geri, show them what you're made of,' I told myself, trying to sound convincing.

Nomis Studios was located in a low building, surrounded by terraced houses with net curtains. The foyer was quite dark and the receptionist didn't look up as I gave her my name. She pointed me towards a cafeteria set off to one side and told me to wait until I was called.

I hadn't been quite sure what to wear, so I'd settled for a pair of hot pants, a Barbie T-shirt and platform shoes, with my hair in plaits and a pink bobble jumper flung over the top. Cute and quirky – my normal style. There were other girls waiting, and I could sense them sneaking a look over their magazines, summing up the competition. I couldn't blame them, I did the same. I noticed a girl with short blond hair and a long nose. She didn't look particularly attractive, but I soon discovered that she had a great voice.

One by one our names were called. Inside the studio, there were several chairs arranged in front of a low stage occupied by a keyboard and a dozen stools. The management team, Bob and Chris Herbert, were father and son.

Bob looked like an extra from *Miami Vice*. He had a suntan and wore a white suit, pale-blue shirt and brogues. He had gold rings on his fingers and looked like he was in his late forties. His son, Chris, was long and lean, with a Timberland shirt hanging out of his jeans and his hair slicked back. I think he quite fancied himself.

'Tell us about yourself,' he asked.

I showed them a few of my best modelling shots and began relating my musical background, exaggerating like crazy. Describing the demo, I made myself sound like a seasoned session singer. In reality, I hadn't sung since then.

'How old are you?' asked Chris.

'I'm as old or as young as you want me to be,' I said. 'I can be a twelve-year-old with big boobs if you like.'

Then I sang my old favourite, 'I Wanna Be A Nightclub Queen'. I have quite a deep voice, with a whisky and cigarettes kind of sound that suits slow, sexy numbers.

I couldn't properly gauge the competition because I only managed to catch the girl before me and the one after.

Melanie Brown looked incredibly beautiful and cool, with huge brown eyes and amazingly big hair. She wore a cap on back to front, knee socks and a little mini skirt, all in beige. She looked wicked!

Then I spied Victoria Adams from the *Tank Girl* audition and she smiled in recognition.

All of us were called into the studio and divided into

two groups of six. Immediately, I realized that I'd made the reject pile, with the girls who weren't as pretty or as talented. Mel and Victoria were in the other bunch.

Bob gave us a cassette player. 'I'm giving you a song. I'm sure you'll know it – 'Just A Step From Heaven' by Eternal. Each group has to put together a dance routine and come back.'

I trooped into the corridor outside, already fearing the worst. I'm fine doing my own dance steps, but lousy at learning a routine. A girl with blond curly hair and a loud northern accent took it upon herself to choreograph our group.

'All right, we're gonna do this and then this,' she said, showing us the routine. God, it was crap! Real Eighties-style body-popping and head-rolling stuff. I had trouble picking it up, and halfway through our performance I lost touch and just freestyled. It probably saved me because it marked me out as being a little different.

The other group was great. They had some really cool and funky moves – pure Janet Jackson – and I so wished I was one of them. Well, that's it, I thought, end of audition.

Then Bob motioned to me, 'Geri, I want you to change groups. Go off and learn the routine.'

Part of me froze. Victoria and Melanie had both obviously had some dance training and made it all look so easy. I was terrible at picking things up. The other group also had Michelle Stephenson, a well-spoken student from Oxfordshire, and a Welsh girl who sang like an angel.

Thirty minutes later we reappeared, and I managed to keep up for the first bit before I lost it totally. Again, I kept smiling and improvised with my own little wiggle, trying to pick it up again. Bob and Chris didn't seem to mind.

Afterwards, they got each of us to do another solo number. Melanie sang 'Queen of the Night' by Whitney Houston and I thought she sounded fantastic. She was clearly a favourite.

As the audition ended, I went up to Melanie and told her, 'You really are beautiful.' She had a booming northern laugh.

'Where are you going now?'

'Home to Leeds.'

'Do you want a lift to the station?'

'Sure. Why walk, eh?'

As we chatted in the car, we just clicked. We seemed to have so much in common. She'd left school at sixteen and danced in nightclubs. And for two years she'd been turning up at auditions, hoping for a break.

Bob and Chris had narrowed their list to five girls, but none of our places were guaranteed. So far they had only heard us sing individually. The next step was to see how our voices blended as a group. We were each given a tape of a song they wanted us to learn: 'Signed Sealed Delivered I'm Yours' by Stevie Wonder.

I practised the song every day for a week until I was virtually singing it in my sleep. There were builders outside, painting the various cottages at Fairlawns, and each time I walked outside they shouted to me, 'Sounding good, Geri,' or 'Getting better, love'.

I still had dark days, when I struggled to get out of bed. Life seemed pointless. Why bother rehearsing? The spring flowers were blooming outside and the trees were in full leaf, but I didn't see the colours. The world had become almost monochrome since Dad's death.

A week later the final candidates met again at Nomis Studios for a second audition. For some reason the Welsh girl didn't turn up. Another girl had taken her place, Melanie Chisholm, aged nineteen. She came through the door wearing a black top with two white stripes down the sides, an A-line skirt and trainers. Her hair was in a plait that fell down her back.

Mel C had a dancer's air about the way she walked and held her shoulders like a gymnast about to perform a floor routine. She had taken part in the original audition of 400 girls and had made the shortlist. Unfortunately, she'd had tonsillitis and couldn't make the previous week's try-out. Tonsillitis plagued her until she had them out.

Bob and Chris had us stand around a piano and sing the Stevie Wonder song. Victoria, who had been in a band before, automatically assumed that she was the lead singer and began dominating the vocals. She was very showy, as if she was auditioning for a role in a West End musical.

The rest of us looked at her strangely, thinking, What's going on here?

Mel B's voice was quite deep, as well as strong and soulful. Beside her, Mel C seemed confident and relaxed, as though she'd been doing this all her life. Michelle's voice was the most controlled and well trained. Her breathing was perfect. And she could hold notes with an operatic resonance and power.

All of us were a little hesitant at first. I probably hung back the most. I tried to half sing and hide myself among the others.

We had no experience at singing harmonies and sounded terrible. Each of us had a different interpretation of the song and was either half a beat slower or faster. The end result sounded more like a pub karaoke night than a polished quintet.

Bob and Chris didn't seem too concerned. The next stage of their plan was to see how well we combined and if we had the right personal chemistry to get on with each other. Bob planned to put us up in a guesthouse in Surrey for a week. During that time, we would put together a routine and perform for the mystery backer of the enterprise, whom none of us had met.

'We start a week on Sunday,' said Bob, giving us the address of the guesthouse.

'What if we've got jobs?' asked Michelle Stephenson, who had a rather clipped, private-school accent.

'Resign.'

'What about money?'

'Go on the dole.' Bob fixed her with a stern look. The message was clear; anybody not totally committed to the band should leave now.

I didn't know what to do. Richard, the agent in Chiswick, had been really encouraging me to write my own songs. He seemed confident that I could have a solo career. Should I go with the girls, or stick with him?

I asked a DJ friend what I should do. 'Girl bands don't work,' he said bluntly.

I disagreed with him. The music scene *needed* young, positive female recording artists. At twelve years old I had Madonna to look up to. The teenagers today needed someone like that.

Why should boy bands dominate the charts? There hadn't been a major all-girl group since Bananarama in the mid-Eighties. The time was right.

Although I barely knew any of them, I chose to stick with the girls. Nothing I did was half-hearted. I now had a mission. I was going to be in an all-girl band and we were going to be bigger than Take That and New Kids on the Block.

Only a few days earlier I'd been drowning in self-pity. My elusive big break seemed further away than ever. Suddenly my life had been transformed. I'd been thrown a life-line and grabbed it with both hands.

All my daydreams became filled with images of pop-music stardom – limousines, press conferences and appearances on *Top of the Pops*. What would the doubters say when I proved them wrong?

I had always loved music, but I had never tried to determine what made a song popular or memorable. As a child I used to make up my own little tunes and, later, in my teens, I often put lyrics into instrumental bits of songs. A melody either stuck in the mind or it didn't. Now I listened to songs with a totally different mindset. I tried to break them down into parts and listen to the harmonies and vocal styles.

Because I had no formal singing training, I tried to pick up hints and strengthen my voice. I listened to the radio constantly, often singing along in my car as I drove to the gym. God knows what other drivers thought when they stopped at lights and looked across to see me belting out the latest Janet Jackson hit.

On Sunday afternoon I drove to the guesthouse in Surrey. It was run by a scout master and seemed to be full of insurance salesmen. I hadn't seen the girls since the audition, although I'd phoned Victoria during the week just to make sure the whole scheme wasn't a figment of my imagination.

We shared a room at the guesthouse, although Victoria took up most of it with her two massive suitcases.

She was a girl's girl, very feminine and soft, and she went straight to my bag and began talking about clothes. Like me, she could remember where she'd bought every item in her wardrobe and how much she had paid, including the discounts.

'I should take you to the car-boot sales,' I told her. 'You get some amazing bargains.'

Victoria looked bemused at the thought of wearing second-hand clothes. She bought directly from the high street.

That afternoon we drove ten miles to Trinity Studios, an ageing dance hall with paint peeling from the walls and rusting radiators that rattled but remained permanently cold. It was the sort of place where they had old ladies tap-dancing at three o'clock, ballroom dancing at five and the church bingo sessions on Friday nights.

The song we had been given to learn, 'Take Me Away', was a mid-tempo ballad written by a songwriting team and no doubt rejected by half a dozen bands. None of us particularly liked it. The lyrics were awful and completely negative.

Our first attempts at the song were abysmal. Enter Pepi Lemer, a singing teacher who looked like a pint-sized version of Barbra Streisand. She must have been about forty, and had great legs and a greasy patch of hair on the back of her head.

Pepi was enormously patient and sweet-natured. Right from the beginning we decided there would be no lead singer. None of us wanted to feel like a bridesmaid, singing, 'ooh aah ooh' in the background. Instead, we would try to become a perfectly blended five-part vocal group. This obviously made Pepi's job that much harder.

We delegated who was to sing a particular section of the song and then combined for the chorus. Each of these attempts was recorded on a cassette player and then played back to us. We sounded awful.

Pepi pulled my shoulders back. 'Try to blend, Geri. Can you hear it?'

I nodded.

'Mel, you're flat,' said Pepi.

'No, I'm not.'

'Yes, definitely flat. And, Michelle, you were too slow.' She clapped her hands to the beat.

Poor old Pepi. It can't have been easy. Michelle sounded like we were at Covent Garden opera house. I lacked confidence or any formal musical training. By comparison, Mel C seemed incredibly relaxed, as though she had done this a thousand times.

The name of the song turned out to be very appropriate. Poor old Pepi's nerves steadily deteriorated over the week. Finally she snapped and shrieked, 'Take me away!'

This seemed more like slow torture than training. Each morning we arrived at Trinity Studios at ten o'clock and didn't leave until late afternoon. As well as singing, we choreographed a dance routine, practising the steps until we could have done it blindfold and not missed a beat.

'Right, come on, we're gonna do this,' Mel B said in her booming northern voice. She showed us an idea and Mel C would suggest an extra move. Both of them had been trained as dancers, particularly Mel C, who had won awards for gymnastics and ballet when she was at school.

Victoria had also done singing and been to dance school as a youngster. I marvelled at how quickly they picked up new routines.

Mum could never afford to send me to ballet lessons. I remember being eight years old when I finally cajoled her into letting me go to dance classes that were held in a hall on a council estate. When I arrived, I discovered that the other girls were all aged five and younger. I felt stupid and went home.

How I wished I'd stayed. Podium dancing at raves and Greek nightclubs was no substitute for formal training. At times I felt like I had two left feet, and Mel B grew increasingly frustrated at my lack of co-ordination.

Michelle also struggled, although she didn't seem as bothered. I desperately wanted to get it right, fearing they might drop me from the band.

At night we went out to the pub or the pizza parlour. The others ate second helpings, while I picked at the edges. We had been together only a few days yet I felt an amazing affinity with the girls. Our lives had been remarkably similar, except perhaps for Michelle, who'd had a more middle-class upbringing.

'I had posters of Adam Ant, Bruce Willis and Madonna,' said Mel C as we discussed our teenage fixations.

'Adam Ant?' bellowed Mel B. 'Who?'

We all laughed.

'I was dead cool,' announced Mel B. 'I liked Neneh Cherry and Bobby Brown.'

Victoria had a confession to make. She had once wanted to marry Matt Goss from Bros. We howled her down. 'It gets worse,' she said. 'My first-ever favourite band was Bucks Fizz. They had a song where the men ripped the skirts off the girls. My mum made me a skirt just like it.'

After a week of rehearsing, we had our showcase for the silent partner in the management team. We all dressed in black and white, but in different combinations. I wore hot pants and a T-shirt; Michelle Stephenson wore a baby-doll dress and the others had black trousers and white shirts.

An E-type Jag delivered a tall man in his sixties, who strolled into the studio with the casual walk of somebody who owned the place. Four steps behind him came a short, tubby sidekick.

Bob did the introductions. 'Hello, girls. This is Chic Murphy. He's paying for all this.'

The tall man grinned. He had grey hair and a small cross tattooed on one ear.

'Nice to meet you, girls,' he said in a thick cockney accent.

Chic looked like an endearing old rogue, the sort of character who I imagined would have known all the East End haunts in the days of Reggie and Ronnie Kray. He claimed to have once managed one of the Three Degrees – 'the famous one'.

Two chairs were found for Chic and his sidekick. We launched into our one-song repertoire, trying to ignore Pepi at the back of the hall, who made all sorts of gestures about breathing and tempo.

Chic was snapping his fingers. 'Ya gotta do like the Four Tops, girls . . . Yeah, that's the way . . . Ya gotta do it like that . . . Smokin'!'

Afterwards he announced, 'Yeah, that's good, girls, I think this could work.'

None of us knew what the next step would be. A week's work and one song hardly equipped us to take the pop world by storm. Bob and Chris chatted with Chic and then came back with a proposal. Chic had a vacant house in Boyne Hill Road, Maidenhead. Us girls were to move in together and spend the spring and summer rehearsing. He would cover our expenses.

We were given a fortnight to sort out our affairs. I held on to my lovely little flat in Fairlawns, not willing to burn that bridge just yet.

To complicate matters, I had a phone call from a producer at L!VE TV. It had been a year since I'd made the pilot for *London Live* and 'Fashion Police' and the fate of the show had been in the balance since then. A decision had finally been made and the new head of programming at the channel, Janet Street-Porter, wanted to see me.

I took the call at Mum's house.

'What shall I do?' I asked Max. 'Should I go? This could be five grand a week.'

'What about the band?'

'I know, I know. But what if it doesn't work out? What if we disappear without trace?'

I was torn between being sensible and pragmatic or following my gut instincts. Did I take the money and short-term security of L!VE TV? Or stick it out with the girls, getting paid nothing? Having fought so hard for so long to get interviews I didn't have the courage to turn one down.

L!VE TV had moved into offices at Canary Wharf in London's Docklands. I clipped the visitor's pass to my jacket and followed the security guard through the open-plan office. Boxes were still being unpacked and wires snaked across the floor and dangled from open ceiling panels. The station wasn't due to begin broadcasting until September.

Janet Street-Porter had a panoramic view of London from her office, stretching along the Thames as far as the Houses of Parliament. Her unique voice could be heard from halfway across the room.

Plastic sheets covered the new carpet in the conference room. Janet and Nick Ferrari sat opposite me at a long table. I thought it was quite ironic to be meeting Janet Street-Porter. Five years earlier, she'd been a fleeting figure in my life when I shook my butt at *Dance Energy*, trying to get noticed by the roving cameraman. Since then she had left the BBC, although as far as I knew Normski was still her boyfriend.

'So what have you been doing?' she asked.

'I've been making music. I'm in a band.'

'Sounds great,' she replied, totally uninterested. 'Do you still want to do this show?'

'Um . . . I think so.'

Janet was quite up-front about interviewing a range of people and tinkering with the format of the show. She has so much energy and enthusiasm that I should have been bouncing out of my chair, raring to go. Instead I felt vacant.

It was the worst interview performance I have ever given, and I could see Nick Ferrari thinking, What's going on here? Where's the bubbly girl I met a year ago?

Not surprisingly, I didn't hear from Janet again. I had made up my mind before I even left her office that my heart wasn't in L!VE TV. I had incredible faith that the band could make it. If I walked away now, perhaps we'd never know.

Later, at home, I told Max, 'Look, I can be a TV presenter any time, but I can only be a pop star once, when I'm young.'

Back at my flat in Fairlawns, I loaded up the Fiat Uno with suitcases, boxes, a beanbag and two potted plants.

Maidenhead is about thirty miles west of London. It has a working-class end of town and a middle-class end, with Boyne Hill Road somewhere in the middle. Chic's house was semi-detached by a matter of inches and sat on a hill about five minutes' drive from the town. At the bottom of the road was a pub, a corner shop and a railway bridge.

The old-fashioned semi had a back garden full of rubbish and mounds of soil behind the washing line. Our neighbours consisted of an elderly couple on one side and a fireman and his pot-head mate on the other.

Inside, the house was clean and functional. It had obviously been decorated cheaply – blue-grey carpet covered the floors, the curtains were pink and the rooms were full of second-hand furniture.

There were three bedrooms. The two Melanies shared the main one, along with the double bed until we could find some more furniture. Victoria and Michelle had the second bedroom, while I had a shoebox-sized room all to myself.

I had never lived with so many people and it took a while to get used to the general level of mess and noise. On the first morning, it took me three-quarters of an hour to get into the bathroom. Inside, I found more shampoos and make-up than you'd find in your average Body Shop.

Downstairs there were coffee cups piled in the sink, shoes tossed casually beneath the coffee table and knickers drying over the radiators.

None of this bothered me. It felt like a summer camp or an extended pyjama party.

On our second night, we discovered the salad bar at the local Pizza Hut. It cost £2.50 to stuff your face. Discussions turned to the band and we decided to lay down some ground rules.

'If anyone has a problem, they speak up or shut up,' I said, kicking off the policy discussion.

'We don't let boyfriends get in the way,' contributed Mel B. She raised an eyebrow at Victoria and Michelle.

'We make decisions together,' I added.

'All expenses are shared,' offered Mel C. 'But that doesn't mean I'm paying for other people's phone calls.'

'We'll have an itemized bill,' suggested Victoria.

There was an electricity in the air, a sense of expectation that we were all involved in the beginning of something big. And no matter how different each of us was, there was something embedded within us that was very similar: ambition.

We had the same hunger. Maybe to different degrees, but the dream was the same – all of us except one. I had my doubts about Michelle. Freckle-faced and cuddly, she could have stepped straight out of a Charlie Brown cartoon.

From that first week in the guesthouse I had sensed that Michelle was more ambivalent about the outcome. She didn't have the same hunger. Perhaps it had something to do with her age and background.

Michelle had so much going for her. She had breezed

through her A levels and been offered a place at university. She had grown up in Oxford and now lived in Kensington. She worked at Harrods on Saturdays. The rest of us were more working class – even Victoria, whose father was a self-made man with his own building company.

Michelle seemed polished round the edges while the rest of us had a certain roughness. Nothing had been handed to us on a plate. We had worked hard and taken the knocks.

However, none of these things would have made any difference if Michelle had shown the same drive and determination as the rest of us. We were starving for it. Too many promises had been broken; too many doors slammed in our faces.

We were the 'If Only' girls, who had spent our lives saying, 'If only they'd choose me' and 'If only I could get a break'. Our dreams had started in the days when we sang into hairbrushes in front of the mirror. We had never grown out of them. The fantasies weren't childish to us; they were just as vivid and real as ever.

The way I figured it, people fell into three major categories: those who have little ambition, achieve nothing and complain about what a rough deal they get; those who are comfortable with their lives and feel no need to rise – perhaps they peak at school but go no further, like the star of the drama club or the captain of the football team – and finally there are people like me – restless dreamers who refuse to accept that the cards they are dealt in life can't be changed. Let's redeal.

The two Melanies and Victoria were the same. Dreamers like us rarely doubt that it will come true. We just have to work hard and wait for our turn.

Each of us had an imperfection, some small flaw or weakness that undermined our confidence and stopped us fulfilling our potential. In each case the blemish was different, but that didn't matter. Together we could hide them. Together we could be perfect.

What were these flaws? I had a wild imagination and chaotic creativity, but I didn't have the skills or training to channel them properly. Mel C had a great voice, but was camera shy and introverted; she hated even talking on the telephone. Mel B had amazing energy, but was like a loose cannon who never quite knew what she was aiming at or why it was important to her. Victoria perhaps wasn't the most creative, but she had something far more valuable and important to the group: a sensible and normal outlook on life. She could keep our feet on the ground when our ambitions outstripped our abilities.

Each morning, we piled into my Fiat Uno and drove the thirty miles to Trinity Studios. Now we had three crap songs instead of one to practise.

Michelle and I tried to rewrite the lyrics to 'We're Going To Make It Happen', turning it into an up-beat song. I reworked the first verse until it began:

The time is right, we want release.
Break on through and get the system moving.

It was supposed to be about being on the dole, but the girls laughed and said it sounded as though we all needed the loo.

Pepi persevered with teaching us harmonies and proper breathing. Bob and Chris turned up periodically, but mostly left us to our own devices.

As we made up dance routines for our three songs, the Michelle situation became a more obvious problem.

The dance routine for 'We're Going To Make It Happen' was quite complicated. Mel B had choreographed a hip-hop step that Michelle and I struggled to pick up. 'Up, up, up. Lift your knees,' she shouted, sounding like a regimental sergeant major on a parade ground.

At lunch, I stayed back to practise; Michelle went and lay in the sun. This had become a habit. She lacked the same intensity or enthusiasm to learn and at times it bordered on laziness.

The two Mels grew frustrated at trying to help her. Privately, we called her the Gary Barlow of the group, i.e., the one who couldn't really dance. Take That was then dominating the singles charts and Gary Barlow seemed to have two left feet.

I also thought Michelle's voice was a little too operatic in style. 'Try to imagine you're Tina Turner,' I told her. 'Be a bit more poppy.' This was pretty impertinent coming from me, but I had more cheek and attitude than the others.

Having identified a problem, the group's policy went into effect – lay your cards on the table. Mel B had a long chat with Michelle, telling her in typically blunt northern style to get her act together. Mel might not have the largest vocabulary, but she can use certain expletives with telling effect. Afterwards, Michelle seemed a changed person. She practised harder and put in the hours. We then had a two-week break, during which time she dropped her boyfriend, left her Saturday job at Harrods and deferred her university place.

Unfortunately, without consulting the rest of us, Chic,

Bob and Chris had decided that Michelle didn't quite fit. They didn't get around to telling us until the night before we returned to Maidenhead. Tears were spilled as Michelle said goodbye. Although I felt sorry for her, I knew that she would go on to university and another life. She had opportunities that the rest of us had never enjoyed.

Now we had to find a new member for the band – somebody young, fresh and vibrant, who could sing and dance. Just as importantly, she had to have the same dream as the rest of us.

'She should be blond and fresh,' I said.

'And dedicated,' added Mel C.

We were sitting in a pub in Windsor, contemplating the search for a replacement.

'But where do we find her?'

After lunch we wandered the streets of Windsor, half expecting to find this new girl window shopping or listening to music at Cut Price. We all saw her at the same time. Young, blonde, attractive – just what the shopping list said.

'Hello, sorry to trouble you, but can I ask you a question?'

'Sure.' She turned at the sound of my voice and looked slightly alarmed at how closely Mel B seemed to be peering at her.

'Can you sing?' I asked.

'Well, I . . .'

Mel B interrupted, 'Can you dance?'

Again the poor girl didn't get a chance to respond before Mel C asked, 'What's your name?'

'Melanie.'

We looked at each other and had precisely the same thought. We can't have another Melanie.

The poor girl was nonplussed as we turned on our heels and left her.

Chic Murphy lived close to Windsor in a large rambling house with painted white walls and a golden stork statue in the garden. His initials were spelled out in tiles on the bottom of the swimming pool. Chic's wife was much younger and they had the most beautiful blond-haired children.

Chic was a Flash Harry with a heart of gold and I found him very endearing. I never discovered how he made his money, but he obviously did well for himself.

On Victoria's birthday he took us to a swanky casino, The Cromwell Mint, and gave us each £100 to spend. The place was full of rich Arabs and serious gamblers who were a little put out by our giggling and hollering each time one of us had a win.

Afterwards, he took us to dinner at a Chinese restaurant attached to the casino and we finished up having a huge cake fight that ruined Victoria's suit.

Pepi Lemer found a fifth member for the group. She had a student, Emma Bunton, who had just turned eighteen. Emma had spent six years at the Sylvia Young Theatre School and had also done some child modelling.

She didn't audition, but instead went on a week's trial. She arrived with her mother, Pauline, on a rainy afternoon in late July at Maidenhead train station. The rest of us were waiting on the platform, wanting to make the right impression. I wore red cut-off dungarees, black tights and platform shoes. It felt like a strange sort of blind date.

'God she's young,' muttered Victoria, as Emma stepped from the train behind her mother.

'Just a baby,' agreed Mel B.

Emma had big blue eyes, blond hair and a huge smile. Straight away I knew she was the one.

Pauline was catching a train back to London. She and Emma hugged tearfully. 'You'll be home by the weekend,' she said, brushing Emma's hair from her eyes.

Afterwards, we squeezed into my car, with Emma in the back, alongside Mel C and Victoria. Mel B sat next to me in the front. She always took that seat, like a co-pilot or navigator, and her favourite catchphrase became 'I know where we are'.

I tend to stare at people when I first meet them, and I couldn't take my eyes off Emma in the rear-view mirror. She looked so shy and anxious.

'Have you ever lived away from home?' I asked.

She shook her head.

'You'll have great fun. I promise.'

Looking at Emma, I realized what products of our upbringing we all are. At eighteen I was the wild child of Watford and getting into all sorts of scrapes. Emma had never left home. Her mother had signed her with a modelling agency at a young age and then sent her to stage school. I guess some people are born under a lucky star; others have to find one.

That night, as I lay in bed, I heard a soft knock on the door. Emma sat on the edge of my bed. I could see that she'd been crying.

'What's wrong?' I asked, giving her a hug.

She shook her head and sniffled.

'Are you homesick?'

She nodded.

'That's not a bad thing,' I said. 'Just think how much fun it will be when you get home again.'

'Don't you get homesick?'

'Not any more.'

From that night on I always defended Emma. The others would say that I let her get away with murder, and they're right. I'd always wanted a younger sister, and that's what Emma became. She could do no wrong in my eyes.

The rest of us had been singing and dancing for weeks. I thought it might be hard for Emma to suddenly fit in, but she slipped perfectly into place. In terms of the music, she took over Michelle's lines and carried on. In the house, she shared a room with Victoria, and we discovered that beneath her baby-blue eyes Emma had the heart and soul of a true party girl. She'd often stay up until two in the morning dancing to R & B songs, and then I'd wake to find her in the kitchen with Mel B, cooking a massive fry-up.

We were all very different. Mel C was quiet and accommodating, but she stood her ground during disagreements. She and Mel B would occasionally have 'sibling' scraps and I'd try to be the diplomat. Unfortunately, this meant getting the odd accidental whack when caught in the middle.

Emma shared a room with Victoria, which worked out well because they would drive home together to see their families in Victoria's Clio when they were homesick.

The one certainty of a shared house is that the empty yoghurt tubs, diet-Coke cans and skimmed-milk cartons always reappear in the kitchen within twenty-four hours, no matter how many times you throw them out. In addition to this, Mel B and Emma would leave the aftermath of their chicken Kormas on the kitchen benches and Mel C would eventually clean up. Taking charge of the situation, I drew up a roster delegating chores and stuck it on the fridge. Nobody took a blind bit of notice. They simply used the roster to jot down notes and phone numbers.

'What do you do?' asked Mel B, studying the list closely for the first time.

'I organize.'

She laughed. 'OK then, I'm having your job.'

We had to live on a strict budget. Once a week we all trooped down to Sainsbury's and bought our weekly shopping. We tended to each have our own food because our tastes were so different. Emma, for instance, ate an endless supply of baby food. She would buy dozens of little jars of stewed apple and custard.

Mel B had the most conventional diet and would cook herself proper meals like corned beef and rice. Mel C ate things like mashed potato with tomato sauce. Victoria seemed to live on cheese and crackers, or perhaps a bagel with honey.

Although not consciously starving myself, I remained very controlling when it came to my diet. My idea of a main meal was bean sprouts, rice and a splash of soya sauce. Mel B tried to help me and encourage me to eat more. I'd forgotten how normal people enjoy food.

I continued going to the gym and found a willing partner in Mel C. Although she had played a lot of sport and done gymnastics, Mel had never been to a proper gym or aerobics classes. Eventually we joined a place round the corner. Occasionally Victoria came along, or went running with us. Mel and I had this image in our minds of creating perfection – or at least becoming as good as we could be.

Mel C was the most disciplined of the five and I was the most militant. After getting back from the gym each morning, we had to drag Mel B and Emma out of bed. I used to bellow like a platoon commander, but Mel C was far gentler. She would make them tea and toast, before gently urging, 'Come on, here's your tea. Rise and shine.'

Victoria would already be up, curled in front of the TV in her dressing gown.

I crashed my car seven times that year – mostly little scrapes and knocks in carparks and on country lanes. Imagine the chaos of trying to drive with four girls in the car, all singing, laughing and generally mucking about.

Coming out of the gym one rainy evening, I failed to see a cyclist who was flying down the hill. He crashed into the back of my Fiat, smashing the window and sending shards of glass flying through the car. Miraculously, he didn't seem to be too badly hurt. I insisted on taking him to hospital, along with his mangled bike.

Victoria had a spot of blood on her cheek from a piece of glass. She completely panicked and demanded that the doctors see her first. The poor cyclist had to wait his turn.

'Don't worry. We're in a pop band,' I told him reassuringly. 'I'll give you free tickets to our first concert.'

He smiled painfully and I decided not to tell him about our three-song repertoire.

Another of my accidents happened when I stood on the brakes to avoid hitting an injured dog on the road. The car behind couldn't stop in time and tail-ended me. A frail old woman, who must have been in her nineties, was standing at the side of the road. She wore a tattered cardigan and seemed distressed.

Her bristly old mutt lay in the centre of the road, already stiff as a board. It had died hours earlier, under the wheels of a car, and the old woman didn't know what to do.

I lifted the dog into the back of the car and let her sit beside him, cradling his head.

'We'll take him to the vet,' I said. 'He'll know what to do.'

The dog was long past saving, but I didn't want to break the news to her. Mel C came with me and we listened as the old woman described having raised the dog from a puppy. He had been her best friend for nearly sixteen years. It was heartbreaking.

Later, we drove her home and promised we would visit.

On most mornings we arrived at Trinity Studios at about 9.30 a.m. and didn't finish until 5 p.m. As the weeks went by, the hours tended to drift until we started at eleven and finished at three. Afterwards, we'd race home to watch *Home and Away*.

Of an evening, we'd muck about at the house. Mel C and Emma were big Take That fans and we'd watch their videos and mimic all their moves.

'OK, let's do a Madonna medley,' I'd shout, and we'd be off again, belting out old hits such as 'Like a Virgin' and 'Papa Don't Preach'. Next would be a Tina Turner or Queen medley. Standing in the lounge, clutching mop handles and brooms, we'd pretend to be singing at Wembley with stand-up mikes.

Mel B had pretty much abandoned her life up north and stayed in Maidenhead at weekends when the others went home. I decided to stay as well. Apart from sharing the dream, we were best friends and 'partners in crime'.

Mel had a friend turn up unexpectedly one afternoon.

'I've got to get him out of the house,' she whispered as he lounged in front of the telly.

'Just tell him to go.'

'No, I can't. You think of something.'

I shrugged in defeat. 'I'm always doing this for you.'

Giving a squeal of alarm, I rushed to my Filofax. 'Oh my God, we've got tickets to the opera. We've forgotten.'

Mel screwed up her face and mouthed, 'Opera?' Then, out loud, she said, 'Oh dear, you're right.'

'Come on. We can still make it.'

I rushed upstairs, threw on a dress and put my hair up. Melanie did the same. I could hear her saying to him, 'I'm sorry about this. Maybe next weekend. Geri booked the tickets ages ago, and I promised to go with her . . .'

The plan was to pack him off home, but he seemed in no hurry to leave. He suggested letting himself out after the televised football game finished.

'Come on, Melanie, we have to go.'

We bundled ourselves into my car and drove off down the street.

'What sort of idea was that?' said Mel incredulously. 'He's in the house and we're out here.'

'He's your friend.'

'What are we going to do?'

'We could go out to a club.'

'Not like this. I'm dressed for the bloomin' opera.'

Instead I drove back and forth past the house with a skirt over my head so he wouldn't recognize me. His car was still there. We parked down the street and waited for over an hour until finally he left.

'Thank Christ for that,' said Mel. 'Where are your house keys?'

'You've got them.'

'No I haven't.'

We stared at each other in disbelief. We'd locked ourselves out of the house. There were no windows open downstairs and only a small one open on the first floor. The next scene was pure farce – the two of us, dressed to kill, carrying a ladder down the road while teetering on platform shoes.

'OK, up you go then,' said Mel, as we leaned the ladder against the wall.

'Why me?'

'Because you're smaller. Look at the size of the window.'

'You always make me go first.'

'Stop faffing and hurry up. I'm freezing.'

Muttering curses, I climbed the ladder and squeezed through the window. I bruised my knee and hobbled downstairs. 'Bloody opera!' said Mel. 'As if.'

We seemed to specialize in adventures like this. One night we both dressed up in office clothes and went to a bar. I was Felicity and she was Stephanie and we worked together in advertising. We ordered champagne and kept the pretence going as a string of businessmen hovered like bees around a honey pot.

At other times we'd choose a nightclub from *Time Out*

and drive down the M4. It might be a hip-hop club one Saturday and a salsa club the next. The two of us were perfect company; we didn't need anybody else.

Of a Sunday we'd go shopping at Camden market, dressed in funky clothes. Heads would turn and I could see people wondering, Who are those girls? We might not have been famous, but we weren't going to be ignored.

Chic dropped by to see us at the studio, showing all his usual enthusiasm.

'I've got it!' he announced. 'How about Take Five?'

We all sighed. 'No, that sounds too much like Take That,' said Mel B.

'What about High Five?'

There was no response.

'Plus Five? Five Alive?'

We all giggled. Finding a name for the band was proving to be difficult. Bob and Chris had initially suggested Touch, which was OK, but perhaps a little wet.

That night I went to an aerobics class with Mel C. I often seem to get my best ideas while working out. Bouncing along to some techno music I suddenly flashed, 'Mel, I've got it!'

'Got what?'

'The name. What about Spice?'

Back at the house, I called up the stairs to the others, 'What do you think of Spice? We're all so different.'

Mel and Emma peered over the banister. I could see them thinking about the name, as if trying it on for size.

'Yeah, I like it,' said Mel.

'Me, too,' added Emma.

The band had a name.

Bob and Chris had been conspicuously absent for most of the summer and autumn. Occasionally they invited people to the studio to listen to us – usually producers who might be interested in working with us.

Collectively, we'd written our first song together, 'It's Just One Of Those Days'. We sat around the table in the dining room one night and someone started humming a melody. I chipped in with a line that fitted and then someone else added another.

After much chopping and changing, with entire verses lying in balls of paper on the floor, we finished the song. If nothing else it proved we could do it. It also meant we didn't have to put up with songs we didn't like; we could write our own.

We'd been practising for nearly five months, and it was time to see if we'd been wasting our time. A showcase performance was planned for a group of producers.

Bob gave me £125 to buy outfits and I went to Camden market with Mel B. We bought matching Adidas T-shirts for everybody and planned to wear Levis jeans and trainers with them.

We had a trial run. I did Victoria's make-up, putting her hair into two plaits and giving her a look that could have come straight out of the *Face* magazine. Unfortunately, she felt completely ill at ease. She and her friends had always aspired to wear designer labels that were instantly identifiable. Her clothes had to make a statement and clearly jeans and a T-shirt didn't send out the right message.

The showcase took place in early November, back at the same studio in Shepherd's Bush where we'd first met.

Two dozen writers and producers turned up – some of them established and others on the way up.

I was so nervous beforehand. Pepi's daughter did our make-up and I sneaked a look outside at the audience. The wooden stage was raised only a few inches. We had to take our places before the music started, which only increased my nerves. There was a moment of silence when I looked at the faces watching me and thought, What on earth am I doing here?

'We're Going To Make It Happen' was the first song. It had a little rap section halfway through, which meant I didn't have to do the full dance routine. Phew!

My butterflies didn't disappear until all three songs had finished. I felt enormous relief; I hadn't screwed up. Then the exhilaration kicked in.

For a small crowd they made a lot of noise. We had people coming up to us afterwards saying how great we sounded. We sat down on the stage and answered their questions.

Up until then, none of us knew if we were any good. Bob and Chris hadn't been sure. Now we had industry people giving us positive feedback. And they weren't just patting us on the head to encourage us. They really, really liked us.

Afterwards, around the snooker table, I met Mark Fox, who worked for a music publisher. We chatted about the industry and he gave me his business card. 'If you ever need advice, give me a call,' he said.

Following our showcase success, Bob and Chris realized that Spice was a valuable commodity. Until then they'd left us to our own devices, with very little daily contact.

None of us had been asked to sign any form of contract. This worked both ways, of course. Bob and Chris had no formal commitment to us and vice versa.

Until now, it hadn't been an issue. But once contracts were produced we would have to make a decision. Do we stay with this team or do we strike out on our own?

# MAD MARY AND THE PSYCH WARD

Being in a band was the most exciting and liberating experience of my life. I could lose myself in the music and revel in having four friends who could share the moment with me. I could be artistic, creative, spontaneous and outlandish, yet people would say, 'Yes, but what do you expect? She's in a band.'

My boundless energy had direction. I had been born to do this. This was the best fun imaginable. Yet deep down where the butterflies gathered in my stomach I knew that something was wrong. My preoccupation with the band had distracted me from other problems. I'd been running on empty since my father had died. Sue Joblin had been right when she'd recognized the signs of anorexia and self-loathing.

When I joined Spice, it was as though my problems were packed in a box and put into storage at the back of the wardrobe, top shelf, behind the old cassette case of compilation tapes that I took as mementos from Dad's flat after he died. And while I lived in Maidenhead and we rehearsed each day the problems remained locked away. I was still very skinny – barely seven stone – and controlling about what I ate. My portions 'wouldn't feed a rabbit', according to Mel B.

The others grew accustomed to my obsessive behaviour and gradually I began to relax into the security of a busy routine and a shared goal. On the positive side, the binge-ing had stopped. I hadn't vomited in almost a year.

Only Mel B knew about my problems then. I shared a lot with her – personal secrets and dark fears. She had become so close a friend that sometimes I worried the other girls might feel left out.

We had the strongest personalities in the band, which made for a fairly fiery relationship with lots of heated dis-agreements. Many of Mel's beliefs were based on her gut feelings, whereas I was more exact and backed my opinions with things I'd read or been told. The other girls stayed out of these debates because the next minute Mel and I would be best friends again.

At times I thought Mel B was the kindest, sweetest, most considerate friend in the world, but at other times I felt I was living with the complete opposite. The bond between us was so strong that it was a huge wall for any-body to break down or reach through. Together, we felt as though nothing was beyond us. We could take on the world and win.

During a break for Christmas, Mel B and I booked a package holiday to the Canary Islands for £200. We knew the country, but had no idea which area we'd be staying in. It turned out to be a hotel in the capital, Gran Canaria.

Built into a cliff-face, the rooms stepped down in a series of tiers. It was possible, we discovered, to go from top to bottom, leaping from balcony to balcony. It's not the sort of thing anyone would try unless they were completely pissed.

Ralph and Sue, a couple from Lancashire, were staying at the same hotel. Sue knocked on the door one morning, asking if we'd seen Ralph.

'He didn't come home last night. I waited up for him.'

Suddenly I remembered where I'd last seen him. He was balcony-hopping to the hotel carpark. That's where Sue found him, fast asleep in someone else's jeep.

The hotel was quite new, with cool marble floors and its own pool. The beach was a ten-minute drive away, so Mel and I rented an awful purple hire car – a Twingo – which had the acceleration of a lawn mower.

Some of the days were quite hazy, so we went into town shopping for summer dresses and souvenirs. We'd noticed something strange about the men in the Canary Islands. From the back they looked incredibly slim, but when they turned round they could have been six months pregnant. We nicknamed this condition 'Canary Belly'.

Mel tried to help me eat sensibly by ordering proper meals. 'Just copy me,' she'd say, spooning more food onto my plate. She found it completely incomprehensible that I considered food the enemy. Mel had always been relaxed about what she ate and had never dieted. She had a fantastic figure.

On Christmas Day we ate French fries and ketchup on the beach, washed down with ice-cold bottles of beer. The sun shone and we fell asleep on beach towels, waking as the afternoon cooled down. Mel and I could paddle in the shallows and walk along the beach without having to make small talk; we were comfortable with silences. It was the best Christmas of my life.

Back in Maidenhead, I was alone in the house for the final few weeks of our holiday. The other girls were spending the New Year with their families. I wanted the time to pass quickly so we could be back together.

A strange thing happened in those long empty days. All my excitement and optimism began to leak away, and in its place came a flooding tide of depression. All those dark thoughts that had crippled me when my father died came rushing back. The self-loathing, sickness and abuse. Nothing can describe how out of control I felt. It was as though the energy and enthusiasm of the girls had pre-occupied me for the previous nine months but, once I was alone, I couldn't stop myself from focusing on the negative thoughts.

The girls weren't due back for another two weeks. I wouldn't go to Watford to see my family because I didn't want them to see me like this. Natalie was about to have a baby and I should have been with her. That's what sisters are supposed to do. Yet I knew that I couldn't visit my problems on her at the happiest time of her life. It wouldn't be fair.

I desperately wanted my family to be proud of me. For months I'd been telling them how great things were with the band and how focused I'd become, but if they saw me now they'd see that nothing had changed – the same old Geri, chasing her impossible dreams and getting all screwed up.

Once or twice in Maidenhead during the previous year, when the girls had all gone home for a weekend, I'd suffered similar attacks of depression. A dark cloud would settle over me and the self-loathing would return. That's when my old reliable friend was there for me again; the one that never leaves, the one I can control – FOOD!

Thankfully, these bouts of bingeing were quite rare. Come Monday, when the girls returned, all would be well again.

Who was I kidding? Ever since Dad's death I'd been treading water. Each time I stopped, I started drowning.

I binged my way into the New Year. I cleaned out the cupboards and the fridge, and the contents were flushed down the toilet, via my stomach. Then I went to the supermarket. As the checkout girl rang up the groceries, I began eating again. On the drive home I ate two Mars bars. I forced myself to throw up again, scratching the back of my throat with my fingernail.

That night I wrote:

*I am lonely. I want someone to hold and tell me it's going to be all right. There's no-one. I'm bingeing again. I haven't done that in a long while. I feel hateful and disgusted with myself. I'm paralysed by a black relentless cloud.*

The next morning, I felt exhausted and out of control. I had frightened myself so badly that I couldn't spend another night alone. I needed help.

I arranged to meet Karen at a pub near Watford. We sat at a table near the fire and I couldn't look at her face. What would she see?

'Karen, I think I'm going mad. Please, I need help.'

Karen had suspected for a long time that I had an eating disorder, but assumed that I was over it. Now she began to see how debilitating and dangerous it had become.

I can't recall much about what happened next, except that I told her, 'Take me to hospital, I think I need help.'

Karen phoned Dr King, and then she took me to the psychiatric unit at Watford General Hospital.

In the admissions area, a young doctor with curly hair and five-o'clock shadow began asking me questions. He'd obviously been working all night.

'Are you on any medication?'

'No.'

'Do you take drugs?'

'No.'

'Are you allergic to anything?'

'No.'

He ticked off the answers on a form. He looked up and studied me closely. I normally look people directly in the eyes, but I couldn't hold his gaze. 'What seems to be the problem?' he asked.

I shook my head tearfully.

'OK, don't worry. Just tell me how you're feeling right now.'

'Terrible. Out of control.'

'In what way?'

'I can't stop bingeing. I've been throwing up.' I knew the term was bulimia, but I struggled to say it. Instead, I told him I had an 'eating problem'.

'How long has this been happening?'

'Not for a long time. I thought it had stopped. Now it's come back . . . worse than before.'

After weighing me and doing general tests for blood pressure and reflexes, the doctor introduced me to a nurse. Kate was from Birmingham and had the sort of solid ankles that you associate with nurses who spend all day on their feet.

She gave me a quick tour of the facility and then showed me to my room. It was on the second floor, with a window overlooking the hospital. The bed had crispy white sheets and was so well made that I could have dropped a pound coin in the centre and it would have bounced straight back up.

Karen had gone home to pick up a nightdress and some toiletries for me. I lay on the bed and listened to the hospital hush. Occasionally, I heard a moan or a trolley rattling in the corridor.

Rather than being frightened any more, I felt amazingly calm. Everything in the psych ward was so white, clean and peaceful that it felt like a neutral country surrounded by war. 'I'm safe here,' I told myself. 'I'll be OK. I'll talk to doctors. They'll know what's wrong with me.'

Next morning I went exploring. The place was full of an odd bunch of nutty geriatrics and young people who were addicted to tranquillizers, painkillers or alcohol. A couple of them were solid-gold lunatics, like Mad Mary. She was Irish, with black penetrating eyes, and used to walk the corridors in her nightie, muttering, 'Mother of Mary. Mother of Mary . . .', in her very strong Irish accent.

Another patient, Danny, played an air guitar and wore headphones that weren't plugged into anything. He had spiky hair and ear lobes that were pierced half a dozen times.

The obvious lunatics tended to congregate in the

smokers' room. The carpet had cigarette burns that ringed the chairs like crop circles. People sat talking to themselves, having animated conversations that were so detailed and well acted that I could almost believe there was actually someone next to them answering back. It made me think of Jimmy Stewart in *Harvey* – one of Dad's favourite movies. Perhaps they all had six-foot pet rabbits.

I smiled at people in the corridors and said good morning. They seemed surprised.

The large lounge had been furnished with old chairs and cheap carpet, and had a TV showing cartoons. As I turned to leave, I spied a skeleton in the corner with lanky blond hair and dull grey eyes. She must have been about seventeen and seriously anorexic. It shocked me. Compared to her, I didn't look ill. How was she still alive?

Midway through the morning, a young counsellor came to see me. I expected him to start asking me questions about my childhood, digging for answers. What about that word-association game? Or the ink-blot tests? Maybe I'd seen too many movies.

He was in his mid-thirties and had dimples when he smiled.

'How did you sleep?'

'OK.'

'What have you eaten this morning?'

'Eggs on toast.'

'Good.'

He started searching through the notes on his clipboard, struggling to find what he wanted. Mumbling an apology, he handed me a piece of paper.

'What's this?'

'A diet sheet. You'll also be taking Prozac.'

He disappeared just as suddenly as he'd arrived. Is that it? What about the couch and confession bit? Don't you want to find out why I'm like this?

Kate would escort me to the cafeteria at mealtimes and make sure I picked something off the menu. It was fairly typical hospital food: spaghetti bolognese, tinned pasta, cauliflower cheese and buttered bread. Pudding was a choice of trifle, or jelly and custard.

Mostly, I sat by myself at first, but eventually I started chatting to people, wanting to know their stories. One lady in her forties was hooked on tranquillizers. She was almost childlike, with her grey hair pulled back into a ponytail by a ribbon. She sat hunched over, which made her seem even smaller, and spoke in the sing-song voice of a child.

Another lady, a manic-depressive, had legs that were knotted with purple veins. She'd lost touch with her grown-up children. None of them came to visit her or answered her letters.

'I have four grandchildren,' she said proudly, at the same time as tears welled in her eyes. 'My youngest just had her first baby. A boy. I hope I get to see him.'

Many of these people had sorry lives with little hope of turning them around. If given the choice, I wondered if it was better to be a shambling lunatic with a permanent smile than have to live with the reality of knowing you were mentally ill.

A nice black nurse with pillow-shaped breasts took me along to the expressive-art classes. These were in a separate room, which had paintings drying on washing lines and half-finished sculptures covered in damp cloth.

I started carving out a mound of clay. The cool white

mud felt nice as I squeezed it between my fingers and shaped it, unsure of what I was making. It finished up looking like my version of *The Scream*. Afterwards, I did a painting of a girl with long hair and very sad eyes that stared out at me. She looked almost haunted by a distant memory.

Although these images were dark and bleak, I didn't feel that way in the hospital. On the contrary, I felt quite safe. It was my sanctuary from the world, a refuge from all the pressures of life outside. I had no responsibilities or decisions to make; everything was done for me. I didn't have to make excuses or justify what I did. Being mad is the ultimate get-out clause.

During that next week I was a model patient. I ate my three meals a day and then queued with the rest of the zombies for my happy pills. Twice a day we stood in line for our day meds or night meds in little paper cups, then I shuffled down the corridor to the lounge, or back to my room.

Karen came to visit me every day. She said things like 'Everything will be OK' and 'You'll be better in no time'.

'Of course, I will,' I replied with certainty. The doctors were going to make sense of it all and take the burden from me.

After two or three days, I realized this wasn't going to happen. No attempts were made to analyse my problems or discover the cause of them. Instead the doctors seemed happy to keep me on Prozac and monitor my diet.

If they wouldn't do it, then it was up to me.

## Wednesday, 4 January 1995

*Having talked to some of the people in here, my problems seem almost irrelevant. Yet I feel as though I've opened a Pandora's box which I can't close.*

*Why do I make the same mistakes time and again? Attracting bad men, never finishing what I start, not expressing myself clearly, not thinking before I speak, thinking too little, thinking too much, feeling too much, being too selfish . . . the list goes on and on.*

*A child who falls down normally remembers to put their hands out next time. Not me.*

I did a lot of thinking in hospital. I sorted through all the baggage of unanswered questions and tried to make sense of Dad's death. Why was I so hell-bent on becoming famous? Why did I court rejection and risk failure for a lottery ticket that might never come up?

After ten days I began to grow restless in the psych ward. Perhaps the novelty had worn off. I didn't have any clearer picture of what had gone wrong, but I felt as though I'd given my mind an MOT test or a grease and oil change. Everything was now in working order.

The girls had been back in Maidenhead for a few days when I arrived. The only person I told about my stay in hospital was Mel B.

I came off the Prozac soon afterwards. It stole my creativity, and to be able to write songs you must be sensitive and in touch with your emotions. Instead of making me feel happy, Prozac made me numb. Ignorance may be bliss for some people, but I didn't like feeling distant from life. It was time to get back to reality.

* * *

'All right, Gorgeous?' yelled Mel B. 'Come on, you can go faster than that.'

We were passing a group of cyclists who were up out of their saddles and climbing a hill. Mel B loved to catcall from the front seat.

'Have you ever used your girl power to get what you want?' I asked the girls.

Mel C looked at me uncertainly.

'You do know what your girl power is, don't you? It's tapping into your inner resources to help you achieve your goals. If a girl has brains and femininity, and most importantly inner strength and determination, then, my dears, she has a very deadly weapon.'

Victoria and Mel B knew exactly what I meant.

'If a bloke can flex his muscles in a room, why can't a woman flex her femininity?' said Mel.

'A girl shouldn't feel guilty about being attractive and wearing nice clothes,' echoed Victoria.

Emma took it all in.

The term 'girl power' wasn't my invention. It had become one of those hip phrases on the street, and I liked what it stood for. I felt as though I'd tapped into my girl power to get on in my life. I've always felt very lucky to be living now. A century ago, suffragettes had to chain themselves to railings to get women the vote. And in the Sixties, feminists chipped away at the glass ceiling and guaranteed my generation of women had a better future. Now, in the Nineties, women no longer have to shy away from being feminine. It's not a sign of weakness, it's a strength.

Girl power became an important philosophy when Bob and Chris finally produced a contract. Songwriters and record producers had been showing an interest in us, and suddenly it became necessary to lock us up like teenage daughters.

It was too late.

During our Christmas holiday together, Mel B and I had talked about our management problems. We agreed not to sign a contract unless we were sure.

From her dancing days in Leeds, Melanie was used to having contracts. Right at the beginning she had asked Bob and Chris, 'Aren't we supposed to sign something?' Thankfully, they'd fobbed us off and we now had a choice.

We said nothing to the others. We had to be sure they felt the same way. If not, one of them might go to Bob or Chris and accuse us of dissent. We might be thrown out of the band and replaced. Instead, we had to approach the subject carefully.

Even before the showcase in November, I had talked to Victoria about another manager who we both knew, Albert Samuals, who looked after Right Said Fred and Sonia. I'd been introduced to Albert by Ellena, the girl who got me started in topless modelling. Victoria had met him separately.

'Do you think he's any good?' I asked her, as we drove to the studio one morning.

'I don't know. He's got some good names.'

'Well, if it doesn't work out, we could always go and see Albert. Can't we, Tor?'

'Sure. It's a good idea.'

I had a similar discussion with Mel C as we worked out at the gym. She had no great faith in Bob and Chris. Belief is a two-way thing.

By the time we were handed contracts in late February, none of us intended signing until we'd read the small print and talked it over.

'We'll just take them away and read them,' announced Mel B, making sure the others could hear her.

'I'm going to show it to my dad,' echoed Victoria. 'He knows about these things.'

'There's no rush, is there?' said Mel C.

That night we had a band meeting in the bedroom. We read through the contract and discovered that Bob and Chris wanted 25 per cent of everything. I already knew that fees like this weren't unusual in the music business, particularly when so many of the artists are young and desperate.

'I'm not having that to start with,' declared Victoria. 'They don't deserve a quarter. How much work have they done?'

The terms of the contract were couched in all sorts of clauses and legalistic handcuffs. Although I didn't know much about contracts, this one seemed to be very much to their advantage.

Effectively, we'd be owned by the management team and have no say in the music, marketing or promotion of Spice.

No-one suggested leaving, although it was now firmly on my mind. Instead, we kept our mouths shut and simply asked that certain details of the contract be changed. Rather than list these all at once, we introduced them slowly, making sure the process was long and drawn out. Meanwhile, we continued rehearsing at Trinity Studios.

By mid-February, we still hadn't signed. At the house one night, four of us were chilling out and toying with the lyrics to a song when Victoria suddenly announced, 'I think we should leave Bob and Chris.'

Instantly, I said, 'Yeah, come on, let's do it.'

'It's about bloody time,' muttered Mel B.

'Does that mean we're going to do it?' asked Victoria, sounding quite anxious at having triggered the coup.

'Yes,' I told her.

'What will we do?'

'We'll find another manager,' said Mel B.

None of us mentioned the possible legal problems, but I knew they existed. Although we hadn't signed a contract, Bob and Chris had invested time and money in helping us develop. They would have to be compensated in some way, but this could be negotiated later. By then, hopefully, we would have a new manager.

On the first Sunday in May I had a phone call from Bob at 6 p.m. He wanted to know why we hadn't signed the new contracts. I tried to wangle my way out of answering, but he wouldn't be fobbed off. Chic had started to suspect.

'I want the contracts signed today. OK?'

'I understand. I'll talk to the others and get back to you.'

Dancing about as if on hot coals, I told Mel B. The others had gone home for the weekend.

'We can't make the break now. What about Tuesday?'

An important meeting had been arranged with the songwriter Elliot Kennedy, who had written 'Everything Changes', a big hit for Take That. We were booked to spend a day in a studio with him, writing a song.

'We have to go and see him,' I said.

'Now?'

'Absolutely. Otherwise Bob and Chic might cancel the session when we don't sign.'

Mel and I looked hard at each other, reading each other's thoughts.

'Come on. Let's do it!'

Grabbing bin bags, we dashed upstairs and began collecting our clothes. Shoes were tossed into boxes and cassette tapes mixed with socks and make-up. We loaded up the Fiat Uno until there was just enough room for us to squeeze in the front.

I wrote a note and left it on the kitchen table:

'Thank you for all you have done. We can't agree to the terms of your contract.'

Then I shut the door, did a U-turn and beeped the horn in farewell.

I glanced at the fuel gauge.

'How much money have you got?'

'Ten quid,' said Mel B.

'I think I've got a fiver. Hopefully that'll be enough.'

Outside it was freezing, and the heater blasted hot air onto the windscreen to stop it fogging. We had just passed Coventry and still hadn't worked out how to find Elliot Kennedy. Neither of us had any idea where he lived. All I remembered was a reference to Sheffield.

In the seat next to me, Mel could barely contain herself. Her eyes were blazing. We both felt empowered. We were on a mission, and together we could make anything happen.

We stopped for petrol at a motorway service station just south of Sheffield. Looking in the telephone directory, there must have been about eighty Kennedys listed. Instead, we started to ring round local recording studios. Most of them operate at weekends, and until quite late, because musicians get inspired at odd hours.

At the second studio I called, a sound engineer picked up the phone.

'Is Elliot Kennedy coming in this week?'

'Yeah, on Tuesday.'

'I'm trying to contact him urgently. We're meant to be working with him and I've lost his number.'

'I can't help you. I've only got an address.'

'That will do.'

Elliot was staying in the country, recording with another girl. It took us two hours to find the place – a big old house in the middle of nowhere. After twice getting the wrong house and almost being eaten by an Alsatian, we arrived after midnight and knocked on the door.

'Try not to look desperate,' I whispered to Mel.

Elliot opened the door.

'You don't know us. We're from a group called Spice. We don't like our management and we're leaving them. Will you still work with us?' I gave him my flirtiest eyes and biggest smile.

It came out in such a rush that Elliot laughed. We were like two stray puppies, pleading to come inside. Finally he shrugged and said, 'Sure. Why not? Come inside and have a coffee.'

Elliot found us a place to stay for the night. The next morning I phoned Mel C in Sidcup and broke the news. She took a train to Sheffield and joined us. I also phoned Emma and Victoria, who arranged to meet up with us on Tuesday.

When Mel C arrived, we started to write a song with Elliot called 'Love Thing'. It was the first track we put down without our management.

That night, we stayed in a small guesthouse and then arranged a bedsit. By clubbing our money we scrabbled together just enough to cover the cost of the studio time.

In the longer term, we had accommodation problems. Mel C had kept her flat in Sidcup and Emma and Victoria could always live at home, but I'd given up my place at Fairlawns and had nowhere to live.

Mel B moved in with her boyfriend in St Albans, and for a few weeks I stayed in their spare room, which had a bed base but no mattress.

At the showcase in November, several important introductions had been made. The first was to Mark Fox, a music publisher at a company called BMG Publishing. Although now in his late thirties, Mark used to be a drummer in a band called Haircut 100.

I remembered him because he made a special effort to come and say hello to us after he heard us sing. Together with the two Mels, I drove to BMG's offices in Putney. While they waited in the car I went up to see Mark. I felt terrified. I didn't know what to say to him, or what he could do. Finally, I blurted out, 'Can you help us?'

Mark became very excited. 'Of course I will. You girls were great.'

He was so sweet and charming that he refilled my reserves of confidence. And he could always make me laugh with his wonderful impressions of Kenneth Williams in the *Carry On* films. 'Ooooh, I knooooow.'

Mark immediately began arranging interviews with various record companies and managers. He took us to many of the meetings, briefing us beforehand on who we were going to see.

A few weeks before our midnight flit, we had started working with a production team at a recording studio called The Stone Room in the City. Matt Rowe and Richard Stannard – better known as Matt and Biff – had worked with East 17 and had seen us perform at our showcase in November.

They're like Laurel and Hardy. Matt is tall, slim and a bit preppy, while Biff is round and cuddly.

Initially, we spent a few days recording a half-written ballad called 'Feed Your Love'; now we started working with them again on a new song called 'Wannabe'. It was very much a team effort.

The song itself took only about twenty minutes to write. We started off simply mucking about with chords and raps. Right from that moment, I think we all realized that this was something special. It happened so naturally that the song seemed to symbolize what we were about.

The genesis of any new song is normally quite spontaneous. One of us would come up with a top-line melody and the others would begin adding ideas. Some of my best thoughts cropped up while I was lying in the bath or about to fall asleep at night. Then I'd sing the melody into a tape recorder or down the phone to the studio.

Producers would take the idea and incorporate it into a song. If it seemed promising, we'd all start adding lyrics and harmonies.

Through Mark Fox we were also introduced to the Absolute boys, another production team, consisting of Paul Watson and Andy Watkins. People like this would come up with backing tracks and new ideas to bounce off us. Then we'd sit around the studio and start chipping in with suggestions. Slowly, a song would emerge, with the lyrics changing constantly as we agreed on something better.

We each had our traits in the songwriting department. Mel B was very good at quirky lines and coining phrases like zigazig ha. I seemed to come up with the hook, or the play-on words that triggered a chorus. Mel C could fill up a song with harmonies, or take what I had done and add vocal flourishes. Emma had an ear for really sweet melodies and ballads, while Victoria would suggest a chant here or there.

In between the studio sessions, we spent every spare moment visiting record companies, music publishers, writers and would-be agents. Mark Fox had been wonderful setting up these meetings and taking us to dinner when we looked underfed.

Each morning we gathered at Emma's flat in Finchley, and her mother would make us toast and jam.

Once on the road, my Fiat Uno became a mobile head-quarters and my Filofax was our personal assistant. We did our homework. For each would-be manager, we knew who they'd represented and their reputation. Certain people were rumoured to be very controlling and Svengali-like – I was very conscious of this. Other managers were obviously out to make a quick buck.

We didn't want somebody who would try to run our lives or get rich at our expense, we wanted an employee who would facilitate and manage our affairs.

Some of the candidates were awful. One manager of a well-known singer had a flat in Notting Hill Gate. He invited the five of us to dinner, and we turned up to find a plate of doughnuts on the table.

'Help yourself,' he said.

'Oh no, it's all right, I'm saving myself,' said Mel B, meaning that she'd wait until the proper dinner came. But the doughnuts *were* the dinner. We looked at the crumbling pink icing and listened to this guy talking about how good he was at looking after women.

Another name to strike off the list.

We had an appointment to see an old-fashioned heavy-weight manager with an office near New Bond Street. It had been a long day in the studio and we were all tired. We started bickering in the car and were still arguing as I knocked on his big black door.

'For God's sake, why don't you shut up?'

'Don't tell me to shut up.'

'I'll say what I want.'

'You started this, you grumpy cow.'

'Who are you calling a cow?'

The door opened and we put on these enormous smiles.

'Hi, we're the Spice Girls.'

We launched into a performance that had been honed to perfection. I made the pitch: 'We've got the name, the personalities, the image and the songs. You're looking at the complete package. We're going to be huge . . .' Meanwhile, like a real live wire, Mel B jumped on the table; Mel C was enchanting; Victoria looked poised and aloof and Emma batted her baby blues. We left this guy dizzy and breathless. Once you'd been 'spiced', you didn't forget it.

We sang a harmony from 'Wannabe' just to drive the message home.

I looked at him and could see the pound signs ringing up in his eyes. Quick buck. I'd seen it before with some of the other managers we'd interviewed. In each case we unanimously agreed that they weren't for us.

It was strange having so much power. We had no record contract or performing background, yet we were turning heavyweight managers down.

Breaking the bad news seemed to be my job. I complained about this, and Mel C was delegated a few softer rejections, like the doughnut man. I had to say no to the old-school heavyweight.

'I'm dreadfully sorry, but we don't require your services,' I told him.

He was very put out. 'You know nothing, lovey. You don't know the game. You listen to me . . .'

'No, we've made our decision. Thank you very much.'

He rang me back ten minutes later and started barking at me down the phone. This time he wasn't so polite. 'You'll never make it without me,' he yelled, finally showing his true colours. It guaranteed that if he was the last manager on earth we wouldn't choose him.

At the time I felt quite shaken, but later I found it amusing.

My enthusiasm never wavered, despite the setbacks. When the going got tough, and we all began feeling downhearted, I tried to find ways to keep our spirits up. It was so important to be positive because we were selling a dream. Our confidence and enthusiasm had to be contagious for others to see what we had to offer.

The Absolute boys, Paul and Andy, lived south of the river, near Richmond. They had a large house and a studio on an island. After recording a song one afternoon,

Mel C and I chatted on the dock. Paul and Andy had a manager who was in partnership with an agent called Simon Fuller. Fuller had been managing the solo career of Annie Lennox.

'Maybe we could get an introduction,' I whispered to Mel C.

We didn't take it any further, but coincidentally, Paul and Andy had passed on a tape to Simon of a song we'd written called 'Something Kind Of Funny'. Having heard it, Simon asked to see us. He called us before we called him – a good sign.

Again we did our homework. Simon had been a publishing scout for Chrysalis Records in the mid-Eighties, then he left to set up his own management company. He started with two acts: a rock band and an unknown youngster called Paul Hardcastle who had written an anti-Vietnam war song called '19'. The single was a huge number one hit, selling 65,000 copies a day. Afterwards, Simon called his company 19 Management.

From there he picked up Cathy Dennis, a session singer from Norwich, who went on to have two number one hits in America and another three songs in the top five. Annie Lennox split with the Eurythmics in the early Nineties, and Simon turned her into Britain's richest solo female artist.

The curriculum vitae looked pretty good.

We first met Simon at his office in Rampton's Dock, just off Battersea Bridge. He had a buddhalike calm as serene as the river outside. Having dressed to impress, we gave him the full Spice treatment.

'We're a finished product,' I told him. 'We have half

the songs for the first album, we have the right image and the time is right.'

'We want to be as famous as Persil Automatic,' added Victoria.

Simon laughed, but he got the message – world domination might just be enough for us. We wanted movies, merchandising, TV specials and to conquer America. As for a manager, we needed somebody with a silky touch, but not a Svengali. A mastermind, but not a manipulator. Could Simon do that for us?

Having met so many aggressive managers, it was a relief to discover someone totally the opposite. Simon was quite soft and gentle. He wore jeans and had his hands folded in his lap. When he spoke, I almost had to lean forward to hear him.

'I think you're fabulous. With or without me, you girls are going to make it. But if you tell me where you want to go, I will try to take you there. You tell me to stop and I'll stop.'

Clearly, Simon wasn't a stereotypical music agent. He had a quietly confident air, but with no sign of cockiness, and he seemed immeasurably wise.

'I love watching artists grow,' he told us. 'Not just professionally, but personally. That's the great thing about this business.'

Simon knew exactly what we wanted to hear. I looked at each of the girls' faces and could read their thoughts.

Yeah, he's the one.

That night, I wrote in my diary:

*Well, after a good six months of living, breathing, sleeping, eating, chatting, partying, fighting, arguing and plotting, we have surprisingly stuck it out and are still together. We have one major thing in common which holds us together, and that is ambition.*

*Although we have been down different roads and come from different backgrounds, our lives have remarkable similarities. We have struggled through the mediocre jobs, hoping to get the break we needed to fulfil our dreams. Until now, that 'lucky break' had passed us by.*

*The five of us know that, without the other four, we cannot function. Our ability to work, create and make good music, while remaining friends, is our strength. Although we are five separate individuals, we have an enthusiasm that seems to increase when we are together. It's as if we know instinctively how the others feel.*

*Although the journey has been short so far — compared to the one ahead — we have shared many laughs and also tears. Pride has had to be swallowed. Characters have been finely tuned to fit the group. We are five captains all steering the ship, and we have taken on board a fine navigator in Mr Simon Fuller . . .*

*We have many challenges ahead. Perhaps we are chasing a rainbow and will never reach the end. But together it feels so much better — I know I am not alone.*

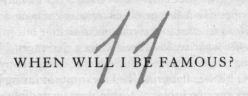

# WHEN WILL I BE FAMOUS?

For two months we had knocked on doors selling our dream and searching for a manager. At times it had seemed a thankless task, but it had a lot of positive side effects. As well as showcasing our talents, we proved how hard we were prepared to work.

Our efforts had created a hype about Spice within the music industry. This buzz seemed to grow as news spread that we'd signed with Simon and 19 Management. Suddenly we had record companies and music publishers queuing up to negotiate, fearing they might miss out on the next big thing.

I know this might sound a little too easy, but a lot of the hard work had already been done by then.

All record companies were basically the same, according to Simon, although they each had slightly different management styles. Sony is considered to be quite corporate, London Records is strongly into pop and Virgin is very hip and cool.

I wanted to sign with Virgin. I liked the fact that they had artists like Neneh Cherry, Isaac Hayes, Culture Club and Massive Attack, but no-one like us. We weren't following in anyone's footsteps or being compared to any similar bands.

London Records had been desperate to secure us. On the day before we signed with Virgin, Tracey Bennett, the head of London Records, took us all on a boat down the Thames and tried to convince us to change our minds.

'Look what we've done for East Seventeen,' he said, and then gave us the whole we're-a-big-happy-family spiel. This was flattering, and also quite amusing because I knew the executives at Virgin were incredibly worried about somebody poaching us at the last minute. I half expected them to have rival speedboats jostling in our wake.

Since signing with Simon at the end of May, three of the group had moved into a three-storey terrace in Cyprus Road, North London. Emma and Victoria were still living at home.

The two Mels took the largest bedrooms and I had an attic room that was just big enough for a double bed, the radiator and a little desk by the window where I would write my diary. The room was full of odd angles because of the sloping roof, but I liked being high up. On clear nights I could see stars above the neighbouring chimney pots.

The Spice command centre had switched to Simon's office in Battersea. I felt relieved to no longer have the responsibility. The previous four months had been stressful as we kept ourselves on track. Now Simon took over things, briefing us every few days.

The image of the band had occurred naturally and there had been no need to invent characters. Each time we launched into our sales pitch for record companies, our different personalities were obvious. Each of us added a distinct essence to the cooking pot. Mel B was the bold, aggressive Amazon, full of high-octane vitality. She had a natural musical rhythm that came across in her personality. There were no half measures with Mel. She would swear like a trooper and pick her nose in public without giving a toss what people thought.

Victoria had an aura of cool sophistication that was quite ironic. With her moody, pouting face, she always looked composed, yet she had a fantastic sense of humour.

'Yeah, I'm as deep as a puddle,' she'd say, laughing at herself.

In her baby-doll dresses and pigtails, Emma came across as being sweet and pure, all apple pie and spring-time. She had a childlike enthusiasm and a naivety that kept us laughing. Even kittens have claws, however, but thankfully Emma hadn't learned to scratch.

Mel C had a dancer's air and balletic grace that gave her an amazing physical presence. At the same time she was really appreciative and never self-absorbed. She was a shy dreamer whose real passion could only be unleashed on stage when performing.

And then there was me. What did I bring to the party? I was the flame-haired live wire with a mad imagination and a never-ending supply of ideas. I never lost my enthusiasm as I cajoled the others with my constant gift of the gab.

None of these traits was manufactured. Nobody got shoe-horned into being somebody they weren't. That's why Spice was such a perfect name. We were different flavours in the same recipe.

Right from the outset we made everything bigger, bolder and larger than life.

I had been dyeing my hair different colours since I was eleven years old. It had been pillar-box red when I'd joined the band. My friend Janine had been doing my hair ever since I could remember, and one day I walked into her salon in Watford and asked her to put six blond strips through my red hair.

'Are you mad?' she said.

'Trust me. It'll be great.'

'But blond strips aren't fashionable any more.'

'I know, but they soon will be.'

That was how confident and bold we had to be, even with our friends. We had to establish an identity that set us apart from other bands – not just all-girl combinations, but the dozens of new faces that are constantly being launched by the music industry.

The biggest music buyers are teenagers, and their tastes change quicker than street fashions. The five of us were very aware of that. After all, we were barely out of our own teens. How long had the pictures of Bros, Wham! and Madonna stayed on our bedroom walls? Barely a year or two.

Why would the Spice Girls be any different? We'd talked about this a lot. Two years seemed to be the general consensus. We'd give it everything in that time. In, out and shake it all about, that was the philosophy.

Right up to the last moment Virgin fretted that we wouldn't sign. The fact that London Records was pushing so hard increased the tension. We were due to sign the contracts at Virgin's head office at 6 p.m. on 13 July 1995.

The managing directors and staff were waiting. Two stretch limos pulled up outside, the drivers opened the doors and out popped five inflatable dolls. No Spice.

There were almost heart attacks.

We were five minutes away, heading towards Virgin. The morning had been taken up by a meeting at Sony Publishing and another with our lawyers to discuss what Simon labelled 'the deal of the decade'. Managers are prone to exaggerate, as I was quickly learning.

I sat in the back of a car, staring out of the window and wondering what difference it would make. How was it going to feel? Would it change my life? Would it change us?

We were like sisters now. We borrowed each other's clothes and helped each other get rid of unwanted boyfriends. We fought like sisters and made up afterwards. Would it always be like that? We were going to be famous. Do you hear that! FLIPPING FAMOUS! I wanted to stand at the top of Big Ben and yell it across London.

As the car stopped outside Virgin Records, I suddenly realized that I'd been in Kensal Road before. There was a photographic studio a few doors down, where I'd done pin-up sessions for a snapper called Trevor Watson. It was also where I'd met Derek, the bewigged music manager who wanted to turn me into the next Betty Boo.

We signed the contracts on the rooftop of Virgin Records and had our photographs taken. As the cameras whirred, we tossed the dolls over the edge and watched them slowly float down to the Grand Union Canal below.

The champagne corks popped and everyone wanted to congratulate us. Someone told me that George Michael had signed for Virgin that day, too. That made me feel special. I was joining the right team.

Afterwards, Paul Conroy, the co-managing director of the company, handed us each a cheque for £10,000. I'd never seen that many zeros on anything with my name on it. I kept sneaking a look at the cheque, just to make sure.

Simon took us to dinner at Kensington Place, a restaurant in Notting Hill that was a favourite of Princess Diana's. We were all quite drunk, but Victoria was totally smashed. We wrestled her knickers off in the cab, spilling beer everywhere, and I threw them out the window. The driver earned a big enough tip to cover the cleaning. Then we staggered into this really posh restaurant, reeking of alcohol.

I could see people thinking, Who on earth are they?

A year from now, you'll know.

I didn't phone anybody like Natalie, Max or Mum. I didn't have to. This was *our* day and *our* victory. I couldn't look at the others without beaming. Emma looked like she'd never stop smiling; Mel B grinned; Victoria had a champagne hangover already and Mel C kept doing soccer celebrations. I sneaked another look at my cheque.

After dinner the five of us went back to the house in Cyprus Road. Victoria was so drunk we put her straight to bed. The rest of us slumped into armchairs and onto the sofa, holding the huge bouquets we'd each been given by Virgin.

Mel C put on a Blur tape and cranked up the volume on the song 'Girls and Boys'. Emma hit Mel B playfully over the head with her flowers, and suddenly it was every girl for herself. We were smacking each other with flowers, petals twirled through the air like snowflakes, and we bounced from cushion to cushion laughing. Eventually we had nothing but broken stems and torn cellophane.

'Now I know what it's like to trash a hotel room,' I yelled.

'Rock 'n' roll!' screamed Mel.

A strange thing happened the next morning: I woke up and didn't feel any different. Somehow I'd imagined that I would. We had a record contract that was huge for an unknown band and people were falling over themselves to work with us. I *was* going to be famous; there was no doubt any more. Yet it felt almost like an anticlimax.

I guess I expected that once I'd had a day like yesterday, every day would be like that. Why didn't the high last?

'Don't worry, Geri, you just need a bigger and better day,' I told myself.

A week later, the sense of anticlimax was still with me. After a fortieth-birthday bash for Mel B's mother, I wrote in my diary:

> *Today I feel numb. No, not even that. I feel that I am on the outside looking in on the world (once again).*
>
> *I remember the line, 'When I get rich and famous . . .' People deliver it as if everything is going to be OK when it happens. But will I be OK? Will it be all that I am expecting and more?*
>
> *I am still living in hope.*

The stretch limo had parked behind a blue and white Chevrolet taxi. Looming overhead was a floodlit billboard with a seventy-foot-high picture of Kevin Costner.

Emma pointed to the limousine. 'Is that for us?'

Simon nodded and smiled.

The driver wore a neatly pressed shirt and tie. 'Welcome to California,' he said, raising his cap. He was totally bald.

'Leather seats,' said Victoria.

'Tinted windows,' added Mel C.

I opened a compartment behind the front seat. 'Will you look at this. It's a television!'

I fiddled with the controls, but could only pick up the NBA basketball.

Virgin Records had given us a camcorder as a present and we were supposed to be filming every precious moment of our big trip. Everyone was too exhausted to bother. I felt disorientated and longed for a bed.

'You should try to stay awake to beat the time difference,' warned Simon.

It had been two weeks since we'd signed with Virgin Records. The trip to America was a separate project. We wanted to meet with TV and film executives to promote the idea of a Nineties-style *A Hard Day's Night*.

From our first meeting with Simon we'd stressed that we wanted to do a film together. It must have sounded as though we lived in a dreamland, and in many ways we did. We were still totally unknown and a year away from releasing our first single.

The power of people combining is an amazing thing. Privately, we may have had occasional doubts – at least I did – but together there was no question of our future success.

I don't know where this self-assurance sprang from. Perhaps we had each suffered enough setbacks to make it our turn. This was no guarantee, of course. Whoever said that luck evens itself out should read the headlines and see what appalling misfortunes some people suffer over and over again. Perhaps it stemmed from our youth. All teenagers have a sense of immortality and unbridled expectancy. Among us, there was never a sentence that began, 'If it doesn't work out, we can always ...' The opposite was true. We put no limits on our success, or boundaries that might fence it in. Some British bands give up on America or dismiss it as being too hard to crack. Take That hadn't made it, and neither did Bros, despite their UK success.

Making a movie was a separate ambition. It had more to do with our childhood fantasies than music. All of us had dreamed of being a big Hollywood movie star. Our generation had grown up watching American films and TV shows like *Fame*. We were slaves to West Coast fashions and had owned Levis 501s, Ray-Bans and Reeboks.

Having been fed on such a diet, it wasn't surprising that we wanted a piece of the great American dream – Hollywood stardom.

The limo pulled up outside the Four Seasons Hotel, in the shadow of palm trees. As I entered the foyer, I could smell the lilies. Vivaldi's *Four Seasons* was playing. Everything about the place oozed class and I wanted to collect matchboxes just to prove to my friends that I'd stayed there. I wondered if the concierge had postcards.

I didn't pinch myself, I was too busy enjoying it. So much had happened to me in the previous month that I hadn't had time to contemplate how far I'd come. It was certainly a long way from a flat-faced terrace in Jubilee Road, Watford, to the Four Seasons Hotel.

'I could get used to this,' Mel B announced, as she popped her head through the adjoining door to our rooms. 'Have you seen the bathroom? Someone could drown in that tub.'

'I could swim laps.'

Mel had already tried on the white towelling robe.

None of us felt much like eating. Simon took us to a Rib Shack, full of large portions and large people. I couldn't believe the size of the salad bar, it must have been sixty feet long, heaving with every sort of bean, pasta, potato, coleslaw and salad combination ever conceived, as well as tropical fruit salad and cake.

Our meals were so large we barely made a dent. The waiter wrapped up the leftovers in tinfoil in the shape of an animal. Mine was a duck.

'What's this?' I asked.

'It's your meal.'

'But I've finished eating.'

'You might get hungry later.'

I could just imagine walking back into the Four Seasons Hotel carrying a tinfoil duck full of soggy salad.

Mel B was the only one to take hers.

'What are you going to do with it?' I asked.

'Find a homeless person who's hungry.'

'Like that film with Richard Dreyfus and Nick Nolte? *Down and Out in Beverly Hills*.'

We doubted whether we could find any such needy soul in real life. Yet it didn't take us long to discover that behind every beautiful façade and expensive address in Los Angeles there are always places where the poor and homeless lead a different existence.

\* \* \*

Next morning, after breakfast, I slipped into my silver Pamela Anderson bikini. Mel B had a matching one, and we spent all day hanging out by the hotel pool, trying to spot celebrities. We knew Elton John was staying and I'd walked past Morgan Freeman in the corridor.

It was Sunday and we didn't have to start working until the next day. I wanted to go rollerblading at Venice Beach or window shopping on Rodeo Drive. Then I could see the footprints outside Mann's Chinese Theater, or visit Universal Studios.

It was manic, five girls all wanting to do different things – some to go shopping, others to lie by the pool or go sightseeing. Afterwards, each shopping bag had to be unpacked, each outfit displayed. Then the next big question: 'What do we do now?'

'Quick, everyone, I saw Bon Jovi at the gym.'

Another mission.

'Let's get ready for dinner.'

'What are you going to wear?'

'Can I borrow that top?'

'Does this eyeshadow match my lipstick?'

It was so frantic and non-stop that there was no time to be homesick or to feel intimidated by my surroundings. I felt as though I'd become part of a secret club with five members.

This sense of belonging was enormously important to me. If I'd been walking into meetings or restaurants by myself, I might have felt shy and vulnerable, but now I knew that I wasn't alone. People weren't just looking at me, they were looking at a pack. We had a singular presence that turned heads and gave us each a heightened sense of boldness and confidence.

Simon had ties in America with the William Morris Agency, who represent Annie Lennox. Such a powerful agency has enormous pulling power and could easily arrange meetings for us. First thing on Monday morning, several white Cherokee jeeps arrived to take us to Jeff Frasco's house – one of our US agents. He had an amazing home, with a black-bottomed pool and a carpet whiter than his children's perfect teeth.

Jeff had organized a string of meetings with Hollywood film producers and TV executives. Most of these would take place at Arnold Rifkin's house – the head of William Morris – who looked like an older, albeit still handsome, version of Richard Gere, with a wider waistline. He had a mansion in Beverly Hills, with high ceilings, polished wooden floors and a massive swimming pool. Is everything in the US big?

We set up a table on the patio beside the pool. First up was Tod of Fox Studios, who gave us a frosty vibe. I could see him thinking, OK, you've got my time. Make your pitch. I've got a squash game in twenty minutes.

We launched into our routine. I did most of the talking, Mel B leapt onto the table, Victoria remained cool and elegant, Mel C played the Scouse football fanatic and Emma batted her baby blues.

It was amazing to see the transformation in Tarquin. It started with something as simple as tapping his foot. Then both feet. Then I knew we had him. He had forgotten about his next appointment. We had won him over. To finish, we took Tarquin into the lounge, sat him on a chair and played a tape of 'Wannabe' as we danced about. He seemed overawed.

The bigger studio bosses came next, and we repeated

the performance another five times on that first afternoon. It became very tiring after a while and we had to lift ourselves for each meeting. If one of us showed signs of flagging, the others would pick her up.

On Tuesday we had a meeting on the Dreamworks lot and another at Disney. A fat, balding executive with his two sons from the bubblegum factory in tow said to us, 'Are you signed?'

'Yes.'

'What do I want to see you for?'

I pulled up a chair. 'Hey! I know you're probably a very important man, and I don't want to patronize you, but sit down and listen. You might learn something.'

We weren't pitching film ideas or scripts. We were selling ourselves, our music and our energy.

By the third day, despite the positive feedback, we were all tired. By then we'd seen most of the big studio bosses, as well as music publishers, producers and executives from NBC, CBS, Fox TV . . . Simon did his best to keep us focused.

Whenever we teased Simon or became too cocky, he would produce an imaginary red card from his pocket, like a soccer referee.

I loved Los Angeles. It had a nervous energy and was full of characters who seemed larger than life. People acted as though they were permanently auditioning for a role – even the waiters. The entire city was like a movie set. It all looked beautiful from the front, but when you looked behind the classy shopfronts and piazzas there were alleys full of trash cans and rubbish. And LA didn't seem to have a heart. There isn't a central place where everybody hangs out, instead there are dozens of different areas, like Hollywood and Santa Monica. Where was the city's soul? It reminded me of an enormous bus station, with people coming and going, but nobody staying very long.

At an Italian restaurant that night we met Harvey, a fifty-year-old wannabe with silver-grey hair, a wide waist-line, cowboy boots and a gun in his ankle holster. He reminded me of what Burt Reynolds might have looked like if he hadn't quite made it. Harvey told us stories of all the film tough guys he knew and the wild things he'd done in bed with various screen beauties. Dream on, I thought.

Afterwards, walking in the parking lot behind Spagos, Simon asked me, 'Have you noticed how when you walk into a place, instead of saying, "Here come Spice", people say, "Here come the Spice girls"?'

'Mmmm, you're right.'

'What do you think about calling yourselves the Spice Girls?'

It made a lot of sense. If people were going to lengthen the name anyway, why not make it official? Apparently, there was also an American rapper called Spice, who was moderately well known.

We discussed it with the others and we all agreed on the change of name.

Back at the Four Seasons, we pressured the waiter until he cracked and brought us a round of pina coladas. The alcohol laws in America meant that Emma and Mel B couldn't legally drink.

We sat around on sofas, eating caramelized nuts from a silver dish and ordering more cocktails. Normally I drink very little, but I found myself getting quite tipsy.

We were flirting with a group of boys at the bar, which annoyed Simon.

'Who wants another drink?' I asked.

'I think you should go to bed now,' he said.

'Come on, Mel, share a cocktail.'

Simon began to stand. 'Listen, Geri, I think you've had enough. Time for bed.'

'Don't tell me to go to bed. You're not my father.'

I wasn't about to be lectured by Simon. I'd been independent for too long to let somebody start bossing me about. I'd earned the right to make decisions for myself. To stress the point, I stayed up until two in the morning.

Despite my protests, it was quite natural for Simon to feel like a chaperone. He was in his mid-thirties and some of us were barely out of our teens. He felt a responsibility towards us and he cared about our welfare. The truth is, I didn't always feel grown up or in charge of situations. I missed my dad, and perhaps subconsciously I looked upon Simon as a father figure. I know I thought he was very wise.

The next morning as we left the foyer a limousine pulled up. The back door opened and a woman tumbled out, almost in slow motion. She wore bright-red lipstick, dark glasses and a big floppy hat with a red rose on it. She fell awkwardly in a tangle of arms and legs, causing her dress to ride up. It took several seconds for the next detail to register with me: she wasn't wearing any knickers.

Brushing herself down, the blonde walked smartly inside.

'Do you know who that is?' I said to the others.

'Who?'

'Courtney Love.'

Wow! In *our* hotel – the ultimate bad girl and punk priestess. Her husband, rock star Kurt Cobain, had committed suicide only a year earlier. They were the Sid and Nancy of the Nineties.

The meeting with ABC went well. Back at the hotel, I was still on a high. I spotted a bellboy with a bouquet of flowers. The card had a French name on it, but for some reason Mel B had an inkling they were for Courtney Love.

I picked up the phone. Mel B wandered in as I made the call.

'Oh, hi, Courtney, it's Geri here. I'm a friend of Amanda de Cadenet's. She told me to give you a call when I was in LA.'

'Hiiiii there,' she drawled. 'Don't you sound sweet with that accent.'

I'd never even met Amanda de Cadenet. I just remembered reading a magazine story about the two of them going to the Oscars together wearing matching dresses and tiaras.

Mel was lying on the bed next to me mouthing the words, 'What the hell are you doing?' and putting a pillow over her head.

Courtney, inexplicably, began telling me how hard it was to find a decent nanny for her daughter. 'Listen, Geri, come on up,' she said.

'When?'

'Now, of course.'

'OK.'

I put the phone down.

Mel was in shock. 'You *cannot* be serious. What if she finds out you're a sodding nobody? She might

287

ask you about Amanda de Cadenet.'

'Come on, it's gonna be fun. Let's get leathered up.'

We pulled on our leather jackets and wore John Lennon-style glasses, trying to look really cool.

Upstairs, the door was slightly ajar. I knocked and pushed it open. My knowledge of Courtney Love was pretty limited, but I vaguely knew she was due in court, accused of punching Kathleen Hanna, the former lead singer of the group Bikini Kill.

The curtains were closed and the room lay in semi-darkness. Courtney sat on a sofa in a baby-doll see-through nightie and a pair of knickers. Someone was leaning over her and I could see wires and tubes coming from her head. Oh, my God, what's happening?

I didn't know whether to stay or run. I could smell smoke. Then I realized that a hairdresser was burning the extensions out of Courtney's hair.

'Come on in, come on in,' she drawled.

Mel took a single chair and looked really cool as she lounged casually, still wearing her sunglasses. Meanwhile, I perched on the end of the sofa and felt uncomfortable about being able to see so much of Courtney.

'So what are you doing in LA?' she asked.

'We're in a band,' I said.

'Good for you.' Then she started talking about her years in Liverpool, when she hung out with Julian Cope, the frontman for the Eighties pop group The Teardrop Explodes. This seemed to trigger a whole series of memories and her life story came tumbling out.

Mel B said almost nothing as she peered over the top of her sunglasses, looking very cool. I tried not to look at her because I knew I'd explode into giggles.

Courtney suggested she give room service a call and order tea. Mel was so nervous she only asked for one cup.

The TV was on with the sound turned down. *Congo* was showing and every so often Courtney would make some comment about it. I knew that she'd acted before, but none of her films had been big hits. A year later she won an Academy Award nomination for *The People vs. Larry Flynt*.

Then a guy with a ginger beard walked in, wearing grunge clothing. He sat next to me.

'This is Mel and Geri. They're in a rock group,' Courtney said.

I didn't catch the name, but I recognized him from the Stone Temple Pilots. What if he started asking questions?

Thankfully, the tea arrived – a lone pot with a single cup. Mel pretended it was a room-service mistake. The cool persona was starting to fray.

The telephone rang for Courtney.

'Oh, my God, it's Danny de Vito. He wants me to be in his new movie. What am I gonna do? Oh God! I've got twenty minutes. I look a mess.'

She slid sideways on the sofa and began pinching her thigh. In a little-girl-lost voice she asked, 'Do my legs look fat?'

I patted her hand. 'Courtney, don't worry. Put a bit of lippy on. Where's your floppy hat? You'll be fine.'

'I'll never make it.'

'Of course you will.'

She seemed to cheer up and regain her confidence.

'We should go now,' I said. 'Good luck.'

She gave me a hug. 'Well, make sure you all come back

now. I've ordered tea for three.' She said it in a Miss Hannigan manner.

Around the corner, out of sight, Mel and I started giggling. It was just so unbelievable. Two absolute nobodies had just spent an hour with Courtney Love talking like old friends. Wait until we tell the others.

Yet as we walked down the corridor, the feeling slowly crept over us how sad it had been. Our cheeky prank had been cruel and intrusive. Courtney Love might have been famous, but all we saw was a woman who opened her door and then her heart. She didn't deserve to be made fun of.

After six days in Los Angeles we flew to Hawaii for a holiday on the island of Maui. Simon returned to Britain. We stayed at the Kea Lani Hotel, on Polo Beach, a resort with acres of tropical gardens and three lagoon-style pools.

I loved the place. We chilled out on the beach, but had to be careful about sunbathing topless. For some strange reason, the country that gave the world *Playboy* magazine has an aversion to nipples on display.

Later, by the hotel pool, we were accused of being trespassers by the security guards and I had to complain to the manager. He was very apologetic. Apparently, girls our age didn't normally travel in groups of five and stay at luxury resorts.

The same poor manager had to deal with the complaints when Mel B and I went rollerblading through the corridors. Girls will be girls.

### Saturday, 5 August 1995

*Frosties on a warm sunny balcony, gym, postcards and off to Makena Beach, over a mountain. This is the local nudist beach, where we finally found a place to go top-less. Willies, ginger pubes, big bums and saggy tits. What a sight! But a good vibe. We sat and fried all day.*

*I've just finished reading Boy George's biography. I, too, feel an inner karma today, completely at ease and chilled, like a still pond with no ripples.*

*Tomorrow is my birthday. I hope they don't make a fuss – just remember and be nice. That's enough. Exhausted. Good night, Geri.*


I had a great birthday. The girls gave me a personal CD player; I was really touched.

Some cute surfers asked us to go out with them, but we decided to make it just a girls' night out. I made them come to the movies with me, and we saw *Waterworld*, which had Kevin Costner playing a Mad Max character with webbed feet. Afterwards, we partied back at the hotel in our room.

During the day, Emma and Victoria preferred to lie by the hotel pool, while the rest of us went off to the beach. We met some American college guys on holiday – Adam, Paul and Troy – and hung out with them.

During one spontaneous party, Troy decided to strip for Mel B, Emma and me. We egged him on, convinced he'd stop when he reached his underwear, but he carried right on going. Screaming in horror, we threw his clothes out the door and ran back to our rooms.

At Little Makena Beach I had a glimpse of Maui's

famous waves. They were huge, with a backwash so powerful that it kept sucking me in, filling my knickers with sand. Each time I tried to empty them, I was sucked back into the white water and they filled with sand again.

Back on my beach towel, I started reading Shirley MacLaine's autobiography, *Out on a Limb* – a very spiritual book. Ever since Dad's death I'd been reading stories like that, often carrying two or three with me at a time. I was particularly fascinated by death and the way different cultures deal with the subject. When Dad died, nobody had a clue what to say to me, or how to act. I grieved for myself and what I had lost, not for the person who'd gone. Lots of Eastern religions celebrate death and seem to have a far healthier attitude.

As I finished a page, I turned to say something to Paul. My jaw dropped. He had taken all his gear off. I went seven shades of red. Why is it that when a man is naked, no matter how hard you try *not* to look . . . well, you know what I mean.

### Wednesday, 9 August 1995

*Dreamt of vampires. How odd. Water in my ears and I feel beaten up by the waves. Mel and I went to the big beach and chilled out. I'm loving the Shirley MacLaine book.*

*Later, I went to the market with Adam and Victoria. There was a tarot reader who did my cards. He said that I was moving on to the next level. The highest card, 'Fool', means freedom. Everything he said seemed to make sense.*

*We are now bored with the boys – new ones please.*
*Good night.*

Long before our suntans had faded, we were back in the studio in London watching raindrops running down the windows. We had another six songs to write and tracks to record and remix.

During the week, we seemed to divide our time between recording studios in Richmond, Hammersmith and Old Street. Although I enjoyed the work, I felt under pressure not to let the others down. The two Mels, in particular, could nail their vocals first time. I often had to spend an extra hour or two in the booth, trying to get it right.

'We're going to drop you in on the last line,' said Biff. His voice came through my cans (headphones). I could see him behind the viewing window, sitting at the console. 'This time I want you to hold that last word a little longer.'

'OK.'

The backing track for '2 Become 1' began playing through my cans. Alone in the booth, I closed my eyes and thought, It's coming. It's coming. My bit. Get it right.

Biff hit a button on the console and said, 'Sing along, Geri.'

I picked up the early lyrics until my lines arrived:

> Any deal that you endeavour,
> Boys and girls feel good together.
> Take it or leave it. Take it or leave it.

Straight away the music stopped. 'Much better,' said Biff. 'Do you want to try again?'

I nodded. It still wasn't there. I didn't have the right passion. Having had no vocal training, I found it difficult to relax and deliver emotion. Nervousness tends to make your voice go higher and thinner.

We tried again. I came in a fraction late and felt like screaming in frustration.

'You're tired, Geri,' said Matt. 'Let's try again tomorrow.'

'No, I want to get this. Drop me straight into the last line.'

'OK.'

I tried to think of the saddest thing possible: Dad's death. I missed him so much. I could feel my eyes go misty as the music started.

Take it or leave it. Take it or leave it.

There was a long pause from the studio. I glanced up to see Matt and Biff grinning at me. They both gave me a double thumbs up. Thank God! It was 4 a.m.

Strangely, I dreamt about Dad that night and woke in tears. In my dream I was running through the park in Gannon's Lane, Watford, just next to my junior school. Matt and Biff were running ahead of me as I chased them back to the studio.

Dodging through the crowd, I suddenly saw an Asian man pushing an old pram. I looked at him again and he turned into my dad.

First I took his hand and then I hugged him. I could feel his heart beating.

'How's my little girl?' he said.

'Guess what, Dad, I'm going to be rich and famous.'

He smiled.

'Can you hear my thoughts?' I asked. 'Are you watching over me?'

He had disappeared.

Recording studios make you go stir crazy after a while. They're always situated in the bowels of buildings, away from any windows and traffic noise. That's why the producers and music engineers have 'midnight tans', because they never see the sun.

The sessions were often long and tedious. All of us went through crises of confidence at various times.

There was a lot of waiting around in between individual vocals and while the guys were toying with new mixes.

It meant lounging on sofas, reading magazines and eating takeaways. Victoria and I seemed to live on fruit and bottled water.

Sometimes I felt something was missing. I wrote in my diary that maybe the answer was sex. But who with? I didn't have a boyfriend and there hadn't been anyone since Sean. That didn't bother me. I didn't have the time. But there were nights when I would have liked a close companion. Someone creative, who could make me laugh. A man who had power or a bit of get up and go. At the same time, I didn't want somebody who would demand too much of me or distract me from the group.

Everybody wants to fall in love. It's a magical feeling. Broken hearts are pretty commonplace, but they teach you to be more careful next time. It had taken me three years to stop thinking about Niam. I only knew for sure that I was over him when I bumped into him at a set of traffic lights in Watford. He looked across and smiled. My heart didn't skip a beat or my breathing quicken. At that moment I realized there was nothing there. I didn't fancy him any more.

Oddly, it felt a little sad, because now I had nobody to have that feeling about, no long-lost love to pine for when I was lonely and melancholy. Everybody needs someone to think about when that sad song comes on the radio.

With my first cheque from Virgin Records I bought an MGB 1967 Roadster, classic red with all the original features. It was my father coming out in me. Although he could only ever afford old bangers, he loved the classic sports cars and used to point them out to me as we drove to auditions or car-boot sales.

Paul and Andy, our producers, were both car fanatics and took it upon themselves to help me choose the car in between our recording sessions. Unfortunately, the MG couldn't be delivered until after Christmas, so in the mean time I had to rely on my trusty Fiat.

The MG arrived in early January and I was so excited. I drove it to the studio, beaming with pride. I could see people turn their heads to watch me. Could I really be the owner of a shiny bright-red sports car?

The heater didn't work and I nearly froze to death, but that didn't matter. This little beauty warmed my heart.

A day later, I parked in front of Karen's house and locked it up. I walked to the front door and, as I raised the door key, something made me turn.

In one of those terrible slow-motion moments, I watched my new car rolling away down the hill. I didn't know whether to run or scream. It didn't matter. The MG picked up speed and then singled out the only telegraph pole in the vicinity. Crunch!

Everything I wanted seemed to end up damaged or destroyed – it made me realize that you can become too attached to things.

By then I'd moved out of Cyprus Road and was back living with Karen and her family in Chorley Wood. The two Mels needed somewhere to stay and I found the perfect place.

My Auntie Doreen had lived across the road from us in Jubilee Road. After she died, my mother and Steve bought her house and did it up. Since then, they'd been renting it out.

The two Mels took over the lease and we saw almost as much of each other as before. Just as in Maidenhead, the other girls would clear off and spend the weekends with their families, leaving Mel B and me to amuse ourselves, only this time we had the advantage of having money to spend.

## Saturday night, February 1996

*Stayed in with Mel to watch Stars in Their Eyes on TV. Like the rest of the country, we constructively criticized the contestants. Later, went clubbing at Heaven. Wicked night out. We blagged our way onto the guest list. There were loads of drag queens. What a vibe!*

*Melanie declared me her true friend tonight so I guess it is true. We have been through a lot, perhaps more than most people do in relationships that have lasted much longer. It has been demanding, intense and hectic, confusing, frustrating but good. I think I can truly say that I, too, have found a friend, a bloody good one . . .*

It seemed obvious to all of us that 'Wannabe' would be our first single, but the boss at Virgin, Ashley Newton, couldn't stop tinkering with the song. Ashley had a real passion for R & B and he sent 'Wannabe' to an American producer called Dave Way, who had a reputation for creating an R & B swing sound. The result was bloody awful. 'Wannabe' sounded totally different and certainly not pop.

Soon there were jungle mixes, as well as hip-hop, and a version that sounded almost West Coast. The arguments raged over the different versions until Mel B and I took matters into our own hands and dictated how the final mix should sound. Eventually, we went back to the original mix on the demo, with some of the tinniness taken out.

Although there were arguments and occasionally harsh words, I felt enormously close to the girls during the song-writing and recording phase. So much so that I wanted to do something for them. Exactly a year after our midnight flit from Maidenhead, we were back at Fon Studios in Sheffield remastering 'Love Thing' with Elliot Kennedy. For those few days we all stayed at Mel B's parents' house. Victoria and I had to top 'n' tail in the same bed.

I slipped out of the studios and found a jeweller's shop in Sheffield town centre, where I bought five identical gold rings.

'Do you do engraving?' I asked.

He shook his head. 'There's a shoe-repair place up the road. They also cuts keys.'

I found the shop, but didn't hold out much hope. The key-cutter had forearms the size of football posts and didn't strike me as a craftsman.

'Yeah, love, what can I do?'

'I want you to put the word "SPICE" on the outside and "one of five" on the inside of the band.'

He held one of the rings and examined it closely. 'It's gonna be a squeeze.'

Back at the studio I chose a moment when we were all together. 'I want to have a little anniversary ceremony,' I said, suddenly feeling self-conscious. 'It's a year since we recorded our first song on our own.'

I handed them each a ring box. 'We've overcome a lot to get here. And soon all that hard work will have paid off. I hope that we're always this close. We're each one of five. Together we can do anything.'

# NUMBER ONE

Outside the tight-knit circle of the music industry, nobody knew about the Spice Girls. We had a record contract but no profile. This began to change on Monday, 19 February 1996 at the annual Brit Awards. This was the music industry's night of nights, a home-grown version of America's Grammys.

Virgin had several tables booked for the ceremony and invited us to come and soak up the atmosphere. Days beforehand I began getting excited. I spent hours contemplating what to wear. Eventually, I settled on bright liquid-green lurex trousers that flared at the knee, along with a vest top. I'd bought the material at Berrick Street market and made it myself with Karen's help.

No detail was overlooked. In America I'd picked up some Sobranie Cocktail cigarettes, which were all different colours, and I chose all the green ones to match my outfit and put them in a silver cigarette case.

We dropped by to see Matt and Biff at their studio, The Stone Room, before we left for Earls Court. They told us we all looked fabulous, and I felt as though we were about to 'come out' at a debutante ball.

As we arrived at Earls Court, there were photographers lined up outside, waiting for the stars. A limousine pulled up and Tina Turner stepped out. A wall of cameras lit up the pavement.

'Tina, Tina . . .'

'Over here!'

'Give us a smile.'

'Show us some leg.'

'We love you, Tina.'

God, she looked great. Like a real star.

There were 2,000 people at the awards ceremony – writers, artists, producers, sound engineers, publicists and record-company employees. We were totally unknown, but we turned heads anyway. I would see people watching and wondering. Occasionally, someone nudged their companion and asked, 'Who are they?'

Our table boasted the dreadlocked funkster Lenny Kravitz, French songbird Vanessa Paradis, and husband and wife Ken and Nancy Berry, who headed Virgin and EMI records.

I spied Nikki Chapman, our PR lady, sitting at a table with Take That. I went up to say hello to her, but avoided looking at the boys in case I was caught staring. I kept thinking of all those nights we spent dancing around the living room in Maidenhead singing Take That songs. I was too old to be one of their fans.

A bit later, I went to Nikki's table again, this time with the girls. Jason Orange said, 'Hey, Geri! You all right then?'

Jason had obviously asked Nikki my name, and I could see the girls wondering how he knew me.

The night had some unforgettable moments on stage. You can't gather the biggest names in music without accommodating their egos. Liam Gallagher of Oasis accepted the award for Best Video from INXS star Michael Hutchence and then challenged him to a fight. Noel Gallagher went one step further and said, 'Has-beens shouldn't present awards to gonna-bes.'

Things got even more interesting when Michael Jackson was introduced as the world's most famous pop star. He began singing his chart-topping 'Earth Song' while a chorus of children surrounded him on stage. Somebody in the audience had a laser pointer and kept aiming the red dot at Jackson's head.

As the song ended, a mobile crane hoisted Jackson towards heaven in a Christlike pose, as smoke billowed beneath him. The crowd was horrified, and so was Jarvis Cocker, the gangly lead singer of Pulp, who stormed the stage and waggled his bum at Jackson.

The controversy continued as Oasis picked up two more awards. Lenny Kravitz presented Liam Gallagher with the Best Album award for *(What's the Story) Morning Glory*, and Liam pretended to put the award up his butt and then sniffed it. He challenged anyone to come and fight him if they were 'hard enough'.

It was all very rock 'n' roll.

Nothing could spoil my night. I loved the fact that people were looking at us and wondering who we were. I loved having Tina Turner smile at us and Jason Orange say hello. We were part of modern music history.

Tony Blair was then the Leader of the Opposition and was sitting on a table with Simon and Annie Lennox. High on happiness — I didn't dare drink — I fronted the future prime minister with a proposal.

'Mr Blair, I'm Geri and I'm in an all-girl band. We're going to be huge. We're about to make our first video, would you be interested in appearing in it?'

He chuckled. 'I'm pretty busy at the moment, Geri.'

'OK, I'll go and ask John Major.'

I have no idea what possessed me to ask him, except perhaps that our video for 'Wannabe' was going to have a whole collection of people in it – old, young, rich, poor, politicians, butlers, tradesmen . . .

Annie Lennox picked up the award for Top Female British Artist, and at the end of the evening we finished up on her table, where her statuette nestled between empty bottles of wine and beer.

Annie started talking to us and we crowded around her like hungry children, waiting for scraps of wisdom to fall from her plate. She was the first big star I'd ever met, apart from Courtney Love.

'You've got to keep your heads down and concentrate on the music,' she said in her soft Scottish accent. 'Do you know why?' She took another sip of wine.

I shook my head.

'Because the rest is bullshit. Do you know what I'm saying? This industry is full of wankers.'

I wrote in my diary:

### Monday, 19 February 1996

*Tonight was by far the most exciting night for the band yet. Everyone had been nervously excited about sharing a table with Lenny Kravitz and Vanessa Paradis. We were all on top form. I felt dead confident and proud.*

*What a night! Michael Jackson was booed. Noel Gallagher was a knob. And Lenny Kravitz told me that, with our attitude, we would make it. We hung on his every word . . .*

Our first single was to be released in early July – another four months away. This meant we were still in the honeymoon period between actually signing a contract and being launched on an unsuspecting public as the 'next big thing'.

Although the publicity campaign hadn't officially started, a lot of work was being done behind the scenes to introduce the Spice Girls to the music press and radio stations. A typical example was a day at Kempton Park racetrack, where Virgin Records was sponsoring the main event.

None of us had a clue about racing, but we weren't there for the horses. At one point we bowled up to the producer of *Live & Kicking* – a children's TV show that featured bands – and did an a cappella version of 'Wannabe' in the ladies' loo. The acoustics were fabulous. She agreed to put us on the show when the single was released.

We also managed to create a ripple by clambering all over the famous statue of Desert Orchid, one of the world's greatest ever steeplechasers. In the background of the photographs, you can see the racecourse marshals running towards us.

These sorts of high jinks did us no harm at all, but we were very aware of not going too far. It was OK to be outrageous, but we had an image to promote that didn't include drugs, swearing or drunkenness. Saying that, Mel B and I seemed to break most of the lesser rules and get away with it. It seemed to be an accepted part of our 'characters' to be a little more rebellious than the others.

The band's image had been refined even further. At the November showcase with Bob and Chris, we had all worn similar clothes. Since then we'd decided to celebrate our individuality, wearing outfits that matched our different personalities. Similarly, we tried to play down the perception that we were a manufactured group. Although that was nothing to be ashamed about – the Sex Pistols were manufactured – the music press seemed to look down their noses at such bands. We also decided not to advertise the fact that some of us had boyfriends. This would hopefully attract young male fans. Mel B and Victoria were in long-term relationships, but the rest of us would play down any romances.

In March, as part of the early publicity, Simon set up a meeting with the assistant producer of *TFI Friday*, Suzie Aplin. TV exposure is a priceless commodity for any new band and this was a top-rating show, especially among teenagers.

'Is Chris Evans going to be there?' I asked.

Simon shrugged. 'Suzie says he might be. He's a busy man.'

Despite his having humiliated me on *The Big Breakfast* by ridiculing my audition tape, I regarded Chris Evans as perhaps the most talented TV presenter I had ever seen, particularly when working live. That's why I was so excited about the possibility of meeting him.

We met Suzie Aplin at the studios of Radio 1 and sang

'Wannabe' for her. She seemed impressed. As we finished the impromptu performance, I glanced up and noticed Chris Evans looking through the glass doors. He has such a cheeky little boy face, with a shock of ginger hair.

How much had he heard? Did he like it?

As I waited expectantly, he mouthed the words through the glass, 'Why don't you just go back to *Live & Kicking*?' In other words, we were a shite teen band who didn't deserve to be on his TV or radio shows.

Then he spun on his heels and walked away. There was a long, embarrassing pause. Nobody knew what to say. I put on a brave face in front of the girls, but felt gutted. I didn't want them to see my disappointment. I wanted to show them it didn't matter what one person thought.

Mel B came back to Karen's house with me and we sat in the attic bedroom feeling bruised and unfairly treated.

'He didn't even listen to us,' I said.

'Stuff him. What does he know?'

'Let's send him a fax.'

'Yeah.'

I found a piece of paper and a marker pen and wrote:

*Dear Chris, (ginger bollocks!)*
*Hi, this is the Spice Girls (Melanie and Geri). Don't judge this book by its cover, mate. There's more to us than that!*
*We are sure you appreciate balls and honesty. We are the same breed.*
*Spice Girls.*

Karen had a fax machine downstairs in her office. As the

page disappeared we both giggled and pretended that we felt better.

After Mel had gone I went to the fridge. Cutting myself a slice of carrot cake, I sat at the kitchen table feeling sorry for myself. I went back to get another slice and then another. The cake was gone. I found a packet of biscuits and began eating them, then I looked through the cupboards and found packets of crisps and a box of chocolate dinner mints. Eating and moving all the time, I didn't stop until they'd been consumed.

Afterwards, I swept up the crumbs and I hid the biscuit wrappers deep in the bin. Then I knelt in front of the toilet, resting my head in my hands. Here we go again, it's finger-down-the-throat time.

The release was enormous. All the anxiety of the previous months and the tension of important meetings were suddenly flushed away. This must be how alcoholics feel when they finally succumb and open that bottle of whisky.

Chris Evans had been someone I'd admired. I cared what he said.

That night I wrote:

*I am lonely. I want someone to hold me and tell me it is all going to be all right. Things must be bad – I made myself sick after bingeing and I haven't done that in a long while.*

*It was such a relief, but now I feel hateful and disgusted with myself.*

*So I continue what feels like a quest. It doesn't taste that good, you know – not yet. Why can't I just enjoy it?*

*Do you know what I feel? That Simon is laughing at*

*me. He thinks I'm stupid, running around like a headless chicken, trying to make sense of the deals and different plans. Maybe I am. But I want to get to grips with this. I really want to know what's going on and to see things clearly. When I read this back, I'm probably going to think, Oh, what the hell am I on about?*

*Get back in line, you silly cow.*

Unexpectedly, Simon announced that he didn't think 'Wannabe' should be our first single. Neither did Virgin Records, who wanted us to launch with a song called 'Love Thing'. I was shocked. Up until then, as far as I knew, we were all singing from the same song sheet. Suddenly, someone had switched pages on us.

I was the only girl in Simon's office as he and two A & R bods from Virgin tried to convince me of their reasoning.

'First songs tend to disappear,' Simon said. 'It's the second single that makes or breaks a new album . . .'

'You want a song that's more mainstream to kick it off,' said one of the others. 'You don't want anything too radical . . .'

I thought, This is bullshit! 'Wannabe' is our signature tune. The more they tried to persuade me, the more certain I was that they were wrong. I felt anxious, but also empowered. I knew what the other girls thought; we were agreed on this.

I called each of the girls from a phone box down the road.

'What do you think? Do you think we should do it?'

Emma was the most clear-cut. She had a childlike certainty that couldn't be shaken. Mel C automatically said, ' "Wannabe" is the one.'

I told Simon, 'It's not negotiable as far as we're concerned. "Wannabe" is our first single.'

I drove home in the dark, freezing my butt off in the MG. For the sake of our long-term relationship, I hoped that Virgin would see things as we did.

On Monday, 19 April, we filmed the video for 'Wannabe'. It was shot in an empty building next to St Pancras station, which had been decorated to look like an old mansion house, with velvet drapes on the walls and echoing corridors.

The central idea for the video was to re-create the same energy and dynamism that we showed when we crashed into record companies and did the frenetic hard sell. We invaded places and left people breathless. The director, Johanne, came up with the location. The station building had been transformed, and populated with odd characters and stereotypes. We had to bounce through the place singing 'Wannabe' and sweeping away the cobwebs.

I wore an outfit which had cost me £20 at a second-hand stall at Notting Hill market. The showgirl outfit was a leotard with sequins on the front and back. Unfortunately, I also insisted on wearing a pair of towering platform shoes, à la Vivienne Westwood. I could hardly walk in them and I certainly couldn't run. I fell over so many times that Johanne grew hoarse yelling, 'Cut!' I wobbled through the entire video, nearly wiping out a lampshade and almost toppling down a flight of stairs. All because I wanted to look tall.

The video appeared to be shot as one continuous take from beginning to end, but was in fact two takes, so perfectly synchronized that no-one could tell.

*The Big Breakfast* sent a crew to do a story on the shoot. They chatted to us between takes – our first proper TV interview – and we spent the entire time talking over the top of each other. We were all learning how to do this, nobody had given us any media training.

On Saturday afternoon I binged again. I can't remember why. I polished off half a birthday cake that had been left in Karen's fridge and felt terrible because it didn't belong to me. I wrote a note to Karen apologizing.

Afterwards, I cleaned the toilet bowl to make sure there was no trace of sick. I kept thinking of all the starving people in the world and there I was wasting food. I hated myself.

There was only one answer: I had to do something good to make amends.

I drove to Tesco in the MG and bought fifty bananas, fifty apples, a dozen loaves of bread and sandwich filling. Then, back in the kitchen, I began making packed lunches.

Mel C phoned. 'What are you doing?'

'Making lunches.'

'Oh.' Mel didn't know how to respond. 'Are you going out tonight?' she asked.

'Yeah. Do you fancy coming down to London with me?'

'Where to?'

'I'm going to deliver some food to the homeless.'

Mel thought about this for a second. She was getting used to my flights of fancy. 'Yeah, I'll come.'

We drove to Charing Cross first and found people sleeping in doorways along the Strand. I kerb-crawled until we saw someone, and then stopped on a double-yellow line, jumped out and ran across the footpath.

'Here you go, mate. Have something to eat.'

A young face looked up from a sleeping bag. I couldn't tell if it was a boy or a girl. The sandwiches were wrapped in clingfilm and Mel had the fruit in carrier bags.

'There's another one over there,' she said, dashing over the road.

Further along the Strand we found four people in a doorway opposite Australia House. They asked for money. 'This is better for you,' I said, handing out the food. They seemed appreciative.

From Charing Cross we drove down to 'Cardboard City' beneath Waterloo Bridge. Parking the car, we walked down the dark steps and discovered a whole new world, a slum township fashioned from cardboard, ply-wood and old blankets. The stench was unbelievable and I felt quite frightened. It was nice to have Mel with me.

Cardboard boxes and packing crates had been made into makeshift dwellings, with just enough room for people to crawl inside. An old guy with a blanket around his shoulders sat beside a trolley full of aluminium cans.

'Here, have something to eat,' I said.

At first he looked at me cautiously, as if he feared I might be trying to poison him, then he accepted the food and put it under his swag. I thought he'd be starving and scoff it down; maybe he didn't want to eat in front of me – even broken men have their pride.

Peering inside a large cardboard box, I noticed a bundle of rags. It began moving. I left the sandwiches and fruit at what seemed to be his feet.

'I wish I'd made more,' I told Mel as we drove home.

'We can always come back another time. It's really sad, isn't it? It sort of opens your eyes and makes you appreciate how lucky we are.'

Although I felt good about helping others, I knew my motives had been purely selfish. I'd been so disgusted with my bingeing that I'd tried to cleanse myself. I wasn't trying to show anybody that I was a nice person. Instead, I wanted to compensate for what I'd done.

Mel came back to the house and we listened to music. The two of us could sit for hours discussing creative ideas, writing lyrics and talking about being famous. All Mel had ever wanted to be was a pop star. Nothing else would do. It had made her one of the most motivated and driven people I have ever met, and one of the most kind-hearted.

Although we'd seen rushes of the video during filming, the final version was eagerly awaited. We gathered in an editing suite in Soho to see the end result.

Simon made an announcement, clearing his throat first, which seemed to signal bad news. 'Virgin want you to reshoot the video.'

'What?' I almost laughed.

'They don't like it.'

'You *are* joking?'

'No.'

I struggled to get my head round the implications. The video had cost £130,000, and the costs were split half and half between the record company and the future earnings of the Spice Girls. Even allowing for the fact that certain people might not like the video, how could they just scrap it? It was a criminal waste of money.

'Simon, I'm sorry, but we can't pull it. I think it's

immoral. You can buy a house for that sort of money. We're talking about a hundred and thirty grand.'

'But they don't like it.'

'I don't care.'

'They've also suggested shooting a different video for America.'

'Why?'

'The Americans are used to slicker, more highly produced music videos.'

'No. The video is great,' I insisted. 'It shows who we are and what we're like.'

That seemed to put an end to the suggestions. In May, Virgin decided to trial the 'Wannabe' video on The Box, a cable pop channel, two months before the single was officially released.

I enjoyed the feeling of nervous excitement. There was a tension in the air and I could feel it whenever I walked into the offices of Virgin or 19 Management. This was the first big test of whether 'Wannabe' was capable of launching the group to bigger things.

In that first week there were seventy requests from viewers to play the 'Wannabe' video – more than for any other song. The signs were good.

Everything that happened to us from now on seemed to be a first. I felt as though we were at the top of an enormous pyramid of people who were working behind the scenes to launch the Spice Girls. Fortnightly planning meetings were held between Virgin, 19 Management and Brilliant, our public relations company. Every aspect of marketing and promotion was discussed, from the artwork on posters to the TV and radio campaigns.

Our first TV appearance took place in April on

*Surprise Surprise*. This is the show where Cilla Black tries to make people's dreams come true. In this case, she wasn't interested in *our* ambitions, but that of a teenage Manchester girl who had bombarded her local radio station with letters, asking if she could become a DJ. She'd even offered to clean the presenter's shoes.

Cilla surprised her with the news that she would become a disc jockey for the day, spinning her favourite discs and interviewing an authentic, honest-to-God bona-fide pop group.

The poor girl had no idea who the Spice Girls were. She looked totally underwhelmed. I think she was hoping for Take That. We didn't have a single to give her, so we signed a poster.

At least they played 'Wannabe'. We'd filmed a special video for the show, showing us singing in a multi-storey carpark in Manchester. The choreography was really tacky, with each of us leaning out from behind a pillar to sing our bit.

*Surprise Surprise* showed the segment on a Saturday night in early May. Mum told everybody about it beforehand, all the other cleaners at the Harlequin – the shopping mall where she worked. She didn't get excited in front of me. I think in the back of her mind she still thought, Why couldn't you just be a teacher?

Even after the show she wasn't overly enthusiastic. Mum has this habit of ignoring the whole package and picking up on obscure details, like my shoes or the location.

'Where was that place you were singing?'

'A carpark.'

'Why you sing there?'

'Because that's what the show wanted.'

'OK.'

For an honest opinion I talked to Janine. She'd always given it to me straight, telling me the unvarnished truth, whether it involved boyfriends or fashion disasters.

'You looked and sounded great, but the bit with the pillar was pretty naff.'

My sentiments exactly.

A few days later, on 16 May, we filmed a segment for *Hotel Babylon*, a late-night music show hosted by Dani Behr. The programme was recorded in a beautiful old manor house in Aylesbury which used to belong to George Harrison.

Loads of my friends from Watford came up to be in the audience when we filmed on Saturday morning. We sang 'Wannabe', and I had never been so nervous. There were no rehearsals or second chances. What a buzz! There must have been at least a hundred people in the audience.

Dani Behr gave us the big introduction and then suddenly the cameras were on us. There was a moment of blind panic in that first few seconds. My legs were shaking and I was certain everyone could see. What on earth were we doing? People were going to see right through us. We weren't pop stars.

Mel C was next to me, and by the second chorus I sneaked a look at her. She was beaming. Then I noticed that people were dancing. They were smiling and clapping. My God, they like us. Does that mean we're good?

'You were fabulous,' said Natalie.

'Really?'

'Just brilliant.'

Still on a high from the show, I drove to Oxford that afternoon to see a friend. A demo tape of 'Mama' blared from the car stereo and I sang along at the top of my voice. It sounded as though there were sirens mixed onto the track. How strange! I looked in the rear-view mirror and saw the flashing lights.

I pulled over and waited on the verge as a young policeman stepped out of the patrol car and strolled up to my window. They had clocked me doing 85 mph.

'Did you see us flashing our lights?'

'No, I'm sorry, I didn't. I was concentrating on the road ahead.'

He had a two-way radio clipped to his shirt. 'We clocked you doing eighty-five miles an hour.'

'It was down hill. This car can't usually go that fast.'

He took my licence and asked me to follow him back to the patrol car. I sat in the back seat while he and his partner did a licence and car-registration check.

The young policeman kept staring at me in the rear-view mirror. Finally he said, 'I know you; you were on that Cilla Black show the other night, *Surprise Surprise*.'

'That's right.'

'Yeah, I recognized your face. You were in that . . . er . . . that . . .'

'Pop group. The Spice Girls.'

'Yes.' He started telling his partner all about it.

I went all bubbly and sweet. 'Did you like us?'

'Yeah, I thought you were good.'

'I've just been filming another show, *Hotel Babylon*. We're on this Friday night.'

'I might watch that.'

Having grovelled enough, I dropped the big question. 'Does that mean you'll let me off then?'

They looked at each other. 'Nah.'

Quite clearly, I wasn't yet famous enough to avoid £30 speeding tickets.

A week later we flew to Japan for a promotional tour. The single was being released there a month in advance. Hopefully, we could use it as a springboard to launch the Spice Girls in the Far East.

Simon had suggested the strategy. Most bands leave the Far East market until last, tackling Europe and America first. But Western pop music had exploded across Asia, and more and more bands were having an impact. It was a massive market that hopefully we could crack.

We travelled by ourselves, with just one PA, Camilla. Simon had stayed in the UK. Local record-company people met us at the airport and arranged transport. From then on it was a jam-packed schedule of interviews, photo shoots and record signings.

The Japanese are very warm and friendly, always smiling and bowing. For once I didn't have to peer up at people; even the men were on my level. The trouble was that nobody in Japan seemed to be big on eye contact. They're not into kissing, either. They shake hands instead. I found this strange because I love to hug.

Some of the interviews were hysterical, particularly for radio, as they struggled to pronounce our names. Geri sounded like Jelly, and they pronounced Victoria as though it was a brand of air freshener. All day we were ferried from studio to studio.

The novelty of being interviewed kept us bright and

bubbling. We swept through places like a force-ten gale, with words tumbling out in a rush. Mel B and I did most of the talking, because we were the loudest and had the most to say.

Sticking to the set pattern, we described how the Spice Girls had formed and what great friends we were.

'Do you have boyfriends?'

'No, not all of us. But we're looking.' Nudge, nudge, wink, wink. 'I quite fancy a Japanese boyfriend.'

'You could put him in your handbag,' yelled Mel B.

### *Tuesday – (Third day in Japan)*

*Well, it's the morning, and Emma and I are lying in bed after an erratic sleep. We've both decided we can't face any more Japanese food. Sometimes this feels like a school excursion – too many rules.*

*Only four more days to go. The photo shoot is today. Great.*

It was decided that 'Wannabe' would be released on Monday, 8 July. A month beforehand it had been put into the clubs. This meant that DJs were playing the song in nightclubs and discos, although it wasn't available in the shops.

The reports filtering back were favourable. The record would be played on the radio several weeks before release. When a band is generating a buzz, this is usually reflected in the pre-sale figures. This is the number of records the shops order, ready for the day of release. The figures were surprisingly strong for 'Wannabe', and there was a growing air of confidence that Virgin might have a hit on its hands.

I had just finished reading a book by Louise Hay called *You Can Heal Your Life*. She had come up with a technique to build self-belief and confidence, which she called a cosmic shopping list. Basically, it meant writing a list of everything you want, but doing it in the present tense, as if these things have already come true. If you believe and visualize things, they will happen for you.

I wrote in my diary:

> *'Wannabe' is the biggest-selling single in 1996.*
> *The video is the most-shown and best-selling video of the year.*
> *The Spice Girls are a huge success.*
> *I am slim and beautiful.*
> *George Michael is my husband.*
> *I am respected.*
> *I am happy and in control.*
> *I have very special friends.*
> *My life is in order.*
> *I feel loved.*

I put George in there because I still thought there was a possibility that he and I were meant to be. You don't lose *all* your schoolgirl crushes.

A month before the launch we began touring UK regional radio stations, being interviewed by dozens of DJs with their up-and-down voices. We travelled in a minibus as far north as Aberdeen and as far west as Manchester. Edinburgh's fourth biggest radio station put 'Wannabe' on their A list, which meant it was played at least six times a day. Pretty cool for a first single. I lost count of how many radio stations we visited and journalists we schmoozed with.

By the second week in July, everything focused on the charts. Would all the hard work pay off? Was 'Wannabe' the right choice?

That Sunday, I invited the girls round to Karen's house to listen to the Top 40. We set a picnic rug out on the lawn and had a bottle of champagne ready and waiting.

'This is the most exciting moment of all,' I said. 'The hoping. The expectation. Remembering how we got here. And now it's all come to this.'

Dr Fox on Capital Radio had counted down from forty to number ten. It reminded me of my schooldays, when I used to huddle around the radio and get excited when Madonna held on at number one. Now we waited for *our* song. The mid-week chart had put 'Wannabe' at number six. Could we go higher?

The sun was shining and I could hear children playing in their back gardens. Number nine was Toni Braxton's 'You're Makin' Me High'. I wanted her to sing faster so we could move on.

Number seven was Celine Dion with 'Because You Loved Me'. Number five was Peter Andre and 'Mysterious Girl'. The tension was unbelievable; we were somewhere in the top four.

Foxy held us in suspense through an ad break. He then announced the highest new entry for the week: 'Wannabe' by the Spice Girls. We were number three! We hugged and danced around the garden in bare feet.

Karen took a picture of us all sitting on the picnic rug holding up three fingers. Later I had it framed, because it showed such a wonderful moment in our lives. We looked so innocent and young.

On Thursday the *Daily Star* ran a headline, HOT SPICE. THESE GIRLS JUST WANNABE DATING!

With the single at number three and tipped to go higher, we were suddenly newsworthy and, more to the point, photogenic 'pop babes'.

The interview had been in a corner pub in East London, with all of us squeezed around a table. Instead of asking us about music and the band, the reporter wanted to talk about sex and what sort of blokes we liked. The *Daily Star*'s readers are mostly working-class men, so we told the reporter what she wanted to hear.

'None of us fancies celebrities that much,' Emma told the reporter. 'They're not real people. We all prefer salt-of-the-earth men, like builders, bricklayers, telephone engineers – those kinds of guys.'

These brief comments were miraculously transformed, and the Spice Girls emerged as a 'sizzling sex-on-legs' treat for honest, hard-working lads.

It wasn't until I saw the story in print that I realized how many people were going to read it and perhaps believe it was true. This was like playing a game. The Spice Girls needed publicity, and the newspaper wanted a sexy picture and story.

'That's how it works,' said Simon. 'Everybody wins.'

The following day we flew back to Japan for more pro-motional work. *En route* we received word that *Top of the Pops*, the most important music programme in the coun-try, wanted us to perform. They had arranged a satellite feed from Tokyo to London. Stepping off the plane, we were rushed to a hotel near the airport. After quickly getting changed, we were taken to the nearby temple that had been chosen as a backdrop.

The summer temperature had climbed into the mid-nineties and we sweltered in the blazing heat. Already exhausted from the flight, I had heavy make-up hiding the dark rings under my eyes. It made my skin feel even clammier, and I had visions of mascara leaking down my cheeks. We used the same dance routine as for our appearance on *Hotel Babylon*. It took an hour to film and I felt dehydrated and jet-lagged by the end.

This was hardly how I envisaged my first appearance on *Top of the Pops*. Instead of hospitality rooms at the BBC and a celebration afterwards at a club or restaurant, we had to settle for bottles of mineral water and a bus trip to the hotel.

The clip went to air on Thursday night and the 'from Japan' introduction made us sound like a big international act. 'Wannabe' was still at number three, but the new chart would be out on Sunday.

It was early evening in Tokyo when the call came through. We were all sitting around in the lounge opposite the hotel reception. The waiter had just delivered a tray of cold drinks.

Camilla walked in with a smile on her face. 'Simon has a message for you all. He says you should crack open a bottle of bubbly.'

'Why?'

'Because "Wannabe" is number one.'

Our hollers and whoops brought the hotel to a standstill as people turned to look at us hugging each other.

'I want to get pissed,' said Mel B, ordering champagne.

'We have to be up at eight.'

'So what? We're NUMBER ONE!'

We celebrated at a Chinese restaurant in the hotel. Mel B kept ordering bottles of champagne and we kept coming up with new things to toast. I drank enough just to get tipsy and to feel a little sad. I didn't want to be on the other side of the world. I wanted to be at home.

This was the moment I'd been waiting for – my ultimate revenge on all those people who had dumped, doubted or ridiculed me. It was also my way of saying thank-you to all those people who had supported and encouraged me.

I wanted them to see me, so I could say, 'Look at me! I did good! I told you so!'

# SCARY, GINGER, SPORTY, BABY AND POSH

*13*

$\mathrm{F}$ame is a gradual thing and I didn't have time to really think about it then. In many ways it's like an addiction that creeps up on you unexpectedly. There are pivotal moments, but for the most part it happens out of sight and is controlled by other people.

When 'Wannabe' stayed at number one for seven weeks, I suddenly found myself being recognized in the street. It also happened to Mel B – perhaps because we were the loudest and most outspoken.

I pulled up at a set of traffic lights in north London as a group of kids were crossing. Suddenly they stopped and one of them pointed. I gave a little wave. Within seconds they were at my window, asking for an autograph. The lights had turned green and the drivers behind were honking their horns, but I found a pen in my bag and wrote 'Love Geri' on the back of my old speeding ticket.

It was nice to be recognized, but I still didn't feel any different inside. I found myself thinking, Is that it? Why am I still here? Somehow I imagined it was going to be something like *Let's Make a Deal*, the game show in

Turkey. 'Geri Halliwell, walk through door number three.' And off I'd go to a place where famous people live – a kind of parallel dimension, where I didn't have the same fears and insecurities as before. Or maybe I just expected the thrill to last longer.

Instead, hard work got in the way. After Japan, we visited Germany and Holland on promotional tours. By then, the commotion in Britain was so great that film crews and photographers were waiting at the airport when we arrived home.

From then on we had no time to ourselves. A typical day went something like this: up at 6 a.m., picked up and driven to TV studios, make-up, rehearsals and an interview on breakfast TV. Back in the cars for the drive to Central London. Two teen magazine shoots, with different outfits, hair and make-up. Interviews with the *Sun*, *Daily Mirror* and the *Independent*, a radio phone-in programme and a charity appearance.

A week later we performed at a Capital Radio Roadshow concert on Clapham Common. Dr Fox joined us on stage after our set. 'I've got some great news to tell you, girls,' he announced. 'You're number one for the fourth straight week.'

The crowd cheered and Foxy asked, 'What do you think about that, Geri?'

'Fucking excellent!'

Oops! I had just sworn live on radio and in front of 10,000 people.

From then on, every time we appeared on a children's TV programme, I was a little nervous about getting overexcited and swearing.

It wasn't always my fault. Virgin Records organized a

Spice Girl party and we expected an informal celebration to thank everyone who had worked so hard on the launch. We sang a few songs from the up-coming album and I started mucking about, pulling faces. The others joined in and we finished by collapsing in a fit of giggles. What I didn't realize was that many of those present were international music journalists and reporters from UK teen magazines.

From then on, I realized that whenever someone organized a Spice Girls party they were never for us.

There were dozens of interviews every day, including one with *Top of the Pops* magazine. The reporter, Peter Lorraine, had lunch with us and did a quirky piece with the headline SPICE RACK. He gave us each a label, which he based on our personalities. With my liveliness, zest and flaming red hair I became Ginger Spice. The others were Posh Spice (Victoria), Sporty Spice (Mel C), Scary Spice (Mel B) and Baby Spice (Emma).

The tags were a marketing man's dream. From that moment on we began using them as alternative names. There was an element of truth in each of the labels, but we pushed them even further. Our characters became more and more cartoon-like. My hair became redder, my lipstick brighter and my outfits more outlandish; Mel C wore tracksuits and did backflips on demand; Mel B's untameable Afro grew even wilder until she looked truly scary; Emma wore pigtails and baby-doll dresses that made her look fifteen years old; and Victoria acquired twenty-five pairs of Gucci shoes.

Emma Forrest of the *Independent* commented that although we were all attractive there was something slightly rough about the Spice Girls. Our make-up was

Maybelline rather than Yves Saint Laurent, she said, with even the 'posh one' having a touch of vulgarity about her.

'Places, everyone. Pay attention, Geri.'

The photographer wore a Lakers baseball cap, blue jeans and running shoes.

We were back in America to film our second video and to do a photo shoot for *More* magazine at Venice Beach.

A crowd of people had gathered to watch us, most of them tourists. The locals were obviously used to seeing film crews and photographers. They live in a kind of human zoo, full of odd and exotic characters.

Although I wanted to go rollerblading along the seafront, work came first. The photographer wanted us to visit stalls, try on clothes and have our tarot cards read. The street stalls smelled of surfboard wax and incense.

'Hey, hey, hey! Over here!' Mel B had discovered a tarot reader who called himself Captain Jim and looked like an old sea salt.

'How much does he want?' Emma asked.

'He'll do us all for eighty dollars.'

'Who's got any money?'

We all shrugged. 'Hey, Camilla, can you lend us eighty bucks?'

None of us carried money any more. It wasn't a conscious decision. We didn't have time to go to the bank and often it meant being recognized or drawing a crowd.

Captain Jim started with Mel C.

'I can see that you've got a really bad diet and you're living on junk food.'

We looked at each other in disbelief.

Emma was told that she'd have a drinking problem,

Mel B was going to do charity work in the Third World, and I'd marry young, settle down and live quietly in the country. By then we'd heard enough.

Afterwards, we posed for photographs at the open-air gym. The body builders were oiled up, with their veins popping out of their forearms. One guy had a neck the size of my waist and looked pumped full of steroids; he was so covered in fake tan that it dripped off him when he sweated. The photographer wanted us to hang off him and we all complained.

'That's disgusting,' said Emma.

'Too many steroids,' whispered Mel B.

'How do you know?'

'Check out the lunchbox.'

When the shoot finished, we still had another assignment at the beach. The Spice Girls had a quarterly magazine, and I came up with the idea of doing a photo story parodying *Baywatch*. In the back of the Land Cruiser we all changed into bright-red one-piece swimming costumes.

'Who hasn't got a whistle?'

The girls nodded.

'OK, we'll do some shots at the lifeguard tower and then on the sand.'

We clambered onto the tower and struck various poses, scouring the shoreline. I had this vision of a swimmer getting into difficulties and mistaking us for real lifeguards.

A jeep appeared from further along the beach. The driver looked nothing at all like David Hasselhoff.

'Hey, have you guys got a permit?'

Camilla and the photographer looked blankly at each other.

'We're taking some holiday snaps for our friends back home,' I said, giving him my cutest smile.

'You need a permit from the sheriff's office to film or photograph commercially on the beach.'

Emma batted her eyelids and flirted.

I started blagging. 'Oh, the permit. Yes, of course we have permission. I'm sure if you check with the sheriff's office you'll find all the paperwork is in order.'

The lifeguard eyed us suspiciously. 'OK, I'll go and check. In the mean time, you'll take no more photographs.'

The jeep disappeared down the beach.

'Quick, let's do this bloody thing before he comes back,' I said.

I had a list of shots that I'd written down earlier. Marshalling everyone into position, we managed to get through them all. Spicewatch later became a hugely popular poster, selling around the world.

Four days later we drove into the Mojave Desert. When the scrapyards and roadside diners disappeared, I knew that we were truly in the wilderness. When the billboards stopped it felt like a different planet.

I'd never been into a desert before. I imagined miles and miles of emptiness, with barely a hint of green, yet there was nothing bleak about the Mojave. The salt flats and gravel basins were dotted with cactus and sagebrush. And the sky stretched upwards almost endlessly, passing through different shades of blue.

The heat was unbelievable, topping 112°F at midday. Air-conditioners hummed at full power on the trailers and awnings were rigged up to provide shade.

The video for 'Say You'll Be There', our second single,

was to be radically different from the first. It had a science-fiction feel and was loosely based on the movie *Faster Pussycat! Kill! Kill!* Dressed in figure-hugging leather and PVC catsuits, we were all transformed into freedom-fighting superheroes. In keeping with the B-movie flavour, I dreamed up some names for each of us. I was Trixie Firecracker; Victoria became Midnight Suki; Mel C was Katrina High Kick; Emma, Kung Fu Candy and Mel B, Blazing Bad Zula.

I wore skin-tight PVC hot pants and a zipper top, as well as thigh-length boots with lethal-looking spiked heels.

Filming started early each morning in a bid to escape the heat, yet by the time we finished wardrobe, hair and make-up it was already stifling. At times I waited for hours between scenes. My make-up melted like ice cream and the frames of my sunglasses were too hot to touch, yet there was something wonderful about dressing up and escaping into a fantasy world.

Poor Victoria wore a full PVC catsuit and the director had her balancing on the back of a car for more than an hour. She nearly fainted in the heat just for three seconds of footage.

In one scene I had to balance on my three-inch heels and throw a heavy martial-arts blade. The silver disc had three spikes and skimmed through the air. I had to throw it off to one side of the camera, just above head height.

'Try that again, Geri. See if you can throw it a little straighter,' said the director.

'It's impossible to balance in these shoes.'

'I know. Just concentrate.'

The crew was off to one side, watching from a safe distance.

I wound up and launched the blade. It curved through the air like a boomerang and I could hear people shouting.

Our poor hairdresser, Denilio, the boy genius, looked up in time to see this thing skimming towards his head. It sliced off the very tip of his right ear.

'I am so sorry. I'm a bit dangerous,' I told him. He was relieved to still have his head on his shoulders.

In the evening, we drove back to a small hotel on the edge of the desert, where the beer was cold and the rooms were air-conditioned. We were up again at four in the morning and arrived on location when it was still dark. The silence of the desert had the same effect as a vast, empty cathedral. Conversations automatically dropped to a whisper. I lay alongside Mel B on the roof of a car and we stared upwards. I'd never seen so many stars. I felt as if the roof of the universe had come down to touch my nose.

'What are you going to do when you're really famous?'

'What do you mean?' asked Mel.

'I want to do something good. I want to stand up and speak out about an issue that doesn't normally get raised, or for a group of people who struggle to be heard.'

Mel thought about this for a while. 'I'm going to speak out for people of mixed race,' she said.

Until I met Mel, I'd never been very aware of racism. She had shown me how it existed everywhere. From the earliest stages of our friendship she described what it was like to walk into a place and to be aware of your colour because everybody else was white.

And she would say, 'I am not black. I am not white. I am mixed race.' She was very proud of the fact and I admired her strength and certainty.

'I feel like Thelma and Louise,' I said, staring at the desert sky.

'Yeah. I know exactly what they'd be doing.'

'What's that?'

Mel grinned at me and pulled off her top. She's such a free spirit that she seizes moments like that. She knew I'd follow.

We stripped naked except for our bovver boots. It was pitch-black and we could barely see each other, just hear our voices. The rest of the crew were busy setting up or doing their own thing in the caravans.

'Come on, let's go,' said Mel. We went sprinting across the plateau, with everything bouncing. I've never felt so liberated and alive. Mel caught up with me and we ran side by side, then we skipped around the sagebrush, feeling like desert nymphs or flower children.

The sky turned a brilliant midnight blue just before the dawn. We barely noticed that it was growing light until the rocky outcrops began to emerge.

Suddenly we realized that we had to get back or everyone would see us. We sprinted towards the car and laughed as we pulled on our denim shorts and tops. It felt wonderful to have shared the moment with each other.

Despite the success of 'Wannabe' a lot of the so-called experts considered the song to be a lightning bolt that wouldn't hit twice. The Spice Girls were written off as being a one-hit wonder. One music magazine editor dismissed us as 'vaudevillian girls with pushy mothers'.

Yet the pre-sale figures for 'Say You'll Be There' were the highest ever taken by Virgin Records. It meant that we were almost guaranteed to enter the charts at number one.

In the mean time we had a tour of the Far East that included Japan, Hong Kong, Thailand and Korea. 'Wannabe' had reached number one in seventeen countries and sold more than six million copies. I could have sworn that I had personally met every one of the buyers over the previous two months. Of course we complained to Simon about the workload, but none of us really minded. We had given ourselves two years to make the most of it, and it was only just starting.

Simon had business to discuss over dinner. Pepsi wanted us to star in a TV advertisement and marketing campaign that would put our photograph on 100 million cans of soft drink. There were other deals being negotiated to launch dozens of official Spice Girl products, from duvets to dolls.

Simon mentioned the figure Pepsi were offering.

'Is that all?' I asked. The others looked at me in disbelief. 'Is that the first offer or their final offer?'

'The first offer,' said Simon.

'Good. Then I'm sure you'll be able to get more.'

I sensed that Simon wasn't impressed, but it was part of my nature to haggle over prices and strike better deals. I was my father's daughter.

On long flights, Simon and I sat together and talked about 'the big plan'. He knew I was interested in the business side of the Spice Girls and he treated me like his little protégée.

We had a brilliant time in Hong Kong. On our way to a gig at Planet Hollywood, we decided to walk instead of taking cars or taxis. Mel C had a beatbox on her shoulder and a Backstreet Boys song, 'We've Got It Going On', was playing.

We skipped and danced down the street, oblivious to the stares of pedestrians and drivers. Slipping round the back of Planet Hollywood, past the smelly bins and through the kitchens, we emerged on stage. The place was packed with a real melting pot of nationalities, including a bunch of British lads who gave us a huge cheer and lots of cheek.

We did a showcase of three songs and left them wanting more. That's the way to do it. Later, as I shimmied out of my red dress to go to the toilet, I marvelled at how well all five of us were getting on. There were no fights or arguments; we had naturally sorted ourselves out during interviews so that everybody had their turn.

I didn't realize then that exhaustion would change things. By the time we reached Bangkok we were all tired. Instead of sitting and chatting in our rooms, the girls' doors were closed and they slept.

At 11 p.m. I wandered downstairs to the bar, looking for company. I just needed somebody to talk to. Although I loved the girls, I found it very difficult to reach out and pick up the phone, or knock on a door and say, 'I don't feel so good.' I had always tried to be the strong one who didn't need reassurance. There was nobody in the bar except a pianist and two businessmen having a nightcap.

Outside, it was hot and muggy. Dad, who suffered from asthma, used to say, 'It feels like I'm breathing through treacle.' Now I knew what he meant.

I began walking along the road. Traffic had banked up on the busy main road and red tail lights glowed in the distance. The barrow stalls and kiosks had been boarded up and padlocked for the night and the air smelled of over-ripe fruit and petrol fumes. In the alleys I could see stray dogs picking through torn rubbish sacks.

The first few drops of rain were so large that they hit the footpath and seemed to explode. Within seconds it was teeming down and I was drenched. I turned and began running back towards the hotel, dodging dark shapes that huddled beneath umbrellas. Rain stung my eyes and my shoes had filled with water. My jeans and shirt clung to my skin and water poured from the peak of my cap. It felt wonderful. The walls had been closing in on me, but now I felt free and alive. Why did I feel boxed in by my own anxiety? What was I afraid of?

Back at the hotel I had a shower and then heard Simon knocking at the door. He wanted to talk. Why was I constantly questioning his decisions?

'Geri, you need to let go,' he said. 'I am the manager. Don't always feel you have to control everything. Just concentrate on what you have to do.'

He didn't understand that I'd always been independent. At six years old I was getting myself off to school. I left home at sixteen. I had survived by myself. Suddenly I was in a band and had to think about everybody else, and I found it very difficult to lean on the others.

'You're in a group now,' said Simon. 'Let me deal with things.'

I knew what he meant. This was his platoon and I had to fall into line.

'You don't think I fit in, do you?'

'I'm not saying that.'

'Do you want me to leave?'

'Don't be silly. I just want you to relax a little. Don't feel as if you're responsible for everything.'

I knew he was right about me worrying. I couldn't help it. It might all end tomorrow. We might fail or break up or make the wrong decisions. I couldn't let that happen. Succeeding meant too much to me.

After Simon had gone, I rang room service and ordered five servings of chicken kebabs. When they arrived, I pulled the chicken pieces off the skewers onto a cotton serviette. Then I wrapped them up and went downstairs in the lift. It was 2 a.m. and the lobby was deserted except for a girl on reception. It had stopped raining.

I walked to a bus stop outside the hotel and began whistling. The first stray dog had a mangy coat and limped as though it had taken a kick or a knock from a car. It was soon joined by others as I shared out the chicken pieces.

'I am a good person,' I told myself. 'I am doing something good here.'


'Say You'll Be There' had gone straight to number one, breaking all sorts of records and creating a media frenzy. Photographers screamed out our names while jostling and wrestling each other.

The cheeky, bum-pinching, knicker-flashing antics of the Spice Girls had captured the public's imagination. The tabloid newspapers went to town, demanding interviews, door-stepping our homes and wanting to know every detail of our backgrounds. It was said that a Spice Girls front page could increase daily sales by 10 per cent.

The *Sun* and the *Daily Mirror* – arguably the two most

competitive and aggressive newspapers in the world – were trying to outdo each other with various Spice stories.

After we'd finished shooting a commercial for the album, a *Mirror* journalist came to our hotel for an interview. She began asking questions about the holiday Mel B and I took to the Canary Islands. Despite the smiles and light-hearted banter, it was clear she was digging for dirt. The girls seemed to close ranks and grow very protective. What did the *Mirror* have?

As a tease, we convinced the reporter to get dressed up in our clothes and become the sixth Spice Girl. We made her do a series of racy poses, knowing that she'd be embarrassed later.

The paparazzi behaved like pigs all day. Victoria had a snapper put a camera up her skirt as we arrived at Radio One. They were crouching beside the car doors, hoping to get a flash of gusset as we stepped out.

The *Daily Mirror* revealed its hand the next morning. They had photographs of Mel B sunbathing topless in Gran Canaria. I was on the sunbed next to her but, just for a change, I had my top on. Phew!

Ralph and Sue, the couple we'd met on the holiday, had flogged their holiday snaps and a story about us. They described wild parties in their apartment and claimed that Mel and I were always prowling for men.

The next day we flew to France. That evening I had a phone call from Simon. Somebody from my old modelling agency was threatening to sell topless pictures of me to the newspapers. Apparently, one of the shots showed my crotch. It had been taken without my knowledge by a photographer who claimed to be changing film.

I felt sick. Just when I thought things could only get

better my past began catching up with me. It was like a runaway train that was going to squash me flat.

I'd known this day would come. In the very early days of the group, I had discussed it with the girls. I made them sit down at Fairlawns and I showed them my modelling portfolio. I wanted them to know exactly what my past had been, so that it didn't come as a surprise later.

'When we become famous, people are going to start looking for skeletons,' I said. 'I guess you could say that my skeletons are these pictures.'

'What's the problem? Madonna did it,' said Mel C.

I appreciated the support. We all knew that our pasts would be scrutinized. Former boyfriends and lovers would be tracked down. Friends and relatives would be asked for stories and pictures.

'We have to be ready to answer the questions,' I said. 'If there's something embarrassing, we have to know about it in advance. That way we can decide how to limit the damage.'

Even then, I don't think I fully appreciated the impact my glamour modelling might have on the Spice Girls. Now I'd been given a very short, sharp lesson on how others would try to profit from my past.

'The story is going to run anyway,' I said to Simon wearily. 'There are too many photographs of me out there. We can't buy them all up.'

*Friday, 25 October 1996 – Paris*

*Today we had four interviews, which were OK. I hardly spoke. I have no confidence whatsoever. Everyone is*

*really tired. We sang 'Wannabe' on a TV show, which
gave me a lift. It was a joy to perform after all this time.
Performing is when we are most at ease.*

*There were loads of feisty fans grabbing at us as we
left Paris on the Eurostar. That's where I'm writing
now.*

*I am very conscious of my position in the band.
Perhaps I have even taken two steps back in the last
couple of days. That's because I have been with the girls
constantly. There is no breathing space to collect my
thoughts and assess who and what I am.*

*Now, to make matters worse, the papers are going to
find out about my topless modelling.*

I started bingeing in my hotel room. Old habits die
hard. I woke next morning feeling and looking awful. I
started eating straight away, before I'd done my make-up
and hair. Emma and Mel B were feeling unwell and they
wanted to cancel the planned trip to Rome, but Simon
wouldn't hear of it.

We had to do a TV show and photo shoot before they
managed to see a doctor, then we caught a plane to
Rome. I fell asleep, only to be shaken awake by severe
turbulence. I started to think about the La Bamba disaster
and imagined us all perishing in a crash like Buddy
Holly and Ritchie Valens.

The Italian fans were brilliant. There were dozens of
them waiting outside the hotel and they gave us an
enormous cheer. It made me feel wonderful. On top of
that, I was put in the same room that Madonna had stayed
in and got to sleep in the same bed.

It had been a better day. Emotionally, I still felt quite

low, but on the surface I was funny, talkative, cheeky and optimistic. If only I could stop eating.

For two days reporters from the *News of the World* and the *Sunday Sport* had been chasing the story that I'd once been a topless model. By Saturday morning it appeared likely that they had photographs and would run them the following day.

In fact they had nothing, but they bluffed a Virgin publicist into confirming the story.

On Sunday the *News of the World* announced, SPICE GIRL'S NUDE PHOTO SHOCK.

From that moment on every glamour photographer, studio and picture library in the country began searching their archives for topless or nude shots of Geri Halliwell. It was only a matter of time before they found them.

That morning, I woke in sunny Rome feeling tired and rather large around the waist. After a coffee, a cigarette and a bath, I went downstairs. We had teen-magazine interviews first thing in the morning. It wasn't until nearly lunchtime that I managed to call Karen in Watford and ask about the UK papers.

The fact that nobody had photographs was no comfort to me at all. It meant the story would keep running until the pictures surfaced. And how long would it be before an interviewer raised the subject live on TV or radio? I had to be ready.

That evening we did an Italian TV show with a smarmy host and loads of pretty girls in high-cut leotards. We sang 'Say You'll Be There' and then smudged the host with lip-stick kisses. Back in my hotel room, I took two tranquillizers, ate too much and fell asleep. I could hear the Italian fans outside, chanting our names.

'Emma . . . Emma . . .'

'Geri . . . Geri . . .'

They were still there when I woke up. I opened the window and gave them a wave from the balcony. What a lovely way to start the day. I wanted to take the Italian fans with me; they could be my alarm clock every morning.

Another day, another night, another hotel room. This one in Bologna. I pigged out on room service until I felt ugly and bloated. 'Why do I keep going round in circles?' I asked, as I cleaned another toilet bowl. 'I should be on top of the world.'

'Wannabe' had gone to number one in twenty-two countries and the album had already been released in Japan, where the Spice Girls had become the biggest-selling British band since The Beatles. What is wrong with me?

I woke late and had to dash downstairs to the lobby. The girls were waiting impatiently. We caught a flight home and I felt incredibly relieved.

As I walked into Karen's house my depression and sadness seemed to lift. Natalie and Janine were there. I gave them enormous hugs and listened to all the local gossip about friends and babies.

'I think I'm pregnant,' said Janine.

'You're not?'

She nodded excitedly.

'Come here. I want another hug.' I was so happy for her. 'You're pregnant and I look pregnant. We make a good pair.'

They managed to cheer me up, as we sat on my bed and began flicking through holiday brochures. Where could we go over Christmas? Somewhere nice, warm and away from it all.

That night I wrote:

## Tuesday, 29 October, 1996

*I've come to the conclusion that family and Janine definitely come first. My energy has been spread too thinly.*

*I really want to start tomorrow with a good approach and attitude and maintain that throughout this next trip to Sweden and Norway. I want to enjoy it.*

The next morning I discovered that *Here* magazine had published pictures of me naked, reclining over a tree trunk. The *Sun* reprinted the same photographs on page three, under the banner SPICE TO SEE YOU TWO! 'Exclusive: chart-topper Geri's greatest hits.'

The shots had been taken in Burnham Beeches, Buckinghamshire. They dated back to my earliest days of modelling, when I was trying to get a decent portfolio together. Surely now the floodgates would open. What would the girls think? What would they say?

We had a day off before flying to Sweden. I went for a jog, five times round the football field just up the road from Karen's house. A couple of young boys were kicking a soccer ball at the goals and a man tossed a stick to his dog.

As I ran, I made up little chants to myself.

'I am confident . . . I am great . . . I love my friends . . .

they love me, too ... I am confident ... I am great ...'

I also used my old traffic-light technique to push myself harder. 'If I don't finish another two laps, then I'll never be anything,' I'd tell myself. Run, Geri, run.

There were 500 fans waiting for us at Stockholm airport. The interviews started in the limousine on the way to a chatshow and they didn't stop all day. The same question kept cropping up. 'Would we strip for a million dollars?' Apparently, a cable sex channel had made the offer.

'You must be joking,' said Emma, giggling.

'That's not our thing,' added Mel B.

I said nothing.

The last interview of the day was terrible. In the middle of it, the woman reporter pulled out a photograph of me naked and said, 'What do you think of that?'

Oh my God, I thought. 'Well, yes, that is something I did in the past. Thank you very much. Let's move on.'

The other girls were quick to back me up. They, too, didn't want the media to focus on my past. They wanted to move on and talk about the Spice Girls.

I had become very conscious of not saying too much. I even measured it. I spoke only two lines in one interview. Similarly, I was careful about barging or butting in, or having a strong opinion. Instead, I went along with the majority.

I didn't want to reveal private things about myself to journalists. They could have my smile, a little chat and a bit of humour, but that's all. Unfortunately, I hadn't yet learned that the more you hide, the more people want to see.

\* \* \*

From Stockholm we flew to Oslo in Norway. Victoria had been vomiting all night and she showed a lot of courage by keeping going. I fell asleep on the flight with my head on a food tray – how attractive!

We went straight from the airport to a children's TV show and then did another round of TV interviews. During one of them I had the same stunt pulled as before: a topless photograph was shoved under my nose.

The interviewer asked, 'Are you proud of your topless modelling, or do you regret it?'

I looked him directly in the eyes and said, 'It is something I did. As we point out in "Wannabe", if you want to know me now, forget my past.' My heart was pounding.

Victoria felt so unwell that she couldn't rehearse for that night's TV appearance. Our sweet and very funny young assistant, Rachel, stood in for her.

During the day we heard that one of the girls from Abba wanted to meet us. I don't know whether it was Agnetha or Frida. None of us could be bothered, which really shocked me. I felt terrible. I'd been an Abba fan. I used to sing 'Super Trooper' into my hairbrush.

Yet in truth, after working so hard during the day, there was no energy left to go out socializing. It took a lot of strength of character just to keep smiling and be polite no matter what.

The TV appearance went well. My favourite moments were performing. For those few minutes we sang and moved in harmony, just like in the days at Trinity Studios when the bonds were so tight between us.

Victoria managed to get through the show without vomiting, but we still had to do Germany.

It was late on Friday night in Oslo. Mel C had gone to

bed. Emma and Mel B were at a restaurant somewhere in the city and Victoria was making phone calls home to her boyfriend. I didn't feel sleepy. Dozens of fans had braved the cold and were standing outside the hotel.

Putting on an old tracksuit, I pulled my hair back and pushed it beneath a baseball cap. I wore no make-up and had Jamiroquai coming through the earphones of my personal CD player. Keeping my head down, I strolled from the hotel, past the waiting fans and into the night.

As I walked the streets, I saw couples kissing in the shadows and teenagers hanging out in restaurants and bars. A saxophonist was busking in a city square and I gave him the last of my change. Normally, I didn't carry money, but I'd found a handful of coins in my hotel room.

A black guy was preaching from a soapbox about the evils of the world and how we live in a 'virtual insanity'. I walked on, unnoticed, revelling in the fact that nobody recognized me. Eventually I felt confident enough to make eye contact with people and smile. I used to do that all the time. I was one of those people who started chatting to the stranger next to me on the tube. Now I couldn't travel on trains or buses. The only strangers I met were businessmen in the first-class sections of planes. We'd chat over coffee and after-dinner mints.

I didn't regret one moment of the Spice Girls, but it was nice to be normal for a while and to do something as simple as taking a late-night stroll, looking in the shop windows.

Stopping outside a church, I climbed the stone steps and pushed at the large doors. My footsteps echoed in the emptiness as I walked inside and sat down. Churches have such a strange vibe. I lit a candle and watched the molten wax slide down the sides and cool. The flame could never hope to illuminate such a massively dark place.

I could hear the faint strains of laughter and music outside. I wished that Dad were alive. I had this vision of him sitting in a leather armchair in his study and saying, 'Geri, let me tell you about life.' And he would give me all this wonderful advice about how to overcome unhappiness and loneliness.

He'd say things like, 'The path of true love never runs straight,' and, 'Don't be the last to leave the party.'

Of course, this was just another of my show-reels. My dad never owned a leather armchair, or had a study. His advice was always that of a romantic who had read too many soppy love stories, rather than a practical man full of homespun wisdom. It didn't stop me loving him just as much, though.

I felt safe in the church – protected from the world outside. For those few minutes, nothing could intrude and touch me.

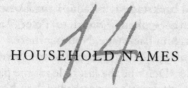

# HOUSEHOLD NAMES

## Sunday, 3 November – Munich

*10 p.m. I've just got in – another long day. I had another horrible dream last night that I had boils growing on my legs. I was exhausted when I woke up. Went for a little jog in the bright Munich sunshine.*

*Then went to the studio for the Bravo photo shoot. That was OK, although my make-up artist was a bit dodgy. We did Bravo TV and Bravo sex talk – what great fun!*

*Afterwards we did our 'thang' at the House Party gig. It all went well. We met Gloria Gaynor. 'Your song is an anthem,' I told her.*

*OK, so there is my day.*

Not quite. The first gut-wrenching news of the morning came courtesy of the *Daily Star*. The front-page headline read, HOW I COULDN'T MAKE IT AS A MODEL.

It went on to claim that I had failed as a glamour model, which had been my 'life-long ambition'. Oh please!

It shouldn't have come as a complete surprise. Two months earlier the same newspaper had claimed that my motto was 'A lover a day keeps the doctor away'. It described me as having gone absolutely 'bonkers' over pop star Peter Andre – bombarding him with phone calls after we'd chatted backstage at a Radio 1 roadshow.

I had never spoken a word to Peter Andre. I had brushed past him backstage. Nothing more.

'How can they write that?' I asked Simon. 'It's not true.'

'I know, Geri, but it's more trouble than it's worth to do anything about it.'

Later, I bumped into the reporter who wrote the story, Linda Duff. 'How could you write that?' I asked her.

She shrugged. 'I couldn't go back to the office with nothing. I'd get in trouble with my editor.'

Apart from my supposed failure as a model, another 'exclusive' story appeared on the same weekend, this time in the *News of the World*.

SIZZLING SPICE GIRL WAS TOO FLAMING HOT IN BED

A muscle-bound fitness instructor claimed that I left him a panting physical wreck after a sex marathon. I was an absolute man-eater, he said, who screamed and shouted during sex, wore knee-length leather boots in bed and left claw-marks on his back. I even answered my mobile phone while naked on top of him. Apparently, all of this had taken place in Dave's bedroom while his mum, Norma, was downstairs.

More like in his dreams!

The entire story was a fabrication. Dave was the male model I'd met at the Pink Floyd video shoot. I had been on one date with him, in Greenwich, which ended with a peck on the cheek at the railway station. The only room I saw in his house was the kitchen when he made me a cup of tea.

After the final paragraph, the newspaper asked its readers if any of them had ever romanced a Spice Girl, or had early photographs of us. If so, they were to call on a special hotline.

I rang Mum from Germany to tell her the story wasn't true.

'Geri, don't worry, I know it,' she said. 'Nobody has sex for four hours.' We had a laugh.

I also wanted to call the editor of the paper and complain, but again Simon told me to forget about it. 'You'll only turn it into a bigger issue.'

'But it's a lie.'

'Yes, and tomorrow it will be fish-and-chip wrapping.'

He was right. 'Muscleman Dave' was a wannabe trying to make a name for himself – the worst kind.

I plodded through the day, feeling lonely and under siege. That evening everyone went out for dinner except Mel B and me. After knocking gently on her door, I sat on the end of her bed in my nightdress as we chatted about the past few weeks.

'I can't understand how you've coped through all this,' she said.

'I'm asking myself that.'

Mel could be quite deep and whenever we talked like this the conversation always drifted down a similar path, with Mel saying things like, 'We're all on a learning curve.'

'Life is just one big lesson.'

'Everything happens for a reason.'

'You gotta take the rough with the smooth.'

She didn't half go on sometimes, but I appreciated her being there. She seemed to care. My relationship with Mel had been one of the most demanding, intense, hectic, confusing and frustrating in my life. Behind her loud voice and aggressive style, I could recognize a truth and honesty. She could do the same with me. It felt pretty cool to know somebody that well.

Although I chose fame, my family didn't. I hadn't realized how the Spice Girls would impact upon their lives. I thought it would just be me. When 'Wannabe' came out, Mum didn't understand the huge marketing campaign being planned. She told me, 'Don't worry, Geri. I've been telling everybody about the group. All the teenagers at the mall.'

'Please, Mum, you don't have to do that.'

'No, I tell them. I am very proud. This way you sell more records.'

Now she was beginning to regret having opened her mouth. Teenagers followed her around the shopping mall as she cleaned, constantly asking her questions about me.

The *Daily Mail* ran a photograph of Mum with a mop in the hand, standing beside a rubbish bin. The headline read, SPICE GIRL'S MUM CLEANS BINS FOR £4.33 AN HOUR.

The inference was unmistakable. Here I was, a successful pop star with two number-one singles, but my mother still worked every day as a Mrs Mop, cleaning at a shopping centre. I was clearly too mean-spirited and penny-pinching to help her out.

Yet I'd begged her to give up her job and avoid the hassle.

'No, I want to continue it,' she said.

'You don't need the money any more.'

'I like my job.'

'OK, but you simply have to learn not to open the door. Ask who it is first. And when reporters phone up, you say, "Thank you very much, no comment." Never engage in conversation.'

It was very hard for her. She had been taught that it was rude to shut the door or hang up on people. The reporters were so polite and charming that Mum wanted to invite them inside and make them an omelette.

'I'm sorry, I can't talk to you,' she'd say, and ten minutes later she'd still be chatting away on the doorstep, too polite to shut the door in their faces. And when she came home to discover teenage fans waiting outside the house, she took them inside, made cups of tea and acted like an old mother hen, solving all their teenage problems.

Some of the journalists went to extraordinary lengths. My Aunt Maria in Spain had the *Sun* arrive on her doorstep. They took her out to dinner and, glad of the company, she chatted away about my childhood holidays in Spain. She even gave them photographs.

Another newspaper published a photograph of the Walter de Merton Junior School netball team, showing a rather toothy Geri Halliwell in the front row. The paper had tracked down my team members and asked them about me. For God's sake, what were they going to say? I was only eight years old.

All of the girls encountered similar stories. Just before Christmas, the *Sunday People* ran a photograph showing people allegedly snorting cocaine at a party Mel C had been at. The whole premise of the story seemed to be guilt by association. Of course, anybody who remotely knew Mel found the suggestion absolutely ridiculous. She treated her body like a temple, exercising constantly and eating the perfect diet. She'll live to be 120.

Emma and Victoria had both been stitched up by former boyfriends, who'd sold pictures and details of their sex lives to the tabloids. Afterwards, Emma and I would plot our imaginary revenge, fantasizing about a well-aimed drop-kick and pouring pints of beer over their heads. They deserved far worse.

### Thursday, 6 November 1996, 4 a.m.

*I didn't get in till 3.30 a.m. Spent all day filming the video for '2 Become 1'. They shot everything on a blue screen so that the backdrop of New York can be super-imposed later. Seems a little silly considering we'll be in New York next week. Why not use the real thing?*

*We all had to wear winter coats, and at the very end a little deer wandered in. It was the director's idea. God knows what a deer is supposed to be doing in New York! It gave us a running gag all day. Whenever someone made a mistake it was, 'Oh, dear.'*

*During hair and make-up at midday we did an interview with the NME and then dashed across the road to do a promotion at MTV. We made a five-minute trailer advertising a competition to take 170 children to Lapland with the Spice Girls in December to meet Father Christmas.*

*After all that, I had to wait until eight o'clock tonight for my scenes in the video. I've been anxious and*

On our way to a holiday in Maui in July 1995 – our first overseas trip. Back then we carried our own bags.

SKOOLS OUT!!

1116. Naughty Girls

Backstage at *Top of the Pops*.

A champagne moment with Simon.

Best friends. Janine came to visit me in a Paris hotel in autumn 1997 – she kept my feet on the ground.

The fans, photographers
and frenzy at another public
appearance.

We're number one!
'Wannabe' tops the UK charts
and we celebrate in Japan.

The president, the prince
and the showgirls. South
Africa, November 1997.
*People in Pictures Ltd/John Hogg*

Photograph: Richard Young, Rex USA

Photograph: Mark Seliger © Straight Arrows Publishers c

Photograph: © Hachette – EMAP Magazines Ltd

Photograph: Christophe Gstadler
© The Condé Nast Publications Ltd

Photograph: Peter Robathan © The Face

The Brits 1997 – the Spice
Girls come of age.

Hiding in St Tropez. © *Alpha*

The biggest stage of all.
Addressing the world's press at
the United Nations. *PA News*

Breast Cancer Care – a cause close to my heart. *PA News*

Singing 'Happy Birthday' to a prince – the perfect laxative. *PA News*

My guardian angel. George rescued me when I had nowhere to go.

Who knows what tomorrow will bring? *Dean Freeman*

*stressed all day. That's why I stuffed my face with comfort food. Same old bollocks. I thought I was getting over this.*

*At least the rushes of the video were good. Emma and I looked almost like twins.*

'Are they waiting for us?' asked Mel C as she pulled the curtain back a few inches. Below us in Oxford Street 5,000 people were chanting for the Spice Girls.

We were holed up in the Berkshire Hotel, waiting for our cars to arrive. I looked over Mel's shoulder. There were mothers with strollers, fathers carrying children on their shoulders and hundreds of teenagers waving sparklers.

'Listen to that, will you,' said Emma, getting misty-eyed. Mel C was also blinking back tears.

Sections of the crowd were singing 'Wannabe', spontaneously taking the different parts. It gave me goosebumps.

We were in a hotel room overlooking the crowd. The Spice Girls had been invited to turn on the Christmas lights in Oxford Street. Beforehand, there were competition winners to meet and some wonderfully brave young kids with eczema and asthma. It was amazing to see their strength and courage.

'OK, the cars are ready,' said Jerry Judge, our head of security. He's an Irishman, but he reminds me of John Wayne. There was another bodyguard in the hall and a third minding the lift. A fourth fell into step as we crossed the foyer.

Jerry paused at the doors and waited for a signal from the police. He loved all this cloak and dagger stuff. He made it seem as though there were snipers waiting on the rooftops to pick us off.

'OK, go, go, go! Move, move!' He urged me forward, aware that I couldn't run in platform shoes. The doors to the Jags were open and the engines were running. Police motorcyclists with blue flashing lights had taken up positions at the front and on either side.

The cars edged off and moved slowly round the block, approaching Oxford Street again. Suddenly it seemed as if a thousand stars had burst from the footpaths. I could hear the crowd screaming and see their faces lit up by the strobe-like flashes of the cameras.

I sat next to Simon and he gave my hand a squeeze. He knew the previous few weeks had been difficult for me, with my glamour-modelling pictures splashed over the papers. 'Don't worry, Geri, this has made you seriously famous,' he said.

Rather than damage the Spice Girls, my naughty past seemed to have simply added to the appeal. Whereas a drug scandal would have killed our popularity stone dead, sexy pictures were evidently OK. Parents were still happy for their youngsters to listen to the band and apparently the lads seemed to have a soft spot for me.

We pulled up outside the HMV store, where a cherry-picker stood ready to carry us aloft to turn on the Christmas lights. As the doors opened the sound hit me. Unbelievable! My heart pounded. They were screaming for us! There were banners everywhere, saying things like MARRY ME, EMMA! and I LOVE YOU, GERI!

I skipped over towards one of the barricades and a sea of hands shot out, just wanting to touch me. I couldn't hear what they were screaming. Most of it was simply noise. I could see Jerry Judge near by. He didn't want us doing anything that could cause the crowd to surge.

This is what it must have been like for The Beatles, I thought.

The Lord Mayor was waiting for us, along with Dr Fox from Capital Radio, which was broadcasting live. It took them five minutes to round up the girls from various corners of the clearing. We climbed into the cherry-picker and rose slowly to the platform.

I felt completely overwhelmed. Is this it? Is this what I wanted?

Dr Fox did the introductions, and each time he mentioned a name the crowd went wild. The poor old mayor looked totally overawed.

'So tell me, Geri, what are you doing for Christmas?' asked Foxy.

'I'll try to keep my clothes on,' I replied and the crowd roared again.

Then it was time for the countdown. We led the crowd.

'TEN!'

'NINE!'

'EIGHT!'

As much as I had dreamed and fantasized about such a moment, nothing matched the sound and colour of this chorus. It was as though we were being held aloft by the hopes and dreams of another generation.

'FOUR!'

'THREE!'

'TWO!'

'ONE!'

We all hit a button and Oxford Street lit up in a blaze of neon. I glanced across at Emma, Victoria and the two Mels. Their faces were beaming. All of us knew this was a special moment. For the first time, we felt truly famous.

The cherry-picker carried us down and we skipped across to the crowd again, scrawling autographs and kissing cheeks. I threw a young boy over my shoulder in a classic fireman's lift and carried him down the street.

Jerry Judge was motioning for us to leave. I wanted to stay. I wanted to shake the hand or kiss the cheek of every person who'd braved a cold winter night to see us.

Afterwards, we went to Debenhams department store to meet the families of the Oxford Street Association, which had organized the event. Then we could relax for a couple of hours at a hotel before the big bash to launch our album at the Oxo Tower, overlooking the Thames.

'Why do we have to go so late?' I asked Simon.

'So the guests can eat first.'

'But isn't it *our* party?' chimed in Mel C.

'Theoretically, yes.'

'But not in reality,' I said.

Simon shook his head.

After watching *EastEnders*, I put on a foxy purple PVC dress that Karen had helped me make.

We arrived at 10 p.m. and were whisked through a back entrance and up a kitchen service elevator that smelled of rotten vegetables. We huddled together, trying not to dirty our clothes.

One of the odd things about being famous, I'd discovered, is that you never get to use the front door. Every time we arrived somewhere it was always through the kitchens or via the service lift. I could even recognize the aroma — ah, we must be here, I can smell the rubbish bins.

What a palaver! There must have been 300 people, all trying to grab our attention. Most of them were distributors, salesmen, pluggers and music publishers.

After standing on the stage and showing our gold discs, we were divided up and expected to circulate. This meant being pulled and pushed from one group to the next, meeting and greeting total strangers who wanted us to sign serviettes and menus for their children. I didn't get a drink or a snack. Every time I saw someone I knew and tried to talk to them, someone would whisk me away to meet another group.

This went on for nearly two hours, until I felt totally exhausted. Then I spied Matt and Biff in a corner, eating canapés and trying to find another bottle of champagne.

'Biff, Biff, my saviour,' I said, slipping behind his ample frame. 'I'm just going to hide here, OK. Don't tell anyone, please.'

They kept me hidden until the music started and the lights were dimmed. The other girls were still being dragged around on meet and greets. Then I looked out and noticed that a young girl had found me. She was staring, wide-eyed, and seemed too shy to say anything.

'Do you want to dance?' I asked.

She looked behind her.

'No, I mean you. Can you dance?'

She nodded.

'Will you dance with me?'

She nodded again, her mouth falling open.

And so I pushed out of my hiding place and took her by the hand. We found a space and started bopping to the Spice Girls. She knew the words to every song on the album.

Whenever someone from Virgin or Simon's office tried to pull me away, I told them, 'No. I'm dancing with a friend.'

The evening included a £65,000 fireworks display on

the Thames. The Metropolitan River Police had to close the river for an hour. I thought it was a little over the top and stayed inside in the warmth.

The following morning, 9 November, we flew to France.

Photographers took snaps of Mel B and me whizzing around the airport terminal on a trolley. East 17 and Gabrielle were on the same flight and also at the same hotel in Paris.

Most of our luggage had failed to arrive, but I still had my acoustic guitar. I'd been having lessons for six months.

## Sunday, 10 November – Rome

*Tonight we appeared on the same TV show as a few weeks ago – with a smarmy host and a co-host who looks like Madonna. Why do all Italian girls who work on TV seem to look like Madonna?*

*E17 were there and we played British Bulldog with them. When E17 performed we pulled silly faces at them and I did a runner across the screen. The show was going out live. We were like kids mucking about at school.*

*Afterwards we had a dash to the airport for the flight to New York. It was bedlam.*

*We had a three-hour stopover at Heathrow – which is quite odd because you know that you're in your home country but you can't go home. Then it was six hours to New York with a really snotty air steward.*

*Our hotel, the Royalton, is extremely dark and modern – a bit depressing really. I'm exhausted. Sleep now. Good night.*

The good news was that the album *Spice* had gone straight to number one and was outselling the next five albums by four to one. The Spice Girls fan club had new people joining at a rate of 10,000 a week.

On Monday morning the circus started again in New York. This time we had a cameraman following us making a *Spice* documentary, along with a photographer from *Top of the Pops* magazine, which was planning a sixteen-page poster book on the Spice Girls. He arranged to shoot us in Times Square, outside Radio City Music Hall, in Central Park and on top of the Empire State Building.

We all went shopping at Macy's and in Greenwich Village. Because we each liked such different clothes, it was easier to split up. Mel C went to Nike Town, Victoria to Prada, and Mel B, Emma and I went looking at second-hand shops and antique jewellery boutiques in the village.

Since signing with Virgin we'd each been living on a modest monthly allowance. With two worldwide hits and the album at number one, we knew the Spice Girls were making good money, but we had no idea of the actual amounts.

Occasionally, one of us would ask Simon 'How much money have we made?' or 'When are we going to see any of it?'

'In a few weeks,' he'd say.

'Can you be a bit more specific?'

'Before Christmas.'

'Cool.'

At a photo studio in downtown Manhattan we did a shoot for *Interview* magazine and chatted to the reporter Katie Puckrik. I was so tired that I fell asleep on a sofa, while the others scoffed a Chinese takeaway and danced to the Backstreet Boys. I felt depressed and quite ill, but tried to pick myself up. I knew I had to be on song for an important dinner that evening with MTV.

I had the head of US Virgin Records, Phil Quartararo, on my table. He told me that somebody had anonymously faxed him a picture of me nude.

'Oh, my God!' My hand flew to my mouth.

'Hey, I thought you looked great.'

I blushed.


Peter Lorraine, the reporter from *Top of the Pops* magazine, had been interviewing each of us over the previous few days. I glanced at his notebook and saw a reference to my topless modelling. It made me very defensive and tearful. This was a teen magazine, for God's sake! We were co-operating on their photo shoot and now they were going to stitch me up.

After being put on the spot, Peter assured me that it wasn't going to happen. Maybe I was getting paranoid about negative publicity.

That evening we flew to Los Angeles, and I woke the next morning in the Beverly Wilshire, where *Pretty Woman* was filmed.

As I stepped into the lift, I remembered the elevator scene in the movie when Julia Roberts shocked an elderly couple by announcing, 'I'm not wearing any panty hose.'

Now, on the final leg of the tour, I felt relieved. It had been a roller-coaster few weeks of feeling happy, sad, ugly, pretty, lonely, insecure, loved and unloved.

I wrote in my diary:

*Isn't it funny how the most enjoyable events seem to be the least pleasant for me? Perhaps I'm tired. Or maybe*

*I have such high expectations that I can't help being disappointed. Take me home. That's where I want to be right now. Far, far from here.*

*Where is home? I've been living in rented accommodation and other people's houses since I was sixteen. Home keeps changing.*

There was high drama at the *Smash Hits* Awards Ceremony – the very best kind. Robbie Williams, ex-Take That, was thrown out of the dressing room he was supposed to be sharing with gangsta rapper Mark Morrison. Morrison and his sullen entourage simply took over like henchmen.

I'd met the rapper once before at a Radio 1 roadshow. He wore his trademark big fur coat and was surrounded by bodyguards, as if he thought he was Michael Jackson.

Mel B and I looked at him and thought, What a prat! Mel grabbed the collar of his coat and I nicked his cigar. His bodyguards were laughing, but Morrison got really angry at being teased.

His biggest chart success had been a song called 'Return of The Mack', but we changed it to 'Return of The Prat'. During the *Smash Hits* Awards Ceremony, we decided to wind him up. Backstage at the London Arena, Mel B and I crept into Morrison's dressing room and left a note on his mirror, saying, 'Return of The Prat!'

We were only teasing, but our publicist, Muff Fitzgerald, almost had a heart attack. Morrison had a reputation as a hard man and Muff was afraid he'd have to defend our honour and get his head knocked off.

The concert went brilliantly. During 'Say You'll Be There', I launched a few kung-fu kicks – wearing big, black granny knickers this time. Even so, the photographs made the newspaper the next day.

The Spice Girls picked up awards for Best New Act, Best British Group and Best Video for 'Say You'll Be There'. There were 12,000 people in the arena and a TV audience of millions. What a buzz!

Afterwards, backstage, we were interviewed by Simon Sebag-Montefiore for a piece in the *Spectator*, a right-wing political magazine. He had convinced his editor to take a tongue-in-cheek look at British politics and international affairs through the eyes of five young women who, he reasoned, knew nothing about it.

First he had to explain to his readers who on earth the Spice Girls were and why anyone should care. He described us as a popular singing ensemble that had dominated the culture of those aged between five and twenty-five in most countries of the world. Then he rattled off some of the sales figures for the singles and album.

I loved doing the interview. Although I knew that Sebag-Montefiore was a smiling cynic, I enjoyed the fact that somebody was asking me intelligent questions. I might not have been an expert on politics but I had an opinion.

I was in my element, declaring that Margaret Thatcher was the original Spice Girl and a pioneer of Girl Power, having risen from humble beginnings as a grocer's daughter to become prime minister.

The other girls were angry at being labelled Conservatives, particularly Mel C, who is an out and out Labour voter from working-class Liverpool. Victoria leaned further to the right than me, Emma was apolitical, while Mel B came across as a complete anarchist.

With tongue firmly in cheek, Simon likened Girl Power to the 'People Power' that had overturned Ferdinand Marcos in the Philippines. He claimed that young people believed we were modern-day philosophers.

'Should Britain ever join a single European currency?' he asked, before rattling off questions on the future of the monarchy, the class system in Britain and the personalities of John Major and Tony Blair.

The article appeared on Friday, 13 December 1996. As expected, it was quirky and funny, with Sebag-Montefiore poking gentle fun at us. Thankfully, no-one came across as an idiot.

None of us realized how famous the article would make us. Within twenty-four hours our views were all over the BBC's six o'clock and ten o'clock news. Jeremy Paxman pondered the 'Spice Vote' on *Newsnight* and the Prime Minister talked about us on the *Today* programme.

John Major had just lost a crucial by-election and needed some good news. The right-wing newspapers picked up on the *Spectator* article and ran with it. Spice Girl song lyrics were analysed for Thatcherite leanings and editorials pondered what impact the 'Spice Vote' would have on the national polls.

Partly, this reaction stemmed from the fact that pop stars aren't supposed to be right wing. They're supposed to be anti-establishment and trash hotel rooms, snort cocaine and swear on TV.

Most of the popular rock bands, like Oasis, are gung-ho Labour supporters. Yet I've always felt it is a little hypo-critical to have working-class boys earning millions of pounds and at the same time criticizing self-made people and entrepreneurs. Despite what the newspapers said, the

Spice Girls weren't Tories. Instead, we reflected almost perfectly the politics of our generation. We had one and a half conservatives, an out-and-out socialist, an anarchist and one who didn't have a clue. How's that for an instant vox pop?

I was seven years old when Margaret Thatcher came to power, and although I admired her I had no idea what her policies were. If I had, I might not necessarily have agreed with them. In reality, like most people, I picked up my politics from my parents, particularly my dad.

I'm all in favour of the conservative values of personal responsibility, hard work and enjoying the fruits of your success. At the same time, my social conscience is strong. We need the safety net. We have to care about the community from the bottom up and look after the environment.

In the wake of the *Spectator* article we had calls from every Conservative Association in the land, and offers of free membership to the 'Say No To Europe' groups. Politicians were desperate to be photographed with us and we had dozens of invitations to dine at the House of Commons. Political editors were told to doorstep the Spice Girls and there were countless requests for more serious interviews.

All of these offers were declined, but the result of the mayhem couldn't be ignored. Up until then, the Spice Girls were known to anybody under the age of twenty-five. Afterwards, not even the crustiest, most out-of-touch judge in the land could claim ignorance. We were household names.

## PATTY PICKLE

A dozen builders, with pot-bellies and bum-cracks showing, were hanging off the scaffolding of a construction site in Birmingham.

'Hey, Geri, we love you!' they shouted.

'I love you, too, Spice Boys,' I yelled back. They loved it.

We ducked through the back entrance of a Virgin Megastore. There were thousands of people out front, waiting for the Spice Girls. It was supposed to be the opening of a new music store, but it had turned into a huge crush. The surrounding streets were blocked off and dozens of extra police had been summoned to control the crowd.

Inside the crammed store we stood on a makeshift stage. A local DJ asked us questions and we drew the winner of a platinum disc. Photographers, reporters and fans jostled for space. Mel B had a bash on a drum set and I held up a pair of men's underpants that had been thrown onto the stage.

After saying our goodbyes, Jerry Judge took us to a

sealed-off area. 'I'm not happy with this. The police aren't totally in control. We can only get one car through. When I give the word, you head straight for the limo. No stopping. If this crowd surges forward people are going to get hurt.'

Jerry had a habit of overdramatizing things, but this time he wasn't exaggerating. Security guards cleared a tunnel to the door and across the footpath. Jerry kept in touch with the police and his own men on a two-way radio.

Given the all-clear, we started moving like a rugby scrum. Any moment I expected to trip and disappear under a crush of bodies. I kept smiling and waving as we marched across the footpath and dived into the car, finishing up on top of each other as the door slammed and we started moving.

The crowd had surged forward and there were hands and faces pressed up to the glass. People were hammering on the sides and roof. Emma and Victoria looked worried. I tried to absorb every moment because I knew that adulation like this wouldn't last. I also trusted people like Jerry to look after us. I could hear him talking on the two-way. Someone had been crushed against a barrier. A St John's Ambulance officer was there.

Edging through the crowd, we reached clear road and accelerated away. At a service station ten minutes down the road we rendezvoused with the convoy of other cars.

Jerry and his men did a quick post-mortem while the rest of us swapped stories from the front line. Sometimes I didn't appreciate how dangerous crowd situations could be and how easily they can get out of hand. I always assumed that Jerry was being ultra-cautious because he was paid to be, but he wasn't just looking after us, he had to be equally conscious of the fans and their safety.

Unfortunately, I was the worst offender when it came to ignoring instructions. During an interview on Capital Radio, I told listeners, 'Come down and see us. We're live on air.' Within twenty minutes there were hundreds of people outside.

'You have to get out of here quickly,' said one of the producers. 'We've been in trouble with the police before about this sort of thing.'

Jerry looked at me sternly as we made our escape through yet another back door, past the rubbish bins and milk crates.

Along with Mel B, I was also the most likely culprit when it came to ignoring instructions and spontaneously running forward to meet fans, shaking hands and signing autographs.

'Oh, God, there they go again,' our security would mutter.

Afterwards, I'd get told off for ignoring procedure. It wasn't premeditated. Meeting the fans was exhilarating.

Our third single, '2 Become 1', was the unbackable favourite to be the UK Christmas number one. It would sell more than 200,000 copies in its first week and would mean the Spice Girls had achieved three consecutive number-one hits.

Everything we achieved from now on seemed to be unprecedented. There was no handbook I could read beforehand. Even Simon and Virgin Records had had no experience of this kind of hysteria and madness. They, too, were blagging.

Switching on the Christmas lights in Oxford Street had been a defining moment. Up until then the reality of being a celebrity hadn't really sunk in. Now I slowly began discovering the limitations it would place on me.

On a Christmas shopping trip to Harrods, the store provided me with a 'shopper' to make sure I found everything I wanted. As I watched a toy being wrapped, I kept thinking about my very first trip to Harrods. I was fifteen years old, and I'd bought a novelty bag of jelly beans so I could get the famous dark-green Harrods shopping bag. Now I had my own credit cards and a personal shopper taking care of me.

At one of the cosmetics counters I tried a lipstick sampler using the make-up mirror. In the reflection I noticed that people were watching me. I didn't turn round. A while later I was at the toy store and the group following me had swelled to almost twenty or thirty. When I stopped walking, so did they. It was like playing a game of Statues.

I smiled at them and they grinned back. Some of them were Japanese and Spanish. Eventually one plucked up the courage to step forward and ask for my autograph. Suddenly they all moved in.

I didn't mind. I love meeting people. But I left Harrods without having done half my shopping.

'Next time take a bodyguard,' said Jerry.

'But I don't want to be chaperoned. It feels pretentious. And I don't want people to think they can't say hello to me.'

He laughed. 'You'll learn.'

On 10 December we flew to France to do a gig at a Virgin

Megastore. Coming home, we picked up twenty competition winners who had won a day with the Spice Girls. We planned to take them on a tour of London and then to a studio in Hampstead where they could see us work on a new song.

All of us were exhausted and fighting sleep. To make matters worse, we had a TV crew following us all day for the documentary. I couldn't even go to the bathroom without looking over my shoulder and finding the camera bobbing behind me.

'Where do you think you're going?' I asked.

'Forget I'm here.'

'Not likely. This is one place you're not coming.'

Arriving in London, we took our twenty French fans on an open-top bus tour. Every time I started chatting with someone the camera appeared, and it started to get on my nerves.

As we crossed London Bridge and headed through Clerkenwell, Mel B looked at me.

'Are you sick of this?'

'Uh huh.'

'Let's do something about it.'

'I'm right with you.'

The bus stopped at a set of traffic lights and we sprang to our feet. Racing down the stairs, we leapt off the back of the bus. Emma, Victoria and Mel C were right behind us.

As we sprinted down the street, laughing all the way, I could hear Camilla screaming, 'Come back! Come back!'

She got straight on the phone to Simon. 'I've lost them.'

'What do you mean you've lost them? How can you lose the Spice Girls?'

'They did a runner from the bus.'

'Find them, for Christ's sake. They can't just walk around the streets.'

Camilla had people chasing us as we dodged pedestrians and swung off lamp posts. The bus eventually caught up and she yelled from the top deck, 'Get back on! Please!'

She was so annoyed with us. 'Imagine if the fans had run off. What if we'd lost one of them? What would their parents say?'

For one moment I didn't want to think about what people would say. I was on a high. The Spice vibe was back. That's what we were about – being spontaneous and having a laugh. We'd started off like that in Maidenhead, but had become very serious and businesslike. Too much work and not enough play makes Spice Girls very dull indeed.

## Thursday, 19 December 1996

*I am knackered. Cream-crackered. This morning we got up at the crack of dawn to do GMTV. Can't stand early-morning TV appearances. They were created by a masochist. Plus I look puffy in the mornings.*

*Afterwards we did Capital Radio and Radio 1 – loads of fans outside, screaming for us.*

*Can you believe it! The Sun readers have voted me 'sexiest female' in their annual awards. The Spice Girls are 'best band'.*

*I'm quite proud of my award, considering I feel so hideous. Funny how life has so many twists and turns . . .*

Journalists were writing stories about how rich we had become. According to some reports, the Spice Girls had estimated earnings of £10 million after only six months. I don't know where the figures came from because we hadn't seen any of the money.

Since signing with Virgin we'd been on a modest monthly allowance. The royalties had yet to filter through, which meant that I didn't feel particularly rich. I was still living with Karen, although for a while I had a flat in Morehouse Road, Notting Hill. I had wanted to be closer to London to cut down on the travelling.

Simon held a Christmas party at a big old house in Fulham. There were about fifty guests, mostly writers, producers, record-company executives and publicists – all of Simon's best contacts in the industry. I felt nervous beforehand. I knew that Annie Lennox would be there, along with Cathy Dennis and Gary Barlow. It had been a hard week, so I didn't want to stay late.

During the evening, Simon whispered to each of us that he had something for us. We gathered in the wood-lined dining room, where a long mahogany table had been polished to a brilliant sheen.

'I have an envelope for each of you,' he said.

'Oh, Simon, a Christmas card. And I haven't got you anything.'

'Just open it,' he said.

'We're rich. We're rich,' declared Mel B.

'I'm gonna buy my mum a house,' said Emma.

'Think of how many pairs of shoes you can buy, Victoria,' said Mel C.

I looked at all those noughts and felt a tremendous sense of relief. All my life I had worried about money. My mum had scrimped and saved on cleaner's wages to keep three children fed and clothed. Back then I'd scrabbled for pennies in coat pockets and behind sofa cushions. Later, when I supported myself, I used to fret whenever the phone or gas bill arrived. I'd pinched toilet rolls from the gym and would take home any unclaimed towels. I'd never been able to afford freshly squeezed orange juice or exotic fruits.

Now I held in my hand a cheque that could have bought my family home in Jubilee Road twice over. It felt good. Very, very good.

With her job in the travel industry, Natalie had booked me a holiday for my three weeks off over Christmas. Janine came with me to Antigua in the West Indies. Of all my long-time friends, she had remained the closest. And she still did my hair for me, putting the blond streaks in my fringe.

Mel B had also booked a holiday in Antigua with her boyfriend, staying at the Sandals Resort a few minutes up the road. Emma was taking her entire family to Barbados.

We all needed a break. The previous six months had taken their toll, particularly on me. Very few people recognized the change, but one who did was Louise Gannon of the *Daily Express*. She had interviewed us in the very early days of Spice, and again in December, just before our Christmas break.

She wrote that I seemed to be the most altered by fame. Having been bombarded by page-three skeletons from my past, I now looked more vulnerable than vampish. I was quieter and more defensive; thinking carefully before I spoke.

Our hotel in Antigua was clean and simple. The white-washed apartments were right on the beach and there were surprisingly few people. Some days we seemed to have the sand to ourselves, except for the coconut sellers and girls offering to bead our hair.

I found it hard to slip into the slow rhythm of the Caribbean because I'd been moving at such a pace for so long. Despite being three months pregnant, Janine also didn't stop. She came jet-skiing with me and trekking up mountains.

One day we took a taxi ride to see Mel B. Her resort was far more luxurious, with beautifully landscaped gardens, waterfalls and native parrots. She came to meet us in reception, looking relaxed and tanned, with her big brown eyes and golden hair. It was so lovely to see her that I lifted her in the air and spun her around.

'I've really missed you,' I said.

'It's only been ten days,' she said, laughing.

'I'm so used to having you around.'

That evening we went to a help-yourself barbecue on the beach, with live music and limbo dancing.

Mel explained that she was having some trouble at her resort because people recognized her.

'It's not as private as I'd hoped.'

'Come and see us,' I told her. 'There's hardly anybody there.'

She dropped by the next day and we lay on the beach. The jungle greenery came right to the edge of the sand and occasionally I wondered if someone might be hiding in there, taking photographs. When I bent over, or reached across to grab my book, I suddenly thought, Wouldn't it be horrible if they took a shot now. Eventually

I found myself sitting, bending and lying in positions that didn't show any unflattering bits. I simply couldn't relax.

During her holiday in the Caribbean, Emma stayed at a family resort in Barbados. It didn't have the same level of privacy as the places Mel B and I had chosen. Unbeknown to the family, a paparazzi photographer had managed to track Emma down and booked into an adjoining room at the resort.

He photographed Emma and her mum by the swimming pool from behind. They both have almost identical long blond hair.

A few days after arriving back in London, the *Daily Mirror* published the photograph under the banner, GUESS WHICH ONE IS THE SPICE GIRL? It was a cheap, tacky gibe at the size of Emma's bum. The story was picked up by breakfast TV and radio stations.

Emma had always been happy with her figure, but I knew that she'd be terribly hurt. I phoned her straight away. She'd been crying.

'It doesn't matter, Emma,' I said. 'It's just the press. This is what they do.'

'The bastards! The bastards!'

'Don't let them do this to you. You have to be strong.'

I drove round to her house and formulated a plan on the way. 'Right, you're coming out with me tonight,' I said. 'We're going to show how beautiful you are.'

She dressed in a pair of black trousers and my bustier. With her hair and make-up done, she looked fabulous. Then we went out to a showbiz club in the West End that's popular with celebrities and the paparazzi.

There were yells from the photographers as the first of them clocked us. Others joined in and the motor drives whirred. Emma gave them an enormous smile. The photograph was on the front page of the *Sun* the next morning. She looked stunning.

Quite rightly, there was an enormous backlash against the *Mirror* for publishing the shot of Emma and her mother. Women in particular were outraged. Why should a twenty-year-old be scrutinized in such a way? No wonder we have so many young girls with eating disorders. I knew this more than anyone.

In the middle of Montreal, in freezing weather, I had a temperature of 102°F. I thought I was going to die. Mel B had the same flu and both of us were popping antibiotics.

The Spice Girls were two weeks back at work and already I felt exhausted and run down. This is hardly how I wanted to start the big North American push.

'Wannabe' had entered the Billboard Hot 100 at number eleven, the equal highest entry by a début act in the chart's history. It had also become the highest entry by a British band, beating a thirty-two-year record held by The Beatles with 'I Want To Hold Your Hand'.

The strategy had been to tackle America last. Hopefully, the excitement and demand for the Spice Girls in the rest of the world would have created a buzz of expectation. For months America had been reading and hearing small things about us. We'd kept the dam gates closed until the trickle banked up. Now for the big splash.

Canada, unfortunately, was a disaster. Mel B and I were both so ill that we had to miss an MTV special. The others went ahead without us. It was the first time that all five of us had failed to appear together.

The Spice Girl flu proved to be unstoppable. By the

time we arrived in New York, it was Victoria's turn, but she soldiered on.

## Monday, 27 January – New York

*I'm writing on Four Seasons Hotel notepaper because I've forgotten my diary. Bizarre is the word to describe this trip to the US of A. Tonight was a real twister. A local radio station organized a bus tour with competition winners. Along the way we had personal backrubs, transvestites delivering food and loads of fans from God knows where. It felt like an episode of Saved by the Bell, only worse. I did laugh.*

The contest winners had won a bus tour of New York with the Spice Girls. Having filled the coach with alcohol, the radio station let us loose in the Big Apple. The idea was to do a tour, stopping at various locations to cross live back to the DJ in the studio. We had to make it sound as though we were partying all over the city.

Most of the time it seemed like chaos. At the back of the bus Mel B played psychotherapist to a queue of men whose girlfriends didn't understand them. Emma chatted to a journalist from *The Face* and announced, 'I don't want to be a cutie any more. I want to be a *sexy bitch*. I want to be a hot sexy bitch.'

He seemed surprised. 'You never liked being a cutie?'

'I like it sometimes. I can get away with murder.'

Victoria sounded like death warmed up, with her head full of flu and her stomach rattling with antibiotics and lozenges. I finished up talking to Colleen, a schoolteacher who'd had a breast-reduction operation. She fancied Richard, one of our security guards, and was making him very nervous.

Each time the DJ crossed to the bus, everybody started hollering.

'Hello, Noo Yaaaaawk,' I yelled. 'What a wicked party. You're missing a great night.'

They played 'Wannabe' and we all started dancing in the aisles.

'I want to drive the bus,' I declared.

'No way,' said the driver, a black guy in a blue uniform.

'Oh, come on. Please let me drive the bus.'

'I could lose my job.'

'I won't tell anyone.'

I sweet-talked him into letting me get behind the wheel at the next set of lights. I could barely reach the pedals in my platform shoes.

He hovered over my shoulder as the lights turned green. 'Just take it easy.'

'Where am I going to go? Nothing moves faster than six miles an hour in this city.'

I managed to drive two blocks before his nerves were shot and I took pity on him.

More than 150 radio stations across America had 'Wannabe' in heavy rotation on their playlists. These included trendy stations like Power 96 in Miami and Z100 in New York. Some of the US music critics had dismissed us as a throwaway pop band, but they couldn't argue with the charts.

By 7 February only Toni Braxton's 'Un-Break My Heart' stood between 'Wannabe' and the number-one spot. A week later we owned it.

I can't remember where we were when the news came through, and I don't think any of us realized the size of our achievement until everybody around us became so excited. People were queuing up to congratulate us at the record company, our PR agency, in the newspapers and teen magazines. No British band had made it big in America for so long that this was a major breakthrough.

Apart from the success of 'Wannabe', the album *Spice* had débuted at number six on the US Billboard Album Charts. It was destined to spend nearly five months in the Top 10, reaching number one on 31 May 1997.

'My God, it's me,' I said.

Jennifer Saunders grinned and struck a Ginger Spice pose, giving me a V-sign.

I was gobsmacked.

'How on earth do you wear these shoes?' she exclaimed.

A make-up artist and hairdresser had transformed the comedienne into a redhead with blond streaks. It was surreal watching her. Jennifer had also been studying TV footage of me, so she could copy my mannerisms and gestures.

We were filming a video for the charity Comic Relief. Our single 'Who Do You Think You Are?' was being released on Red Nose Day, with all the royalties going to famine relief in Africa and other good causes in Britain.

Dawn French had been transformed into Posh Spice, tottering on high heels and flicking back her hair. She'd even captured Victoria's pout.

'Why don't you ever smile?' Dawn asked her.

'Because I get dimples,' explained Victoria. 'They make me look thirteen.'

Kathy Burke, who plays Waynetta Slob in Harry Enfield's TV show, had become Sporty Spice. The ageless Lulu became Baby and Llewella Gideon from *The Real McCoy* looked scary enough to be Mel B.

Comic Relief had taken over a theatre in Willesden and filled it with an audience of jugglers, snake charmers and tattooed ladies. Our Spice doppelgangers were called The Sugar Lumps and were brilliant at mimicking us.

The video was shot in a mock-up disco and the director had us mixing and matching on stage with the fake Spice Girls. Sometimes there would be four of us, and a fake Posh or a fake Scary. In the editing suite they cut the film around and created a wonderfully bizarre performance.

On the first day of filming, we didn't finish until 1 a.m. We agreed to meet back on the set at eight. My driver picked me up from Karen's house and we headed towards Willesden. I glanced at the morning papers and absent-mindedly scratched inside my ear with my little finger. Suddenly, my false nail pinged off and lodged inside. I tried to pull it out, but it wedged in even further.

'Ow! Ow! Ow!'

The driver pulled over on the A40 and tried to help. He had hands like a professional wrestler's. I was lying on the seat, screaming, 'Get it out! Get it out!'

He was at a total loss. 'I can't. My fingers are too big.'

'Then get me a doctor.' I had visions of the nail being stuck in my brain.

He found a surgery in Ealing and rushed me straight into the waiting room. A handful of old ladies and a very pregnant woman looked up in amazement as I pleaded with the receptionist. It felt as though my eardrum had ruptured.

The doctor sent me straight to the casualty department at Central Middlesex Hospital in Park Royal, West London. I tottered in wearing my platform boots, flares and a big coat, looking every inch a Spice Girl.

The nurse at reception began taking details. I was leaning over, filling in a form and tearfully holding my ear when a young guy appeared at my elbow.

'Can I have your autograph?'

I didn't say a thing, I simply signed a piece of paper.

The nurse reassured me. 'I'll find the doctor now.'

'Ow! Ow! Ow!'

Down a corridor, a young Pakistani doctor appeared with a stethoscope slung round his neck ER-style. As I lay on the examination table, he produced a frightening-looking instrument that looked like something from the London Dungeon torture display.

'Just hold still. This will only take a second.'

He pulled out the false nail and presented it to me on a paper towel.

'Congratulations.'

I was so grateful that later I sent him a signed photograph for being so nice.

Somebody at the hospital couldn't resist phoning the papers and it turned into a front page for the *Sun*: HOSPITAL DASH FOR GERI, and then in smaller print – 'Over Fingernail!'

How embarrassing! I am so clumsy. I used to buy a comic book called *Twinkle* as a kid and it had a character called Patty Pickle in it – so-called because she always got herself into a pickle. That was me – Miss Sound Bite and the human headline.

No wonder photographers and reporters followed me about. I made wonderful tabloid fodder because I was so ungainly and haphazard. I was always going to say something they'd love, or flash something I shouldn't.

The Brit Awards were being handed out again. This time the Spice Girls had star billing. A year ago we'd been unknowns, gawping wide-eyed at the music legends. Now we were being billed as the hottest band in the world.

I still had the same old problem, of course. What am I going to wear?

Five days before the awards, I came up with an idea for a Union Jack dress. 'Look, this is what I want,' I told Karen, drawing the design on a piece of paper.

I'd learned to sew in grammar school doing textile design. Ever since then I'd been chopping and changing clothes to make different outfits. Although I have a creative mind, I'm not very good on the finishing and finer details. That's why I always got Karen to go over the patterns and either resew the seams or start from scratch.

I asked Karen to go out and buy a Union Jack flag.

'Are you sure it isn't against the law to deface the flag?' she asked.

'Nobody's going to mind.'

'What am I going to sew it on?'

A week earlier, while recording at Abbey Road Studios, a designer had sent me a black dress that featured a boned corset tied at the back. Karen sewed up the crotch and stitched the Union Jack over the top. It was very short and skintight.

One of our stylists wasn't convinced it was such a good

idea. 'That's the symbol of the National Front. People might think you're a racist.' Just in case, I arranged for a huge peace symbol to be stitched onto the back.

I had Karen make me another dress for the presentation phase of the awards' night. Again I sketched the design on a piece of paper. I called it my Jessica Rabbit dress because it was red, low-cut and tight at the waist, with a revealing split up one leg.

The Spice Girls had been nominated for five awards at the Brits. We would also open the show with a huge production version of 'Who Do You Think You Are?'

We spent two days rehearsing. We had choreographed the majority of the dance routine in the studio while we were writing the song. Our dancing coach, Priscilla, added a few extra moves and polished us up.

Now I had to remember the routine while all sorts of cannons and fireworks greeted our appearance on stage.

My nerves were jangling. Michael Jackson had been booed by this same crowd a year earlier. Liam Gallagher of Oasis had already announced he wasn't coming because 'he might chin the Spice Girls'.

Earlier in the day we'd done a full dress rehearsal for selected photographers. These pictures would make the next morning's editions. It had all gone well, but performing to an empty auditorium is no preparation for the real thing.

That afternoon the others went shopping or home to rest. I stayed behind practising the dance routine with Priscilla in the dressing room. I had never stopped being self-conscious about my dancing and knowing I had to prove myself to the others.

As the show approached, the backstage area buzzed

with excitement and celebrities wandered back and forth. At this level, a lot of the meetings and photo opportunities are set up by publicists and assistants.

'Do you want your picture taken with Elton John?' asked Muff Fitzgerald.

'Yeah, great!'

We all crowded around him.

'Hi, girls.'

'Hi, Elton.'

He swept off again.

Diana Ross was also performing. We met her outside her dressing room and had a picture taken. Her eyelids were very large and she blinked slowly.

'Everyone is talking about you in America. Congratulations on your number one,' she said.

At that moment I spied Clive Black, the managing director of Warner Music. He is the man who famously turned down the chance to sign the Spice Girls.

'Hey, Clive, how come you passed on our demo tape?' I shouted.

'Yeah, Clive. Bet you're glad you did that,' added Mel B.

He laughed. 'I think you did OK without me.'

As the big moment drew closer, we gathered in our dressing room and closed the door. There was chaos outside with television crews, photographers and technicians falling over each other in the narrow corridors.

Mel B pretended she wasn't nervous, but she bounced around and couldn't stop talking. Mel C was totally the opposite and talked to nobody. Right up to the last minute she rehearsed the song in her mind, and if anyone tried to give her a hug she went rigid.

Emma occasionally got the giggles, but she seemed quite relaxed. Victoria said she'd been really nervous before she arrived but now felt better.

'It doesn't matter if we don't win an award,' I told them. 'I've got one for us anyway.'

I gave them each a small golden cherub candle that looked like a statuette and read out one of my corny poems.

Finally, I said, 'This is going to be the greatest night of our lives. Let's just enjoy it.'

A production girl with a microphone in front of her mouth and a clipboard knocked on the door. 'OK, we're ready for you now.'

We followed her out and down several corridors until we reached a big ramp. Put in position on top of a big catwalk, we had our backs to the arena and a huge screen in front of us. A lead-up trailer was being shown to the crowd.

There were 5,000 people in the auditorium and 30 million people watching on TV worldwide. I stood second from the end, with Victoria next to me. We glanced at each other out of the corners of our eyes. The look said it all: Oh, my God!

She reached across and gave my hand a squeeze.

Ben Elton welcomed the audience to the 1997 Brit Awards.

'Ladies and gentlemen, Margaret Thatcher was due to appear with the Spice Girls, but unfortunately her belly button ring has gone septic. Please put your hands together and welcome Posh, Sporty, Ginger, Scary and Baby – THE SPICE GIRLS!'

Cannons suddenly exploded and the lights came up.

The first bars of 'Wannabe' reverberated through Earls Court. We turned and strutted down the ramp and the music flowed into 'Who Do You Think You Are?' The crowd roared.

I walked down the catwalk to the opening line, and suddenly I was filled with a rush of adrenalin. I could feel my heart pumping. Those next few minutes passed in a blur. All the dance practice and rehearsals came together and I simply enjoyed myself rather than worry about things going wrong. It didn't. The routine went off perfectly.

I could have listened to the applause for ever. Better still, I wanted to freeze that moment and lock it away so that I could go back there any time and stand on that catwalk with my heart pounding and my legs shaking, listening to all those people cheering. It doesn't get any better than this, I thought. We've made it!

Backstage, we quickly changed so that we could get to our table for the award presentations. Shimmying into my low-cut Jessica Rabbit dress, I took a final look in the mirror. That morning I'd been to Rigby and Peller to have the corset fitted to make my waist look smaller. I also bought a basque to wear under the dress, but I hadn't had a chance to test it while wearing my outfit. I discovered that it actually made the dress slip down when I walked and I had to constantly keep tugging it up. I felt very voluptuous but a little nervous.

Sitting at a table quite near the front, we watched as people like Gabrielle and The Fugees were given awards. As 'Wannabe' was announced Best Single we all gave a scream of delight and hugged. Then Jerry Judge cleared a path for us to the stage. It felt wonderful to clutch the trophy, knowing that my friends and family were watching. Even Victoria couldn't stop smiling.

Mel C decided to issue a challenge to Liam Gallagher after his earlier comment about 'chinning' the Spice Girls. 'Come and have a go, if you think you're hard enough,' she cried. The crowd loved it.

A little later, 'Say You'll Be There' won Best Video. Again, we danced onto the stage to accept the award. The comedian Frank Skinner made the presentation, giving us each a kiss.

Mel B said a few words, thanking Simon, Virgin Records and all the people who had helped us along the way.

'And most of all we'd like to thank our fans,' I said. 'You're the best!'

I thrust the trophy above my head in triumph and screamed, 'Yeah! Girl Power!'

As my arm went up, my Jessica Rabbit dress slid down, giving all present a glimpse of more breast than I'd intended. There are no prizes for guessing what story dominated the tabloids the next morning.

LOVELY BRITS, said the *Daily Star*. SPICE GIRLS WIN TWO BIG ONES AT POP SUPERSHOW.

Patty Pickle had done it again. 'For God's sake, Geri, can't you keep your tits in?' laughed Mel C.

On top of that, every front page featured a photograph of the Union Jack dress.

Ten days before the Brits, I'd written a 'cosmic shopping list':

*I am happy, confident, satisfied and fully in control.*
*I am slim, beautiful and fun to be with.*
*We perform really well at the Brits.*

*'Wannabe' wins Best Single and 'Say You'll be There'
wins Best Video.
We're on the front page of every newspaper.
I look great and everyone loves my outfits.
We have a fantastic year ahead and everything goes as I
want it to.
I have spirit, focus and kindness.
The girls love me.*

All the list had so far come true. Well, almost all.

# 16

## A LIPSTICK KISS

My childhood fantasy of fame had no down side at all. There were no press intrusions, or exhausting schedules, or sniping columnists, or former boyfriends who kissed and told. However, like most things in life, once you put them under a bright light you begin to see the flaws and imperfections.

My expectations were unrealistic, but the fantasy wasn't entirely wrong. The trappings of success were obvious. Every time the Spice Girls moved, we did so in a convoy of Jaguars and Mercedes. Jerry Judge and half a dozen minders flanked us as we stepped from the cars. Policemen also stood guard to keep the fans at bay. At airports, our bags were always checked through in advance and we swept through passport control to the VIP lounge. Only after all the other passengers had boarded the flight were we escorted from the lounge to the departure gate and welcomed on board.

Flying First Class had become a necessity rather than a luxury – we needed the sleep. The first time I sat up front I felt like Alice in Wonderland, who'd been shrunk and put in this enormous seat. My feet could barely touch the floor. I flicked between personal video channels and pressed all the buttons to see what they did. The nuts came in china bowls, the champagne in proper glasses and there was a seat opposite each chair so that I could invite someone to join me for dinner.

This was all very civilized, but by the third or fourth time I flew First Class I had stopped noticing these things. More often than not I was asleep before the wheels left the tarmac.

Our normal entourage consisted of two or three bodyguards, two PAs – Rachel and Camilla – a make-up and hair stylist, a Virgin publicist and occasionally Simon. Throw in one or two journalists and we made it to fifteen.

Rachel and Camilla shadowed us everywhere. If hotel staff forgot to put mineral water in the minibar, I didn't have to pick up the telephone; Rachel or Camilla did it for me. If I wanted a sunbed or a massage, they made the booking and a driver would be waiting outside the hotel to take me there and bring me back.

I didn't have to carry a passport or money, or worry about dry-cleaning or balancing my cheque book. I rarely had to shop for birthday presents, or remember to send thank-you cards or flowers on Mothers' Day. All of this was done for me. I was safely cocooned from the mundane and menial realities of life.

Four weeks after the Brits, the Spice Girls were guests at another awards ceremony, this time at the Royal Lancaster Hotel in West London. The Capital Radio Awards were used to launch the Help a London Child charity weekend.

The biggest patron of the charity was George Michael, who over the years had donated more than £1 million to Help a London Child.

George arrived dressed all in black, with dark-rimmed glasses. He told a hushed audience about his mother's battle against cancer and his grief at losing her.

He explained that soon after her death he went into the studio and recorded a song that he hoped might help his father over the loss of someone he had lived with for forty years. It was called 'Waltz Away Dreaming', and it was to be used to raise funds for the Help a London Child appeal.

As he finished and returned to his table, George was given a standing ovation.

The awards ceremony continued and the Spice Girls were named Best Female Group. When Oasis won the award for Best Male Group, Noel Gallagher couldn't resist having a dig at us.

'Don't you think it's about time the Spice Girls did a gig?' he announced bluntly.

Mel B hit back on stage, saying, 'Did you notice that Noel ran straight out after he said that?'

I kept glancing across at George Michael's table. A part of me wanted to reach out and tell him that I understood how he felt at losing someone he loved. I wanted to introduce myself, but what could I say? Deep down I was still the little girl who'd stuck his photograph in my diary.

Choosing a quiet moment, I slipped away from our table and walked across the room.

'Hello, I'm Geri Halliwell.'

George glanced up at me and reached out his hand. I gave him my biggest flirty eyes. 'It's a pleasure to meet you, Geri.'

'I've got all your records. I was a really big Wham! fan. I come from Watford, too.' Oh, God, Geri, can't you think of anything more intelligent to say than that?

George laughed. He could see I was nervous.

We chatted for a few minutes, and later I gave George's manager my telephone number and said, 'Please get him to call me.'

Ever since Dad's death I had taken an interest in spiritualism, reading about various Eastern religions and looking hard at the big questions. Death is such a taboo subject in the Western world. We don't know how to deal with it, or what to say to people who are grieving.

George and I talked about this. When Dad died, I remember feeling sorry for myself and what I'd lost, not for the person who had gone. Everybody around me seemed to want to hide and avoid the subject. Yet in Eastern religions they celebrate death as a rebirth. People escape so much of the pain and fear because they look forward rather than back.

Although we didn't get the chance to talk very often, because of our busy schedules, we became telephone buddies.

The Spice Girls juggernaut rolled on. After signing with Pepsi, Simon had struck endorsement deals for products such as Walker's crisps, Impulse deodorant, Polaroid cameras, Cadbury chocolate bars, Chupa Chup lollipops and Sony video games. On top of this there were dozens of official products in the shops, including dolls, cards, posters, magazines, bicycles, skates, helmets, schoolbags and pencil cases.

When added to the hundreds of unofficial market-stall

rip-offs and counterfeit merchandise, I couldn't walk down the street without seeing my face on a T-shirt or a coffee cup. It was quite mad. Initially, Mum tried to collect all the different things, but finally she admitted defeat. It simply wasn't possible to keep track of them all.

In April we flew to New York to continue the Stateside push. The album *Spice* had moved to second place in the Billboard charts. We spent five days rehearsing for a coast-to-coast appearance on *Saturday Night Live* singing 'Wannabe' and 'Say You'll Be There'.

Up until then we'd mimed our hit songs when appearing on televised shows. This had given ammunition to our critics, who claimed that we were avoiding performing live, and prompted headlines like CAN THEY SING . . . CAN THEY REALLY, REALLY SING?

This made the *Saturday Night Live* performance very important and also nerve-racking. We rehearsed in a studio a few blocks from Times Square, working with our own band and a voice coach.

On the night we were all on tenterhooks. Joe Pesci, another of the guests, came into the dressing room and got mobbed. 'We're gonna do it, yeah,' he bellowed, looking quite scary. A few minutes later, Robert De Niro poked his head around the corner. He was a lot smaller than I'd expected, with greying hair beneath a peaked cap.

'I think he quite fancied you, Mel.' I winked at Mel B.

'Nah, he's too old for me.'

Hair and make-up had finished. Mel C put on her vocal tape and occasionally one or more of us joined in with her. Performing live on stage is very different from working in a studio. Voices can crack under pressure or nerves can make you squeak. Victoria and I had a harmony in the chorus that wasn't pitched off the music. We simply had to remember what note to hit.

I wore my white dress with the words 'Geri' and 'Girl Power' printed across the front and back. After a group hug in the dressing room, we took our positions. The live studio audience numbered several hundred and we could hear them laughing at the comedy sketches.

The music started and the lights came up. Please, God, let my voice be strong enough. I tried to focus on a face in the front row – a young girl in a Yale sweatshirt – pretending I was singing just to her. That way the audience wouldn't seem so large.

One of my lines sounded a little squeaky, but overall we did a good job. Backstage we high-fived, and I felt enormous relief as well as excitement. We had proved something, perhaps even to ourselves, and we deserved to celebrate.

Dan Aquilamte, the rock critic of the *New York Daily News*, declared that we had silenced a lot of people in America who thought we were manufactured and therefore no good. We had male hearts beating a little faster and had proved we could sing.

Similarly, Sam Wood of the *Philadelphia Inquirer* admitted we might not be Montserrat Caballé but we knew how to belt out a good tune.

After promotional tours of Taiwan, South Korea and Bali, Simon had arranged the schedule to give us nine days off. Ooooh!

I stayed in Bali and asked Natalie to join me. We rented a lovely villa in the mountains where Princess Diana had spent some time when she visited the island. I felt so lucky to have a sister like Natalie. She was like a best friend and understood me better than almost anyone. She had seen my best and worst – all my faults and insecurities – yet she loved me unconditionally.

As a youngster I had idolized her, but now I had become virtually the big sister. I guess I'd grown up more quickly and discovered more about the world. After finishing college Natalie had joined a travel company and eventually married – never leaving Watford.

I spent much of the holiday working. Our ambition of doing a feature film was about to become a reality. The Spice Girls were to produce and star in *Spiceworld, The Movie*, which was to be filmed during the summer on location in London and the Home Counties.

The general idea was to do a send-up of rock stars and pop culture. We wanted to poke fun at ourselves, the media and the hype that surrounded us. Kim Fuller, Simon's brother, was writing the script, and he saw it as a mix between *A Hard Day's Night* and *Spinal Tap*.

It was to chronicle a week in the lives of the Spice Girls, including rehearsals, recording sessions, press conferences, photo shoots and interviews, in the lead-up to our first-ever live concert at the Royal Albert Hall.

Having worked on the script for almost a year, it was now just down to fine-tuning the various characters and trying to make the lines sound convincing. Kim had written some great TV comedy and worked with Tracey Ullman and Lenny Henry. A little older and greyer than Simon, he had a soft voice and a lovely wry sense of humour.

I got on really well with Kim and we spent hours on the phone and fax, bouncing ideas and storylines off each other. He had managed to capture the franticness of our lives brilliantly – whizzing from place to place and rarely stopping to draw breath. He had also littered the script with weird adventures and lashings of chaos. There were cameo appearances from Elton John, Bob Geldof, Jennifer Saunders and Jonathan Ross.

Richard E. Grant had been cast as our manic, stressed-out manager Clifford. I had suggested Alan Cumming for the role of Piers, the hapless documentary-maker. I remembered how moved I had been when I saw Alan play *Hamlet* on the night before my father's funeral.

'It looks as though we might get Roger Moore,' said Kim.

'You're kidding.'

'No. He's up for it.'

Kim wanted a mysterious Svengali-like figure in the film, who was secretly pulling the strings, because people had always assumed that such a person existed behind the Spice Girls. Roger Moore was perfect for the role. With tongue firmly in cheek, he could play a classic Bond-style mastermind, pulling the strings in the background while stroking his cat and talking New Age nonsense.

The six-week shoot was due to start on 9 June in London. During the same period we would have to write and record songs for a new album in a mobile studio that would follow us to the various locations.

In the mean time, royalty called.

'You should address Prince Charles as Your Royal Highness,' said the palace aide, looking rather shaken by the amount of flesh on display in the dressing room. 'You may curtsy, and if His Royal Highness offers his hand you may shake it. On no other account are you to touch the prince.'

Out of view, Mel B stuck her nose in the air and started Emma giggling.

Prince Charles had invited the Spice Girls to perform at the Prince's Trust concert in Manchester to raise funds for his favourite charities. It was to be another live performance; this time in front of our home-grown fans.

The palace aide had come to discuss royal etiquette before our meeting with the prince. This would take place in the foyer of the Manchester Opera House. I wore a trapeze outfit with a white bodice which I'd bought in Majorca years earlier when I'd been dancing. Karen had put panels of blue sparkly material in it and the whole outfit had cost me only £20.

'Maybe he'll invite us for tea,' whispered Mel B as we waited in the foyer for Prince Charles to arrive.

'If only I could meet Princess Diana,' said Victoria.

'And the boys,' added Emma.

According to the papers, Baby Spice was Prince William's favourite and a poster of Emma had replaced Pamela Anderson on the wall of his room at Eton.

Prince Charles arrived and waved at well-wishers as he strode into the foyer flanked by security guards and detectives. He wore a classically tailored dinner jacket and was a little shorter than I'd imagined. He had a very warm and gentle manner as he greeted his guests. As he reached me, I pulled him forward and gave him a kiss on the cheek which left a big red lipstick smudge. At the same time, I gently patted his bum – a very Spanish thing to do.

The kiss caused quite a stir. The press loved it because it

made for a wonderful photograph – the prince and the showgirl. His Royal Highness didn't seem to mind. He was just about to walk away and came back again, as if to say, 'Whooah, that's a nice change.'

Like most of my antics this was entirely spontaneous and very much Ginger Spice in action. I've always had a problem with anybody demanding that I conform to protocols or rigid formalities. I've always been greeted in that warm Latin manner and I've been raised to believe that everybody is equal, from the postman to the president. We all get cold in winter and hot in summer. We all enjoy a laugh. Prince Charles is no different.

That night I lay in my bed trying to sleep, but my body felt as though it was flying around the room. It had been such an exciting day and I knew that I wouldn't have time to appreciate it properly. The next morning the Spice Girls would be on a flight to Cannes to publicize the yet-to-be-made film.

We stayed on a luxury cruiser and felt like real film stars as a speedboat came to take us to shore. I had taken to curling my hair, and I boarded the boat wearing a head-scarf so my curls wouldn't drop in the wind. Combined with my sunglasses, it gave me the look of a 1950s screen siren trying to slip into Cannes unnoticed.

'Let's all do it!' announced Emma, who sparked to life after sleeping in.

Headscarfs were found for everyone and we giggled as we tied them on. Our driver let me take the wheel of the speedboat on the way to shore. There were paparazzi and press photographers following us in their own boats.

'Hey, there's Andy Coulson,' said Victoria, pointing

into our wake. Andy was the showbiz editor of the *Sun*.

'Hi, Andy.' We all began waving and encouraged him to try to catch us.

His photographer, Dave Hogan, was trying to hold on and shoot pictures with one hand.

'How are you, Dave? How's the family?' I yelled.

'Good. Good. Slow down.'

'You'll just have to catch us.'

That evening we went to a film party at Planet Hollywood – one of the dozens in Cannes that were competing to attract celebrities. Our van took ages to reach the doors because the crowd of onlookers was so huge. People were hammering on the side and rocking the van back and forth. For the first time in a crowd situation I felt a slight prickle of fear and a sense of vulnerability. What if the van tipped over? What if we couldn't get out?

A guy filming us for a documentary was punched in the face as he tried to intervene. Eventually, the van reversed up to the red carpet and we managed to get inside, where it was very dark and smoky. The first person I spied was Iggy Pop, bare-chested and sweating. Kate Moss, Johnny Depp and Naomi Campbell were hanging out, looking extremely cool.

The place was too crowded and not bright and showbizzy at all. I felt really square and not with it. I didn't want to be there. Emma gave me a look that said, Thank goodness we have each other. Both of us laughed.

The others felt the same, and being totally uncool we skipped out and went back to the boat. It felt nice to be together and I curled up in bed with that comforted feeling, listening to the water lapping against the hull.

The next morning, before leaving Cannes, we all

climbed out on top of an awning at the Hotel Martinez overlooking the plaza. In the distance I could see the bay – a brilliant patch of blue. A sea of photographers had gathered below us, where thousands of fans were blocking the street.

This is what Marilyn Monroe would have done, I thought, or Brigitte Bardot. I'm really a part of all this, even if it's just for a few hours or days. Tomorrow I'll be in America and a week from now I'll be back in the UK.

There was no time to rejoice in our success or savour the moment. As Clifford, our manager in *Spiceworld, The Movie*, would say, 'You girls don't have a life, you have a schedule.'

I knew there was a reason for this, but just for a little while I wanted to stop the roller-coaster and get off. Then I could sit back and say, That was so great. Haven't I done well? or, What does all this really mean?

We were in Monaco to do a TV show, and were staying in the same hotel as Lionel Ritchie and the Bee Gees, who were in town for a concert. As I sat in the bar that night with Emma and Mel C, the pianist suddenly struck up 'Hello'. I looked up to see Lionel Ritchie coming through the doorway.

His assistant weaved between the tables until he reached us. 'Lionel Ritchie has asked if he might join you for a drink.'

'Sure, why not,' I said.

Lionel came across with a glass in his hand. He looked exactly the same as I'd imagined – tall and lean, with a big warm smile.

We chatted about how quickly it had all happened for

us. 'It creates extra pressure when you become so big so quickly,' Lionel said. 'It's a very hard thing to maintain that level of success.'

'Do you think it's better to have things build up more slowly?' I asked.

'Maybe. I don't know. I can give you one piece of advice.' He leaned closer. 'What you need to do is to live here' – he put his hand at about chest height – 'and earn here' – he put his hand above his head. 'That way you never have to get out of bed to pay your bills. You go to work because you *want* to, not because you *have* to.'

It was all about freedom. Doing things because you enjoyed them, not because you are obliged to do them.

Not long afterwards, in Japan, I had a very similar conversation beside a hotel swimming pool. One of the members of Boyz II Men started talking about fame, money and artistic integrity.

'You see this,' he said, showing me his Rolex watch. 'It cost me eight grand. I can afford it because our last album deal was worth seven figures.'

I knew he was going somewhere with this, so I sat and listened.

'When we first started it was all about *our* music. That was the motivation. We were really proud of it and we still are. But now there's something else that's pushing us, and that's the lifestyle. I've got used to owning nice things and buying what I want. That's why if they want us to get out of bed now they're going to have to pay for it.'

I compared this philosophy on fame to what Lionel Ritchie had told me. Lionel had been right. It's far better to do something because you want to, not because you have to pay the bills, or want to buy another Rolex.

There seemed to be two traps that I could fall into. One was financial – having to fund an expensive lifestyle. The other was psychological – becoming addicted to fame. I didn't want to suffer either fate. One of the main reasons I had pursued fame and refused to give it up during the tough years was because I wanted to be free. I didn't want a department-store manager or a hair-salon boss leaning over my shoulder telling me what to do. I wanted to make my own way in the world, on my terms.

Six weeks were set aside for filming *Spiceworld, The Movie*. It was nothing like I'd imagined in my childhood show-reels. I hadn't factored in the regular 6 a.m. starts and the interminable waiting between takes. Three minutes of film could take two or three days to shoot.

After long periods of sitting around we had only one or two chances to deliver our lines and get them right; this made it a little difficult to sound honest and real. At the same time, I knew the logistics and cost of filming from having done music videos.

Our very first scene on the opening day of filming was at a manor house on the outskirts of London. Hair and make-up took a few hours before we settled around a large table in a panelled dining room.

We were all a little anxious, but Richard E. Grant kept up a running series of gags and kept filming us for a home movie he was making to show his eight-year-old daughter.

The director, Bob Spiers, got us to run through the scene several times, trying to help us relax. I had the opening line, where I had to ask Clifford about his love life. This prompted a story from Clifford about the girl who stole his heart.

'OK, let's do it,' said Bob. 'Places, everyone.'

A clapperboard snapped shut.

'Camera. Speed. Action.'

My heart suddenly leapt and my voice went squeaky. Despite having barely a dozen words to say, I sounded more wooden than the dining table. All of us were pretty terrible.

'Maybe you shouldn't tell us that you're filming,' Mel B suggested. 'We're much better when we don't know.'

'You'll get more confident,' Bob reassured us.

We did another dozen takes before finishing the scene. Richard E. Grant was incredibly patient and utterly professional. Even so, I wasn't surprised to find out later that the entire dining-room scene had ended up on the cutting-room floor.

Despite the secrecy surrounding locations, we had a running battle with the paparazzi, who were desperate to get the first shots of the Spice Girls on location. At times this turned into high farce, as security guards plucked photographers out of trees and haystacks. Some of them had blacked-up faces and wore jungle greens.

Two of them dressed up as a cow and were caught wandering over the meadow towards the manor house. We waved as they were marched off, with a cow's head tucked under one arm and cameras under the other. We all knew it was just a game. The photographers would be dumped outside the main gate and come back to try again the next day, and the day after that.

When it came to fluffing lines, Mel B and I shared the title. My memory is lousy, particularly when I'm nervous. Suddenly, my mind would go blank halfway through a scene or I'd get tongue-tied, which would set the others off giggling.

The dialogue was very bang, bang, bang, with lots of one-liners. My longest speech was only about four lines. On top of this, we had five people delivering lines in one take, which meant having to stop and start as camera angles were changed.

It was silly to imagine that such a movie could be deep and meaningful, but I wanted us to be as natural as possible. There was only one moment in which I felt I came close to being emotionally honest and real. It was at night, beside the Thames, when the Spice Girls seemed on the verge of splitting up after an argument.

As we sat on a park bench eating hot chips, we contemplated whether we'd changed since we'd become famous. Victoria claimed to still be the same, although her tastes had become more expensive.

The major difference, I said, was that we now worried about different things. In the past we'd lived almost hand to mouth, never quite knowing where the next meal or pay cheque was coming from. Now we talked about hit singles and chart positions. Money was no longer an issue.

As the scene ended, Victoria raised the question about when our success might end. At that moment a boat cruised down the river with coloured lights spilling across the water. I could see silhouettes of people dancing or sitting on the foredeck. The music grew louder. It was 'Get Into the Groove' by Madonna. I remembered being twelve years old and dressing up to get into a Watford cinema to see *Desperately Seeking Susan*. I'd come a long way since then. No, I'd come *all* the way. The dream had come true. Now I didn't want it to end.

Looking at the rushes after each day's filming, I was happy with the movie. We were poking fun at ourselves, at the tabloid press and at the self-importance of some music critics, some of whom were already writing the movie off without having even seen it; but I was confident that none of the fans would walk away disappointed. Ultimately, it was a film made for them and nobody else.

We had virtually no songs for the new album when filming started. We had to write these at the same time as we were doing twelve-hour days on set. A mobile recording studio had been set up in a Winnebago, and in between takes we could lock ourselves away and begin writing.

Lying in bed one night, I came up with the first few lines of a song. I dashed downstairs and sang them into a dictaphone. The next morning, at the mansion house, I played the tape to Andy and Paul, the Absolute boys, who had earlier helped us co-write 'Who Do You Think You Are?' They picked up the melody line and began toying with it. I wanted something with a Motown feel. Mel C eventually finished off the chorus and, later, when we had more time, the other girls came in and helped write the verses and bridge.

The song, 'Too Much', had its beginnings while we were filming in London's Docklands on a large closed set. Security had to be especially tight because of the intense media interest. As I left the set in a car, the large metal gates opened and there were hundreds of fans and local youths trying to storm inside. They had to be held back by security guards.

Sitting in the back seat of the car, I scrawled a few lines

in my little red book about love being blind and how so often words can appear deep but are in fact meaningless. I thought it might be the start of a verse. Later the others helped fill in the gaps. Mel C and I wrote the middle eight at Andy and Paul's studio in Richmond. On my way to the session, I turned up at the wrong studio because the boys had moved.

'Is the studio not here?' I asked the security guard.

'No.'

'Oh.'

'You're Geri, aren't you?'

'Yes.'

'Can you sign this for me?'

'Sure.'

He gave me his T-shirt, which had a printed message on it: 'What part of no don't you understand?'

Having found the right studio, I added the line to the song and Mel C finished it off.

This is normally how our songs were created. When writing for five people, it's difficult to create lyrics that are especially personal. Instead, the songs had to be more ambiguous, with the meanings open to interpretation so that each of us could read into the lyrics what we wanted to.

At the same time, the songs had to suit our various vocal ranges, and decisions had to be made about which bits we were each going to sing. Usually, high bits went to Emma, ad libs to Mel C and the low bits to Mel B, Victoria and me.

# Monday, 28 July – London

The last week on set and then it's a wrap. We filmed the title sequence today – a mix between Tales of the Unexpected and James Bond – silhouettes with long arms and bodies moving.

It's been so draining doing the album and the film – all the umming and ahing and waiting around.

I'm glad it's almost over. Which reminds me, I've got lines to learn.

Good night.

## SPICE KAMPF

Life began imitating art. The Spice Girls took over a mansion in the South of France to spend four weeks rehearsing for our first live concert at a stadium in Istanbul.

In *Spiceworld, The Movie* the same scenario had been acted out at the manor house where we prepared for the film's big finale at the Royal Albert Hall. In both cases we called our bolt-hole Spice Camp, although, thankfully, in France we didn't have the gloriously manic Michael Barrymore as our sergeant major and dance teacher.

The beautiful old villa cost £10,000 a week to rent. It had seven bedrooms upstairs and another two below. There were several drawing rooms and a large lounge with ornate ceilings. A marquee had been erected on one side of the house and been transformed into a makeshift dance studio and gymnasium.

The acres of gardens surrounding the house were enclosed by a high stone wall and patrolled by security guards to prevent unwanted paparazzi sneaking inside and snapping pictures of us beside the swimming pool.

There were only eight people in the house – the five of us, plus Simon, Camilla and a cook, Cresida.

'This is like a bloody convent,' we muttered.

We entered Spice Camp on 17 September, with twenty-five days until the concert. The previous few weeks had been frenetic as we bounced back and forth between America and Britain. In early September we had the MTV awards at Radio City Music Hall in New York, where 'Wannabe' had surprised all of us by picking up Best Dance Video. Luckily we'd arranged an acceptance speech just in case.

I wrote in my diary:

Met Madonna. She said she liked our album – her favourite track is 'Mama'. What a buzz! Also briefly met Puff Daddy and Will Smith. At the party afterwards, I said hello to Janet Jackson. She was very sweet.

I wore my US flag dress. The make-up artist did this really weird make-up job on me. I felt so ugly. I looked like Alice Cooper. I wasn't me any more.

We filmed our new video for 'Spice Up Your Life' in the building where *The Witches of Eastwick* had been filmed. It was a two-day shoot. The first day was Princess Diana's funeral.

I tried not to cry.

I failed miserably. I sat in a limousine, watching the funeral on the small screen. It was early in the morning in New York and I had just spent an hour having my make-up done at the hotel. I wore a thick black mask of eye shadow to cover my sad face.

The make-up was leaking down my cheeks. Black tears for a black day as I watched Prince Charles and the young princes following Diana's coffin through the streets of London.

We all have snapshot memories of events that are so important or terrible that every detail seems to be burned into our minds. A generation before me, millions of people around the world remembered where they were when they heard that John F. Kennedy was assassinated. For my generation, perhaps Princess Diana's death has a similar resonance.

A week earlier, I had been at Max's thirtieth birthday party, which didn't finish until the early hours of the morning. I had rented a little farm cottage not far from Berkhamsted because I needed a base in England for the next twelve months, most of which would be spent overseas.

As I drove home from the party, I turned on the radio. The announcer's voice began breaking as he relayed the news that the princess had died in a car crash in Paris. It was surreal. Numbing. I didn't feel anything because I couldn't take it in. I couldn't understand it. How could she be dead?

A few days later I left the UK after saying goodbye to a lot of friends who I wouldn't get to see very often in the next twelve months. During that time, the Spice Girls would do a massive promotional tour for the film and second album, as well as nearly a hundred concerts in Europe and America.

News of Diana's death overshadowed everything. Only a few weeks earlier, I'd been involved in a car chase with photographers. It was after the wrap party for *Spiceworld*,

*The Movie*, when Emma and I were being taken home by Neil, a lovely driver in his mid-sixties. Neil looked like the sort of conscientious motorist who had spent forty years behind the wheel and never collected so much as a parking ticket.

As we left the party he noticed several paparazzi following in cars. Emma had just moved into her new house in North London and didn't want the press discovering where she lived and staking her out.

Suddenly, Neil turned into a demon driver. He was hurtling through the streets, doing U-turns and darting down backstreets, trying to shake off our pursuers. In the back seat, Emma and I were hurled from one side of the car to the other. It had seemed like great fun at the time, but Diana's death put a harsh new light on high jinks like that.

The rehearsals at Camp Spice were more intense than any before. We had so much to prove in Istanbul. Performing on *Saturday Night Live* and at the Prince's Trust Concert had gone some way towards answering those critics who said the Spice Girls were a manufactured band, who couldn't deliver the goods without the safety net of a studio and a producer. Yet there was still a question mark over whether we could maintain this for an entire concert and not just two or three songs. Could we cut it as a live band?

I knew that we didn't have to prove anything to our fans – they never doubted us – but the music press and industry critics were waiting for us to fail. Then they could tell each other, 'I told you so,' and continue penning our obituaries.

The decision to stage the first concert in Istanbul had been a purely marketing one. Pepsi had sponsored the show and organized a massive push into Turkey. From our point of view, the location didn't conflict with our world tour itinerary. It also had a nice East meets West tag-line.

Up at 7 a.m. every morning, I spent thirty minutes on the treadmill in the gym before breakfast. Mel C would already be there; her normal workout had stretched to two hours a day.

Twenty minutes away from the villa, an arena had been hired with the same stage proportions and set design as in Istanbul. This is where we rehearsed with the band and we practised our dance routines in a nearby studio. I arrived an hour before the other girls so that I could spend extra time with Priscilla, our dance teacher. She would take me through the steps she would be teaching that day, breaking the routines down into small parts to make them easier for me to learn.

Although dancing was still my weakest area, I was getting better at picking up routines. The mind is like a muscle and, if you get used to learning, it becomes easier.

After an hour of dance rehearsals, we had lunch with the crew and band; then we began working through the various songs.

After the band rehearsal, we had a session with our singing coach, Kenny, and another dance lesson. Then the girls would head back to the villa, while I stayed behind with Priscilla to keep practising. On the ride home with Paul Attridge, our chauffeur, I would sit in the back of the stretch Mercedes, tapping my feet on the floor as I tried to remember all the steps I'd learned that day.

I arrived back in time for an aerobics class with an overenthusiastic instructor who looked like Anthea Turner. Normally it was just Mel C and I, although sometimes Victoria came along.

Cresida prepared the meals and we each ate different things at different times. Mel B and Emma liked more traditional English food, like mashed potato, chips and chicken, whereas Victoria, Mel C and I were happier with fish and salad.

Physically exhausted, I fell asleep every night with my legs feeling like lead weights. The next day it would all begin again. I didn't mind. It felt as though we were on a mission, with everything focused on Istanbul.

At the end of the first week, we flew back to Britain to be among the celebrity guests on a TV special, *An Audience with Elton John*. We had to sing a live version of 'Don't Go Breaking My Heart', and my line was quite high. I struggled with the top notes during rehearsals. Please, God, don't let me screw it up. I looked across at the others and realized they were just as nervous. These were the moments that we seemed to pull together. The attitude was, What the hell, let's go for it.

On a very rare day off, I flew my mother to Cannes and we took a helicopter to Monaco. I wanted to treat her to a special day, where we could do all the things rich people do, like taking a boat ride in the bay, eating lobster and caviar at an exclusive restaurant, and then going to the casino in Monte Carlo.

She loved being on the water, cruising past the huge whitewashed mansions, with their motor launches and yachts moored out front. She gazed in amazement. Were there really so many wealthy people in the world?

Every child experiences a moment in their lives when they suddenly realize that their relationship with their parent or parents has almost come full circle. As I showed Mum the sights of Monte Carlo, I suddenly felt as though I was the parent and she the daughter. It was like a scene from my own childhood, like the day trips to the beach, and I could hear myself saying things like, 'Are you hungry yet?' and 'Do you want to go to the toilet before we leave?'

At the restaurant she nearly had a heart attack when she saw the prices.

'Don't worry, Mum, just enjoy it.'

'But look at the cost. You'll run out of money, Geri.'

I laughed. 'I don't do this all the time.'

Mum had always had to be so careful with her money, collecting coupons to get a few pence off items in the supermarket and scouring the aisles for discounts. I had been exactly the same and was still very careful. It's nice to enjoy your money, but I had read too many stories of former pop stars who'd gone from rags to riches, and then back to rags again. When all this was over, I didn't want to finish up living on social security in a council flat or working at Tesco.

At the casino, I realized that I'd forgotten my passport and only had one credit card on me. The only place that we could use a credit card was in the high rollers' room with all the serious gamblers.

I got bored after a while, and I could see Mum was horrified at how much money was being wagered by some of the gamblers, so I took her back to the hotel.

My relationship with Mum had changed a lot since I

was a tearaway adolescent. As a child, her accent used to embarrass me as much as my dad's age did. I didn't want my friends to meet either of them. Later on, Mum had exaggerated about her ten O levels and degree in Greek philosophy, trying to get me to work harder at school. She had constantly reminded me of how much she'd sacrificed, wielding the fact like a cane to bring me into line.

Now I could understand why she did these things. I appreciated that no parents are perfect and, as much as we try to escape the fact, we are all products of our parents' genes and how they raised us. Mum was no different and had grown up with the same fears, prejudices and guilt about money, sex and religion as her mother. And, in turn, she passed these on to me.

Not only was I beginning to understand this better, I could see myself becoming more like her. We both had the same fiery temperament and worried about things we couldn't control.

### Sunday, 12 October – Istanbul

*Well, tonight is the night! It's quite mad thinking about it. I feel as though I've been training for this moment all my life. It's all I've ever wanted to do – to show off, to sing and entertain.*

*Our posters are everywhere and the whole of the city seems to be waiting for us. The dates of the world tour have been released and the tickets in Amsterdam sold out in fifteen minutes. Tomorrow our new single is released – 'Spice Up Your Life'. I think it will go to number one.*

*I am very excited and I know I would never have done this without the four girls and (not forgetting) Simon. I do love them – all of them – different parts in different ways.*

*You all touch a part of me.*

At the dress rehearsal on Sunday afternoon, I felt my mouth go dry and the butterflies begin to flutter in my stomach. At the same time, I felt a rush of nervous excitement. Nothing could beat this high. Performing live for a huge audience is like being a trapeze artist working without a net. It feels dangerous and invigorating.

The vibe seemed to filter contagiously down through everybody surrounding us, from the caterers, to the security guards and roadies. They had all become infected by the same sense of expectation and anticipation. This was the big show. Everybody wanted to be a part of it.

Reporters and fans had placed our hotel under siege. Each time we arrived there were scenes of general chaos. Suddenly I recognized a face from the past. Ehran, the Turkish game-show host, waved to me frantically.

'Hello, Geri. Remember me? Remember me?'

'Hi, how are you?'

'Good. Good.'

Ehran purposely moved tight alongside of me. Then I noticed the film crew. He wanted to show his TV audience that he knew me.

'Still dyeing your hair,' I laughed.

'Oh, Geri, you're still the joker.'

Jerry Judge appeared and quickly manoeuvred me away. I could hear Ehran going on about 'my good friend, Geri,' as he did his piece to camera.

It was strange being back in Istanbul. In three years I'd made a remarkable journey from being a minor TV celebrity on a tacky game show to becoming an international pop star. Yet I looked back very fondly on that first brush with fame. It had been gratefully received and extremely flattering.

On my twenty-first birthday, in a hotel room not far away, I had vowed to Caro that I would streak at Wimbledon if I wasn't famous by the time I was twenty-two. I missed the deadline by a year. Thankfully, Caro didn't hold me to the bet.

We arrived at the stadium three hours before the concert and I was so excited that I tried to relax in the dressing rooms and conserve energy.

All of us knew how important the concert had become and there was a tremendous sense of unity and shared purpose. Yet at the same time I worried about letting the others down, particularly with my dancing. What if I missed the cue? What if I fell over, or forgot the routine?

Victoria could see this. 'Geri, it doesn't really matter if you do it wrong or not,' she said. 'They're here to see *you*, with your big hair and your Girl Power signs. They don't care about the rest.'

It was so sweet.

The show opened with a big production version of 'If You Can't Dance'. We had to stand behind a huge metal door that lifted mechanically amid bursts of smoke and fireworks. My heart pounded. We couldn't see the crowd on the far side of the ramp, but we could hear them. The first chords sounded from the band and the ramp began to lift. But instead of going up, it swung forward and almost decapitated us. At the last second we had to duck beneath it.

This near disaster proved to be a huge bonus. It completely defused my nerves. I simply reacted instinctively and let all the weeks of rehearsing pay off. I didn't screw up the dance routines and my voice was strong and clear. The costume changes were fraught, but OK.

Our outfits had only arrived a day earlier and mine had too many fasteners, making them difficult to get on and off. As we finished each set, we changed behind black screens at the rear of the stage. Clothes were flying everywhere as hairdressers and stylists did running repairs, quickly retouching the make-up on our sweaty faces.

When the music started up, we only had a few seconds to get back on stage. At one point, getting ready for 'Spice Up Your Life', I had to put on a belly-dancing outfit that I'd picked up from a fancy-dress shop in the East End. The music had started and I still wasn't fastened. I was the last on stage, walking on at the precise moment that I did my vocals.

Eight thousand people danced with their arms aloft, like a human wheat field swaying in the breeze. I looked out across the enormous stadium and felt as though my whole life had been leading to that moment. This is what it was all about. I was doing what I'd always wanted.

As the concert ended, we bounced off stage, dripping with perspiration.

'That was unbelievable,' said Victoria.

'Oh my God.'

Mel C looked ready to do it all over again.

'Did you hear them singing "Wannabe"?' I said,

sipping a bottle of mineral water and signing autographs for the production staff.

All our families were waiting at the hotel, but we couldn't leave until the crowd had dispersed and the traffic jams had cleared. Shutting the dressing-room door to keep out well-wishers, we washed and got changed.

Simon patted me on the back. 'Well done. You've really got over this hurdle.'

From Istanbul we were expected to fly to Egypt, change planes, and then travel on to Singapore, Bangkok, Delhi, Hong Kong and Japan. The punishing schedule would give us no chance to enjoy the afterglow of Istanbul.

In those first few hours after the concert, I rode the crest of a massive high. I thought that nothing could spoil the moment. Perhaps this time it might last. I could still hear the crowd roaring in my ears. Family and friends were hugging or phoning or faxing their congratulations. The champagne tasted sweeter and the smiles were wider than I could ever remember.

At the after-show party I treated myself to some baclava, the lovely sweet Turkish pastry. I'd been dieting and exercising for weeks to lose weight, but once I started eating I couldn't stop. I ate one piece after another.

I knew this feeling. It had happened so often before. I tried desperately to hold on to the good feelings. I kept picturing the last moments of the concert and the sheer elation I'd felt.

But no matter how hard I tried, I couldn't stop sliding.

## Thursday, 16 October – Delhi

*I measure the size of my pain by my belly. At the moment it's rather huge. I don't know what time it is and I can't even be sure about the date. I haven't written anything for days – either too busy, too tired, too happy, just too . . .*

*I have no time for my soul to recharge, or to dream, or simply recuperate. I am tired and I'm fat and I'm ugly . . .*

When I arrived in Singapore on Wednesday, I went straight to the minibar and scoffed the packets of crisps and peanuts. I always chose the most fattening foods. In Bangkok, I tried to stop myself by getting the hotel staff to empty the minibar before I arrived. It made no difference; I simply called room service.

'I'll have a plate of spring rolls, a side order of chips, the apple strudel, the white chocolate mousse and . . . er . . . the cheesecake.'

'Do you want cream with the apple strudel?'

'Yes.'

'And how many people are dining?'

'Three,' I said guiltily.

'Thank you, ma'am. It will be with you shortly.'

The more I ate, the worse I felt. Ugly, bloated, disgusting.

From Bangkok we flew to Delhi to appear on the Channel V Music Awards in front of 15,000 people. I must have created history in India by becoming the first person to be constipated rather than having diarrhoea. Simon had flown directly to Japan from Singapore and missed staying at the fleapit hotel with the drilling and banging that went on through the night.

On Saturday morning we had rehearsals and performed at 7.30 p.m. that night. Straight afterwards we caught a flight to Japan, stopping off in Hong Kong to refuel. We arrived in Tokyo early on Sunday evening.

*We are all exhausted. I told Simon it was a shit schedule. Guess what! We all have to work tomorrow. I'm praying that I get malaria so we get a day off. It's a TV show with Boyz II Men and Vanessa Williams.*

*Simon has done his back in again.*

*I am so miserable and sad. All I do is eat. Is it frustration? Loneliness? Pressure? I don't know why.*

Simon had damaged his back a few months earlier and had needed an operation in New York. The disc problem flared up again in Tokyo and left him flat on his back. He arranged to fly directly back to London for another operation.

I told the girls that I was going to ask Simon for a week off. My bulimia had come back and I couldn't go on like this. Surely we had done enough. We had earned a rest.

When I arrived back in England, I arranged to see him on the evening before his surgery. At the Cromwell Hospital, I found half a dozen people in his private room, including both his secretaries. Simon had a clipboard and was making calls.

I waited until one by one they finished talking business and left.

Simon knew I had something to tell him. I sat on the end of his bed.

'I'm sorry, Simon, I'm really tired,' I said, getting tearful. Then I explained how terrible it had been in Bangkok, Delhi and Japan.

'It's the tiredness that is causing depression. If I could just have some time off I'll be fine . . . As good as new.'

Simon nodded and made concerned noises, then he looked me in the eyes and shook his head. 'There are two reasons, Geri. One, it sets a bad precedent amongst the girls. If you take a week off, then everybody will be asking for one. And two, we sold eighteen million copies of the first album. That set the benchmark. We want to sell nineteen million copies this time.'

I looked into Simon's eyes. Something was wrong. I couldn't see the man that I loved like a father.

'I'll see what I can do about getting you a day off,' he said, expecting me to be grateful.

As I left the hospital I thought, This isn't right. Something has to change.

I called the band's lawyer, Andrew Thompson, because I wanted to know my legal standing with Simon. It had been six months since I'd talked to Andrew and our accountant, Charles Bradbrook. Too long. Knowledge is power.

I arranged a meeting, but it would have to wait until after the Spice Girls returned from South Africa in ten days' time.

## Friday, 24 October

*The last two weeks have been an absolute nightmare.
What have I learnt from all this?*

*This has been a fantasy, a dream. I have worked my
tail off to get this far and it hasn't been easy. I have lost
my faith in Simon. 'A man will break up this group,' he
once said to me. Ironic really.*

*But I do feel for him. We are all only human after
all.*

*Enough of the negativity. Lots of positivity. I just
wish my life could be more balanced . . . I am determined to enjoy life. To soak up everything – the names,
people, places – this won't ever happen again. I have to
absorb it all now and appreciate every minute, hour, day
and week of what is to come.*

On Saturday we flew to Germany to collect an award for
Best Group from a cable music channel. I had stopped
bingeing and managed to enjoy myself. Harrison Ford
was there, looking very Harrison. He blushed when we
said hello.

Late in the evening we flew to Paris. Knowing that
Sunday was officially a day off, I arranged for Janine to
come and join me. We spent the day shopping at the flea
market and having a fabulous lunch. I bought Janine a
suit and myself two coats.

That night we talked until the early hours. I told Janine
about the problems with Simon and my own unhappiness.
We'd been friends since I was seventeen and she knew me
better than anybody.

'Are you saying that you might leave the group?'

'I don't know. Maybe.'

She looked shocked. 'What do the other girls say?'

'I don't know. I haven't talked to them about it.'

Although Janine was concerned about me, she knew I wouldn't do anything without thinking it through first. She had to fly back to England on Sunday night and I felt sad saying goodbye. I needed some company and went to the movies with Verne Hamilton, my bodyguard – a huge black man with a bald head and the softness of a teddy bear. I got on really well with all our security guys. They were paid to do a job, but I didn't look upon them as employees. Verne was a mate and I liked going out with him. We watched *The Full Monty* and laughed ourselves silly. What a wicked movie!

Although I could escape for a few hours into the darkness of a cinema, I couldn't hide from the fact that the Simon situation had to be resolved. He was no longer the same manager whom I had loved and admired two and a half years before. Back then his words had been 'I love watching artists grow. Not just professionally, but personally. That is the great thing about this business.'

Although I respected his diligence and professionalism, things had changed since Simon had uttered those words. Maybe I had just woken up to the fact. I didn't know if the other girls had sensed it.

Before signing with Simon we had been very good at sorting out any internal problems and disagreements. The five of us were so close that we seemed to put up walls to protect each other.

But increasingly, as time went by, we began turning to Simon to sort out our personal problems and misunderstandings. Perhaps that's why the press had labelled him 'The Sixth Spice Girl' and 'Svengali Spice'.

I could see this, but what about the other girls?

We had all complained about Simon at various times. That was nothing surprising – managers normally get the blame for nightmare schedules – but nobody had ever suggested that his heart wasn't in the right place. How could I raise the subject? What if they accused me of being disloyal?

I realized I was now past caring and quite prepared to leave. First I would talk to the lawyers and then make a decision.

For the next four days we jetted back and forth between London and Paris for various photo shoots, a TV advertisement for the album, the Polaroid launch party and the opening of the British Legion's annual Poppy Day Appeal.

By Thursday night we were tired and homesick. One of the girls suggested that we fly home from Paris that night so we could have the whole of Friday seeing friends and family. Camilla checked on the prices and the cheapest private jet would cost us £1,500 each.

I didn't feel the same need to get home and could happily have stayed in Paris and rested. But I agreed to go home for a day before we flew to South Africa on Saturday. Shortly before midnight we left the comfort of a warm hotel room and took a private jet to Luton. From there, a driver took me to my cluttered farm cottage, surrounded by cowsheds and barns.

The driver dropped me at the door and drove away. As I flicked on the light switch in the hall, I discovered there was no power. The telephone and heating had also failed.

I stumbled about in the pitch-black, without a candle, torch, or the slightest clue where the fuse box was located. Welcome home, Geri.

With no way of contacting anybody and no-one I could call at one o'clock in the morning, I put on six layers of clothing and curled up downstairs under a big duvet on the sofa. I left a warm hotel room for this! Nobody will ever believe it!

## *1 November 1997 – South Africa*

*Life has a funny way of balancing itself out. Just when you think everything is going wrong, the tide turns and something wonderful happens. Today has been one of the most memorable, satisfying days of my life.*

It had been a long flight and the moment we landed in Johannesburg a minibus had whisked us away from the airport. Army trucks escorted us through the city amid tight security. Pulling through iron gates, the minibus stopped outside a large house, surrounded by neatly tended lawns.

Walking up the front steps, we entered a dark oak hall and then a lounge. Waiting for us was a smiling Prince Charles.

President Nelson Mandela strolled into the room wearing his trademark African shirt. Immediately, I was struck by his quiet calm. He has the most penetrating yet warm eyes, and a face that looks both innocent and incredibly wise. I felt overwhelmed. As a teenager I'd gone to a huge Free Nelson Mandela concert at Wembley Stadium. Now here he was kissing my cheek and welcoming me to the new South Africa.

We strolled out into the garden, where a red carpet had been laid out. Dozens of journalists and photographers were assembled on the lawn in glorious sunshine, waiting for the photo opportunity.

Coming from the darkness of the lounge, I blinked a little and then took in the view of Johannesburg from the hilltop. The press conference was very polite and formal. Nobody shouted over the top of each other or jostled for position. We all lined up – Victoria, myself, Nelson, Prince Charles, Mel B, Emma and Mel C.

I discovered that President Mandela was slightly deaf in one ear. Reporters were calling out questions and he wasn't answering. 'They want to know if you like the Spice Girls,' I told him.

'I think I'm too old for them,' he said.

'No you're not. You're as young as the girl you feel and I'm only twenty-five.'

The press roared.

Clearly enjoying himself, Nelson then suggested that meeting the Spice Girls was a highlight of his life. 'Having been in prison for twenty-five years, he would say that, wouldn't he?' I said.

Inside the house at least two dozen of the president's relatives and friends had formed a line, waiting to meet us. Many had brought their sons and daughters with them.

'This is my son's friend's brother-in-law, Mtuabu.'

'Hi, nice to meet you.'

'And this is my cousin's next-door neighbour, Medosso.'

'I love your hair.'

I kept praying I wouldn't have to remember all their names.

Afterwards, I went to the bathroom with Mel B and Emma. Mel grabbed some extra sheets of toilet paper.

'It's a souvenir,' she whispered. 'Nelson Mandela's bog roll.'

Later, I stuck them in my diary, just as someone might keep ticket stubs or a concert programme.

That night we were due to perform at a Prince's Trust concert near Johannesburg. An armoured truck with an escort of soldiers and police picked us up from the hotel. It reminded me of the problems still faced by South Africa. The North Gate stadium was packed with 28,000 people. Ten thousand of the tickets had been distributed free in the townships.

Before the show we met Prince Harry in a dining room at the stadium. He was a real sweetheart and we chatted about his school.

The Spice Girls performed three songs at the concert. Thousands of fans came outside the stadium to say goodbye as a helicopter arrived to pick us up. Scraps of paper and dust swirled across the ground as we lifted off and rose higher. A spotlight swept onto the crowd below us, illuminating white and black faces, all looking skywards and waving. What an amazing moment.

The helicopter set us down in the grounds of Sun City, a massive resort and gambling centre that had been plonked in the desert like an African Las Vegas. The hotel looked like a palace, but everything seemed plastic, even the plants.

The other girls were tired, but my mind still buzzed

from the concert. I also told myself that I'd spent too many nights sitting in hotel rooms; it was time to get out and appreciate life a little more.

'Come on, Verne, I want to go dancing.'

'Who with?'

'You, of course.'

Verne looked horrified.

'Don't tell me you can't dance. I want no excuses.'

We found a really tacky club that was absolutely packed with people. I dragged Verne onto the dance floor, where he towered over me and looked distinctly uncomfortable. I wondered what the white South Africans in the club were thinking.

Afterwards, in the casino, we played some blackjack and I finished in front. I fell into bed exhausted, but happy.

I wrote in my diary:

> It has been a good day for the girls and a good day for Geri.
>
> I've been thinking about what I want from life right now. The answer is fulfilment. That means love, creativity, freedom and a reason to go on – a cause, a message to deliver.
>
> I have an obligation to round off the Spice Girls, but I won't be doing another album or another Spice Girls' movie. I'm going to keep searching for truth and compassion . . . This is my life, I am in control.

After our last formal engagement in South Africa we flew to a game reserve in Zululand in a light aircraft. As I sat in the back seat, I picked up a news magazine and began reading a story about the Aids epidemic in Africa and the cultural factors that meant the disease was spreading at a terrifying rate. A man would die of Aids having infected his wife, and she would then be looked after by his brother – often marrying him. And so the disease would spread and wipe out the entire family.

It's such a high-profile disease in the Western World, but often we forget about Third World countries that don't have the money to educate people or give them the means to protect themselves.

I wanted to do something to help and decided to start by filming a documentary in Mozambique – one of the worst-hit countries – concentrating on a clinic that looked after children with Aids.

Perhaps I could film it during my Christmas break. First I would need to do the research and get a producer on board.

Simon had missed the South African trip because of his back operation. By the time we arrived back in England on 4 November he had gone to Italy to recuperate. The following morning I met with our lawyer, Andrew Thompson, and the Spice Girls' accountant, Charles Bradbrook.

We sat in the front room of the farm cottage, which thankfully now had electricity and heating. At least I could make them a cup of tea!

'I am considering leaving the Spice Girls, but I need to know where I stand.'

Andrew and Charles looked worried.

'At the very least I want to be able to go back to Simon and say, Listen, I *will* be taking a week off.'

As Andrew began explaining my legal position, I started to realize that I had forgotten who held the power. We did. I also came to the conclusion that I didn't want to leave the group. Instead, I wanted to get rid of Simon Fuller.

The phone rang. It was Mel B. There was still an intuitive bond between us.

'Are you thinking what I'm thinking?' she said.

'We should sack Simon.'

'I know.'

'I'm with our lawyer right now.'

'I'm coming over.'

I felt a rush of excitement. This was the old Mel B – perceptive, spontaneous and uncompromising. She arrived within an hour.

'So let's do it.'

First we had to consider the other girls. What would they say? I was fairly sure that Victoria would agree, because of hints she'd dropped in Spice Camp and again in South Africa. She had grown apart from Simon.

Mel and I sat in the lounge and began plotting. We were united again, on a mission. How could we break free of Simon's control? It wasn't as easy as simply handing him a P45 and saying, 'Thanks for all your help, but we don't need you any more.' A world tour had been arranged. A new album had to be launched. *Spiceworld, The Movie* was due to have its world première in less than six weeks.

Simon managed our lives. He had all the phone numbers, dates, schedules and contacts that kept this enormously complex machine moving. He had also ensured that people around us – the stylists, drivers, bodyguards, PAs and publicity people – were all on his payroll.

We had a fairly good idea of the up-coming schedule, but we didn't have the finer details of times, places and contacts. These were all kept on a laptop computer and printed out on monthly running sheets.

Without these we were lost. Many of the jobs would have to be cancelled or postponed. Arrangements would have to be remade very quickly.

In a few hours we were due to catch a flight to Rotterdam for an appearance on the MTV awards. Rehearsals would be the following morning for a show that evening.

Mel and I talked for hours – not just about the logistics, but also the reasons. Both of us were tremendously appreciative of what Simon had done for us, but slowly he had become lost in Spiceworld.

Once the whirlwind took over, we didn't have time to question this. Until now, none of us had stepped back to look at the big picture. I wrote in my diary:

*Remember, remember, the fifth of November.*

    *Today, I had a meeting to change the course of history for the Spice Girls. Basically, after hours of talking with financial advisers and with our lawyer, Mel B and I have decided to take matters into hand. We are leaving Simon Fuller.*

    *Girl Power has come into effect. It's time. This will prove that the Spice Girls are the source. No-one else.*

**List of why we should sack Simon:**
*Put spirit back into the group*

*Proves to the world we are not a manufactured band.*
*We have nothing to lose.*
*Just hire someone to finish the schedule up to September.*

That evening we flew to Rotterdam. Mel and I decided
that it couldn't wait. It was time to confront the others.
Finding an excuse to get the girls to my room, we broke
the news.

'We want to sack Simon.'

We all looked at each other.

'Yeah, let's do it,' we roared in agreement. There was a
mixture of excitement and fear of the unknown. The five
of us made a pact that we'd stick together regardless of the
consequences. There was no backing out.

At three in the morning, we were still on the phone to
Andrew Thompson in London, putting into effect the
legal process that would sever our links with Simon.
Catching a few hours' sleep, we turned up at the
rehearsals for MTV. I clutched my scraggy red quilted bag
containing my Filofax, which had all the important diary
dates in it, along with phone numbers for the lawyers,
record company, PRs and producers. I couldn't take
my eyes off it throughout the rehearsal, and I carried my
mobile in case Andrew rang. The scale of what we
planned seemed terrifying, but I had no doubts about its
correctness. God, please help us get through this day.

Simon knew at nine o'clock that morning. Our lawyers
had been in touch with his lawyers and the penny dropped
– or should I say the bombshell. Simon didn't want the
news to leak. If anything, he thought it was a little tantrum
and that we'd come to our senses. He obviously had no idea
of the true situation. The Spice Girls had never been closer.

Ten minutes before the MTV awards ceremony we discovered that we had won Best Group. Considering the storm that was about to break, we needed this more than ever. It was a reminder that this was about music and the Spice Girls – no-one else.

After the nerve-racking ceremony we went directly to the airport. Jerry Judge and his security team had also been told to stand down immediately. Very kindly, Jerry said, 'I'll get you back to Britain. After that, you're on your own.'

The private jet took off from Rotterdam just before midnight. A lot of tears were shed at Luton Airport. We had to say goodbye to people we'd grown close to, like the security guards, Verne and Alan.

Thankfully, three of our drivers were subcontractors and not employed by Simon. They turned up at the airport to take us home.

In the early hours of the morning, I wrote in my diary:

*The 6th of November was a day of anticipation and nerves. We saw a lot of grown men cry and a lot of people deserted us in our hour of need. Then again, there were some great people who stood by us . . .*

*Since making our decision, more and more has come to light that seems to confirm that we've made the right choice. We are going to make it happen. It is going to be all right.*

### Cosmic Shopping List
*Simon makes no fuss about quitting as manager.*
*There is no ugly mess and we part amicably.*

*The five of us are strong. We depend on each other and work happily as a team.*
*We continue to work as planned on all the collaborations and everyone is still behind us 100 per cent.*
*We keep the schedule as planned and it goes smoothly.*
*We make the next ten months the best in our lives together.*

## THE BACKLASH

Early that Friday morning, I drove to Emma's house to pick her up. We had tea and toast in the kitchen, and it felt like the old days, when the Spice Girls used to refuel at Emma's house before knocking on record-company doors.

I had no illusions that hellish times lay ahead. A lot of people were going to struggle to understand our decision to split with Simon. On the face of it he seemed to be perfect value for money, as well as a lovely, passive, caring man. I still didn't fully appreciate how reliant we had become on the people around us. Only two drivers had stayed with us and the cars dropped us at St Christopher's Place where Andrew Thompson had his office.

The car couldn't pull up out front, so we had to walk the last bit. Five of the most recognizable girls in the world were on a busy London street without minders or bodyguards. Pedestrians and office workers did double-takes, not quite believing their eyes. I think they assumed we were lookalikes rather than the real thing.

Paul Conroy, the head of Virgin Records, had come to

435

the meeting. Clearly, he was concerned that his biggest-selling act had gone into meltdown. Together, we explained to him our reasons for sacking Simon and our intention to carry on.

'Nothing has changed,' I said. 'The film, the world tour, the second album – all of them are going ahead.'

After the meeting with Andrew and Paul we were taken to a hall in Brixton to rehearse for our TV special, *An Audience with the Spice Girls*, which was to be recorded on Sunday. Rumours of the sacking had finally leaked and as we left the rehearsal hall there were two dozen journalists waiting outside. I looked up and saw Verne and another security guard.

'What are you doing here? I thought you weren't allowed—'

Verne gave me a hug. 'Looks like you might need some help.'

'But . . . what about Jerry?'

'He let us come. He said, "What you do in your own time is your own business. I'm not going to stop you."'

Rushing back to Andrew's office we agreed the wording of a press statement. Simon's lawyer, Gerard Tyrrell, was there, which made things a little uncomfortable because I liked Gerard a lot. We had a great rapport and I had nicknamed him the Grim Reaper because he always came with bad news.

That night we became free from Simon Fuller when he signed the contract. By the following morning the news had broken.

The headlines declared:

SPICE GIRLS SACK MANAGER.

EXIT SIXTH SPICE, A VICTIM OF GIRL POWER

The inside pages were full of speculation about the split, including overwork, sexual tensions and internal rows over our private lives. Some commentators called it the ultimate act of Girl Power.

From the outset, I was perceived as having been the instigator of the sacking, although I don't know how this information leaked. The five of us were equally committed and nobody could have driven a wedge between us.

The impact of the decision had astonishing consequences. By Monday, shares in EMI – the parent company of Virgin Records – began falling as a direct result of what dealers described as 'fears for the future of the Spice Girls'.

Many commentators and columnists were similarly pessimistic about our chances. Like vultures, they began to circle and wait. It was only a matter of time, they said, before we self-destructed.

## Sunday, 9 November – London

*Another early start, but everything felt different and exciting. Our passion was back. This is our life and our mission.*

*We were quite nervous doing the* Audience with . . . *The all-female audience was made up of celebrities who had brought their children along to see the Spice Girls. The vibe was fantastic. We had arranged for there to be three male gatecrashers hiding in the audience – Jonathan Ross, Richard Madeley and Brian Conley. They had sneaked in dressed as women.*

*Having been spotted, I marched them out on stage.*

*'OK, strip,' I said jokingly.*

*Suddenly they began taking their clothes off. Oh my God, how far will they go? I thought. The sketch worked brilliantly.*

*Unfortunately, there were scuffles as we left the show. The press seem to have it in for us because of Simon.*

The following day we had to shoot the video for 'Too Much' in a London studio. The rushes looked great, but the day proved to be horrendously long. Poor Mel B didn't finish until 5 a.m. and was outside wearing very little.

During the day, I felt under enormous pressure because so many negative things were being written and said about us. I called George and he gave me the outside reassurance I needed. He told me to follow my instincts and to remember what things were like before I started on this journey.

I loved talking to George. We could let off steam and joke about the old days, growing up in Watford. It was nice to reminisce. Nothing can compare to the first time you are dazzled by the bright lights, we decided, but of course the second time you begin seeing who's shining them.

Our new PA, Tor Williamson, arrived the next day, and she proved to be a godsend. Tor had worked previously for both 19 Management and Brilliant, and when she saw that we'd split with Simon she immediately sent a letter offering her services. Before it even arrived, I phoned her to ask if she wanted the job. This was nice because it meant we both wanted each other.

We also hired a new PR man, Alan Edwards, a sweet-looking forty-year-old with a slight cockney accent and almond-shaped eyes. He had worked in the music industry for his entire career and peppered his sentences with words like 'gig' and 'yeah, man'.

Already it felt as though we were gathering a good solid team around us. We were going to need it. With an album and a film to launch, the next few weeks would see us travelling twice around the world.

With the backlash still rumbling in Britain, we flew to Madrid on Tuesday evening. The press seemed to want their revenge, and suddenly we were being portrayed as having manipulated them from the beginning. Of course, it takes two sides to play the game. Now they had decided that we were ripe for the taking, and we were accused of having grown too big for our boots, and a negative spin was put on every story. Although we were out of the country, our families were reading the papers and telling us the headlines.

On Thursday evening, still in Spain, we performed at an awards ceremony for mainly industry people. Beforehand, the photographers refused to sign the standard release form to restrict where and how often their pictures could be reproduced. This had always been our practice to stop photographs being used on kiss 'n' tell stories or unauthorized products. No-one had ever refused to sign before.

Having failed to sign the forms, they were told to put down their cameras or leave. To add to the heated atmosphere, we arrived late, having been delayed at a TV interview.

None of us realized what had gone on before as we

arrived on stage. We launched into 'Spice Up Your Life' and about a third of the way through I suddenly realized that nobody in the audience was responding to us.

When the song finished we were presented with an award. Each of us had a little acceptance speech to give and I had written mine in Spanish, which I thought would be a nice gesture. I had slipped the speech into my sock and was so occupied trying to get it out that I didn't hear the booing and hissing from photographers.

The other girls began walking off. I glanced up and found myself alone. I looked utterly confused.

I felt like saying, Hey, what's the matter?

Instead, I muttered, '*Gracias*. Thank you very much. Bye now.'

Backstage there was a sense of shock. I felt like giggling. Oops!

The English tabloids were going to have a field day with this. They'd be writing our obituaries by the morning.

We went to our rooms and Victoria and I phoned Alan Edwards in London. Hopefully, he could manage the story to make sure the newspapers knew exactly what had happened.

Victoria and I talked about our worst fears. 'We can't let this happen. We cannot fail.'

We tried to reassure ourselves that people would understand what really happened. 'This is not going to beat us.'

Feeling rather dejected and unwanted, we flew to Rome. The Italian fans were the perfect remedy. There were hundreds of them outside the hotel and they chanted all night, calling our names.

When I woke next morning, they were still there.

'EMMMMA! EMMMA!'

'GERRRI! GERRRRI!'

I walked out on the balcony in my dressing gown.

'EEEAAAEEEEEEEEERRRhhhhhh!'

'Morning,' I said, giving them a wave. It reminded me of the famous photograph of Marilyn Monroe waving from a window in her bathrobe.

Later that day I went shopping with Emma and Mel B. A crowd gathered outside the Prada shop and we finished up standing on the balcony. The narrow road had been completely blocked by fans who wanted to catch a glimpse of us.

This was both heart-warming and heartbreaking, because it seemed as though most of our own countrymen and women had written us off.

That evening we appeared on a really tacky live Italian variety show. We were all in great spirits and feeling rather mischievous. Mel B popped her head up between two people during an interview and then dared me to do a sprint across the stage. She knew I couldn't say no to a challenge.

A big song and dance number was in full swing, with loads of people in top hats and tails. Suddenly I began weaving between them and then joined in, doing a little tap-dance routine. The host didn't know what to do, but carried on as if the whole thing had been scripted.

Afterwards, I went clubbing with Mel B, Emma and some of the bodyguards. We polished off seventy-five Belinis – champagne and peach juice – and danced the night away.

Andy Coulson, the editor of the Bizarre column in the

*Sun*, had flown to Rome to interview us. He was probably one of the most powerful men in the pop-music media in Britain, and I've always liked his cheekiness and charm.

People seemed to have been losing their heads all around us, we told him, but as far as the band was concerned we were like the centre of a tornado – everything was dead calm. All that had happened had made us even more determined. No-one could possibly ruin what we had. It's funny how in times of adversity our relationship was at its best. We became stronger and closer and appreciated each other more. It was as though we went back to being the five girls we were at the start. Best friends on a big adventure.

I really appreciated Andy's efforts. The rest of the papers had written us off, but he wrote a positive piece.

In the mean time, with the help of our new team, we began building up a diary of future appointments. There were also dozens of meetings with lawyers and accountants that often didn't finish until well after midnight. Having taken control of our own fate, we had to expect a far greater workload. In Paris we did thirty-six interviews in a single day to publicize the film. The same question was asked every time: 'Why did you sack Simon Fuller?'

## *Monday, 1 December – England*

*It has been a couple of weeks since I last wrote to you and we have three more weeks until we have a holiday.*

*The past few days have been in England. Very strange indeed. Still a bubble of backlash from the media, but it has calmed down a lot. We did the* Smash

Hits *Poll Winners' Party* and the Spice Girls were voted Best Band. I was the Least Fanciable Female and Worst Dressed Person.

*I must admit that, next morning, hearing the radio reports, I started to cry. I was so upset.*

*My morale is pretty low right now, I need a motivator and reminder person who can whisper in my ear all the positive things I have done, otherwise I wallow in the negative.*

*I had a bit of a cry in the car and also in the dressing room. My crying sessions seem to always happen when I'm having my hair or make-up done. Karin, our make-up girl, bore the brunt of it. Poor thing.*

*Although I know how much some newspapers lie or twist things, I can't help but be affected. It's not helped by the fact that I DO actually feel like the least fanciable person in the world right now.*

The Spice Girls had been invited to sing at a Royal Command Performance for the Queen at the Empire Theatre in Leicester Square. The dressing rooms were buzzing. There were dancers from the West End revival of *Oklahoma!* and stars like Celine Dion and Enya.

As always, I had the dilemma of deciding what to wear. I chose the same dress I had worn in the 'Too Much' video, a sequinned, strapless gown that was tight at the waist – à la Rita Hayworth.

After what had happened at the Brits, when my bosom popped out, I wanted to be extra careful. At the last minute, I asked Kenny Ho, our stylist, to get some Sellotape so I could tape the dress to my chest to stop it slipping down. He came back with black gaffa tape, and I put a wad of it inside the bodice.

I was quite nervous beforehand. Our first number was 'Too Much', a slow song, and we all stood on individual platforms that rose up from the stage. Mine went the highest and I found myself on the same level as the royal box. In the darkness, I could see Her Majesty, who seemed to be looking at me like my old headmistress, Mrs Rhodes.

I thought, Oh, my God, she doesn't like us. She's not smiling.

I felt very vulnerable and exposed, swaying in the heights of the theatre. As the song ended, I had to get down some steps and go straight into the second number, 'Who Do You Think You Are?'

The dance routine had been toned down because of what we were wearing. The song started and I strutted forward, giving it some.

> The race is on to get out of the bottom.
> The top is high so your roots are forgotten.
> Giving is good as long as you're getting,
> What's driving you it's ambition and betting.

I turned my back to the camera and looked down in horror. A big black blob of gaffer tape was sticking out from the top of my dress.

For God's sake! What is it with me? My life is like a bloody Carry On film. My intentions are good, but something always goes wrong.

I quickly ripped off the tape and kept going as if nothing had happened. It didn't matter, everybody had seen it. Thankfully, they edited it out for television.

Afterwards, backstage in the line-up, I wore the same dress as I waited in the celebrity line-up for Her Majesty. Photographers were jostling for position to record the moment. I was the showgirl who had patted the prince's bottom – a 'human headline' who was prone to popping out of dresses and breaking royal protocol.

What made me especially nervous was that I had never curtsied before. I had a vague idea of how to do it and figured I would simply copy the others. The main thing was not to look clumsy and unladylike. At the same time, I was afraid the photographers were waiting to get a shot of my cleavage as I curtsied.

As the Queen reached me, I did a very quick, self-conscious dip. She said a few words about being pleased to meet me and then moved on.

A headline the next day read, GERI DOESN'T CURTSY TO THE QUEEN.

## Tuesday, 2 December 1997

*I am now on a plane to LA.*

*Last night I met the Queen, and the tabloids are saying I didn't curtsy. They only ever focus on my bouncing bosom. It's just the male-dominated media going for the cheap shot. They can't handle seeing a woman with brains so they have to shout 'TITS!' It's so crass.*

*But I can take it on the chin. Half of me hurts and needs a cuddle of reassurance, the other says, Hey, it's a compliment, sweetheart. Forget it.*

*We're off to LA. Let's make it a good one, girls.*

The next few weeks passed in a blur of interviews, photo shoots and TV appearances. These had become so routine that I felt like a wind-up doll going through the motions. I almost lost track of time. Was it Wednesday, or Thursday? At least we had a break coming for Christmas. I just had to hang on.

At the US Billboard Awards in Las Vegas the Spice Girls won Best Album and Best Breakthrough Act. I dressed as Elvis in a sequinned white suit. By then my tanks were empty.

The greatest irony about sacking Simon had been the fact that it had been triggered by my not being given a week off. Yet since then we had worked twice as hard to prove that we didn't need him.

Alan Edwards arrived in Las Vegas to join us. He had been working on the pre-production schedule for my Aids documentary in Mozambique. A producer had come on board and there were plans to begin filming a week before Christmas.

Alan took one look at me and his face fell. I had no spark left in me.

'We can't go ahead with this, can we?'

'No.'

I was gutted, yet I knew that physically I wasn't strong enough to spend ten days in the wilds of Africa. Instead, I needed a complete break.

## Saturday, 6 December – Brazil

*I'm lying in bed, fighting off mosquitoes and listening to the sounds of the Amazon. Today has been a comedy of* errors. We arrived this morning from Vegas. The hotel was a nightmare. Dark and depressing, with no security. Reporters and fans were roaming the corridors, knocking on doors.

The local mayor offered us his boat. I expected a luxury motor launch, but this thing looked more like the African Queen. I half expected to see Bogey emerging from the wheelhouse covered in oil and grease.

It's all very charming and olde worlde, but the planks creak, there's no air conditioning and that port in the drinks cabinet was decidedly dodgy.

Never mind. I'm so tired I could sleep standing up. Good night.

### Sunday, 7 December – Brazil

Victoria woke up feeling like death warmed up. Not a good start to the day. They wanted us to go canoeing with the winners of the MTV promotion. None of us fancied clambering about on flimsy wooden boats.

Instead, we did a press conference and met the fans at the hotel.

Victoria still isn't well. We've squeezed all our commitments into twenty-four hours so we can go home a day early. Hooray! Roll on Christmas.

One of our last official engagements of the year was guaranteed to blow away any cobwebs and get the heart racing. Seven thousand fans gathered in London's Leicester Square for the world première of Spiceworld, The Movie.

As the limousines pulled up, Victoria stepped out first and I followed. All of us were dressed in identical pin-stripe suits and I had a big cigar. We loved the fact that we looked the same.

'Geri, over here! Over here!'

'This way, Baby!'

'Give us a smile, Posh.'

'One more, Sporty.'

A solid wall of flash guns kept firing as we waved and grinned.

It had taken the cars almost twenty minutes to move through the crowd spilling from the footpaths. Television stations were broadcasting live, catching interviews with guests as they arrived.

Inside the foyer, we were swept into a private room with Prince Charles and the young princes, William and Harry, along with some of their schoolfriends.

As the lights went down in the auditorium, each of us made a short speech and then I found my seat next to Prince Charles. As the film opened, I couldn't believe how big I looked. The screen was huge and I must have been twenty-five feet high.

I found myself listening to the people around me to gauge their reactions. Charles laughed in all the right places.

We were on the upper tier and sitting below were all my family and friends. Here I am, I thought, watching *my* movie, sitting next to the future King of England, while everyone I care about most in the world is with me. This must be as good as it gets.

# 19

# THE VALENTINE'S SYNDROME

Ireland became our base for the holidays and we jetted
in and out of Britain to see family and friends. I came
back for a day's shopping and took Alastair to Harrods to
see Father Christmas. Now two years old, he had grown
into a really charming, cheeky little boy with big brown
eyes, just like his mother. Sometimes, when I was with
him, I wished I had my own little boy.

As we left the store I pushed Alastair in a trolley. He
had chocolate cake smeared all over his face and it made a
wonderful picture in the *Daily Star* the next morning.

Just as I was about to get into the car, I saw a face I
recognized from the past. Trevor used to work out at the
same gym in Watford where I taught aerobics. I used to
read my English essays to him to get some feedback,
because he worked for the *Watford Observer* and knew
about writing.

I waved and said hello.

'Hi, Geri,' he said, and then suddenly he lifted a camera
and started firing off shots. I had a look of shock on my
face and I quickly turned away and slid into the car.

'Geri, Geri, wind down the window,' he called.

I lowered it a few inches.

'How are you?' I asked.

He didn't answer. Instead, he picked up the camera again and went click, click, click. As we drove away, I thought, What is he doing? OK, he's joined the paparazzi, but why won't he even talk to me?

Trevor didn't see me as a person, I was merely a photo opportunity. There seemed to be a line that I had crossed, a barrier that he perceived, and I was no longer the same person he used to muck about and have a laugh with at the gym. Maybe I should have understood that. After all, he was only trying to make a living. But instead it made me feel enormously sad.

On Christmas Eve I flew back to England. The Spice Girls had become the first band in thirty-two years to have two Christmas number-one singles in a row.

The world tour was only a month away and a lot of the details still had to be finalized, including some of the venues. Without a management team we had been running the ship ourselves, putting added pressure on the band.

I stayed at the farm cottage that night and woke on Christmas morning to the sound of cows in the nearby barns. I ran downstairs to find that Mum had left me a present. Ripping off the paper, I discovered an electronic zapper to kill flies. Why couldn't she just buy me Marks & Spencer's knickers like other mothers? No, she has to be practical and buy me a fly-zapper. I could hear her voice in my head, saying, 'You live on a farm, Geri. Think of the flies.'

I couldn't fault her logic.

After a morning at Watford Hospital visiting the children's ward, I arrived at Mum's house in Jubilee Road for Christmas lunch with the entire family, including children and grandchildren.

As usual, Mum's Christmas dinner had a Spanish flavour. After starting with prawn cocktails, she served up turkey with paella rice and *albóndigas* (meatballs). This prompted our annual competition to see who could eat the most meatballs. Max retained his world title, polishing off twenty-six.

After lunch we all squeezed into the front room to watch *Jurassic Park*, with the children sitting on the floor. I had Alastair squirming in my lap.

When the movie finished, Natalie put on a *Now* compilation album – probably number 102 – and we transformed the front room into a disco. This developed into Spanish dancing, with Mum – tipsy on sherry by now – and Steve tangoing up and down the kitchen, much to the delight of the children.

To complete our annual family rituals, Max drunkenly staggered upstairs and came back dressed in Mum's clothes. His toes were squeezed into black pumps and he couldn't do up the zipper on the skirt. All families are mad – mine just seem a little madder than the rest.

I could count on one hand how many times the whole family had been together in the previous five years. Maybe once or twice for Christmas, and again for Max's wedding. And it didn't matter what I had done in the world during that time, when I stepped through the door in Jubilee Road, I became my mother's little girl again.

She scolded me about not eating enough and not

sleeping enough and how I hadn't called her enough. And when Natalie and I discussed our latest shopping expeditions, Mum would say, 'You throw money away, you two. Why don't you shop at C&A?'

We finished at about 11 p.m. and I stayed the night, sleeping in my old room. There were photographs on the chest of drawers of Natalie and me as children. For all her early reservations and doubts about the Spice Girls, I knew that Mum was very proud of me. Every day she went through the papers and magazines, cutting out stories about us. There were suitcases and plastic carrier bags full of them in the attic.

'One day you might want to look back at them,' she said.

I went back to the farm cottage on Boxing Day afternoon. There was a big ginger cat in the garden sniffing through the overgrown flowerbeds. He looked at me cautiously, unsure of what to do. With a few scars and spots of mangy fur, he was obviously a barn cat who had been through some battles with rats and working dogs.

As I walked to the door, he followed me. I bent down and started stroking him and he automatically followed me inside. I had nothing to feed him except skimmed milk, which didn't impress him. Eventually I walked up to the main farmhouse and asked Jimmy, the farmer, if he had anything.

I came back with a tin of dog food, but the ginger cat didn't seem to mind as he scoffed it down. Unfortunately, it soon came out the other end, leaving a stinking mess on the kitchen floor which I had to clean up.

It was bitterly cold that night and I couldn't decide

whether to put the cat outside or let him stay. I liked having him around because I felt quite lonely. We both craved a little warmth, I suppose, and had been through our share of scraps.

Eventually I took him for a walk in the garden and then let him curl up in front of the TV. That night he sprayed urine all over my clothes.

I had to fly back to Ireland the next day. The cat didn't want to leave the house. Each time I tried to shut the door he would run back inside. Finally I managed to keep him out long enough to lock up.

As we drove away I saw him sitting on the front step. He wasn't there when I came home again.

After Christmas I decided to stay in Ireland, where Natalie found a castle to rent in County Wicklow – a lovely Gothic-looking place with ten bedrooms. It was like something out of an Agatha Christie thriller and I half expected to find a body in the library.

For the first few days, Natalie and I had the place to ourselves, except for the butler and housekeepers. At mealtimes, we sat at an enormous dining-room table – one of us at each end – shouting, 'Pass the salt, please.'

The butler called us 'ma'am' and had this amazing ability to be invisible in a room until we needed him. Then he'd suddenly appear and say things like:

'Would you like some dessert, ma'am? Cook has made apple pie.'

'There's a phone call for you, ma'am. Shall I put it through to the library?'

'Will there be anything else, ma'am?'

It was like a childhood fantasy come true.

I said to him, 'Oooh, what about a nice young man, please?'

'I'll see what I can do about that, ma'am.'

Natalie laughed. 'Isn't it normally about this time of year that you have your seasonal fling?'

'Yeah.'

'And it's all over by Valentine's Day.'

'Exactly.'

She knew me very well. I didn't miss having a boyfriend until I stopped working for a few weeks, then I quickly got bored and lonely. I needed a diversion – a man.

The owner of the castle, a German lady, was meant to be away in Argentina for the polo season, but for some reason she cancelled her holiday and came home. She had her own rooms in a separate wing of the castle. The following weekend she invited house guests, which included a young polo player called Jamie Morrison.

Because I had rented the whole castle for a New Year's Eve party, the owner's guests were accommodated in the servants' quarters downstairs. I felt a little guilty about this.

I bumped into Jamie in the billiard room and his father invited us to play snooker. I teamed up with Jamie and we had a laugh. He was very young and athletic, but quite shy. He plucked up the courage to invite me horse-riding the next day.

Bryan Morrison, Jamie's father, had a barrow-boy charm about him, and a gift for self-promotion. He'd been involved in the music industry for years, with bands such as Pink Floyd and the Bee Gees.

One night we sat by the fire chatting about music –

how some make it and some don't – and the fickleness of the industry.

He told me, 'Milk it while it lasts, Geri, because so many people jack it in and then regret it.'

I could see his point, but I also knew that everything has to end at some point. Isn't it far better to choose the moment?

Just occasionally, I had allowed myself to think about this. It had started in November, before we split with Simon. Afterwards, I put these thoughts to one side as I concentrated on making sure the tour went ahead and that his departure didn't destroy us.

The new challenge seemed to energize me and I became excited about the future. I almost convinced myself that the Spice Girls could go on indefinitely. Right at the very beginning, our philosophy had been, in, out, shake it all about – don't hang around long enough for anyone to get bored or see the imperfections. That's where Simon had proved to be so good at making deals and milking the moment.

But this philosophy seemed to have changed now. We had started to convince ourselves that we *could* go on for ever. Of course, that's idealistic, particularly in pop music where acts go in and out of fashion. I could see why we wanted to believe differently. The Spice Girls had developed as a band and got better. We could sing bloody well and put on a cracking live show. People were surprised at how good we were on stage and Mel C, in particular, wanted to take it further, playing more live shows and continuing to tour.

I listened to her and thought, Yeah, maybe you're right, but everyone eventually moves on and changes. Teenagers put new posters on their walls. We did it ourselves.

I hadn't contemplated life after the Spice Girls. I had no particular plans for the future, although I did want to write a film script and do some charity work. Without a doubt I knew that I'd really miss the girls if I left. Yet instinctively a little voice inside my head kept repeating, Stop come September.

The final concert of the world tour was at Wembley Stadium. What better place to put a punctuation mark on a marvellous adventure, just like Wham! had done a decade earlier.

I wouldn't say anything to the girls just yet. I still wasn't sure.

For New Year's Eve I organized a party at the castle. All my family and friends had arrived by then and the place had come alive. Emma and Mel C were also there. The Morrisons were going out to dinner, but I invited them to the party if they came back early.

A little Irish DJ turned up to run the disco. His record collection consisted of Abba, Wham! and the Spice Girls. When he saw three Spice Girls at the party he got very embarrassed.

The Morrisons arrived just after midnight, when the floor was littered with streamers and balloons, and Jamie and I danced to 'Mama'.

I'd love to romanticize about what happened next, but there isn't a great deal I can say. We were in the library and I asked him to give me a kiss. That, I'm afraid, was it!

He did, however, give me a call when he went back to England. He asked if I'd like to come to Switzerland to see his father play polo in the Cartier Cup, and we made a tentative date.

## Saturday, 10 January 1998 – Australia

*First day back at work after a long flight. I am exhausted, happy, sad and confused. Here I am in Sydney with my four fab friends. And I fully love them dearly. I enjoy the laughs, the screaming fans and the glory, yet I am sad inside. Where I want to be right now is snug, sleeping under a duvet, sleeping for a thousand years. That is how I feel these days. I could sleep for that long. Hibernate.*

My hotel room overlooked the Sydney Harbour Bridge and the Opera House. What a magnificent place. I could see ferries chugging in and out of Circular Quay and buskers encircled by crowds on the surrounding concourse.

After a three-week break I should have been raring to get back into it, with my batteries recharged. Instead, I felt as though I needed longer.

It was great to see the girls again, but I was exhausted already after such a long flight. On top of this, I still felt bloated and unattractive. Everybody expected Ginger Spice to wear figure-hugging outfits and show off her curves, but I didn't always feel comfortable with that image. Perhaps I was growing up.

The girls were great fun and enthusiastic about the upcoming world tour. As the limo approached the George Street cinema complex, there were thousands of teenage fans screaming our names. I never ceased to be amazed by scenes like this. All these people had come to see us. They were waving Spice Girl banners and posters; some of them were even dressed as lookalikes. Young children were perched on top of their fathers' shoulders.

Marvelling at the crowd, we began bouncing around ideas about our future. 'Come on, let's do something else together,' said Mel B.

'Like what?' asked Emma.

One of the girls suggested a TV series, which wouldn't be as hard as making a film.

'What about September?' I asked.

'Huh?'

'The two-year plan.'

They looked at me blankly, and the conversation drifted on to something else.

I could hear the little voice inside me, louder than before, saying, No, I really want to get out of this. There has to be an end.

From Sydney we flew to Melbourne for another première, and then straight to America. Our entire Australian tour had lasted two days. Next stop, Chicago.

Oprah Winfrey breezed into the dressing room and I said hello. I could see her mind ticking over as she prepared herself for the day's filming. She had three shows to pre-record and had an amazing ability to hold details in her head, so that she never forgot a name or what questions she wanted to ask.

I loved doing Oprah's show because the studio audiences are so energetic and up-beat. They're always shouting things like, 'Yeah! Wooaah! Go, girl!' and you find yourself getting into the spirit.

Being interviewed on American talk shows is different from in Britain. The soundbites are shorter and the questions are rapid-fire. The whole pace of the show is cranked up a notch to keep the audience bubbling.

Oprah is a legend and I admire her enormously. She battled to the top of her profession when so many things were stacked against her. She wanted to know how we had all started. Was it really as much fun as we made it seem?

'Of course,' we said. 'We're living out our fantasies.'

After the show I went shopping for new clothes. I wandered into a very fashionable and elegant department store and chose a pristine white shirt, tailored jacket and trousers. Slowly I became aware of how odd it was for me to be choosing clothes that were quite normal and even slightly conservative. My outfits were usually outrageous and daring. For the first time I even bought a jumper that wasn't skin-tight and a plain grey cardigan.

I didn't try to analyse why I did this; it simply felt right.

The next stop was New York. Another day, another city. We did the David Letterman show and then cancelled a trip to Canada. This was quite a landmark event, because we'd never abandoned important dates before. There were mixed feelings among us because we were normally so committed, regardless of how tired or ill we felt, but it did show that we were now looking after ourselves and our welfare.

That night, at the Four Seasons Hotel in New York, we bumped into Jason Orange in the bar. The former Take That band member was studying in New York. I had met Jason once before, very briefly, at the Brits two years earlier. We had a drink at the bar with Emma and Mel B. Victoria and Mel C had gone to bed early.

As we sat around the bar chatting, a woman came up to me. I didn't recognize her.

'Hi, I'm Debbie Harry.'

'Oh, hello.'

Although she looked great for her age, this wasn't the same Sunday Girl who I used to sing along with in my bedroom at Jubilee Road, imagining myself to be a blonde, sexy pop icon.

Everybody grows old, of course, but we seem to imagine that icons stay the same. Some of them do – look at Marilyn Monroe and James Dean. I sometimes wonder what would have happened if both of them had lived long enough to grow old. Would they still be idolized in quite the same way?

Something else had happened that evening, which reinforced the fact that fame fades just the same as youthful good looks. I'd gone to a hotel restaurant with Victoria and a couple of the others. There was a long queue waiting to be seated, but we went straight to the front. I knew they would find us a table. I also knew that this was only because we were the Spice Girls. One day it would be different.

I told the story to Jason and he nodded. 'It happened to me,' he said. 'You find that extra bit of care and attention disappears. Waiters don't try that little bit harder and you don't get that extra smile from shop assistants . . .'

Fame changes lots of things. I used to love that wonderful moment of connection that you get when you catch someone's eye as you walk down the street. And I used to enjoy striking up conversations with people on the bus or the tube, swapping stories and general chitchat. Back then, my clothes and body language had seemed to be saying. Look at me! Look at me!

Nowadays, this didn't happen so much. Instead, when

I went out on my own, away from the Spice Girls, I often tried to be anonymous. It was as though I was searching for the space I needed to be able to slip into the rhythm of a normal life.

Each airport had started to look the same and every arrival had a well-oiled routine about it. VIP handlers rushed us through customs and immigration. Our bags were collected and heaped on trolleys. Our bodyguards waited outside. The head of security paused at the door, waited for a signal, and then put the circus in motion.

'Let's go! Let's go!'

We swept through the arrivals hall. I could hear the fans screaming. My head felt heavy. I'd been ill since New York. It must have been the flu.

A bodyguard held open the automatic doors and another intercepted autograph hunters outside. The police had sealed off a section of the sidewalk and given us a clear path to our limousines. The doors were open and the engines running.

Once behind the blacked-out windows I slumped down and tried not to be ill. The convoy rushed towards the Four Seasons Hotel in Los Angeles. The cars behind contained our PA, four security guards, one international publicist, two US agents, one art director and a stylist.

We arrived at the hotel as our luggage was wheeled into elevators. The check-in procedure had been taken care of. Heads turned as we crossed the lobby. Several teenage fans were intercepted, but a mother and her two daughters managed to get through.

'This is Kimberly and Lacey,' she said proudly. Both of them wore Spice Girls T-shirts.

I gave them each a kiss and signed their autograph books.

We had two more nights before I could take a three-day break, when I planned to go to Switzerland to meet up with Jamie.

Early the next morning we had interviews and then a photo call at Planet Hollywood. Three jeeps dropped us at a back entrance – ah, that familiar smell of rotting vegetables. We swept through the kitchens in a swirl of colour, bowled into the lobby, skipped up the escalators and burst onto the stage. As the fans screamed, we waved and yelled hello.

After five minutes we were off again. I still felt sick from the flu and just wanted to sleep.

An hour before dusk, we left the hotel for the première. It was timed to perfection. The sun was setting as we approached Mann's Chinese Theater and we were standing on top of a Union Jack-emblazoned double-decker bus.

More than 10,000 fans lined the road. Some of them had been waiting more than twelve hours to get the best positions. Police had cordoned off Hollywood Boulevard and redirected traffic. The *Los Angeles Times* called it the biggest première at the Chinese Theater in years.

A podium had been set up outside the theatre and a long red carpet awaited us. We all wore white tuxedos with plunging necklines. I stood between the two Mels, gazing out across the sea of faces and upraised arms. I wondered out loud, 'Are they really here for us?'

Some of the crowd had banners and one of them read, I LOVE GERI. It made me feel better.

Along the red carpet and up the stairs, we gathered on

a temporary stage, where each of us was introduced to the crowd.

This is my big Hollywood moment, I thought. This is what I dreamed about as a little girl. Countless times I played the show-reel over in my head, with the red carpet and the canopy and the photographers calling my name. But as I waved and smiled at the crowd I came to a terrible realization. I closed my eyes and conjured up a memory. Suddenly I understood that the reality would never match the scene in my imagination. The fantasy would always be better.

Each accomplished ambition is a dream that is dying.


Tor, our PA, came with me to the airport, along with a bodyguard and a driver. She made sure my luggage had been checked through and then gave me a hug.

'Now, you have your passport, haven't you?' she asked.

'Yes.'

'And your ticket?'

'Yes.'

'Have you got enough money?'

'I think so.'

'Give me a call when you get there.'

'I will.'

I suddenly felt very small and frightened. The airport looked so huge. People were rushing everywhere. I didn't want Tor to leave. I wanted to say, Come with me, please.

For the first time in two years, I was travelling somewhere without PAs, bodyguards, publicists, or the girls. I had to make the journey alone to Zurich, and I can't describe how terrified that made me feel.

Airport Special Services had sent someone to take me

to the First Class lounge. He wore a uniform and had a peaked cap. Tor gave me another hug and watched me walk away. I turned and gave her a wave and a weak smile. I felt like a six-year-old, with money pinned inside my jacket, on my first day at school.

My VIP handler took me through long corridors to the First Class lounge. Feeling totally disorientated, I wanted to grab his hand and hold it so that he didn't lose me. When we reached the lounge, he turned to leave.

'Where are you going?'

'I'll be back to get you when your flight is boarding.'

I suddenly panicked. 'You won't forget, will you? You *are* coming back?'

'Yes, I'll be back.'

As I boarded the flight, I felt like Macaulay Culkin in *Home Alone 2: Lost in New York*.

I tried to work out why I felt so scared. Did I imagine that suddenly I'd be besieged by fans or that I'd get lost? Was I incapable of looking after myself? All of these things were partly true. I had become so emotionally attached and dependent on the people who normally travelled with me that I'd regressed. I was so used to having things done for me and being cocooned from petty worries and chores that I had lost confidence in my ability to do these things on my own.

I had rarely driven a car in two years, or consulted a road map or had to jot down a phone number. I'd lived inside a bubble that was so complete that nothing from the outside ever intruded. Elsewhere in the world, wars were being fought and icecaps were melting; children starved in Africa and floods ravaged South America. None of this ever reached me, unless I happened to catch five minutes of CNN while getting dressed of a morning.

I didn't consciously choose to live this way, it evolved. We were so busy being busy, being famous, that we simply didn't have time. There weren't enough hours in the day for any sort of normal life. And, as a result, I had become almost helpless.

This change had an even greater impact on me because I had once been so self-sufficient and independent. From the age of seventeen I had lived away from home. I'd paid my own rent, bought my own clothes, got the car serviced, paid the gas bills, did everything to run my own life.

Now I had come to rely on a small army of people assigned to look after me. In many ways they relied on my insecurity for their jobs. The more I needed them, the safer their positions were. Although they didn't intentionally encourage me to become helpless, that is what happened.

And I knew that while I had them around me there would never be a day when I woke to find no milk for my coffee or an unpaid bill in the post. I wasn't dealing with the fundamental, everyday issues of life like normal people. Instead, I had a different set of problems.

### 24 January 1998 – Switzerland

*Just arrived in Zurich to meet Jamie. I am really nervous, excited and apprehensive. I have a three-hour car journey to St Moritz. I have really learned in the past two weeks that sometimes the journey and the expectation of what is to come is almost more exciting than the reality.*

*I am so split in what I want out of life. My priorities have definitely changed. I currently feel a bit sick. Is it the tiredness? Or just the wondering how the next few days will turn out?*

I loved the spectacle of polo on ice – the horses and handsome men. The crowd contained the sort of people whose pictures would finish up in the back of *Tatler*. Afterwards, Jamie and I went ice-skating and drank lovely hot chocolate. The sky was so blue and the mountains so striking that it looked like an advertisement for Viennetta ice cream.

GERI LOVES MR POLO declared the *Sun*, which already had me on the verge of getting engaged. I had fallen head over heels for the dashing Jamie, according to the story, and couldn't stop kissing and cuddling him during a romantic weekend in St Moritz.

It was all over by Valentine's Day. Natalie had been right. My Christmas romance syndrome had struck again. Jamie was lovely, but he was only twenty-one, and we had very little in common.

All my relationships in the previous five years had been at vulnerable moments or when I was bored. They had lasted either three weeks or three months. It was almost a pattern. It would probably take a shrink to sort out the reason.

# BEFORE I SAY GOODBYE

'Five minutes, girls,' said the production assistant. She had a walkie-talkie in one hand and a clipboard in the other.

The butterflies in my stomach suddenly fluttered to my throat. Our singing coach, Dave, had given me a warm-up tape and I started practising vocal exercises. The other girls joined in.

We were backstage at The Point in Dublin, preparing for the first concert of the world tour. Outside in the arena there were 6,000 fans waiting for us. I had put on my sheer tights and a flesh-coloured G-string. All my outfits would go over the top of this, and I made sure I went to the toilet beforehand because it was such a palaver getting things on and off.

A mike pack nestled against my back. It had been tested earlier during a sound check. My first costume consisted of white hot pants, a white top and white boots. To stay warm, I threw on a man's dark-blue heavy cotton shirt which came down to my thighs. It had been sent to me by a fan and I regarded it as being lucky. The other girls wore dressing gowns.

In those last few minutes, we were each lost in our own thoughts. I glanced up and caught Victoria's eye. She smiled at me reassuringly.

Spice Camp in Ireland had been a lot more relaxed than in the South of France. We organized ourselves and created our own pressure to learn the routines and match our expectations. We enjoyed it more, because we were proving something to ourselves.

My attitude towards the dance rehearsals had changed. Now I saw it as a challenge, and collapsed into bed each night with my legs aching and my mind still dancing.

After the success of the Istanbul concert, I had no doubt we could put on a good show for the fans. Whether we could do this night after night, for weeks on end, was a question that still had to be answered.

But I told myself that this was the final chapter. I wanted to savour every moment of the world tour because I knew that it might never happen to me again.

The production assistant reappeared. 'We're ready for you now.'

The five of us stood together backstage behind the screen and began a little chant that had become part of our build-up.

We would repeat over and over – 'Tonight's going to be great!' getting louder and louder.

Then we put our hands in the middle, one on top of the other, building up the stack, higher and higher. It had to be done in a set order, so that my hand was always the last on. It had become a superstition.

Outside, we followed the corridor to a set of small stairs that rose onto a ramp behind a huge screen. Dressing gowns were shrugged off and I put my lucky shirt in the small changing booth that we each had behind the stage.

The music to 'If You Can't Dance' was playing, slowly building up in volume until the crowd was at a fever pitch. The screen in front of us consisted of two massive doors that slid back as if they were part of a spaceship.

The five of us stood in a line. I was at the end, beside Victoria. Mel B was in the middle, then Emma and Mel C next to her.

Suddenly, the voice of William Shatner filled the auditorium as he recited the opening lines to *Star Trek*. Only this time they had been rewritten with a Girl Power theme that had us voyaging 'where no *woman* had been before'.

The doors slowly opened and the crowd roared. What a rush! We held ourselves perfectly still, silently counting down twelve bars of eight. The timing had to be perfect.

'One, two, three, four, five, six, seven, eight.

'Two, two, three, four, five, six, seven, eight.

Three, two, three, four, five . . .'

On the twelfth eight, we came in.

If you can't dance, if you can't dance.
If you can't dance, if you can't dance.
If you can't dance to this you can't do nothing for me baby.

We strutted down to the edge of the stage. Mum said I came down the ramp looking like a bulldog. I had done so much dancing in rehearsals that my legs were all muscle.

This was a totally different show from Istanbul. It had a

space-age theme, loads of video graphics and special effects, and had three costume changes in the first thirty minutes. We had to dash to the changing booths, where each of us had a dresser waiting with the next outfit.

My first change was into a waitress's uniform and roller skates for the song 'Denying'. We had re-created a club scene and had me skating from one side of the stage to the other, almost crashing into the cameraman who was putting the images on the big screen. Then I snatched one of the dancer's hats and skated away again.

Later, as I got better and could do figure-of-eights, the girls confined me to one small section of the stage.

My favourite moment in the show was when Mel B and I went on stage and each took half of the audience to sing 'Wannabe'. My side would start and Mel would lead the other half, and the rest of the girls joined in for the zigazig ha section.

We had both sides of The Point competing to see who could do it the loudest.

'Come on,' I shouted. 'Don't let me down.'

'Let's do it again,' cried Mel.

There was also a lovely, quiet moment, just before the two Mels sang 'Sisters'. I walked on stage and began chatting to the crowd. Victoria and Emma joined me. I didn't feel nervous any more. It seemed like the most natural thing in the world to be standing there in front of 6,000 people who had come to see us perform.

There was a twenty-minute break in the middle of the concert, while roadies dismantled the ramp and changed the set. We had a cup of tea in the dressing room and glanced at the TV. I didn't always like having this break. All our adrenalin had been pumping before the interval and we had to find it again back on stage after the break.

We ended the show with 'Mama' and came back on stage to do an encore of 'Viva Forever', 'Never Give Up' and 'We Are Family'.

My voice began echoing through the arena: 'Spice Girls, calling Spice Girls. Return to the mother ship.'

There were loud booms from fireworks and the drums started beating. We all pretended to be pulled backwards up the ramp as though being sucked into the mother ship. Playfully spinning around and sometimes crashing into each other, we dragged the final scene out, not wanting to leave. Then the doors slowly began sliding shut. It was over.

What exhilaration! What relief! I was so full of happiness I could have burst.

Backstage at the bar, we got sozzled on champagne. I rarely drink, so it only took two glasses. I finished up standing on the bar, with a bottle of champagne in my hand, yelling, 'SPICE GIRLS RULE!'

The next morning, 25 February, the *Daily Mail* wrote that the Spice Girls had come of age as performers in Dublin the previous night. Hysterical screeching and emotion from pre-teen fans had greeted our arrival on stage at The Point for the first concert of our world tour.

According to the reviewer, we had given a dazzling illustration of why we had survived the sacking of Simon Fuller.

If anything, the concerts were to get better and better. On those first few nights in Dublin we were all nervous. As we moved on, we began to relax and enjoy ourselves even more.

Performing isn't tiring; it's the travelling. On stage the adrenalin could pull us through, but the flights were tedious and time-consuming. Very quickly I began to feel like a hamster on a wheel.

From Ireland we flew by private jet to Switzerland for a concert in Zurich. From there we moved on to Frankfurt. A coach met us at the airport and drove us to the hotel. I sat by myself, with Victoria in the seat opposite and Mel C in front. Emma and Mel B were sitting together. Light rain had begun falling and trickled down the windows.

The girls began talking about what we'd do after September. 'First I'm taking a long holiday,' said Mel B.

'Me, too,' echoed Victoria. She was flicking through music magazines.

'But we can't leave it too long,' said Mel C. 'We have to keep the ball rolling.'

There were tentative plans to extend the world tour to Asia and Australia. On top of this, the two Mels had talked about each doing a solo project. There was no suggestion of the group splitting up. They would simply do individual things and then come back together as the Spice Girls.

The rain had grown heavier. I watched pedestrians huddle under umbrellas, or dash between shop doorways. A businessman held a briefcase above his head and dashed to a waiting taxi.

'I'm thinking about not continuing after September,' I said, still staring out the window. The others suddenly stopped talking.

'What?'

'Well, I'm not sure. I'm just thinking . . .'

'Why? What are you going to do?' asked Mel C.

'I don't know. I just think September would be a nice

place to finish. Don't you think? In front of our home crowd . . .'

I threw it out there but nobody reacted. The girls simply assumed that I was joking or having a bad-hair day.

I said nothing more, but I now realized that none of the others had any thoughts of calling it quits after the world tour.

The idea of doing individual projects wasn't entirely new. The previous summer, before Simon had left, we'd decided to maximize publicity by splitting up and doing separate magazine covers and interviews.

Victoria did *Tatler*, I did *Arena*, Mel B did *Pride* magazine, Mel C did *NME* and Emma and her mum did *Woman's Own*. It was a way of covering all areas to promote the second album. I shot *Arena* on my twenty-fifth birthday, but the issue didn't come out until a few months later.

All of us had loved doing something separate. We didn't have to wait for four other girls to be made up and styled before a photo shoot. We had our own space.

Since then I'd been asked to do several other things on my own, but was disappointed to have to turn them down after consulting the others. I found this frustrating. The idea of being a totally democratic pop group had been a very noble one, but it simply wasn't possible for *all* of us to be satisfied *all* the time. Somebody had to miss out and finish up being disappointed.

I regarded each of us as being an individual – one of five rather than simply a fifth of the Spice Girls. Two years earlier I had engraved these sentiments on the five gold rings I'd presented to each of us – '1 of 5'. I had been trying to say that we should never lose our unique personalities or forget that we were friends.

Lying on my hotel bed, I stared at the ceiling. That night's show had been brilliant. On stage the magic was still there. Once the music started and I heard the crowd roar, we gave each other a hug in the dressing room and became five friends on a big adventure. These were always the most exciting and exhilarating moments.

Simon's departure had given us all a tremendous sense of purpose and drawn us together; however, it had also increased our workload. We were five directors of an international corporation, working so hard that we had little time for socializing. Once the lights went out and the crowds had gone home we, too, went to our own rooms.

It was 3 a.m. and I could hear an ambulance siren in the distance – the loneliest sound. I picked up my diary and began writing.

### Tuesday, 3 March 1998 – Frankfurt

*Do I go down a road of turmoil and insecurity, constantly on display, or do I just stop and take a different path and make my own tranquil journey?*

*Deep down, I do love these girls. I do feel part of them. But when that feeling isn't there, I am left with jack. Nothing but a horrible feeling of why am I doing this? For money? Fame? Come September, I just want this to stop. This jamboree. This roller coaster.*

*It is going so fast I can't even think. Yes, I could walk away from this and become a better person and find myself on my own terms. That sounds good to me. Then I have an inner voice that says, 'Stick it out. You couldn't do without it. You'd be gutted.' But my good self says, 'You can't just stay because you're scared.'*

*No, in my frame of mind, I want to stay for the right reasons. The problem is that I can't feel or find them. (That sounds like a song.)*

Six days later, on 9 March, I sat in a dressing room in Milan, waiting to go on stage. I suddenly announced, 'I am definitely going to leave after Wembley Stadium in September.'

There was silence.

'Why do you want to leave?' asked Victoria.

'I've had enough. I just want to finish with a big finale at Wembley.'

Again, there was a long, uncomfortable silence. I couldn't look at the girls.

'This feels like a Take That moment,' said Mel C. 'Is this how it was when Robbie [Williams] left? Are you doing a Robbie on us?'

'No, I'm not. I'm going to stick this out until September. I am committed to the band.'

I didn't have a defining reason for leaving. It was a combination of things, a mass of emotions that were keeping me awake at night. They left me with an overwhelming knowledge that I had to go in September.

The next day, as we flew to Marseilles, on the surface things carried on as usual, but I sensed that the girls felt hurt and let down. This was understandable. We'd been so close. We had shared the same dream. We had been clear about what we wanted. We had fought for it together and broken through. Now I think, deep down, they felt as if I was abandoning them.

Inside, I was also crying. The marriage was over and it was almost like a grieving process. But I hoped that until September, and long afterwards, we could all remain friends. Then I would wish them luck as they carried on without me. In many ways I felt that our friendships might have an even greater chance because we could go back to being mates rather than business partners.

The only people who knew of my decision were the other girls, but the lawyers had to be informed. Andrew Thompson quickly arranged a meeting when we next flew into London.

He advised us to make the news public now, rather than risk having it leak. However, it was thought that it would dominate the tour, so the lid had to be kept firmly in place.

In the weeks that followed, quite naturally, the group began to rebalance itself. The four girls became closer and continued planning for the future. It seemed both strange and sad knowing that I wouldn't be a part of these plans, but I knew this was a stage in the process of withdrawing.

This did bother me, but I encouraged them. If my leaving could draw them together or motivate them, that could only be good for the future of the Spice Girls. Although I found it hard, I was actually far happier than I'd been for months. My decision had been made and no longer weighed me down. Each time I went on stage, I knew that I might never get the chance to do this again. All my senses were heightened. Sad songs became even sadder; happy songs were exhilarating. Every word I sang had new meaning.

One of the most memorable nights of the tour was Wembley Arena, when England were playing a World Cup warm-up game against Portugal next door in the stadium. The atmosphere was electric, and we could hear the roars of our own 12,000-strong crowd, as well as those of more than 50,000 people watching the soccer.

At times like that I would think, Why am I leaving, when nights like this are so good? I seemed to be struggling internally to rationalize my reasons, but the outcome remained the same.

Our second album, *Spiceworld*, had entered the Billboard Top 200 Album Chart in the US at number eight. With *Spice* still selling well, it gave us two albums in the Top 20 – a rare achievement.

We had also picked up three major categories at the American Music Awards in Los Angeles – Favourite Group, Favourite New Artist and Favourite Album. There was similar success at the Billboard Awards.

The Spice Girls had seven entries in the *Guinness Book of World Records* and an official web site that handled 1.3 million hits a week. On top of this, *Spiceworld, The Movie* had grossed US$11.3 million in the first five days of its release in US theatres.

Money wasn't an issue any more. Before we had even performed a single live concert, *Forbes* magazine listed us among the highest-paid entertainers in the world. Saying this, the media always vastly exaggerated our earnings.

What was I going to do with this wealth? I didn't know.

Maybe I would buy my *Gone with the Wind* house, like in my childhood show-reels. Back then, I had wanted to put my dad in one end of the house and my mum in the other. That way I could see them both, but they wouldn't have to live with each other.

I was still frightened to spend extreme amounts of cash. For over twenty years I had worried about money and it's a hard habit to break. I had grown up in a household where every penny had to be stretched and very few presents arrived on birthday or Christmas mornings. You don't suddenly forget all this. If anything, it makes you more aware of the value of things.

At the same time, I knew of bands who had lived the high life and, when the bubble burst, they had no money left. I didn't know exactly how much I was worth, but I knew it would have to last me a long time. I couldn't exactly go and work at Boots if it ran out.

Ginger Spice had been a part of me and my personality. She had become almost larger than life and cartoon-like as the Spice Girls found success. The make-up, the hair, the clothes all became brighter and more outrageous. Yet after two and a half years I was beginning to feel less comfortable with an image that was based on me as a teenager. I'd been wearing platform shoes since I was seventeen; at twenty-five I wanted to come back down to earth.

Again, I can't pinpoint a defining moment of change. Maybe it was in Chicago, when I went shopping and came back with lots of conservative clothes. Others could see it happening, like Ben, my hairdresser, Kenny Ho, our stylist, and our make-up artist, Karin. My costumes had grown too outlandish, too 'out there'. I felt as if I was walking around in fancy dress.

In a bid to cheer me up, Ben suggested I change my hair. He took out the blond streaks and lightened it to a honey colour. On top of this, Karin had been encouraging me to wear less make-up. Slowly I seemed to be taking off the layers.

The changes were quite subtle. I didn't look completely different, simply less loud and gaudy. When I next appeared in public, at a press conference in Birmingham, none of the media seemed to notice. I saw this as a compliment because I obviously looked more natural. What I didn't expect was for them to pick up on my body. I'd worn a very smart and simple Gucci skirt and top.

The papers were delivered to my hotel room the next morning. The first paper I picked up was the *Daily Mirror*. The headline read, SAGGY SPICE! And it claimed that first I was Ginger Spice, then I was dubbed Boss Spice, but now I looked like I was turning into Droopy Spice at the ripe old age of twenty-five. The accompanying photograph seemed to suggest that I didn't have a good bra on.

For ten minutes I felt gutted. I stared at myself in the mirror and wondered how I would get through the day. Then I had to say, 'Snap out of it, Geri. It doesn't matter.'

A few days later I chatted quietly with Kenny Ho in the corner of the dressing room. I wanted to change my bustier costume, which I wore for 'Wannabe'. Maybe I could be more versatile and not simply wear dresses that showed off my breasts all the time.

'I suppose I could wear my "Girl Power" dress,' I said to Kenny. 'But I don't know if I really want to.' At the same time, I held up a long black Versace dress, with a red layer and a high neck.

I glanced up and realized that Mel B was watching me. At that moment I think she finally realized that I'd grown up and was ready to move on.

Before then I think she believed I would change my mind and stay. Perhaps she thought it was a stunt to get attention, or that I was being highly strung and melodramatic. Now she realized that I was serious about leaving in September.

I wore the black Versace dress that night.

For almost a month the *Sun* had been chasing a story about the operation I had as a teenager to remove a lump from my breast. Alan Edwards had convinced them to delay the story by suggesting that I might co-operate and give them an interview.

My first reaction was to say no, I didn't want to talk about it.

'They're going to run it regardless of what you do,' said Alan.

Then I thought more about it. 'It could actually be a very positive story.'

'Absolutely,' said Alan.

'We could turn it into an awareness campaign for breast cancer. A lot of teenage girls think it's a disease that only affects older women.'

'Exactly.'

'OK, let's see what they say.'

Initially the *Sun* suggested I do something with Cherie Blair, the prime minister's wife, appearing on the same platform to warn of the dangers of breast cancer. This couldn't be organized in the time, so I agreed to do a straight interview with the paper on Thursday, 21 May, backstage at *Top of the Pops*.

A day earlier, as we flew back to England from Stockholm, I picked up the book *Before I Say Goodbye* by Ruth Picardie. It is one of the saddest, most moving stories I have ever read. Picardie was only thirty-two when she was diagnosed as having breast cancer. Through a series of articles in the *Observer* she went on to describe the progress of her illness right up to her death in September 1997.

These articles, along with letters that she wrote, were compiled by her sister and husband and turned into a memoir of unbearable sadness. I began reading the final chapters as we came in after midnight on the plane. Tears were streaming down my face.

I was still in tears the next morning as I finished the book. When I walked into the studios of *Top of the Pops*, people began asking me, 'What's the matter?' My make-up artist had to keep retouching my face.

I finally realized how lucky I had been. The lump I'd had removed had been harmless, but girls of eighteen can get breast cancer. They can die. From being rather worried about the *Sun* interview, I suddenly became very passionate about getting the right message across.

I did that interview in a side room at the studio. Afterwards, the Spice Girls performed 'Viva Forever', our up-coming single, while all wearing T-shirts promoting breast-cancer awareness.

The impact of Ruth Picardie's story seemed to compound my own fragile emotions. I felt isolated and alone. There was nobody close to me who I could reach out to.

Instead, I found myself in the bathroom, where I sat and had a good cry. 'Hang on, Geri,' I told myself. 'You can last another ten weeks.'

As we left the studio, Mel C asked if I was OK.

'Yeah, I'll be fine.'

She gave me a hug.

That night I lay in bed at the farm cottage, unable to sleep. Picking up my diary, I began writing:

> *Today I feel such pain inside I can't express it. I can't explain. I keep thinking about Dad's death and Ruth Picardie's story. It feels as though I'm mourning a loss. I am shaking with grief . . .*
>
> *I wonder if anyone cares.*

Chris Evans had been one of those very peripheral figures who kept cropping up in my life. It went all the way back to when he hosted *The Big Breakfast* and I sent in my audition tape for a new show *Trash Talk*.

When the Spice Girls first began having hits, Chris made a point of not playing our songs on his Radio 1 breakfast show. But after seeing one of our London concerts he changed his mind. The next morning he apologized on air.

'Spice Girls, I take my hat off to you. I am very, very sorry. I sat there at Wembley and I felt small. Ridiculously, stupidly wrong. I deserve to be wrong. I am as wrong as I have ever been.'

Chris invited us to appear on his TV show, *TFI Friday*. Ironically, it was filmed in the same studio where, five years earlier, David Cadogan had auditioned me for the naughty nurse role in his new play. I walked down the corridor and peeked inside the room. Fancy being back here, I thought. And this time I'm Geri Halliwell, the pop star.

## Friday, 22 May 1998 – London—Copenhagen

Did TFI. *What great fun. I'm flying back to London on Sunday to see Chris Evans to chat about future TV ideas. The girls have been asking what I'm going to do come September. Maybe I should have a plan.*

## Monday, 25 May 1998 – London

*There's a picture of me in the* Daily Mirror *today. I look like a stunned rabbit. They snapped me as I was knocking on the door of Chris's house. I panicked. How on earth did the paparazzi find out?*

*I had to sneak down a back lane. Max lifted me over the fence and Chris caught me on the other side. Thank God, nobody got a picture of that!!!*

*Chris said Gazza [Paul Gascoigne] had been axed from the England soccer squad. Apparently, they expected him to show up. Just my luck!*

*Had a good chat with Chris. Told him I might be interested in doing some TV around Christmas. Didn't dare tell him about September. He said I should choose things carefully.*

*We went to a great old pub in the same street where Mandy Rice-Davies used to live in the Sixties. Met a nice guy called Matthew Freud – the nephew of Sigmund Freud. He's a publicist. We talked about spiritual books like* The Road Less Travelled.

   *The headline in the* Mirror *says,* SO HOW DOES EVANS DO IT?

   *It says that Chris has come up with a new way to snare women – spend months publicly attacking them with insults and then suddenly transform yourself into their best mate and protector.*

I flew to Helsinki that day and rejoined the group. I didn't worry about the reaction of the other girls. I had told them beforehand that I was seeing Chris.

The following morning, 26 May, the *Sun* ran the front-page headline, GINGER SPICE SECRET BREAST CANCER OP.

It described my emergency surgery at the age of seventeen, when a small lump had been cut out of my breast. I had then had to wait three days to find out if the growth was malignant. If it had been, my breast might have had to be removed.

That afternoon our PA, Tor Williamson, announced that *News at Ten* wanted to interview me about breast cancer.

'They're flying a film crew to Helsinki. It isn't a Spice Girl promotion, it's a really heavyweight piece.'

I felt especially enthusiastic. The ITN late evening news reached a large audience and only did serious pieces. I could make an important point about breast cancer and warn young women of the need to be vigilant.

ITN was so keen that they told Tor it would only take ten minutes. Surely I could squeeze them in after the concert. However, we hadn't all agreed that I could do it. As it turned out, we ran out of time to record the interview that night.

'Geri, they've asked if you can do it tomorrow back in the UK,' said Tor.

Hesitantly, I agreed. I desperately wanted to do it, particularly having read Ruth Picardie's book. Here was a chance to send out a very positive message.

After the concert, we were ferried to the airport and boarded a private jet for the flight back to Britain. There was a strange vibe on the plane. No-one spoke. I didn't want to mention the ITN interview. Far better to let everybody sleep on it. I was sure they'd feel better about it in the morning. They were just tired.

## Wednesday, 27 May (1 a.m.)

*I am totally deflated. I don't believe it. I've just heard the news that the ITN interview has been cancelled. The girls want me to wait until September!*

*It can't wait. The story is out now. Forget the band, this is about saving lives. This is about alerting young women to the dangers of breast cancer.*

*I feel as though someone has flicked a switch and the train that I boarded has suddenly been sent onto a different track in a different direction, totally out of control.*

*I can't understand why the girls won't let me do the interview. What has happened to us? We are in such a different place to where we started . . .*

*Is it me or them who is different? All I know is that I have loved and lost. I give up. It's not the same. My heart is breaking. I can't do this any more. Whatever the motivation for their decision, it isn't the right one for me.*

*Something inside me has died. I feel sick. The girls have always said that they're professional entertainers who have trained all their lives for this. I know they can do it without me.*

*Forget the rest of the European tour! Forget America! Forget Wembley Stadium! Ginger Spice is no more. She has left the band.*

I sat on the floor of the cottage with my head on the sofa. My hands were shaking. I felt as though the last drops of self-belief had been wrung out of me.

Climbing into my car, I drove straight to Max's house. I could barely see the road through my tears. When he opened the door he looked horrified. I was verging on hysterical. There was no way he could console me.

'I can't go back. It doesn't feel right any more.'

'You're mad. Stick it out till September,' he said, as he tried to hold me still.

'I'm leaving. My spirit is dying,' I sobbed.

### Wednesday, 27 May, 10 a.m.

*Dear Diary,*

*I haven't been to sleep. I spent most of the night writing a letter to the girls that I'll never send. I lay on the floor in Max's lounge, scrawling page after page, pouring out my heart.*

*By now the girls know that I'm not coming back. It's such a sad way for things to end. I hope that eventually they'll understand why I've done this. I think it's best for everyone if I leave now. I just wish it was like it used to be. Five little girls chasing a dream together.*

The early morning dew covered the fields outside. I could see where the tractors had been driving that morning, leaving tracks through the wet grass. The milking had finished hours ago and a lovely old cow leaned over my front hedge to graze on the grass. She looked up at me with her big hazel eyes and they seemed incredibly sad. We held each other's gaze for several seconds and then she turned and walked away.

## ON THE RUN

That Wednesday afternoon the girls performed on the *National Lottery* show without me. They explained that I had a tummy bug and sent a very convincing get-well message on air.

Victoria had tried to ring me during the day, but I felt too distressed to talk. There was nothing left to say. I seemed to be riding waves of emotion that drowned any rational thought. Anger gave way to sadness and then fear. What was I going to do? Where could I go?

My life with the Spice Girls had been planned almost down to the minute. I was part of a team. A whole support network backed us up. Now I had to start thinking for myself again.

Max was so worried about me that he took me to see Dr King. He hoped the doctor might at least be able to give me something to help me sleep.

Late that night I threw a few things into a bag and got ready to leave the cottage. I couldn't stay in the UK. I had to find somewhere quiet and remote where I could sit and think. Max didn't hesitate to come with me.

He is such a big softie. I've always been so proud of him. He went to a rough school but was smart enough to get into university and become a government scientist. At the same time, he's a worrier like me. From the age of fourteen, when Dad left, Max had taken on the role of man of the house. He's always been the most sensible one in the family. I'm the dreamer, like Dad, but Max kept his head down, worked hard and achieved things quietly without a fuss. He became the perfect big brother, who never got carried away by the idea of his little sister being famous. He didn't ask questions about pop music, or want to know about the celebrities I met. Instead, he got on with his own life, raising a family and searching for happiness. And when I needed him he was always there.

We took a normal commuter flight to Paris. People recognized me at the airport, but nobody realized that I was making my escape. I wanted to be far, far away before the news broke. Using pseudonyms, we booked into Hotel Le Meurrice in the centre of Paris, where I finally managed to get a few hours' rest.

The next morning, I went across the road to the Ritz to use the gym. Max gave me an impromptu squash lesson on one of the glass-backed courts. At one point I leant down to pick up the ball and noticed Richard Gere on a running machine, watching us. My squash game went totally to pieces.

Back in my hotel room, I sat on the bed and flicked on the television. A photograph of me filled the screen.

'Speculation is rife of a split within the Spice Girls. This follows last night's *National Lottery* show when Geri Halliwell, better known as Ginger Spice, failed to appear. A spokesperson for the all-girl band explained that Geri was unwell, but the press are speculating on a rift in the group. Geri has not been seen publicly since the girls performed at a concert in Helsinki on Tuesday night . . .'

The Sky News presenter ended the segment by saying, 'Geri, if you're watching, give us a ring. Let us know you're all right.'

'I'm here,' I said, giving a little wave to the screen.

Max took me to a seafood restaurant that night in a quiet backstreet along the Seine. Fishing nets were strung from the ceiling and lobster pots had been turned into hanging baskets.

'Come on, let's get drunk,' he said, trying to take my mind off things. My mobile phone rang.

'First, I want you to turn off the damn phone,' Max muttered.

'Sorry,' I mouthed.

Throughout the meal we were interrupted by calls, most of them from my new lawyer, Julian Turton. Andrew Thompson had told me straight away that he couldn't represent me any more because he looked after the Spice Girls. I hired Julian, a very pukka solicitor with a jolly personality. I could imagine him striding through the English countryside in a Barbour and Wellingtons.

Other diners glanced up as I whispered in the corner of the restaurant. I worried that I might be recognized. After two glasses of wine I was tipsy. 'I'm a very cheap date, Max.'

'That's all right. It leaves more for me.'

As we left the restaurant it started to rain. The cobblestones were shining as if someone had polished them and water trickled down the lead drainpipes.

'Do you want to get a taxi?' Max asked.

'No, let's walk.'

Both of us were drunk and we skipped through the streets of Paris, splashing in puddles. I did my Charlie Chaplin jumps, clicking my heels together in the air, and we giggled into each other's shoulders.

My life had become so bizarre that I wanted to keep a record of what happened. My diaries weren't enough because I tended to do most of my writing when I felt depressed, so they gave a rather one-sided view.

Back in the hotel room, I propped my camcorder on the coffee table and began filming a video diary.

'It's Thursday the twenty-eighth of May and I am in Paris,' I told the camera, feeling a little self-conscious. 'Yesterday I left the Spice Girls. I thought it would be a really good idea to record my life afterwards. So much has happened and it's going to get even busier.

'At the moment I'm trying to hide from the media. I feel really anxious, with lots of mixed emotions . . . Please, please, I hope something good comes out of this.'

At that moment I knew the rest of the girls were in Oslo. They had two more concerts to go before they finished the European leg of the world tour. Then, after a ten-day break, the American tour would start. I drew comfort from the fact that the band was so close to a holiday. I also knew how good the girls were under pressure. My sudden departure would draw them together and they would go on stage determined to put on a good show.

Equally, once my departure became public knowledge, they would want to show the world that they could survive without me. It would be the ultimate test of their talent and professionalism. I knew they could pull it off.

The concert went ahead and they reworked the routines and shared out my singing parts between them. My absence, however, was never going to pass unnoticed. The next morning's papers were dominated by the story.

The *Daily Express* said, SPICE GIRLS FACE SPLIT AS GERI STAYS AWAY.

The *Sun* went further and claimed I had walked out on the Spice Girls, throwing the band into crisis. With remarkable accuracy, it reported that I had fled into hiding after refusing to join the girls on TV's *National Lottery Show* on Wednesday night.

The *Sun* also had a 'missing' poster, offering a reward to anybody who knew my whereabouts.

Meanwhile, the legal discussions were already under way. Julian Turton came to see me in Paris and explained the legal situation. Newspapers were speculating that if the American tour collapsed I might be sued for millions of pounds.

'I don't care if I lose every penny,' I told him. 'The money doesn't matter.'

Julian raised an eyebrow.

'I mean it, Julian. I've learnt a far more valuable lesson.'

I passionately believed this. Of course, I was afraid for my future. It now seemed so uncertain. But I also felt enlightened by what had happened. All my life I had been driven by a dream. I was the 'If Only' girl, who desperately wanted to be rich and famous because I thought it was going to fill a void inside me. I was wrong. I had just as many faults, fears and insecurities as before. Material possessions don't change this. And it isn't enough simply to enjoy the lifestyle and public adulation. There has to be another reason for continuing.

I had always talked about wanting to do something good with my public standing; finding a cause and a positive message to promote. The breast-cancer campaign had given me that opportunity.

Suddenly I understood how to fill the void. I had to stand up for what I believed in. Life is about compassion and goodness and having a clear conscience. Without those things, it doesn't matter whether you're a household name or a housewife, because your life will leave a bad taste in your mouth.

Sure, fame is fickle and it doesn't last. But if there is integrity and goodness behind what you do, then the experience will endure for longer, and ultimately leave you feeling happy about what you've done.

I didn't try to explain this to Julian. I was still working it out for myself. But when he told me that I could lose everything I didn't care. Whether you have a pound or a million pounds in your pocket you are still exactly the same person. You take the same weather with you. And you build the same walls around you whether they are based on fear, insecurity or ego.

As long as I walked away with my self-esteem, I was no worse off than when I started. I was scared, but I kept telling myself, trying to sound convincing, Geri, if you want it badly enough you'll bounce back. Or if you want to go and do something else, that's OK, too.

It was Friday, 29 May – Mel B's birthday. I wondered what the girls were saying and doing. Overnight, I had thought a lot about the Spice Girls, and in particular our fans. I didn't want them to feel as though I'd let them down. That was my biggest regret. I would never be able to say a proper goodbye to them. That's what I'd hoped to do at Wembley Stadium in September.

I had planned to take a holiday in Mauritius during our tour break, but it wasn't due to start until 30 May. I had another day to kill in Paris, lying low as the storm broke. Max had gone back to England and Natalie and Alastair had come to join me.

Sky News was now running bulletins every fifteen minutes on 'Missing Ginger Spice'. The worldwide search had begun.

'I can't stay cooped up in here,' I told Natalie. 'I need to clear my head.'

'But what if you're recognized?'

'I'll take the chance.'

My hair had already been dyed a less striking colour and closer to its natural shade. I had no make-up on and wore a pair of jeans, a T-shirt and a flat pair of shoes. I tied back my hair and put it under a baseball cap.

Taking Alastair's hand, we walked to a nearby playground with a climbing frame and swings. It had an old-fashioned steam-driven merry-go-round, with brightly painted horses and piped music. I joined the queue to buy a ticket from the booth. As I held a twenty-franc note in my hand, I tried to think when I'd last had money in my pocket. I couldn't remember.

Alastair tugged at my hand excitedly.

An old man tapped me on the shoulder. He was with his grandchild, who was staring at Alastair shyly.

'I have a spare pair of tickets,' he said, offering them to me. 'I thought you and your little boy might like them.'

'Well, thank you. Let me pay you.'

'*Non, non.*'

I was so touched. He was a complete stranger who had no idea who I was. He asked for nothing in return. He was simply a grandfather out playing with his grandchild who did a very nice thing for a young woman and her nephew.

Both sides agreed to release formal press statements on Sunday afternoon. That morning I wrote my statement in long hand as I waited to catch the flight to Mauritius. I suddenly realized that I should show it to somebody first. The girls had a whole team of PR advisers, but I had no-one.

Then I remembered Matthew Freud, the publicist I'd met at Chris Evans' house. I phoned Chris and got Matthew's number. He called five minutes before I boarded the plane and I read the statement to him.

'That sounds fine,' he said.

Both sides were to swap statements to make sure that each agreed to the wording. Throughout these negotiations I sat in the First Class cabin of the flight to Mauritius, wearing dark glasses and avoiding eye contact with other passengers. It felt like the final scene of a movie – I was flying off into the sunset, making my escape to a place where nobody knew a thing. I could relax and switch off.

From the airport, I took a helicopter to Le Saint Géran, a lovely resort on the beach, overlooking the bay. The manager welcomed me with a huge cocktail, complete with umbrella. 'I've heard about your departure,' he said, smiling broadly. His teeth were as white as his shirt.

'Oh . . .' So much for being anonymous.

The sun had been shining when I arrived, but the clouds now moved in and it started to rain. I hadn't realized it was the rainy season in Mauritius.

I turned on the TV, hoping to find an old movie. Instead I discovered that Sky News and CNN were both running the story. Every few minutes the Sky announcer declared, 'Any moment now we'll be crossing live to hear an announcement on whether Geri Halliwell has left the Spice Girls . . .'

I felt nervous.

Julian Turton stood on the steps of Andrew Thompson's office. He was besieged by dozens of TV cameras and more than a hundred photographers. 'Surely there must be more important things happening in the world,' I muttered. 'I'm only leaving a pop group, for Christ's sake.'

Julian read my statement:

> This is a message to the fans. Sadly, I would like to confirm that I have left the Spice Girls. This is because of differences between us. I am sure the group will continue to be successful and I wish them all the best. I have no immediate plans. I wish to apologize to all the fans and to thank them and everyone who has been there.
>
> Lots of love, Geri.
> PS. I'll be back.

I had mixed emotions as I watched. I tried to remove myself from it all, as if it no longer concerned me. Perhaps

I was trying to convince myself that I'd already moved on. I told myself that was a good sign.

Le Saint Géran had various lodges that were inter-connected. Mine was at the very end to safeguard my privacy, but instead I felt even more exposed and vulnerable. The worldwide search for Ginger Spice had stepped up a gear. Matthew contacted me every few hours with updates.

Apparently, certain newspapers had put a price on my head with speculative offers of £500,000 for the first photographs. The *Sun* had sent a team to the Maldives, believing me to be hiding there. I was always worried that my holiday plans would leak, so I'd told everyone I was holidaying in the Maldives instead of Mauritius. The *Sun* had been tipped off and some lucky photographer and reporter were getting a free holiday. I had to laugh.

### *Monday, 1 June 1998 – Mauritius*

*Things are going crazy back in England. Everybody is looking for me. A half a million pounds for a photo-graph is an obscene amount. It means I can't possibly hide for ever. But where can I go? I'm too scared even to leave my room in case I'm recognized.*

*I don't feel safe here any more. They're going to find me.*

*How do I get out? I can't use a normal commuter flight.*

From my window, when I peeked through the

curtains, I could see deckchairs on the beach and palm trees dotting the shoreline. Because of the strong winds there were few people on the sand. A boy was sweeping leaves on my verandah. He seemed to be hovering there, not really working. Although he wore a hotel uniform, I grew suspicious and spent the whole day putting on a Russian accent, trying to fool him. Later the manager explained that each of the lodges had a room boy and this young lad had been assigned to me.

The next day, I had a message to call Luciano Pavarotti in Italy. The Spice Girls were due to appear at a concert hosted by Pavarotti in aid of War Child, the tenor's favourite charity. It had been arranged for the following week.

'Please, Geri, come back, we can work this out,' he said, understandably upset. 'We can do a reunion.'

'I'm sorry, Maestro, I think it's a bit early for a reunion.'

'Are you sure?'

'Yes. I really can't do this. I'm sorry.'

For three days I hadn't been outside my room. What a waste of a beautiful hotel. I had visions of the press slowly closing in. Somehow, I had to keep moving. But where?

I thought about chartering a jet back to Britain. How much would it cost? Eighty thousand pounds! Woah! Where would I go then? I had nowhere of my own. Dozens of journalists were camped outside Mum's house in Jubilee Road. Anybody leaving the house was followed in case they might lead them to me. Mum couldn't even go shopping without being trailed through the aisles of the supermarket. It was the same for Natalie, Max and Karen. No matter where I went, the press would find me.

I lay on my bed, feeling vulnerable and frightened. I

could understand the media had a job to do, but surely there were more important stories in the world. I was still so fragile and off-balance emotionally that I didn't want to be photographed or have to answer questions. For three years I'd enjoyed their attention, but now I realized that you couldn't turn it off.

The phone rang. It was Ken Berry, the boss of Virgin Records, calling to see if I needed any help. He had a house in Tuscany and offered it to me as a sanctuary.

'I've also just heard from George [Michael]. He told me to tell you that, if you need somewhere to stay, he has places in St Tropez and Los Angeles. You're welcome there.'

I hadn't spoken to George for a while. Now, in my hour of need, he came to my rescue. I felt as though an angel had been sent down to me.

Somehow I had to slip back into the UK unnoticed and then I could get a private jet to the south of France. Normal commuter flights were out of the question because I knew that somebody would tip off the media.

As I apologized to the hotel manager and thanked him for his help, he told me that the owner of the hotel, Sol Kerzner, was arriving on Wednesday morning from South Africa on his own private jet. I wondered if he might lease it to me.

Later that day the manager came to my lodge. 'Mr Kerzner is flying to London tonight. He will happily give you a lift.'

'That's very kind of him.'

'His daughter, Chantel, is in an all-girl pop group called N-Tyce. You once said very nice things about them on TV.'

I remembered the interview. I said how pleasing it was to see more all-girl bands breaking into the charts. That's what Girl Power was all about.

That evening, I left the hotel in much the same way as I'd arrived – being rushed through the foyer and into a waiting car. I hadn't seen the bars, or restaurants, or swimming pools. I just assumed they existed.

My houseboy came to say goodbye. 'I know who you are. Cross my heart, I won't tell anyone.' He had known all along. God knows what he made of my Russian accent.

The executive jet touched down at Farnham airport early on Thursday morning. I had no idea who was coming to meet me. What if nobody turned up? What if the press were waiting? Suddenly I felt like a little girl lost again. 'Please, please, someone be there,' I whispered.

The jet taxied to a stop and a car drove across the tarmac. It parked beside the steps and Tor Williamson, my former PA, stepped out. She had left the Spice Girls only days after I did. We gave each other a hug.

'I'm here as a friend,' said Tor. 'If you need any help, just ask.'

I had never doubted Tor. She'd always been there for me.

'How are you feeling?' she asked.

'Like an outlaw on the run.'

'You're going to have to come out of hiding some time.'

'I know. But I'm not ready yet. I just want to be some-where I can feel safe and get my head together.'

'George is in St Tropez. He'll see you there. We'll have to smuggle you through Cannes airport.'

Tor and a security guard carried big golfing umbrellas,

and as I came down the aircraft steps they were opened to shield me from view.

'Isn't this a bit over the top?' I said, feeling ridiculous.

'Just in case.'

A room had been booked in a private hotel just up the road. I had to wait there until 3 p.m. before catching another private jet to Cannes. In the meantime I tried to get some sleep, but my body seemed to be floating about the room. I turned on the TV. Richard and Judy were doing the morning show. They introduced a new all-girl group from Ireland called B*Witched, who sang their début single 'C'est la Vie'. It had just gone to number one in the UK. The group had a blonde, a redhead and two brunettes. They all sparkled with enthusiasm and were obviously thrilled to be there. It made me smile. Hopefully they'd still be bouncing in six months' time.

I called Max and told him I was OK.

'It's like a zoo outside,' he said. 'The cars have been there for days. Some of these guys must never sleep.'

'How's Mum?'

'She's had to move out of home. She and Steve have gone to stay with his sister in Portsmouth. Steve got into a fight with a photographer who jumped on their car and wouldn't get out of the way.'

I couldn't imagine Steve getting into a scuffle; he's such a lovely, placid bloke.

'I went to the farm cottage today,' said Max. 'There were a dozen cars parked in the lane. Jimmy [the farmer] told me they tried to move closer but he got his shotgun out and told them to get off his land.'

'Bless him.'

'When is this going to end, Geri?' said Max, sounding strained.

'I don't know. I'm so sorry to put you all through this.'

That afternoon I flew to St Tropez. I had to sneak through Cannes airport and use a decoy car to get me away from the terminal. When I finally arrived at George's villa it felt like a sanctuary.

George came down the stairs in a baggy T-shirt, with his hair tousled. He made me feel so welcome and we sat on the terrace overlooking the Mediterranean. I tried to tell him everything that had happened and it came out in such a rush.

As I went to sleep that night, I finally felt safe. No more running, Geri. I didn't wake for ten hours.

Over the next few days, George and his partner, Kenny Goss, were like big brothers to me, making sure I had plenty of rest and ate well, and giving me the support that I needed as my head swam with questions that had no immediate answers.

'What am I going to do?' Most people are just starting their careers at twenty-five. Mine seemed to be over. What future is there for a former Spice Girl?

I desperately wanted to find answers straight away. Otherwise the world would move on. Nobody would wait for me.

'Don't rush, Geri. Take your time,' said George. 'You have longer than you think before the attention goes away.'

'Fancy going for a run?' said Kenny.

I thought for a moment. He and George had spent all

evening telling me that I couldn't let the press dictate my life.

Right. Starting today, no more running. I take control of things.

'Just give me a few minutes, Kenny. I'll be right with you,' I said, pulling on tracksuit pants, a T-shirt and a baseball cap.

We jogged along the drive and the big electronic gates swung open. Suddenly a dozen photographers appeared from nowhere, with cameras flashing. Game over! I'd been found.

A part of me wanted to turn and run back to the house. Then I told myself, No, if I'm going for a jog, then I'm *going* for a jog.

'Come on, Kenny.'

We legged it, racing past them. As they gave chase, Kenny turned off onto a bush track. We half slid, half rolled down a steep hill and then weaved through bushes. It was like an army obstacle course.

For twenty minutes we ran along mountain tracks and fire trails, finally stopping to rest when we emerged onto a six-lane motorway.

'Do you know where we are?' I asked.

'Not a clue.'

'Do you know the way back?'

'Nope.'

We began laughing. I had half the world looking for me and I'd managed to get lost. We stood on the hard shoulder, with the traffic whizzing by.

'Which way?'

'Your choice.'

We turned left and walked until we found a little

restaurant. Kenny called a taxi which took us back to George's place. The photographers were still waiting outside as we swept through the gates.

George had business in London and Kenny was going back to California. 'Why don't you come to LA, Geri?' asked Kenny. 'You'll be on your own if you stay here.'

I took his advice and flew via England for a meeting with Matthew Freud, Julian Turton and Charles Bradbrook. It seemed unlikely that I'd be sued. If anything, the massive publicity surrounding my departure had boosted sales for the Spice Girls' American tour. In New York, 13,000 tickets for Madison Square Garden sold out in twelve minutes, prompting a police investigation. Tickets were later being offered on the street for US$600 each.

That night I flew to Los Angeles. For the previous ten days I'd been a pinball bouncing around the world. I hadn't stayed anywhere long enough to get used to the time zone.

Paparazzi were waiting at the airport and scuffles broke out when photographers tried to reach me. This ended with a two-hour cat-and-mouse game as we tried to lose them before I reached George's house. It didn't take them long to find me, of course, but I was past caring.

I just wanted to stop and lose myself for a while. What better place than Los Angeles? It still reminded me of a massive bus terminal, with people coming and going but rarely staying. Perhaps here I could be almost anonymous.

## Monday, 15 June 1998 – Los Angeles

*I know I've made the right decision in leaving, but what will be the outcome? What will happen to me? I want this break to be clean. I want us to be friends.*

*There are so many different stages of this divorce. At first I was really angry. Now I'm going through a sad period. I wonder if it's the same for the others . . .*

*Good night.*

# WALK AWAY?

I didn't leave George's house for the first week. Kenny would keep me company, and we'd sit by the pool and read, eating cream-cheese bagels and drinking diet cola.

'You should borrow the car and go for a drive,' he told me.

'I'd probably get lost,' I said, making excuses. 'Maybe tomorrow.'

Photographers were still camped outside the house. One of the British tabloids had claimed I was in LA auditioning for the remake of *Charlie's Angels*. It was news to me.

Although I stayed in the house, I didn't feel depressed or under siege. Instead, I was fuelled by an amazing energy. The future seemed to hold countless possibilities and I wanted to seize the day and do something positive with my fame. It was as though I'd said to the world, 'Hey, stop! I want to get off,' and now I could take a new direction.

First, I had to learn to look after myself all over again. After so long in the bubble I had forgotten how to do ordinary things, like balancing a cheque book and reading a street directory.

One morning I heard the Spice Girls' new single 'Viva Forever' playing on the radio. The release had been delayed because of my leaving. The DJ announced, 'Coming up, we're gonna give away some tickets to the Spice Girls' big concert tour. The girls are in LA next month and it's gonna be a sell-out . . .'

Rather than feeling any pangs of regret, it all felt like a distant memory. I had been through such an emotional journey in such a short space of time that the Spice Girls felt like something that had happened in a previous lifetime.

That afternoon I began surfing the Internet on George's computer. In particular I looked for information about breast cancer. The cancelled interview with *News at Ten* had been the catalyst for my leaving the Spice Girls. If I really felt so strongly about the issue, I couldn't just forget about it. If anything, it made me more determined.

In the mean time, I'd developed a nervous sort of cough. It happened hundreds of times a day – a dry tickle at the back of my throat – which seemed to be getting worse. Kenny took me to a doctor on Rodeo Drive who had signed photographs of all the celebrities he'd treated on his wall.

I just wanted some cough mixture, but he treated me as though I had my vocal chords insured and my entire career could be threatened. I didn't care. I didn't imagine ever singing again.

'Have you been under any stress?' he asked.

'A little,' I said, trying hard not to laugh.

'You have a nodule on your throat. That's why your voice sounds a little husky.'

'It's been like this since I was a little girl,' I explained.

The doctor diagnosed hay fever and gave me an injection that he said would clear up the problem immediately.

Three days later the cough had worsened and my eyes had puffed up due to an allergy. I went back to see the doctor again. Sitting in the waiting room, I kept thinking back to all the research I'd been doing on breast-cancer research and awareness. What could I do to help?

Two years earlier, as we lay in the desert looking at the stars, Mel B and I had talked about how we'd use our fame. We both wanted to promote a worthwhile message or find a cause to champion. Having been so lucky – thanks to millions of people – we wanted to repay that gratitude by giving something back and using our fame positively.

I didn't want to put my face and name to the first cause that came along. Instead, I wanted to understand the issue and believe in it.

I'm in America. Why not find the biggest breast-cancer charity and ask for information? I told myself. The doctor examined my throat again and gave me another injection. The bill came to US$600 – which had me coughing all over again.

It took an age for my credit card to be accepted, and every delay seemed to irritate me. I couldn't wait to get back to George's house and begin my research again.

As the receptionist handed me my receipt, I asked, 'Do you know the name of the head of a breast-cancer charity?'

'Yes. There's a lady called Lilly Tartikoff. She's one of the doctor's patients.'

'Now I'm going to get my money's worth,' I told myself, as I marched back into the doctor's office and asked for the woman's phone number.

The following day I met Lilly Tartikoff at her house in Beverly Hills. A striking woman in her mid-forties, she had a fine-boned face and the grace of a former ballet dancer, yet what impressed me most was her sense of purpose.

Lilly's husband, Brandon, a one-time president of NBC Entertainment, had died of cancer in the late 1980s. Since then, Lilly had devoted herself to fund-raising for cancer research. She was a driving force behind events such as the Fire and Ice Ball in Los Angeles and the annual Revlon Run/Walks for Women in major American cities, which had raised more than US$6 million in eight years.

I knew that the British weren't likely to respond to the same style of events — I couldn't see people jogging through the streets wearing T-shirts and hats saying, 'I've been touched by cancer' — but maybe I could organize a concert instead.

That same week I met an equally inspirational woman, Nancy Brinker. Her sister Susan had died of breast cancer in 1980 at the age of thirty-six. Nancy made a promise to her dying sister that she would dedicate the rest of her life to eradicating breast cancer as a life-threatening disease. She founded the Susan G. Komen Breast Cancer Foundation, which has raised over US$90 million.

As I learned about Nancy's story, I couldn't help being reminded of another pair of sisters, Justine and Ruth Picardie. All of these women had been spurred on by tragedy to do something really positive.

The next morning I started writing letters. If I was

serious about helping, I knew that I needed advice from enterprising people who had been there and done it before. I contacted people like Bob Geldof and Richard Branson for advice.

Kenny handed me a cup of tea and sat on a sun lounger beside the pool. 'So what are you going to do?' he asked.

'You ask me that every day.'

'I know.'

'Why?'

'Because I know that's what you're thinking.'

I laughed. 'I'm going to spend a year giving something back,' I said. 'I've been so lucky and I want to repay some of that support. I don't know exactly what I'm going to do yet, but I want to do it properly.'

Back in the UK, my publicity agent had been deluged with requests for me to give interviews, or make appearances. The offers ranged from the sublime to the ridiculous, and included everything from film roles to invitations to launch fishing boats. The media seemed to be obsessed with what I was going to do next. Clearly, I hadn't stopped being famous when I left the Spice Girls. But how long would that last? Six months? A year? Three years?

Being part of a group had been great, because I could share the triumphs, but it also let me hide from some of the responsibility. I could be more outspoken and outrageous because I was part of something bigger than myself. One of five. There is safety in numbers.

But I couldn't help secretly wondering whether I could make it on my own, especially when I heard the whispers

– she can't sing, she can't dance, she can act a little (as they said of Fred Astaire).

I had seen the down side of fame. I'd been there – homesick and lonely in distant hotel rooms, eating my way through minibars, tearful at the horrible stories. There were nights when I used to sneak a look at the crowd from backstage, hoping to see a banner that read WE LOVE YOU, GERI because I knew it would cheer me up. Surely I'd be happier if I settled down in my nice house, got married and had a family. Why seek recognition any more? It's impossible to please everybody.

Yet for all of the negatives, I didn't want to walk away.

I'd grown up as the ultimate wannabe, but it wasn't naked ambition that was driving me any more. Instead it was a mixture of feelings. My perception of fame had changed. I knew that it wasn't going to fill the void, but it was still a nice place to be while I kept searching.

Whatever I decided to do, it wouldn't be driven by ego. Of course, I can't deny that I liked the attention, but that was only a small part of wanting to go on. By far the most important reason was the chance to be creative and artistic, to push people's buttons and, of course, entertain. That had always been my greatest strength and what I enjoyed most about the Spice Girls. I loved song-writing, especially pop songs with catchy melodies; music for everyday people that would make them smile. I also liked coming up with the imagery for videos and concepts for marketing and promotion. My mind still buzzed with new ideas.

Now I was about to discover if I could make it on my own. I think everyone needs to know this. It's what takes people up Everest, or sailing around the world. It may be about confronting your worst fears, but it's also about emotional independence. Nobody likes being reliant on others to make them feel wanted or worthwhile. And unless we can go it alone and live with the consequences, then all we bring to any relationship, whether with a lover, a friend or the rest of the world, is an invitation to share our emotional baggage.

Why should others have to prop us up? Surely it's selfish to expect so much.

Although I had avoided publicity and hidden myself away, the newspapers continued to write about me. Unwittingly, I had created a media vacuum that filled with negative stories and wild speculation about what had happened to me.

I thought long and hard about how to stop it. Clearly I needed to let people know that I hadn't fallen apart or suffered a nervous breakdown. Finally I decided to do a one-off interview and photo shoot for *Marie Claire* magazine.

I flew to New York at the end of the month, feeling rather nervous about going back into the spotlight. I didn't want to talk about the Spice Girls, but what *did* I want to say? That I was still alive? I didn't quite know who I was at that moment. Instead, I felt like an egg waiting to hatch.

It was probably one of the most chilled-out, low-key shoots I had ever done. I simply walked in off the street and had the hairdresser pull my hair back and put on a light touch of make-up. The stylist had brought loads of clothes for me to try on, all the latest fashions, but I didn't want to commit to any of them. Instead, I stayed in my black trousers and a black shirt. Patrick Demarchelier took the photographs of me sitting barefoot on the floor. It seemed like the most natural thing in the world to me.

The magazine headline read, GERI – AS YOU'VE NEVER SEEN HER BEFORE.

I talked about issues that were very current in my mind. In particular how we often create an image for ourselves that we display to others. And how sometimes we have to peel away the layers, emotionally and aesthetically, to discover who we really are. We only truly evolve as people when we dare to get to know ourselves and remove the layers we hide behind: the make-up, the hair, the clothes and the image.

We have to uncover our true hearts. And if you can do this, then it won't matter if you're not the best singer in the world, or the most articulate speaker. Instead, it's about attitude and self-belief.

From New York I flew to Paris and booked into the Hôtel de Crillon, a Parisian palace that overlooks the Place de la Concorde. From the balcony, high up among the lead-lined turrets, I felt as though I could see the whole city.

Tor Williamson had been working as my PA and joined me in Paris. We began to arrange meetings with charity officials, promoters and literary agents.

The idea of writing a book had always been in the back of my mind. I had been writing diaries and rough chapter outlines since I was twelve years old. I also had scrap-books, school reports, boxes of old letters, family photo albums, modelling portfolios, ID cards, theatre programmes and souvenirs from my raving days. On top of this, I had all the stories of failed auditions and nearly jobs.

I could write about being the ultimate wannabe; the little girl from Watford who never quite felt good enough but kept trying to prove otherwise.

My video diary was proving to be a difficult task. I was much happier writing. Even so, I still liked the idea of documenting what happened to a girl when she left a big pop band. Consequently, I met with the award-winning documentary-maker Molly Dineen.

I knew Molly from an earlier meeting, when the Spice Girls were considering doing a documentary-style film. Although the two of us had clicked the project didn't happen.

We discussed whether we could do a sort of video diary on the next six months of my life. It would mean Molly following me around, filming private and public moments. I didn't actually fully think through where the piece would end up. But I thought it would be interesting to record it regardless.

This surprised a lot of people. On the one hand I seemed to be fighting media intrusion and on the other I was inviting somebody to film me at close quarters for months on end. Molly could see this contradiction, and I think it was one of the reasons she took on the project. She kept gently probing to discover why. Was I an egomaniac? Couldn't I live without a camera pointed at me?

'Does there have to be a negative motive?' I asked her.

'No. But there does have to be a reason.'

I had to think about this for a moment. 'I'm daring to bare my soul,' I told Molly. 'I'm trying to go there. A part of me says that I'm crazy to make a film that could destroy my public image. But I'm trusting my instincts. I'm saying, "Just be yourself, Geri." If I do that, then hopefully I'll show people that I'm a nice person and they'll like me.'

There was a mixture of reasons. Perhaps, if I'm honest, I was so used to having the cameras pointed at me that there was something reassuring about having one there. But, more importantly, I wanted to destroy some of the myths and smash down the pedestals that are so often linked with fame. We are all human, with the same hopes, fears and dreams.

Much later I realized there was another, very simple, reason for doing the documentary. It had to do with Molly, who is so intelligent and lively that she is great fun to be with. The truth is, I loved her company.

The hotel suite in Paris felt almost like a prison cell at times. Although I flew back and forth to England to see friends and family, it wasn't enough. I desperately wanted to be nearer to them.

The whole situation emphasized how different my life had become from those people who I'd grown up with or befriended along the way. They had careers, mortgages and families to support. They couldn't just drop everything to come and visit me.

Tor was in England and the hotel suite seemed very empty and quiet with just me.

All the energy and drive I'd felt when I left the band was like a double-edged sword. While I was acting positively and coming up with ideas, I felt fine, but as soon as things didn't go well the doubts began to creep in. At the worst moments, it felt as though I'd been cast adrift in a big black emptiness, without work or recognition. So much of my identity had been as part of the band that it was quite scary being alone. It was my whole world, both work and play, socially and professionally.

Despite all the new projects I'd put in place, I still felt restless and purposeless. All of my new plans seemed to involve a future time, and until then my life had been put on hold and I was in limbo.

Having a job builds self-esteem. It gives you a reason to get out of bed each day. Being unemployed does the opposite, and that's how I felt in Paris – unwanted and forgotten.

That's another one of the contradictions about me. Overwork and exhaustion can send me down, but so can inactivity and boredom. I *have* to be busy. That's why I began to dread weekends; they were like vast black holes when I had nothing to do.

'You can't stay here by yourself,' said Kenny, when he came to visit me in Paris. He could see I was lonely. 'Come on, let's go back to St Tropez.'

I'll never forget the kindness he and George showed me. They went out of their way to make me feel special because they knew I was homesick and on my own. I ended up spending most of the summer with them, dividing my time between the South of France and California.

In Los Angeles, I drove George's Range Rover to the gym, went shopping and out to dinner. Being out of the bubble felt liberating. I could dress down, in jeans and a sweatshirt, and often avoid being recognized. I could catch a cab, or go to the movies, or stop for coffee. The bubble had been very reassuring and comfortable, but now I had to look after myself, and I loved being independent.

A sure sign of how good I felt was that I started writing poetry and lyrics again. I didn't have any projects in mind

– it was something I'd been doing since I was five years old. The creative urge didn't suddenly stop when I left the Spice Girls.

All summer I found myself writing, whether lying in bed, or by the pool, or sitting on a long plane flight. At George's house in St Tropez I wrote the lines:

> There is a river of tears that I need to cry
> I've been holding back for years.
> There's a mountain so high I need to climb
> to wipe away my fears.

Later it became the opening verse of a song, 'Walk Away.'

I could hear the murmur of the crowd outside in the Sotheby's auction room. My hands were shaking and I tried to hold them still.

I had barely slept the previous night. The same questions kept tormenting me: 'What if nobody turns up at the auction? What if nobody bids for any of the items?'

I had made the decision to auction my Spice Girls clothes for charity two months before I left the band. It wasn't a case of washing my hands of the past, as some commentators said. I was always going to do it. I had a room full of clothes that I would never wear again. What was the point of keeping them? I couldn't imagine my children or grandchildren being interested. They'd be too busy with their PlayStations.

The other thing I'd learned was to travel through life lightly.

It had seemed such a good idea at the time, but now I

wasn't so sure. I kept telling myself that, even if the dresses and shoes sold for only a pound each, at least the money was for a good cause – a children's cancer charity – yet I also knew that others would be quick to label the event a failure.

All my best-known dresses were up for sale, along with my platform shoes, boots, costumes from *Spiceworld, The Movie* and, perhaps the most sentimental item, my classic red MGB Roadster, which I'd bought with my very first pay cheque from Virgin.

I had written a message for the fans in the sale catalogue:

> *My life as a Spice Girl was about hopes and dreams and, thanks to all those young friendly faces, you let mine come true . . .*
>
> *I really hope these mementoes from my past will help to build something for these special children [cancer sufferers]. They too deserve a place for their own hopes and dreams.*
>
> *Much love,*
> *Geri*

I had slipped through a back door at Sotheby's and sat nervously backstage as the main event took place.

I planned to come on stage when the very last lot was being auctioned – my Union Jack dress – and bring down the gavel on the final sale.

This was my first public appearance at my instigation and it made me feel vulnerable. I wasn't the same person I'd been six months earlier. I didn't have the cockiness and confidence of Ginger Spice – and I didn't have the other girls around me for support and reassurance.

I wore a black tailored suit, with my hair pulled back into a ponytail. Clipped inside my jacket, hidden from view, was a small angel brooch, which I wore for good luck. It had been given to me by a fan.

From a corridor just outside the main auction room, I listened as the sale began. The first item was my trapeze outfit, which I'd worn when meeting Prince Charles. Bidding began at £400 and began climbing in bids of £50. Suddenly, it reached £1,000 and began accelerating by £100 a bid. It sold for nearly £2,000 and I felt elated. People had come to buy, not just to watch.

Slowly my past was sold off – the PVC catsuit I'd worn in *Spiceworld, The Movie*; the Chinese-style dress I had greeted President Nelson Mandela in; my Girl Power outfit – all of them exceeded their estimates.

The lady auctioneer introduced the star item and the Union Jack dress was held aloft on a display stand. 'Ladies and gentlemen, I would now like to invite Geri Halliwell to help sell the final lot for sale.'

I took a deep breath and walked on stage. The crowd applauded and flashguns began firing. I was so nervous that I worried I might forget what I wanted to say. I kept telling myself not to focus on the press, but instead to look directly at the kids in the front row. They had come along to represent the charity that would benefit from the auction: Malcolm Sargent Cancer Care for Children.

'I want to thank you all for coming . . . this auction is very important to me because the money is going to some very special children.'

My Union Jack dress had been valued between £8,000 and £12,000. The bidding started and quickly climbed past £15,000. I had the gavel in my hand and kept trying to pick out who was bidding. '£21,000 ... £22,000 ... £23,000 ...'

'I am delivering it personally,' I said, spurring on the bidding.

I recognized Dominic Mohan from the *Sun*. He raised his hand again, pushing the price up to £30,000. A phone-bidder urged it higher. Dominic looked at me and shrugged with his hands, as if to say, 'Sorry, Geri, we can't go there.'

The hammer came down at £36,000. Unbelievable! A home-made dress that had been cobbled together at Karen's house had fetched a fortune. Off stage, I squealed with delight and did a little victory jig.

The buyer was Peter Morton, the owner of the Hard Rock Hotel and Casino in Las Vegas. Later he admitted that he was prepared to go as high as £100,000 to secure the dress for the casino's museum.

As we left Sotheby's photographers and TV cameras were waiting outside.

'Are you happier now that you've left the Spice Girls?' somebody called out.

That sort of question is a nightmare. If I said, 'Yes', the headlines would read, 'Geri admits to being unhappy in the Spice Girls.' If I said, 'No', they'd write, 'Geri misses being Ginger.'

My car had been moved on by parking police, and I was stranded on the pavement, clutching a bouquet of flowers, surrounded by cameras and reporters. Tor called the driver. He was stuck in traffic as he tried to circle the block.

We dashed inside a stationery store and closed the door.

The bemused staff didn't know what to make of it as the manager kept the reporters outside.

'The car's here,' said Tor, clutching my briefcase. 'Let's go.'

Once past the photographers and safely in the car, I sighed with relief. The auction had raised over £150,000 – beyond my wildest expectations.

'They still like me,' I said to Tor.

She laughed at my surprise. 'Of course they do.'

At the beginning of September I moved back to the UK. Max picked me up from the airport and I felt enormously close to him. From now on I decided I would never live too far away from my family.

I still had the farm cottage near Berkhamsted, but builders and renovators had been working on my new house. While still with the Spice Girls I had bought an old monastery, set in eighteen acres of grounds in Berkshire. It had belonged to an order of Roman Catholic brothers and my next-door neighbours were going to be the nuns of St Paul's.

The monastery was a rabbit warren of small rooms and corridors, and it had to be entirely gutted and the interior rebuilt. The work would take until Christmas at the earliest, and in the mean time I planned to stay at the farm cottage.

Typically, Mum had been cleaning up for me. She lifted me in the air and swung me round, thrilled to have me home again.

Waiting for me on the kitchen table was a letter on St James's Palace notepaper. Prince Charles had written saying how sorry he was to hear that I'd left the Spice Girls and wishing me all the best for the future.

Acts of kindness like this gave me an enormous boost because I was still so unsure of my future.

Most of the publicity I'd received had been quite positive, although some commentators suggested there was something fake or insincere about Geri Halliwell, the ex-Spice Girl. The *Daily Express* wrote that I looked so contrite, apologetic and vulnerable that I appeared to be a woman spurned. This apparently went against everything they loved about the old cheeky Geri.

In the past, when people labelled me old and fat and ugly, I would always come bouncing back with shorter skirts and more lipstick. Now, I'd simply become boring, according to the reporter.

Although stories like this upset me, I tried to remain focused on what the auction had been all about: raising money for kids with cancer.

In late September the Spice Girls performed the final concerts of their world tour at Wembley Stadium. It was hard to avoid hearing about the event. Every radio station and TV bulletin seemed to have something about the girls. There was even a rumour circulating that I was going to make a special guest appearance. This was never a possibility; we had all moved on.

In truth, I'd barely talked to any of the girls since leaving the band. I suppose we all needed a little time and space from each other. Like most people, I followed the stories in the papers about their pregnancies and weddings. I hoped the girls were happy.

On the afternoon of the last concert, I stayed at the farm cottage. With the four walls closing in on me, I went for a walk in the fields at dusk. The twilight had turned the farm dams into pools of orange. I sat on a fence and

tried to picture myself at Wembley Stadium. That's how I
wanted to say goodbye – in front of my home fans.

## Sunday, 20 September 1998

*I keep telling myself that it doesn't matter. Then I
question what I am crying about. Sometimes people
think they're upset about sad events in their life when
they are actually crying about something very different.*

*I know this is about low self-esteem – about not feel-
ing good enough. Ever since I was a little girl people
have been telling me that I'm not good enough. It
happened at grammar school. I guess I'm still trying to
prove them wrong.*

*I look at myself sometimes and think, You spoilt brat.
You don't realize how lucky you are.*

*I'm just trying to be happy. Aren't we all?*

The media had continued to speculate about what I might
do next. Opinions were divided, although a career in television seemed to be the favourite choice.

I couldn't decide. I contemplated writing a mind, body,
spirit book, or continuing my film script. Of course, there
were still the charity commitments, but I seemed to want
to keep a finger in every pie.

Although I was afraid to say it out loud, deep down
there was an idea that refused to be pushed aside or
ignored: I kept thinking about going back into the studio
and singing again.

A combination of things made me realize that was
what I wanted to do. On *GMTV* one morning, my mum

saw Dr Fox from Capital Radio discussing what he thought I should do next.

'I don't think Geri should be a TV presenter,' he said. 'She's a pop star.'

Another of the guests, a former editor of *Smash Hits* magazine, agreed with him. 'Geri shouldn't run away from music. It's how she made her name.'

What if they were right?

All summer I had been writing lyrics and toying with melodies. I loved the creative process of writing songs. On top of this, being a pop star isn't a long-term career. It's something you do when you're young. Perhaps I had a couple more years left when I *could* do it, while I still *wanted* to do it.

A different 'if only' entered my head. I kept asking myself, What if years from now, as a grandmother, I look back and say, 'If only I had made a solo album. If only I had tried.'

I didn't want to die wondering.

Secretly, I had already recorded one song that had been recommended to me by George. I think it was his way of building my confidence.

The song was quite challenging and I lacked self belief. Those first few days in the studio were frustrating and at times I felt like walking away. Slowly things began turning around and I started enjoying myself. I also revelled in the freedom of doing an entire song by myself. I didn't have anyone judging me and I could take my time.

There's a temptation, having recorded a song, to push it out there and see what people think. Then I remembered what George had said to me in St Tropez. 'Take your time, Geri. The world will wait for you. If you do decide to put a record out, make sure it's good.'

I loved being back in the studio. My confidence grew and I continued writing.

Now I had a new mission: to write an album.

When I first read the letter I didn't realize what it actually said. I looked at the United Nations letterhead and then read it again. Still it didn't quite sink in.

I was being offered a role as a United Nations goodwill ambassador.

Wow! I thought, rather uncertainly.

I read the letter again. Is this what I think it is? No, surely not.

It wasn't until a meeting in London a week later that it dawned on me how prestigious the offer was and how serious they were about wanting me. In a throwback to my childhood, I never believe anything until I'm actually doing it.

I was asked to work with the United Nations Population Fund (UNFPA) and its UK partners, Population Concern and Marie Stopes International, to publicize the plight of millions of women in developing countries who are denied reproductive health care and family planning.

There were an estimated 350 million couples around the world who wanted to exercise their right to control their fertility but were unable to. As a result, the world population was due to hit six billion for the first time in history in June 1999.

I can't convey how honoured, excited and flattered I felt. I couldn't believe that something had come to me rather than me having to chase it. Normally I'd always had to ask, or put my hand up the highest, or shout the loudest. Now somebody had come and asked *me* to do something.

At my first meeting in London, I couldn't help asking, 'Why did you choose me?'

'We wanted someone with a high profile and an affinity with the issues,' I was told. 'This is about empowering young women to take control of their reproductive health. It's a true campaign for Girl Power.'

Mum couldn't hide her pride. This was better than being a teacher, she decided. Unfortunately, she was sworn to secrecy about the appointment, which had to be kept under wraps until I could fly to New York at the end of October for a briefing at the United Nations. In the mean time, I had another important mission.

The minibus bounced and rattled over potholes that threatened to swallow the wheels. Barefoot children played in the dust, rolling hoops made from old bicycle rims. They paused to wave as we drove past, flashing enormous white smiles.

In the nearby fields, mothers were crouched over, weeding the vegetable gardens, with babies nestled against their backs in brightly coloured slings of cloth.

Despite the dust in Uganda's dry season, the tiny villages of mud-brick huts with thatched roofs were remarkably clean. Each morning the women would sweep the compounds with bundles of thatch and then dampen down the dust by sprinkling water outside the huts.

I was in Uganda for Comic Relief to film a series of

short reports on how some of the money raised in the TV appeal had been spent. This fitted in perfectly with my plans to try to give something back. People had been so good to me that I wanted to repay that faith.

Richard Curtis, the TV and film writer, had been an inspiration. I'd met him two years earlier when the Spice Girls filmed a video to support Comic Relief. Apart from being an amazingly talented writer, Richard had taken a year out and devoted himself to Comic Relief.

If he can do that, I thought, then so can I.

Rather than showing the stereotyped hunger of Africa, the new Comic Relief campaign wanted to remind people how beautiful and diverse Africa can be.

We arrived in Kampala, the capital of Uganda, and spent a night in a hotel before setting off for the distant village of Bulamagi. I was convinced that none of the locals would have a clue who I was, until Tor showed me the front page of a local newspaper, which had a photograph of me in full Ginger Spice costume.

The bus ride was hot and dusty, but somehow Tor managed to sleep through the jarring potholes and blaring car horns. I'd grown up with visions of Africa as a bleak, drought-scarred continent, full of malnourished children. Mum was always telling me, 'Don't waste food, Geri. Think of all the starving people in Africa.' Now I saw a different image. We drove through lush green valleys, past villages where women gathered at water pumps and tended the gardens. The children looked healthy and happy, sitting in outdoor classrooms, reciting the alphabet.

Our destination was the Women's Literacy Project in Bulamagi, which was being funded by Comic Relief. The briefing notes mentioned the University of Bulamagi and

I suddenly imagined an imposing campus, full of students. Instead, we found a blackboard propped in the shade.

As I got off the bus, women hugged me warmly and shook my hand. I felt incredibly touched. They had no idea about the Spice Girls or Geri Halliwell, but they knew that Comic Relief had supported them.

Fifty per cent of adults in Uganda cannot read or write and the majority of them are women. There is so much we take for granted about literacy, yet until now these women couldn't read a medicine bottle to give a child the correct dosage or read their child's school reports. One woman who had learned to read through the project discovered letters from her husband's mistress; until then she hadn't known he was having an affair.

Often the men weren't happy about their wives learning to read. Ignorance was a way of suppressing them.

The women showed us their reading skills and tribal dances. Afterwards, they took me into their huts, proudly showing me their cooking pots and baskets they'd woven.

The human spirit is amazing. So often we claim to be hard done by in life, and complain about not having enough, yet these women continued to smile through appalling adversity. Having survived civil wars, dictators and starvation, they now had Western banks forcing them to grow cash crops to pay off their country's debts when they had barely enough food to feed themselves. Still they kept smiling.

Comic Relief had decided that footage of me white-water rafting would probably raise a few laughs as well as extra donations. What the hell, I'm up for it! I'll even ham it up for the cameras, I thought, imagining it would be like a ride at Alton Towers.

Early in the morning we arrived beside a swift-flowing river that formed the source of the Nile.

'Do I really have to wear this?' I asked, holding up the unflattering yellow helmet.

'Too right,' said the raft guide, Tony, a New Zealander with an accent as broad as his shoulders.

'What about the life jacket? I feel a bit stupid . . .'

'It's compulsory.'

The producer was discussing tactics. They obviously wanted to make the rafting as dramatic as they could. We had four major rapids to shoot and then a nice slow drift downriver to our lunch stop.

The inflatable rafts were on the bank, along with the paddles. Tor wished me luck and drove off with the support vehicles, which would meet us downstream. She left me with Tony, the film crew and a bunch of New Zealand backpackers who'd paid for a day's rafting.

Clambering into the raft, I felt a little anxious, as well as self-conscious – I had a cameraman crouched near my feet, with a camera tied to his helmet.

'Left forward!' yelled Tony, teaching us the manoeuvres. 'Left back!'

When he shouted, 'Hold on!' we had to grab the safety rope along the sides of the raft and cling on for dear life.

Mist still hung over the water as we set off towards the first of the rapids. How dangerous could this be? People do it all the time.

I tried to keep smiling for the camera.

'Keep it steady! Paddle forward! Hard!'

The roar of the white water filled my head and

suddenly we seemed to be paddling towards Victoria Falls. As the front of the raft reached the rapids, I looked down the first drop and my heart stopped.

The raft speared downwards and swung to the right. I could hear Tony yelling, but had totally lost interest in paddling. This was about survival. The raft seemed to be surfing on a wave of backwash that spun us sideways and spat us out. At that moment, one corner of the raft dug deep and the back lifted. My hands were ripped from the safety rope and I was catapulted out.

The shock of the water only added to the confusion. Tumbling over and over, I could see nothing but brown and white bubbles. I had no air in my lungs; it had been knocked out of me. I couldn't breathe. Blind panic took over and I swallowed water. The pressure of the river wouldn't let me go. Is this how I'm going to die?

My life didn't flash before me. Instead, I felt completely helpless and out of control. I stayed underwater for thirty seconds before the rapids spat me out downstream. I came up coughing and spluttering, feeling absolutely terrified. As a result I did a very good Shelley Winters impression, à la *The Poseidon Adventure*, and almost drowned the person trying to save me.

It made for great television, but it took me a long while to overcome the shock. I could barely talk. When the rafts arrived at the island for lunch, I threw my arms around Tor and burst into tears.

I realized something that day: as much as I tried to graft and plan my future, I could never totally control my destiny. Rather than worrying me, I found this liberating. Every day became a bonus and I began to see life from a more realistic perspective.

* * *

Almost before I could clear the water from my ears, I was on a flight to New York for a briefing at the United Nations. My role as a goodwill ambassador was still a secret, but somehow it had leaked to the media and there were dozens of TV crews and photographers waiting for me at La Guardia Airport.

I didn't let this spoil my excitement. In the limousine I told Molly, 'This is so brilliant. I am here doing something I so want to do. It's not every day you feel this happy; that you really think, God, everything is going my way. A part of me says, Be careful, Geri, it can't last. But then I tell myself not to be negative and to enjoy the moment, however long it lasts.'

That night I wrote:

## Monday, 19 October – New York

*I feel like I have a job now. For the last four months I've been virtually unemployed, but now I have a reason to get out of bed.*

*I'm nervous. Who wouldn't be? Tomorrow will be like starting at a new office. Hopefully, someone will show me the ropes.*

*People are often quick to criticize me, but I'm doing this to do good. I don't care if I'm rubbish when I speak, or if I stumble over my words. I just have to remember what I am doing this for.*

*Wrote a song called 'Let Me Love You'. It's about how great it is when somebody, particularly a child, accepts your love.*

The leaking of the news meant that a press conference was hastily arranged by the United Nations Population Fund. Immediately after my first briefing, I would have to answer questions from the world's media.

I had no time to prepare and was really nervous. This was my first proper press conference since leaving the Spice Girls. What if they asked me complex questions about birth control and human rights? I'm no diplomat or politician. I was only just learning about the issues.

The abortion question worried me most. I had to tread carefully because the pro-life and pro-choice camps were so bitterly divided.

The next morning I arrived at the United Nations headquarters on the east side of Manhattan. As the car pulled up, I could see the flags of 185 member nations curling and snapping open in the breeze. They ran alphabetically from Afghanistan on 48th Street to Zimbabwe on 42nd Street.

Photographers and reporters were waiting. I felt jetlagged and puffy from the flight, but tried to stay composed. Introductions were made and UN officials gave me a guided tour of the complex.

I'm terrible at remembering names but great with faces. In particular, I concentrated on listening and learning all I could about reproductive health care and family planning. The press conference was still to come and it loomed like an appointment with a firing squad.

When the media had assembled, I sat at a table, flanked by officials from the UNFPA. There were reporters from around the world, most of them specialists in foreign affairs. I couldn't blag these people.

'This is a tremendous honour for me and I am looking

forward to being involved in this important project,' I announced. 'In the Western World over the last hundred years women have come a long, long way. Often we take our right to make reproductive and sexual choices for granted, but for women in the developing world, who have few real choices in this area, getting pregnant can mean the difference between life and death. These women deserve the same freedom and right to choose.'

A reporter asked me what difference I thought I could make.

'I am famous. Lots of people know who I am. And I am going to use that fame positively. If at the end of the day I can save one person's life, or make it better, then it will be worth it.'

As expected, I was asked about my views on abortion.

'No woman wants, in her heart, to have an abortion,' I said. 'No-one wants to do that. But it is important to give women the choice. You can never say never when you are in that position.'

Far less predictable was a question about the decision by the US Congress to withhold over a billion dollars in funding that it owed the United Nations because of disputes over, among other things, population-related issues.

Apparently, the controversy had blown up that morning. I had no idea what to say.

'Er, well, yes ... er, as you know ... there are lots of complex issues in the world. Look, I'm sorry, but at the moment I'm not equipped to answer that. Give me six months and hopefully I'll be able to give you an answer.'

Afterwards, I felt exhilarated. I knew that I'd done OK. Tor tried to bring me back down to earth by discussing my schedule of interviews and appointments. She knew that I had a habit of becoming overexcited and almost too happy about things.

### Sunday, 25 October 1998

*Mum came and saw the house today. She was lost for words. Typical Mum, she kept saying, 'It's so big, Geri. You're gonna look tiny in that house.'*

*'Look at all those windows to clean . . .'*

*It's starting to look like a home. The staircase is almost finished and they're ready to lay the marble in the main hall. I can't wait to move in. Unfortunately, it might not be until after Christmas.*

*I'm so nervous about singing to Prince Charles on Wednesday. What if I panic and forget the words to 'Happy Birthday'? Please, please let it be OK . . .*

Hundreds of fans had arrived early at the Lyceum in the West End, staking out their positions behind the metal barriers erected by the police. They also spilled off the footpath near the stage-door entrance, hoping to catch a glimpse of the celebrities as they arrived.

A group of teenagers squealed and waved frantically as I stepped out of the car. It gave me a lift. Later I sent Tor outside with an autograph for them.

Prince Charles was celebrating his fiftieth birthday with a gala concert called *A Royal Celebration*. Performers included Robbie Williams, Spike Milligan, Stephen Fry and Roger Moore. Months earlier, Charles had asked me to perform. 'What could I sing?' I asked him. 'I don't have a solo single, or an album.'

There was a thought that I could possibly sing 'Happy Birthday'.

Back then it had seemed like such a good idea. I knew people would automatically think of Marilyn Monroe's rendition of 'Happy Birthday' for John F. Kennedy. I had no intention of trying to mimic her breathless style. I decided to sing the way I normally do and hopefully the audience would join in.

Kenny Ho had designed my dress. It looked like something Deborah Kerr might have worn in *The King and I* – a beautiful blue ball gown, with a tight waist and a large billowing skirt. Walking in the dress took great care and I had visions of toppling over. If that happened I was just going to lie there and pretend to be dead until they carted me away.

George and Kenny came backstage to give me moral support.

'I've been having this recurring nightmare about forgetting the words to "Happy Birthday". I know it's ridiculous – everybody knows the words – but what if it happens?'

'You'll be fine,' said George.

I went to the toilet eleven times that day – singing to Prince Charles is the perfect laxative. Opening the bathroom window, I looked down at the fans spilling onto the street below. Someone spotted me and yelled, 'We love you, Geri.' I waved back.

It's strange how often I struggled to justify to myself why I wanted to be famous, but then a chance encounter like a conversation with fans from a second-floor window will make it all so clear. It felt good to be liked.

'Time to get ready,' said a stylist, knocking on the door.

Standing behind a screen, I peered out and could see the whole audience. Again, I wondered if I had ever been so scared. Oh, my God I'm not going to be able to do this.

Then I told myself, OK, I'm nervous. But at the end of the day, if this all goes wrong, it's not *that* important. Life will go on.

I hitched up the hem of my dress, walked out and smiled.

## Thursday, 29 October 1998

*Last night was incredible. So many things could have gone wrong, but they didn't. I didn't trip up. I didn't panic and forget the words. I did it on my own, a cappella, and then the audience joined in with me for an encore.*

*There were so many things to worry about that I didn't even consider whether people would be judging my voice.*

*The papers are full of photographs. Mum is so proud she can't stop smiling and hugging me. She's been collecting the newspaper cuttings all day.*

*Not bad for a girl from Watford!*

## Epilogue
### A PLACE TO CALL HOME

### Berkshire, England, Sunday, 25 April 1999

I love the smell of newly mown grass; it reminds me of this time of year. Looking out of the kitchen windows I can see Alastair chasing Harry around the garden. Harry's paws have turned green from the cut grass and he'll need a bath before I let him inside.

The apple trees in the orchard are starting to bud and bluebells are coming up in the far corners of the fields. I've been shown photographs of this house in the spring, when it looks like an island in a sea of blue flowers. I can't wait to see that.

The tennis court is dotted with toys and is the perfect place for Alastair to ride his tricycle. I haven't got round to buying a tennis racket yet!

My next-door neighbours are the nuns of St Paul's. I

can just see the roof of the convent if I look past the house-keeper's cottage and the orchard, over the high stone walls.

I took Harry for a walk along the lane last Sunday and I realized that I hadn't introduced myself to my new neighbours. I rang the doorbell and it took ages for any-body to answer. The middle-aged lady who opened the door was wearing jeans and a checked shirt. Her cheek was smudged with potting mix.

'I'm sorry to trouble you. I've moved in next door and I thought I'd come and say hello. I'm—'

'I know who you are,' she beamed. 'Come in, Geri. Come in. I'm sorry about my clothes, I've been working in the garden.'

'Are you a nun?'

'Yes.'

'I thought you'd be wearing a habit.'

'No, not for the gardening. It's not compulsory these days.'

The sitting room contained comfortable old sofas and chairs. Nuns with names like Sister Bernadette and Sister Maria appeared from upstairs. They brought pots of tea and plates of home-made cakes and scones.

'We had lots of calls from journalists when you moved in,' Sister Maria told me. 'Some of them thought that you'd bought the convent and thrown us out.'

The others began laughing. They were adorable and doted on me like maiden aunts.

I told them about the renovations I'd made to the monastery. I'm going to invite them over for afternoon tea and show them. Just like in my childhood show-reel, I've finally managed to get my *Gone with the Wind* house. It has a huge staircase in the entrance hall which divides at the landing and then goes up either side.

I've even labelled one of the bedrooms 'Dad's Room' and put his photograph on the window sill. When I first walked in there I said to Natalie, 'Doesn't this smell like Dad?' It's a shame he didn't get to stay there.

Mum drops by at least once a week and makes sure my housekeeper is looking after me. She sneaks about and gives things an extra polish. She still scolds me about the money I spend.

'You see that sheet? I buy that sheet at Woolworths for £18. How much did you spend?'

'It doesn't matter, Mum.'

'You spend £45 on a single flat sheet. It's crazy!' She waved the receipt in front of me.

'But, Mum, it's Egyptian cotton.'

'So what? Who said Egyptians make the best cotton? Pyramids, yes, but not cotton.'

I don't argue with her any more. I hide the receipts.

A few mornings ago she brought me a cup of tea in bed. I looked at her and thought, I really *do* love you.

This might sound obvious, but I didn't always feel that way. Maybe if I'd loved my father less I would have had more love for Mum. Or perhaps I simply failed to realize how much she meant to me and how much I owe her.

If you're wondering about Harry, he's the man in my life. That's what I tell journalists when they ask me who is sharing my bed. I got Harry from Battersea Dogs' Home last November. George came with me and helped me fill in all the forms. I said I wanted a 'handbag' dog and they found me a shih-tzu.

When I first brought Harry back to the cottage he

disgraced himself totally. Since then I've managed to house-train him a little better. I took him everywhere with me in the beginning, dressing him in cut-off tights or having us both wearing matching striped tops. It's a wonder he ever forgave me.

This whole year has been like creative therapy for me. In writing the album and the book, I've found out more about myself than I ever thought possible. It wasn't until I started analysing my life that patterns and explanations began to emerge. I'd never realized how much I was my father's daughter. I knew I was a daddy's girl, but I hadn't understood the degree to which he influenced me and how much I loved him.

And until I began writing about my failed auditions and looking through my rejection letters I'd forgotten the sheer number of them. Yet I don't regret any of the mistakes and failures. They were all important. Through struggle comes strength. Without the hardship the outcome might have been different.

It's still hard to believe that five years ago I was living in a rented flat in Fairlawns, Watford, and debating whether to get out of bed and go to an audition for an all-girl band. I weighed a little over six stone and was struggling to come to terms with my father's death. I made the right decision and all my childhood fantasies and show-reels came true.

Right now there are tens of thousands of young boys and girls who have the same dream. They are singing into hairbrushes and idolizing pop stars. I'd like to be able to tell them that it all comes down to talent, but that's not true. And I'd like to be able to say that perseverance inevitably pays off, but that's not true, either.

Nor is it about luck, or lottery tickets. You can be the most talented, dedicated, luckiest wannabe in the world and still not succeed. In reality, it's all of these things mixed into a cocktail that's never made the same way twice.

I can tell you some of my ingredients. I had one parent who supported me and my dreams and another who tried to keep my feet firmly on the ground. I went without things and struggled, which made me pursue them even harder. And I had just enough love, being the youngest child, to give me the confidence and belief that anything was possible.

So there you have the secret.

When someone writes a book, I don't think they realize until they finish what the book is truly about. The same is true of their reasons for writing it.

I know that I wanted to exorcize some ghosts and have always believed that everybody has a book in them. But other reasons have become clearer. My dad always talked about writing a book, but he got no further than putting three or four minutes on tape. In a sense, I'm trying to do it for him, completing his unfulfilled ambition.

I also hope that perhaps in some way people will read this and find some connection with me, because we all chase dreams and wonder, What if it happened to us?

My years with the Spice Girls were an amazing adventure. When I listen to our records, I hear five young girls having the best time they could ever imagine. The music was full of mad, youthful optimism and shameless joy.

And when I listen to myself singing, I think, Who is that person?

I know who she is. I know who we all were – 'if only' girls at the top of a dream.

I had two years of tremendous fun and I wouldn't swap it for anything in the world. I am enormously grateful.

Of course, there was a down side – the media scrutiny, the punishing schedules, the need to keep smiling when I wasn't smiling on the inside. But I was elevated to a place that many people aspire to and very few people reach.

At the time I left the Spice Girls I felt emotionally disappointed, but now it doesn't matter. I've let go. Everybody's truth is different, which means that no two people see events the same way.

Before, I used to take things straight to heart, but now I can see where people are coming from and understand their motivations. I realize that we don't have to like everybody or have everybody like us. How you feel inside is more important than what anyone else thinks.

My demons might not have gone for ever, but I know where they're hiding. I'm far more relaxed and balanced than I used to be. I actually distrust the feeling because I've never had it for so long before. Don't rock the boat, Geri.

In two weeks' time my first solo single is released 'Look At Me'. I'm nervous, excited and scared. The sense of expectation is still the best part.

Sometimes I try to imagine what it might feel like if it goes to number one. Great! But what if it doesn't? That's OK, too. It's a lesson learned. Even if it bombs, I can live with that. This time around I'm trying to keep my eyes wide open.

My hunger is back, but I don't have the same sense of urgency about doing everything quickly because there might not be a tomorrow. I realize that you will never die with your in-tray empty. There will always be something left unsaid or undone. Right now I'm happy with my life. Maybe I've finally found a place to call home. It's not just about bricks and mortar. I can look in the mirror each morning and be comfortable with what I see.

Last week, in Los Angeles, I tried on a dress that was a little too tight around the bust. The old Geri Halliwell would have tried to squeeze into the smaller size, but instead I chose the next size up. For me, this was an important step towards self-acceptance.

The future awaits . . . I'm rushing towards it.

My dad used to tell me that if I reached for the stars then I might finish up somewhere near the moon. He also said that I should never say 'if only'.